D1570571

Signal and Power Integrity in Digital Systems:
TTL, CMOS, and BiCMOS

Other Reference Books of Interest by McGraw-Hill

Signal and Power Integrity in Digital Systems: TTL, CMOS, and BiCMOS

James E. Buchanan
Senior Advisory Engineer
Westinghouse Electric Corporation

Drawings by Bert D. Buchanan

McGraw-Hill

New York   San Francisco   Washington, D.C.   Auckland   Bogotá
Caracas   Lisbon   London   Madrid   Mexico City   Milan
Montreal   New Delhi   San Juan   Singapore
Sydney   Tokyo   Toronto

Library of Congress Cataloging-in-Publication Data

Buchanan, James E. (James Edgar) 1936–
   Signal and power integrity in digital systems : TTL, CMOS, and
BiCMOS / James E. Buchanan.
      p.   cm.
   Includes bibliographical references and index.
   ISBN 0-07-008734-2 (hc)
   1. Metal oxide semiconductors, Complementary—Design and
construction.   2. Transistor-transistor logic circuits—Design and
construction.   3. Bipolar integrated circuits—Design and
construction.   4. Digital electronics—Design and construction.
5. Very high speed integrated circuits—Design and construction.
I. Title.
TK7871.99.B55B83   1995
621.39'5—dc20   95-38799
                                                       CIP

McGraw-Hill

A Division of The McGraw-Hill Companies

1 2 3 4 5 6 7 8 9 0 DOC/DOC 9 0 0 9 8 7 6 5

ISBN 0-07-008734-2

*The sponsoring editor for this book was Steve Chapman, the editing
supervisor was Bernard Onken, and the production supervisor was
Donald Schmidt. It was set in Century Schoolbook by Estelita F. Green
of McGraw-Hill's Professional Book Group composition unit.*

Printed and bound by R. R. Donnelley & Sons Co.

McGraw-Hill books are available at special quantity discounts to use
as premiums and sales promotions, or for use in corporate training programs. For more information, please write to the Director of Special
Sales, McGraw-Hill, 11 West 19th Street, New York, NY 10011. Or contact your local bookstore.

This book is printed on recycled, acid-free paper containing
a minimum of 50% recycled, de-inked fiber.

Contents

Preface   xi
Acknowledgments   xv

Chapter 1. Introduction   1

References   7

Chapter 2. Advanced Schottky TTL, Advanced CMOS, and BiCMOS
Logic Families   9

2.1 High-Performance Logic Families   10
    2.1.1   Advanced Schottky TTL Logic Families   10
    2.1.2   Advanced CMOS Logic Families   11
    2.1.3   BiCMOS Logic Families   14
2.2 Timing Specifications   15
    2.2.1   Comparison of Dynamic Operational Characteristics   16
    2.2.2   Timing Parameter Adjustments for Worst-Case Conditions   17
    2.2.3   Caution: Beware of F_{MAX} 18
2.3 Static Input-Output Characteristics   18
    2.3.1   Input Voltage Levels   19
    2.3.2   Input Currents   20
    2.3.3   Output Voltage Levels   21
2.4 Compatibility of Logic Families   25
    2.4.1   Common Ground, Common Supply Voltage, and
        TTL Input and Output Levels   25
    2.4.2   Common Ground, Common Supply Voltage, CMOS Inputs,
        and TTL Outputs   26
    2.4.3   Common Ground, Common Supply Voltage, TTL Inputs,
        and CMOS Outputs   26
    2.4.4   Common Ground, Different Supply Voltage Levels   27
    2.4.5   Dynamic Interface Issues   28
2.5 CMOS or TTL Levels?   28
2.6 Noise Margins of Logic Families   29
    2.6.1   Static Noise Margins of Advanced Schottky TTL Families   31
    2.6.2   Static Noise Margins of Advanced CMOS Logic Families   32
    2.6.3   Static Noise Margins of BiCMOS Logic Families   33
    2.6.4   Dynamic Noise Immunity   33

v

           2.6.5 Noise Margin Summary   35
      2.7 References   36
      2.8 Bibliography   37

Chapter 3. Advanced Schottky TTL, CMOS, and BiCMOS
Logic Circuits   39

      3.1 Advanced Schottky TTL Circuits   40
           3.1.1 Equivalent Circuits for Diodes and Transistors   41
           3.1.2 Functional Operation of the TTL NAND Gate   46
      3.2 Advanced CMOS Logic Circuits   52
      3.3 BiCMOS Logic Circuits   57
      3.4 No Opens or Intermediate Logic Levels on CMOS or BiCMOS Inputs 60
      3.5 Latch-up and Latch-up Prevention   62
      3.6 Electrostatic Discharge Protection   64
      3.7 References   68

Chapter 4. Inductance and Transient Switching Currents   71

      4.1 Inductance   71
           4.1.1 Physical and Electrical Factors that Influence Inductance 72
           4.1.2 Transient Voltage Drop across Inductors   74
      4.2 Transient Switching Currents   75
           4.2.1 Transient Internal Switching Currents   75
           4.2.2 Transient Load Currents   79
      4.3 Ground Bounce   85
      4.4 Guidelines for Reducing Inductance and Transient-Current Effects 89
      4.5 References   91

Chapter 5. Power Distribution   93

      5.1 Component Power and Ground-Pin Connections to Power and
           Ground Planes   94
      5.2 Voltage Loss across Planes   95
           5.2.1 DC Loss   95
           5.2.2 AC Loss   97
      5.3 Circuit-Board-to-Motherboard Connections   99
      5.4 Power-Supply-to-Motherboard Connections   100
      5.5 Voltage Loss in Power Conductors   103
      5.6 Voltage Loss in Power Connections   104
      5.7 Connections between Dissimilar Metals   106
      5.8 Overvoltage Protection   107
      5.9 System Grounding   108
      5.10 Decoupling Capacitors   113
           5.10.1 Local Decoupling   113
           5.10.2 Bulk Decoupling   117
      5.11 Summary of Power Distribution Requirements   119
      5.12 Summary of Techniques for Minimizing Inductance and
           Transient-Current Effects in Power Distribution Networks   120
      5.13 References   121

Chapter 6. Signal Interconnections   123

6.1 Signal Interconnection Categories   124
6.2 Physical Means of Interconnecting Signals   124
    6.2.1   Component-to-Component Connections   125
    6.2.2   Board-to-Board Connections   125
    6.2.3   Unit-to-Unit Connections   126
6.3 Interconnection Impedance   127
    6.3.1   Loaded Transmission-Line Impedance   131
6.4 High-Density Multilayer PC Boards   132
6.5 Characteristic Impedance of Some Common Interconnection
       Structures   133
6.6 Breadboard Interconnections   138
6.7 Routing Guidelines   138
6.8 Crosstalk   141
6.9 Signal Interconnection Summary   149
6.10 References   149
6.11 Bibliography   151

Chapter 7. Transmission-Line Effects   153

7.1 Basic Transmission-Line Theory   154
    7.1.1   Ideal Transmission-Line Response   155
    7.1.2   Transmission-Line Termination   158
7.2 TTL, CMOS, and BiCMOS Device Transmission-Line Response   162
    7.2.1   Typical Advanced CMOS Device Transmission-Line Response   163
    7.2.2   Typical TTL and BiCMOS Device Transmission-Line Response   166
    7.2.3   Controlling Undershoot   168
    7.2.4   Optimum Source-Load Impedance Characteristics   169
7.3 Driver-Receiver Response Test Circuit   170
7.4 Summary of Techniques for Dealing with Transmission-Line Effects   171
7.5 References   172
7.6 Bibliography   172

Chapter 8. Clock Distribution   173

8.1 Universal Clock Distribution Guidelines   173
8.2 Board Level Clock Distribution   177
8.3 Board-to-Board Clock Distribution   187
8.4 Unit-to-Unit Clock Distribution   194
8.5 Test Clock Input Port   196
8.6 References   197
8.7 Bibliography   197

Chapter 9. Device, Board, and Unit Interfaces   199

9.1 Component-to-Component Interfaces   201
    9.1.1   Input Level Requirements   201
    9.1.2   Unused Inputs   202
    9.1.3   Derating Current Drive Specifications   206
    9.1.4   Increasing Drive Capability   207

9.2 Board-to-Board Interfaces   208
    9.2.1   Bus Interfaces   208
    9.2.2   General Requirements for Three-State Buses   211
9.3 Board and System Interface Guidelines   212
9.4 Board and System Interface Protection   213
9.5 Signal Interfaces between Remote Units   214
    9.5.1   Differential Unit-to-Unit Signal Transmission   215
    9.5.2   Low-Speed Unit-to-Unit Signal Transmission   216
    9.5.3   Very Low-Speed Unit-to-Unit Signal Transmisson   218
    9.5.4   Unit-to-Unit Line Terminations   220
    9.5.5   Miscellaneous Unit-to-Unit Considerations   220
9.6 Summary of Interface Guidelines   221
9.7 References   223

Chapter 10. Noise-Tolerant Logic Architectures   225

10.1 Synchronous Design   225
10.2 Important Synchronous Design Issues   227
    10.2.1   Clock Requirements   227
    10.2.2   Hold-Time Requirements   228
    10.2.3   Synchronizing Asynchronous Inputs   230
10.3 Devices Incompatible with Synchronous Design   237
    10.3.1   One-Shots   237
    10.3.2   Latches   239
    10.3.3   Master-Slave Devices   239
10.4 Summary of Synchronous Design Practices   239
10.5 References   240
10.6 Bibliography   240

Chapter 11. Worst-Case Timing   241

11.1 Device Delays   244
    11.1.1   Device Timing Specifications   244
    11.1.2   Timing Parameter Adjustments for Worst-Case Conditions   245
    11.1.3   *Caution*: Beware of F_{max} 251
11.2 Circuit Board Interconnection Delays   251
    11.2.1   Interconnecting Line Propagation Delay   251
    11.2.2   Line Propagation Delay with Distributed Loads   252
    11.2.3   Line Delay due to Transmission-Line Effects   252
11.3 Backpanel Interconnection Delays   253
11.4 Unit-to-Unit Interconnection Timing   254
11.5 Examples of Worst-Case Timing   254
11.6 Signal Timing Summary   260
11.7 Signal Timing Checklist   261
11.8 References   262

Chapter 12. System Initialization and Low-Voltage Sensing   263

12.1 Initialization Signal Generation   265
12.2 Reset Signal Distribution   268
12.3 Reset Signal Phasing   269

12.4 Reset Signal Loading   270
12.5 Reset Signal Timing   270
12.6 Write Protection of Nonvolatile Memories   272
12.7 Logic Initialization to Prevent Hazardous or Damaging Conditions   275
12.8 Summary of Initialization and Low-Voltage Sensing Techniques   276
12.9 References   276

Chapter 13. Memory Subsystem Design   279

13.1 Semiconductor Memory Devices   280
      13.1.1 Typical Memory Device   281
      13.1.2 High-Speed Advanced CMOS and BiCMOS Memory Devices   284
13.2 High-Speed Memory Subsystem Design   292
      13.2.1 Typical Memory Subsystem   292
      13.2.2 Memory Circuit Layout   294
      13.2.3 Control Signal Generation and Timing   295
      13.2.4 Memory Worst-Case Timing Analysis   300
      13.2.5 Crosstalk Control   306
      13.2.6 Data Bus Contention Prevention   307
      13.2.7 Power and Ground Distribution and Decoupling   310
      13.2.8 Failure Rates and Error Detection and Correction   311
13.3 Memory Subsystem Testing   312
13.4 Summary of High-Speed Memory Design Techniques   317
13.5 References   318
13.6 Bibliography   319

Chapter 14. Using PLDs, FIFOs, and Other LSI Devices   321

14.1 PLD Application Tips   321
14.2 FIFO Application Tips   323
14.3 Important Considerations in the Use of LSI Devices   325
      14.3.1 Ground-Bounce and Output Pin Interaction   325
      14.3.2 Proper Connection of Unused Inputs   326
      14.3.3 Proper Termination of Inputs   326
      14.3.4 Decoupling Needs of LSI Devices   328
14.4 Summary of Design Techniques for PLDs, FIFOs, and
      Other LSI Devices   328
14.5 References   329

Chapter 15. ASIC Application Tips   331

15.1 Logic Structures to Avoid in ASICs   333
15.2 Guidelines for Selecting Input-Output Characteristics   334
      15.2.1 CMOS or TTL Levels?   334
      15.2.2 Do Not Let CMOS or BiCMOS ASIC Inputs Float   335
      15.2.3 Output Drive Selection   336
15.3 Early Determination of Number of Ground and Power Pins   336
15.4 Guidelines for Interface Timing   338
15.5 Summary of System Application Tips for ASICs   339
15.6 References   339
15.7 Bibliography   340

Appendix   341

  A.1   Conversion Factors   341
  A.2   Definition of Symbols and Acronyms   341
  A.3   Trademarks   348
  A.4   CMOS and BiCMOS Power Dissipation Calculations   348
       A.4.1 Quiescent Power Dissipation Calculations   348
       A.4.2 Dynamic Power Dissipation Calculations   350
       A.4.3 References   351

Glossary   353
  Index   367

Preface

This book is about signal and power integrity issues and techniques for managing those issues in high-speed state-of-the-art digital systems built with advanced Schottky transistor-transistor logic (TTL) devices, advanced complementary metal-oxide semiconductor (CMOS) logic devices, and advanced bipolar combined with CMOS (BiCMOS) logic devices. It is not about logic design. It is about how to optimize the electrical and mechanical environment for high-speed logic devices. Their very fast edges, low noise margin, and other nonideal characteristics invite signal and power integrity-related system faults; but with attention to basic electrical and electromagnetic principles, they can be applied successfully.

Unfortunately, an introduction to these basic principles appears to be absent from most digital designers' training. Perhaps the material is considered too simple or obvious—and it is simple and obvious when explained and understood. But without an understanding of the simple electrical issues that determine signal and power integrity, there is little likelihood of success when high-speed digital devices are used. Many have learned the hard way in their first encounter with high-speed digital logic devices that the electrical issues cannot be neglected. The purpose of this book is to help those new to high-speed logic design avoid the many pitfalls that await the unsuspecting and to provide those who have encountered some of the problems with solutions.

However, a book such as this cannot provide solutions to all signal and power integrity issues. Each design will have its own unique set of circumstances and challenges. The hope is that the book will at least help the reader develop an awareness of the many critical electrical design issues that may impact signal and power integrity in high-speed digital systems. Understanding that an issue is important is the first step toward its solution.

This book is a combination of *CMOS/TTL Digital Systems Design* (McGraw-Hill, 1990) and *BiCMOS/CMOS Systems Design* (McGraw-

Hill, 1991) with the material updated where appropriate. It follows the basic arrangement of *BiCMOS/CMOS Systems Design,* with material on advanced Schottky TTL applications added from *CMOS/TTL Digital Systems Design* where applicable. Most of the fundamental issues that must be addressed to manage signal and power integrity when high-speed logic devices are applied are the same, and their solution is the same regardless of the technology of the devices being applied. Crosstalk, transmission-line effects, and ground and power supply upsets due to switching currents are universal problems that are controlled by similar techniques. Some of the material in the book may seem at first to be unrelated to signal and power integrity, but managing signal and power integrity in a system in a cost-effective manner involves more than controlling noise and transmission-line effect. It includes structuring systems so that not all signals require special care and using basic design practices that minimize complexity so that those signals which are important can be given proper attention.

Book Arrangement

The book starts with an introduction to advanced Schottky TTL, advanced CMOS, and BiCMOS logic families and their characteristics, followed by a brief review of advanced Schottky TTL, CMOS, and BiCMOS circuits in Chap. 3. Chapter 4 describes some special problem areas and techniques for overcoming them. Chapters 5 through 12 cover circuit analysis and system implementation techniques that are essential for the successful application of high-speed TTL, CMOS, and BiCMOS devices. The final three chapters, Chaps. 13 to 15, cover some of the special system implementation techniques that must be used when one is applying large-scale integrated (LSI) and very large-scale integrated (VLSI) devices, such as memories and application-specific integrated circuits (ASICs). Each chapter stands on its own so that readers with immediate design tasks can go to specific topics instead of reading the entire book. Chapters 4 through 15 end with a summary of the important points and design techniques discussed.

Summary of Chapters

Chapter 1 stresses that the logic design cannot be separated from the electrical and mechanical design when high-speed logic devices are used. Interconnection bandwidth and transmission-line effects and their influence on signal and power integrity are discussed.

Chapter 2 presents a brief overview of the relative performances and specifications of the various advanced Schottky, advanced CMOS, and BiCMOS logic families. A number of tables are provided for quick reference and for comparison of characteristics.

Chapter 3 provides a brief review of advance Schottky TTL, CMOS, and BiCMOS logic circuits. Circuit modeling techniques are introduced that aid in the understanding of logic circuit operation. Several circuit characteristics that designers must understand to successfully apply TTL, CMOS, or BiCMOS logic circuits are reviewed.

Chapter 4 describes the mechanisms that cause internal device and load-dependent transient switching currents and the detrimental effects of inductance in high-speed interconnection. Several examples show the possible magnitude of switching currents and demonstrate the possible adverse effects of excessive inductance. Guidance for minimizing inductance or the effects of inductance in power distribution systems is provided.

Chapter 5 describes the need for low-impedance power and ground distribution networks and describes techniques for achieving them. Techniques for calculating losses in power distribution networks are described. Guidelines for the amount and placement of decoupling capacitors are provided.

Chapter 6 deals with the design of signal interconnection systems for high-speed TTL, CMOS, and BiCMOS devices. Topics include optimum line impedance and how to minimize crosstalk.

Chapter 7 includes a review of transmission-line effects and deals with nonlinear sources and loads as they specifically relate to high-speed advanced Schottky TTL, advanced CMOS, and BiCMOS applications.

Chapter 8 discusses the need for high-quality clock signals in high-speed systems. Techniques for distributing clock signals are described. It is stressed that a sound clock distribution system is one of the keys to a reliable high-speed digital system.

Chapter 9 deals with practical interfacing issues that must be addressed at the device, board, and system levels when high-speed TTL, CMOS, or BiCMOS devices are used.

Chapter 10 describes the importance of synchronous logic design and the necessity for using synchronous design practices when high-speed logic devices are used. Critical design issues for synchronous systems are described, such as techniques for synchronizing signals and metastability.

Chapter 11 provides guidance for determining worst-case device and interconnection delays. A typical board-to-board signal path is analyzed for worst-case signal delay.

Chapter 12 describes techiques for generating and distributing system initialization signals and write protection schemes for nonvolatile memory devices, such as electrically erasable programmable read-only memories (EEPROMs) during power switching or transients. Many critical issues that are often overlooked are discussed.

Chapter 13 covers state-of-the-art high-speed memory devices and the design of high-speed memory systems.

Chapter 14 covers some of the special signal and power integrity issues associated with programmable array logic (PAL), programmable logic array (PLA), and other LSI devices.

Chapter 15 covers some of the special signal and power integrity issues associated with gate arrays, standard cells, and compiled cells.

James E. Buchanan

Acknowledgments

Many thanks are extended to my fellow engineers in the Digital Systems Department at Westinghouse Electric Corporation's Electronic Systems Division, Baltimore, Maryland, who contributed to this book through their efforts as leaders or participants in the in-house digital design course on which this book and my two previous books are based. Special thanks are due to Jim Hudson for his continued advocacy of, and insistence on, good electrical design practices. Westinghouse Electric Corporation is thanked for the opportunity and permission to publish this book. McGraw-Hill, and particularly Steve Chapman, is thanked for this opportunity to revise and update the material in my first two books, and all the readers of my first two books are thanked for their favorable reception of the books and their many gracious comments.

In addition, I want to thank my son Bert for his excellent rendering of the drawings, and my wife Beverly is thanked for her patience and tolerance during the many evenings and weekends that I spent on the book.

James E. Buchanan

Introduction

Today's advanced Schottky transistor-transistor logic (TTL), advanced complementary metal-oxide semiconductor (CMOS), and bipolar combined with CMOS (BiCMOS) logic components require a great deal of careful engineering to manage and ensure the integrity of their power and signal interconnection systems.[1] Their fast rise times cause crosstalk, transmission-line ringing, power supply transients, and ground upsets. Unless power and signal interconnections are designed to minimize these effects of fast edges, there is little likelihood of achieving a sound and robust quality design.

Designers must appreciate that today's high-speed TTL, CMOS, and BiCMOS devices are not easy to use and that certain fundamental electrical principles cannot be neglected without introducing serious power and signal integrity problems and compromising expected performance.[2] These fundamental electrical principles are not complex, and once they have been explained, most seem obvious. However, they are often neglected; perhaps, it is their obvious nature that leads to this neglect.

The two major areas of neglect that cause most of the power and signal integrity problems encountered in systems built with today's digital devices are

1. Inadequate timing margin for worst-case device and interconnection delays

2. Neglect of basic principles of electromagnetism and Ohm's law

It seems obvious that systems must have adequate timing margins for worst-case component and interconnection delays. Too often, though, systems go into production with the expected operating speed based on naive, optimistic assumptions for device timing parameters and little or no allowance for interconnection delays. Often the fact that a breadboard operates at a given speed is taken as proof of the design. Sight is lost of the fact that it is naive to assume that all components in a breadboard have worst-case delays and represent the worst-case combination of conditions that will occur over a production run. Perhaps, in the past when system clock rates were typically very low, it was possible to ignore worst-case timing and interconnection delays without suffering major production disasters. However, when one is dealing with high-performance systems, in the 20-MHz or greater range, causal approaches to establishing operating speed are sure to lead to systems that are difficult to produce. The nearer a system operates to the limits of present-day device and interconnection technology, the greater the chance of serious timing errors. Actual in-circuit worst-case device parameters and interconnection delays must be determined and used to establish system operating speeds. Under ideal conditions, individual devices may operate at very high speeds. However, when many high-speed devices must be interconnected, interconnection delays are often responsible for a significant portion of most signal delays. At 20 MHz, interconnection delays are a significant portion of most signal delays; at 40 MHz, interconnection delays are a major portion of most signal delays. Yet, often interconnection delays are ignored.

To utilize the potential operating speed of today's digital devices, the functional design and the interconnection and power distribution system design cannot be separated. Their fast edges cause crosstalk, transmission-line effects, power supply transients, and ground upset even when the best interconnection design practices are followed. Yet, digital (logic) designers very often fall into the trap of viewing digital circuits as simple functional logic blocks rather than as complex electric circuits. No matter how simple or complex the functional logic being performed, the actual circuitry consists of an imperfect signal interconnection system, an imperfect power and ground distribution network, and logic devices with nonideal internal circuitry. To ignore these imperfections is to ignore basic electromagnetic principles and Ohm's law.

Nonetheless, most of the effort in most digital designs remains focused on the functional logic design even though logic errors or functional concept errors are generally fixable, but systems with poorly designed or conceived electrical interconnection schemes are often not fixable. The steps required to correct functional logic errors may be unpleasant and costly, but they can be accomplished. However, if the electrical system is inadequate, no amount of patching will provide a solid system. One may be able to hand-tune each system as it comes off the production line so that it works for the moment, but whether it will work under all the required conditions or for how long will be difficult to establish. Problems with systems with inadequate electrical systems are often never understood. The problems are blamed on various nebulous causes. Very frequently, the problem is blamed on bad or marginal parts, rather than on the real cause—a poor electrical system or system timing that is not compatible with worst-case device parameters. In such systems, often a given problem will go away following a change to another part or another vendor's part. In the great majority of such cases, the part is not the real problem; the problem is that the part is being used in such a manner that there is very little or no operating margin. Substituting another vendor's part that has a little more margin, or that is a little faster, or slower, corrects the immediate problem, but does not fix the basic problem.

Logic device and interconnection imperfections are more noticeable when high-speed TTL, CMOS, or BiCMOS devices are used because signal edge rates, not clock rates, determine the required frequency response of signal and power distribution systems and the onset of transmission-line effects. The frequency response of digital signal interconnections is important because interconnections act as low-pass networks (Fig. 1.1) and attenuate high-frequency signals. Interconnections will significantly attenuate signals unless they have an upper 3-dB bandwidth sufficiently high to pass the third harmonic of the fundamental frequency component of signal edges. The equation commonly used to express the fundamental frequency f component of a digital signal switching transition t_r is[3,4]

$$f = \frac{0.35}{t_r} \qquad \text{for the general case} \qquad (1.1)$$

Today's 5-V and low-voltage (LV) TTL, CMOS, and BiCMOS devices typically have edge speeds of 1 to 3 ns. Assuming switching transi-

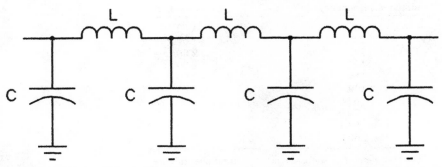

Figure 1.1 All interconnections are low-pass networks when high-speed digital devices are used.

tions are linear, a switching transition t_r that occurs in 1 ns has a fundamental frequency f component of

$$f = \frac{0.35}{1 \text{ ns}} = 350 \text{ MHz} \qquad \text{for 1-ns edges}$$

A linear voltage transition, such as a switching edge, also contains higher-frequency components than the fundamental—the third, fifth, seventh, etc., harmonics. The third harmonic composes approximately 10 percent of the amplitude of a linear ramp.

For a signal with a 1-ns edge, the fundamental frequency is 350 MHz (see above) and the third harmonic is approximately 1 GHz (3×350 MHz). Not all of today's advanced Schottky TTL, advanced CMOS, or BiCMOS digital devices have edge rates as fast as 1 ns, but most have edge rates faster than 3.5 ns, which corresponds to 100 MHz (see Table 1.1), and some may be slightly faster than 1 ns. Thus, today's systems need interconnection networks with bandwidths much in excess of 100 MHz to prevent serious degradation of signals. Digital designers must appreciate that they must deal with frequencies that only a short time ago were considered strictly in the radio-frequency (RF) designer's domain.

Transmission-line effects, at the circuit board or motherboard level, were of little concern with the older, slower TTL and CMOS logic families. Their slow edge rates (5 ns or greater) did not induce transmission-line effects, except on very long signal lines such as long cables between racks. However, when today's digital devices with 1-ns edge rates are used, transmission-line effects are a concern at the circuit board level. For all practical purposes, all signal lines are transmission lines when today's logic components are used to implement digital systems.

TABLE 1.1   Fundamental Frequency versus Rise Time

Fundamental frequency* f, MHz	Rise time t_r, ns
350	1.00
233	1.50
175	2.00
140	2.50
116	3.00
100	3.50
87.5	4.00
70.0	5.00
58.4	6.00
50.0	7.00

*The frequency f is the predominant (fundamental) frequency component in the waveform generated when a logic device switches states.

Transmission-line effects become significant when the signal rise or fall time is less than the two-way propagation delay of the signal line. The line or conductor length where transmission-line effects become significant is commonly called the *critical line length*. The common definition of the critical line length is

$$\text{Critical line length} = \frac{1}{2} \frac{t_r}{t'_{pd}} \tag{1.2}$$

where t'_{pd} is the effective per-unit length (i.e., per-foot) propagation delay of the line and t_r is the rise time of the signal transition.[5,6] The rise time is typically measured between 20 and 80 percent, but sometimes 10 to 90 percent is used. Whether 20 to 80 percent or 10 to 90 percent is used is not significant. The more troublesome issue is that rise and fall times are not specified on TTL, CMOS, or BiCMOS data sheets. Thus, designers are forced to use rise- and fall-time parameters based on past observations or on measurements of current parts. Neither approach provides a great deal of certainty. Nonetheless, Eq. (1.2), even when used with approximated parameters, is very useful for engineering estimates of the possible onset of transmission-line problems in interconnections.

More conservative versions of the critical line length rule cut the ratio to one-fourth or one-fifth of the signal rise time relative to the signal path propagation delay.[7,8] As rise times decrease relative to line propagation delay, transmission-line effects become more pronounced. The typical per-unit propagation delay for tracks on printed circuit boards is 2 ns/ft. Thus, for a signal with a rise time of 1 ns, the critical line length is

$$\text{Critical line length for 1-ns edges} = \frac{1}{2} \left(\frac{1\text{ ns}}{2\text{ ns/ft}} \right) = 0.25 \text{ ft, or 3 in}$$

which means most lines are transmission lines when today's digital devices are used. Even on small circuit boards, many lines exceed 3 in; and in many of today's applications, circuit boards as large as the one shown in Fig. 1.2 are used. On boards as large as the one shown in Fig. 1.2, some lines may exceed 2 ft and most lines will exceed the critical line length, which means most lines on such boards are transmission lines and must be treated as such to control signal quality. All the signal integrity problems associated with transmission lines and transmission-line effects will be present on large boards when today's high-speed digital devices are used, which contrasts sharply with the past when transmission-line effects were seldom a concern at the board level. Today, with the combination of high-speed devices and large boards, transmission-line effects are a major source of signal integrity problems.

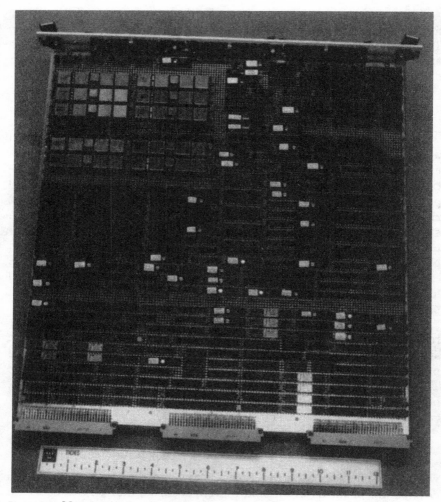

Figure 1.2 Most interconnections must be treated as transmission lines when large circuit boards are used.

Management of signal and power integrity requires a keen under-standing of the transient current generation and noise tolerance (margin) characteristics of today's devices. Today's devices have very little noise tolerance, yet they generate large transient switching currents which cause large amounts of noise. The 5-V advanced CMOS devices with "true" CMOS input thresholds have more noise tolerance than devices with TTL level input thresholds, but 5-V CMOS rail-to-rail output voltage swings generate more noise. Thus, 5-V advanced CMOS devices with true CMOS input levels provide little noise immunity advantage in system application (even though advertisements often stress their greater noise margin). The point that we must keep in mind is that today's devices generate large transient currents which in turn generate large amounts of noise on the power, ground, and signal interconnections of devices that have very little tolerance for noise. Failure to account for the noise-generating characteristics of high-speed logic devices is certain to lead to the design of unreliable systems.

As clock frequencies move up to 100 MHz and above, CMOS and BiCMOS digital devices with either TTL or CMOS signal levels become increasingly more difficult to use. Not only do interconnection delays become significant, but also as frequency goes up, power dissipation goes up, and there is less time for crosstalk and noise to subside. Their large, fast signal swings generate large transient currents. Large transient currents and package pin or interface connector inductance limit the number of signals that can switch simultaneously in a given package or at board or system interfaces without upsetting ground or power levels. Either the signal edge speed must be reduced, or more package and interface connector pins must be reserved for power and ground to reduce inductance, but the number of power and ground pins required to make significant speed improvements becomes impractical. No pins are left for signals. Advanced Schottky and BiCMOS devices with TTL level signals are less of a problem than devices with a 5-V CMOS signal.[9] Likewise, LV CMOS devices offer a great improvement over 5-V CMOS devices with rail-to-rail signal levels since LV (3.3-V) CMOS signals are approximately the same amplitude as TTL signals. Systems built with devices that have TTL, LV, or 5-V CMOS signal levels are speed-limited by their interface levels. Devices with lower voltage swings, such as emitter-coupled logic (ECL), are needed to move to the next level of system performance.[10–12]

In summary, when high-speed logic devices are used, the logic design cannot be separated from the electrical and mechanical design. Power and signal integrity must be "designed in." The "old" approach of treating digital circuitry as functional logic blocks while ignoring the power and signal interconnections is a sure route to the design of unreliable systems. Ensuring power and signal interconnection integrity is a significant and mandatory part of the overall design task when today's high-speed devices are used.

References

1. Ravender Goyal, "Managing Signal Integrity," *IEEE Spectrum*, March 1994, pp. 54–58.
2. Mike Donlin, "Signal-Integrity Concerns Slip into the Mainstream," *Computer Design*, September 1994, pp. 52–54.

3. *IEEE Standard on Pulse Measurement and Analysis by Objective Techniques,* Standard 181-1977, Institute of Electrical and Electronics Engineers, New York, 1977.
4. Robert K. Southard, "High-Speed Signal Pathways from Board to Board," in 1981 WESCON Records, session 18, September 1981, paper no. 2.
5. *Applications Handbook,* Cypress Semiconductor Corp., San Jose, Calif., 1994, pp. 1–5.
6. W. R. Blood, *MECL System Design Handbook,* 4th ed., Motorola Inc., Phoenix, Ariz., 1988.
7. Richard A. Quinnell, "CAD Tools Help Cure Transmission-Line Woes," *EDN,* March 1, 1991, pp. 47–52.
8. David Royle, "Rules Tell whether Interconnections Act Like Transmission Lines," *EDN,* June 28, 1988, p. 131.
9. Dave Bursky, "BiCMOS Process Advances Deliver Bipolar Speed," *Electronic Design,* May 28, 1992, pp. 43–58.
10. Ed Lipsett, "Shift from TTL to ECL," *Electronic Engineering Times,* August 14, 1989, pp. 29–30.
11. Joel Martinez, "BTL Transceivers Enable High-Speed Bus Designs," *EDN,* August 6, 1992, pp. 107–112.
12. Richard A. Quinnell "High-Speed Bus Interfaces," *EDN,* September 30, 1993, pp. 43–50.

2

Advanced Schottky TTL, Advanced CMOS, and BiCMOS Logic Families

To make cost- and performance-effective logic device selections for high-performance system applications, an understanding of the advantages and disadvantages of advanced Schottky TTL, advanced CMOS, and BiCMOS logic devices and families is mandatory. To that end, this chapter presents a brief overview of the various advanced Schottky TTL, advanced CMOS, and BiCMOS logic families [including the low-voltage (LV) logic families]. Emphasis is on speed and interface characteristics. Included are interface requirements between logic families and between devices with different power supply levels.

Each logic device technology has characteristics that must be weighed against system requirements. Tradeoffs must be made based on[1]

Speed requirements

Power consumption

Supply voltage level requirements

Drive capability

Noise margin

Available package styles

Signal level compatibility

Availability

Cost

plus many other considerations unique to each application. Speed is usually a basic selection criterion. If the technology does not meet the speed requirements, there is little point in further consideration. Most of today's high-performance systems require advanced Schottky TTL, advanced CMOS, BiCMOS, or ECL devices; devices from the older TTL and CMOS logic families are too slow for most present-day applications. In the past, ECL was the only choice for high-speed systems. ECL devices are designed with outputs that have controlled rise times and that can drive load terminating resistors. Controlled rise time and control of the match between line impedance and load terminating resistors provide a means of achieving the signal quality needed for high-performance systems. However, ECL terminating resistors dissipate a great deal of power, increase the parts count, and usually require an additional power supply for the termination voltage. Furthermore, ECL circuits inherently dissipate a great deal of power.[2] Advanced CMOS and BiCMOS technologies offer the promise of high-speed performance without the power dissipation of TTL or ECL and without the additional components (terminating resistors) required for ECL systems. However, that promise of high performance cannot be realized without an understanding of the signal integrity issues associated with these technologies and their signal characteristics.

Advanced BiCMOS devices are available with both ECL and TTL levels. The discussion in this book is limited to BiCMOS devices and logic families that have TTL input and output levels. BiCMOS devices with traditional TTL logic levels and interface circuitry coupled to a CMOS core offer the best of both CMOS and advanced Schottky bipolar TTL technology from a system application standpoint.

2.1 High-Performance Logic Families

2.1.1 Advanced Schottky TTL logic families

Today's advanced Schottky TTL logic families are much superior to the original TTL devices which were introduced in the late 1960s. Today's devices have higher output drive, lower input currents, and much improved speed-power products, to mention only a few improvements, compared to earlier devices. However, TTL technology and use are past their peak. The advanced Schottky logic families that are available today were developed in the early to middle 1980s. New advanced Schottky logic families are not being developed. Use of advanced Schottky logic families and devices is on the decline. Manufacturers are discontinuing production of some advanced Schottky devices. Low-voltage (3.3-V) TTL logic families are not available and are not expected to be developed.

The existing advanced Schottky TTL logic families, preceded by their letter designations, are

F   fast advanced Schottky TTL (FAST)

ALS   advanced low-power Schottky TTL

AS   advanced Schottky TTL

In actual system applications, there is little difference in the performance of AS or FAST parts. Certain functions in the AS family are slightly faster than equivalent FAST parts, but the speed difference is usually insignificant. Most static characteristics are similar. Input current and output drive ratings for the two families are about the same. Most small-scale integration (SSI) FAST parts dissipate slightly less power than small-scale integration AS parts, but at the medium-scale integration (MSI) level there is not much difference. If a selection must be made between the two high-speed advanced Schottky logic families, then price and availability may be the best selection criteria since there is little difference in basic electrical characteristics.

The ALS family has never established a clear niche. Most high-performance digital systems have moved to operating frequencies that have bypassed the optimum ALS operating frequency range.

2.1.2 Advanced CMOS logic families

Advanced CMOS technology is used to build a number of what are customarily called *discrete* logic families as well as several bus logic families. Discrete logic families typically consist of small-scale integration devices such as ORs, ANDs, NANDs, and buffers; medium-scale integration devices such as decoders, latches, and registers; and perhaps some small pin count large-scale integration (LSI) devices. Bus logic families tend to consist primarily of octal, or wider, buffers, transceivers, latches, and registers. For classification purposes in this book, advanced CMOS logic families are divided into first-, second-, and third-generation devices or families of devices. As might be expected by the naming of the classifications, the groupings are based on their chronological order of development. First-generation devices tend to have rail-to-rail output voltage swings with no control of slew rate, which can lead to serious system noise problems. Second-generation devices tend to have output slew rate control or TTL level output voltages or both (both of which tend to improve signal quality in actual system applications). Most first- and second-generation devices are optimized for operation with a V_{cc} of 5 V, but most will operate at lower V_{cc} levels including 3.3 V. Speed of operation decreases with lower V_{cc}. Logic families optimized for operation with low-voltage supplies (typically 3.3 V) are categorized as third-generation devices. Any grouping of devices, except by optimized supply voltage (5 or 3.3 V), is dubious at best. Manufacturers are continually changing and improving the capabilities and characteristics of their devices. Some manufacturers have upgraded devices and families without changing the designation used to identify the family, so it must be understood that the grouping shown in Table 2.1 is a transitory ranking. Current manufacturers' device specifications should be consulted for the present status of devices and logic families.

TABLE 2.1   Advanced CMOS Logic Families

Logic family	Manufacturers
First generation, 5 V	
54/74AC, ACT	National, Motorola, Harris
54/74AC11, ACT11	Texas Instruments, Philips
54/74FCT, FCT-A	IDT, Cypress, Harris
29C800	AMD
Second generation, 5 V	
54/74ACQ, ACTQ	National
54/74FCT-T, FCT-AT, FCT-CT	IDT
Third generation, 3.3 V	
54/74LVQ	National
54/74FCT3	IDT
74LVC	Texas Instruments

Discrete 5-V V_{cc} advanced CMOS logic devices and logic families are identified by letter designators such as AC, ACT, and FCT (with a few exceptions). Low-voltage advanced CMOS devices and logic families are identified by letter designators such as LVC, LVQ, and FCT3. Most SSI and MSI advanced CMOS logic devices in the advanced CMOS logic families are pin-compatible with equivalent TTL and BiCMOS logic functions; most have speed and drive comparable to those of AS or FAST devices or BCT or ABT BiCMOS devices. Some advanced CMOS logic families have both devices with the input switching threshold approximately centered (those with letter designators without a T) and devices with input thresholds shifted so that they are compatible with TTL levels (those with ACT, FCT, etc., designators). However, several advanced CMOS logic series are offered only with TTL input levels. One example is the FCT series; there is no FC series. Most 5-V advanced CMOS devices are optimized to operate with TTL supply voltage levels (5 V ± 10 percent), but those with CMOS input levels are specified for operation over a wider supply range, typically between 2 or 3 V for the lower limit to 6 V for the upper limit. Those with TTL input levels are specified with normal TTL supply voltage levels of 5 V ± 10 percent. Yet, most advanced CMOS devices with TTL input levels will operate over the same range as the CMOS level devices in the family; but when the supply level is outside the normal TTL range, input and output levels may not meet TTL level requirements.[3]

Table 2.1 shows some of the major advanced CMOS logic families. Included are some of the major subgroups within the three major groups (at least one manufacturer is shown for each family). Table 2.1 is not an all-inclusive list. It is not practical to provide a comprehensive list of manufacturers and their devices in a book of this type. The situation is so dynamic that the list is certain to be obsolete before the book is published. The current *IC MASTER*[4] is recommended as a source of up-to-date information on the availability of devices and manufacturers.

The AC and ACT advanced CMOS logic families tend to have the widest use and the largest selection of logic functions and accessories. Perhaps next in number of functions are the AC11 and ACT11 logic families, which are similar electrically to the AC and ACT devices but are mechanically different. The power and ground pins are located in the center of the package instead of on the ends, as is customary.[5] The FCT and 29C800 families are not true logic families since they do not have NANDs, NORs, etc. They are often described as *bus interface families*. Bus interface families tend to have only octal or wider parts, but the FCT family does have some counters and multiplexers (the 29C800 family does not). There are a number of speed ranges available in the FCT family. They are distinguished by the addition of an A, B, etc. In the second-generation category, the ACQ, ACTQ, and the improved FCT-T families have slight improvements in speed relative to their associated first-generation parts. The ACQ and ACTQ families are advertised as having a 15 percent speed improvement over the original AC or ACT families. However, the ACQ and ACTQ devices are still slower than equivalent FCT-T devices. One feature that distinguishes the FCT-T family from other advanced CMOS families is the return to true TTL output levels.

Broad acceptance and use of discrete (optimized for 5-V V_{cc}) advanced CMOS logic families has been slow because of the many system-level complications caused by the fast edges and wide voltage swings of the first-generation devices. Acceptance of AC parts (those with true CMOS signal level requirements) has been hindered because of the limited number of AC functions available and because AC parts cannot be mixed with TTL devices without the use of level shifters at TTL-to-CMOS interfaces. This signal-level incompatibility precludes a gradual introduction of AC parts into systems on a one-to-one basis. Lack of direct TTL compatibility also limits the complexity of systems that can be built with AC parts since most random-access memories (RAMs), read-only memories (ROMs), programmable array logics (PALs), etc., are only available with TTL input and output levels. Most system designers have found the risk of having to transition to systems composed entirely of AC CMOS devices with no alternative parts to fall back on (in case of problems with the AC parts) unacceptable. They could not simply substitute an advanced Schottky TTL part because of input-output level incompatibility. To further complicate matters, some manufacturers changed to packages with center power and ground pins (to solve some of the problems caused by fast edges). The new package again created a situation where system designers had no fallback parts. Thus, unless faced with some very compelling reason to do otherwise, in the great majority of cases system designers have found it more prudent to continue to use advanced Schottky TTL for discrete logic.[6] Signal integrity issues are greatly reduced when advanced Schottky TTL devices are used. Second-generation advanced CMOS devices, LV advanced CMOS devices, and the declining availability of advanced Schottky devices are changing that attitude.

2.1.3 BiCMOS logic families

BiCMOS is expected to be the key technology of the late 1990s. It offers the best features from a system application standpoint of bipolar and CMOS technologies by combining advanced Schottky bipolar technology and advanced CMOS technology. Typically, BiCMOS devices have CMOS input structures and CMOS internal logic combined with bipolar output structures. However, some BiCMOS devices also have bipolar input structures as well as outputs. Some BiCMOS application-specific integrated circuits and LSI devices use bipolar drive stages throughout the internal logic. The combination of technologies provides high speed, high drive, and low power. BiCMOS speeds and drive capabilities are comparable to those of advanced Schottky.

A wide variety of digital BiCMOS integrated-circuit devices are available. They include application-specific integrated circuits, RAMs, programmable logic devices (PLDs), and discrete 5-V and 3.3-V logic devices. A BiCMOS logic family that includes SSI devices such as NANDs, ANDs, and ORs is available from Motorola and Toshiba; and BiCMOS bus interface families are available from IDT, National, Philips, and Texas Instruments (Table 2.2). A 3.3-V logic family (LVT) is available from Texas Instruments.[7] All the BiCMOS logic families listed in Table 2.2 have TTL level output swings and TTL level input thresholds including the LVT family. Traditional TTL levels and interface circuitry improve overall system signal quality. TTL levels cause less crosstalk, less dynamic power dissipation, less transient-current generation, and less ground bounce than CMOS levels. TTL

TABLE 2.2   BiCMOS Logic Families

Logic family	Manufacturers
54/74ABT	Texas Instruments, Philips
74BC	Motorola, Toshiba
54/74BCT	Texas Instruments
54/74LVT	Texas Instruments

levels also provide compatibility with LSI devices, such as RAMs, and with test equipment. The advantage of BiCMOS over bipolar TTL is the lower static power dissipation.

2.2 Timing Specifications

Most SSI and MSI advanced Schottky TTL, advanced CMOS, and BiCMOS device data sheets list typical, maximum, and minimum + 25°C timing for devices intended for both the commercial and the military markets, maximum and minimum timing for commercial rated devices, and maximum and minimum timing for military rated devices, as shown in Fig. 2.1 for an advanced CMOS AC and ACT NAND gate. Note that AC devices (see Fig. 2.1, top) are specified for operation with both 3.3-V and 5-V V_{cc}. Traditionally, commercial rated devices are specified for operating conditions of 0 to + 70°C and ± 5 percent from nominal power supply limits, and that is the case for most advanced Schottky TTL devices. However, there is little consistency in the temperature range or power supply range limits for commercial rated advanced CMOS and BiCMOS parts. Some are specified for −40 to + 85°C which is closer to what has traditionally been called the *industrial range*. Some commercial rated advanced CMOS parts are specified with ± 10 percent power supply limits instead of ± 5 percent. Specification limits are much more consistent for military rated devices. Most military rated devices are specified for oper-

AC Electrical Characteristics for AC Devices

Symbol	Parameter	V_{CC}* (V)	74AC $T_A = +25°C$ $C_L = 50$ pF			54AC $T_A = -55°C$ to + 125°C $C_L = 50$ pF		74AC $T_A = -40°C$ to + 85°C $C_L = 50$ pF		Units	Fig. No.
			Min	Typ	Max	Min	Max	Min	Max		
t_{PLH}	Propagation Delay	3.3	2.0	7.0	9.5	1.0	11.0	2.0	10.0	ns	2-3,4
		5.0	1.5	6.0	8.0	1.0	8.5	1.5	8.5		
t_{PHL}	Propagation Delay	3.3	1.5	5.5	8.0	1.0	9.0	1.0	8.5	ns	2-3,4
		5.0	1.5	4.5	6.5	1.0	7.0	1.0	7.0		

*Voltage Range 3.3 is 3.3V ±0.3V
Voltage Range 5.0 is 5.0V ±0.5V

AC Electrical Characteristics for AC Devices

Symbol	Parameter	V_{CC}* (V)	74ACT $T_A = +25°C$ $C_L = 50$ pF			54ACT $T_A = -55°C$ to + 125°C $C_L = 50$ pF		74ACT $T_A = -40°C$ to + 85°C $C_L = 50$ pF		Units	Fig. No.
			Min	Typ	Max	Min	Max	Min	Max		
t_{PLH}	Propagation Delay	5.0	1.5	5.5	9.0	1.0	9.5	1.0	9.5	ns	2-3,4
t_{PHL}	Propagation Delay	5.0	1.5	4.0	7.0	1.0	8.0	1.0	8.0	ns	2-3,4

Voltage Range 5.0 is 5.0V ±0.5V

Figure 2.1 (top) FACT 54AC/74AC00; (bottom) 54ACT/74ACT00 dynamic (ac) characteristics. (*Reprinted by permission of National Semiconductor Corp.*)

ating conditions of −55 to + 125°C and ± 10 percent power supply variations from nominal. The timing information supplied for LSI and VLSI devices is usually less complete than that for SSI and MSI devices; in many cases no typical or minimum data are supplied.

Device timing specifications are tied to loading. Unfortunately, not all manufacturers use the same load conditions when specifying timing. Load resistance does not have a large impact on device timing. However, variations in load resistance and loading network configuration from manufacturer to manufacturer make interpreting and comparing timing specifications difficult when differences are small, e.g., when a logic family is claimed to be 1 or 2 ns faster than another family. For example, when devices are tested to the nominal TTL threshold (1.5 V), loading networks that limit *high* levels tend to improve *high*-to-*low* propagation times. It takes less time to transition a shorter distance. Load capacitance has a major effect on output timing, but fortunately there is more standardization of load capacitance than there is of load resistance. Most SSI and MSI advanced Schottky TTL, advanced CMOS, and BiCMOS logic devices are specified with 50-pF loads. Most LSI and VLSI devices, such as memories, are specified with 30- or 35-pF loads. If the actual load varies significantly from the load used to specify the device timing, the timing must be adjusted to reflect the actual load conditions. However, timing adjustments due to actual load are not necessary in most cases. Signals used for control functions or local point-to-point data paths seldom exceed 50 pF. Thus, in most cases, manufacturers' maximum and minimum specified timing can be used without adjustments. Buses are exceptions. Bus capacitance on large boards or backplanes will usually exceed 50 pF. However, most buses are long line, and thus are not lumped loads and should not be treated as a lumped capacitance [they should be treated as transmission lines (see Chap. 7)].

2.2.1 Comparison of dynamic operational characteristics

Comparison of the dynamic operational characteristics of the advanced CMOS logic families is difficult because these families have never achieved the standardization that exists for TTL logic families. Advanced CMOS devices from different manufacturers tend to have slightly different alternating-current (ac) characteristics even though they have the same letter designation. This variation in specified speeds (of AC and ACT devices) complicates the process of ranking AC and ACT parts on a speed basis to other advanced CMOS and BiCMOS families. However, Table 2.3 attempts to show the relative dynamic performance of the major advanced CMOS and BiCMOS logic families (National Semiconductor Corp. specifications are used for the

TABLE 2.3   54XX240 Buffer and 54XX374 Register Worst-Case Speeds at + 125°C and 5 V ± 10 Percent Supply Levels

Family	Buffer speed,* ns t_{prop}	Register speed,* ns t_{prop}	t_{setup}
ABT	5.5	7.6	2.5
AC	8.5	11.0	5.0
ACT	9.5	11.5	8.5
ALS	22.0	21.0	10.0
AS	7.0	11.5	2.0
FAST	9.0	11.0	2.5
FCT	9.0	11.0	2.5
FCT-A	5.1	7.2	2.0
FCT-T	9.0	11.0	2.0
FCT-AT	5.1	7.2	2.0
FCT3	7.0	11.0	2.0
FCT3-A	5.1	7.2	2.0
BC†	7.5	10.0	2.0
BCT	6.4	11.6	6.5
LVQ†‡	9.5	13.5	3.0
LVT†‡§	4.5	6.1	2.0

*The slower of t_{PHL} or t_{PLH} is shown.
†Worst-case speeds at + 85°C.
‡Buffer speeds for LVT, LVQ, and FCT3 families are for 54/74XXX244.
§Register speed for LVT is for 54LVT574.

AC and ACT families[3]). Table 2.3 is intended as a general guide to the relative performance of the different families. The times listed must not be interpreted as potential system operating speeds. Actual in-circuit operating speed is a complicated function of device input-output characteristics, the arrangement in which devices are interconnected, and the characteristics of the interconnections (see Chap. 11).

Table 2.3 shows that there is not a great deal of difference in the speeds of the various advanced CMOS and BiCMOS logic families. The most notable differences are those for the FCT-A family, which is typically advertised as being up to 50 percent faster than standard FCT parts. First-generation advanced CMOS AC and ACT devices tend to have propagation delays slightly slower than those of advanced Schottky AS or FAST parts. AC11 and ACT11 speeds are comparable to AC and ACT devices. FCT speeds are typically equated to those of FAST parts.[8] FCT-A speeds are slightly faster than those of FAST parts.

2.2.2   Timing parameter adjustments for worst-case conditions

If worst-case device timing is not specified, the system designer must adjust the timing information supplied to reflect actual worst-case operating conditions and process variations. The manufacturer is the best source of information on parameter limits when they are missing and should be contacted for the missing information. However, for those cases where the manufacturer does not have the specific parameter limits needed or is unwilling to supply them, the following rules of thumb can be used to estimate timing parameter limits (for more exact means of estimating timing parameter limits, see Chap. 11):

Rules of Thumb for Timing Parameter Adjustments for Worst-Case Conditions

1. To convert typical + 25°C timing parameters to worst case over the commercial temperature range, multiply typical + 25°C timing parameters by a factor of 1.5.
2. To convert typical + 25°C timing parameters to worst case over the military temperature range, multiply typical + 25°C timing parameters by a factor of 2.
3. To convert maximum (or minimum) + 25°C timing parameters to worst case over the commercial temperature range, multiply maximum (or minimum) + 25°C timing parameters by a factor of 1.25.
4. To convert maximum (or minimum) + 25°C timing parameters to worst case over the military temperature range, multiply maximum (or minimum) + 25°C timing parameters by a factor of 1.5.

2.2.3   Caution: Beware of F_{MAX}

The parameter F_{MAX}, which is listed as the maximum toggle rate or maximum clock rate on data sheets for clocked devices such as counters, flip-flops, and shift registers, should never be used as an indication of the useful speed of a device.[9] It is a measure of what might be achieved with an individual part under ideal conditions with no restrictions on input pulse widths or load conditions.[9] Since most digital systems must operate under conditions that vary greatly from the ideal, and since devices must communicate with other devices to serve a useful purpose, F_{MAX} is of little use for actual system timing. Actual signal path propagation times must be used to determine the maximum operating speed of systems, not F_{MAX}.

2.3   Static Input-Output Characteristics

The static [direct-current (dc)] parametric specifications provided in data books for advanced Schottky TTL, advanced CMOS, and BiCMOS logic families tend to be more complete than those of many of the older logic families. Most device data sheets have three columns of dc characteristics, as shown in Fig. 2.2. In most cases, input-output current and voltage limits are specified for typical operating conditions as well as for worst-case conditions over the extremes of both the commercial and military operating conditions.

DC Characteristics for 'ACT Family Devices

Symbol	Parameter	V_{CC} (V)	74ACT $T_A = +25°C$	54ACT $T_A = -55°C$ to $+125°C$	74ACT $T_A = -40°C$ to $+85°C$	Units	Conditions
			Typ	Guaranteed Limits			
V_{IH}	Minimum High Level Input Voltage	4.5	1.5 2.0	2.0	2.0	V	$V_{OUT} = 0.1V$ or $V_{CC} - 0.1V$
		5.5	1.5 2.0	2.0	2.0		
V_{IL}	Maximum Low Level Input Voltage	4.5	1.5 0.8	0.8	0.8	V	$V_{OUT} = 0.1V$ or $V_{CC} - 0.1V$
		5.5	1.5 0.8	0.8	0.8		
V_{OH}	Minimum High Level Output Voltage	4.5	4.49 4.4	4.4	4.4	V	$I_{OUT} = -50\ \mu A$
		5.5	5.49 5.4	5.4	5.4		
		4.5	3.86	3.70	3.76	V	*$V_{IN} = V_{IL}$ or V_{IH} I_{OH} -24 mA
		5.5	4.86	4.70	4.76		-24 mA
V_{OL}	Maximum Low Level Output Voltage	4.5	0.001 0.1	0.1	0.1	V	$I_{OUT} = 50\ \mu A$
		5.5	0.001 0.1	0.1	0.1		
		4.5	0.36	0.50	0.44	V	*$V_{IN} = V_{IL}$ or V_{IH} I_{OL} 24 mA
		5.5	0.36	0.50	0.44		24 mA
I_{IN}	Maximum Input Leakage Current	5.5	±0.1	±1.0	±1.0	μA	$V_I = V_{CC}$, GND
I_{CCT}	Maximum I_{CC}/Input	5.5	0.6	1.6	1.5	mA	$V_I = V_{CC} - 2.1V$
I_{OLD}	†Minimum Dynamic Output Current	5.5		50	75	mA	$V_{OLD} = 1.65V$ Max
I_{OHD}		5.5		-50	-75	mA	$V_{OHD} = 3.85V$ Min
I_{CC}	Maximum Quiescent Supply Current	5.5	4.0	80.0	40.0	μA	$V_{IN} = V_{CC}$ or GND

*All outputs loaded; thresholds on input associated with output under test.
†Maximum test duration 2.0 ms, one output loaded at a time.
Note: I_{CC} for 54ACT @ 25°C is identical to 74ACT @ 25°C.

Figure 2.2 The 54ACT/74ACT00 static (dc) characteristics. (*Reprinted by permission of National Semiconductor Corp.*)

In addition, output voltage limits are typically specified for several load currents.

2.3.1 Input voltage levels

Advanced Schottky TTL input voltage levels. The input logic level specifications for the F, AS, and ALS logic families are 0.8 V or less for a logic *low* ($V_{IL\ MAX}$) and greater than 2.0 V but less than V_{cc} for a logic *high* ($V_{IH\ MIN}$).[10,11] The nominal input switching threshold is near 1.5 V.

Advanced CMOS input voltage levels. Advanced CMOS logic device input voltage logic level limits fall into two distinct categories: those with true CMOS level inputs (AC) and those with TTL level inputs (ACT, FCT, etc., that end with T). Advanced CMOS devices with true CMOS level inputs (for example, AC devices) have their input thresholds approximately centered between V_{cc} and ground. Actual *low* and *high* logic limits, respectively, are specified at approximately 30 and 70 percent of actual device V_{cc}, as shown in Fig. 2.3, to allow for

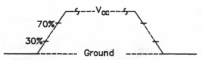

Figure 2.3. Advanced CMOS devices with CMOS input thresholds recognize input levels less than 30 percent of V_{cc} as logic *low* and input levels greater than 70 percent of V_{cc} as logic *high*.

process, temperature, etc., variations. Thus, CMOS devices with CMOS input levels are specified to recognize input levels less than 30 percent of V_{cc} as logic *low* inputs and those greater than 70 percent of V_{cc} as logic *high* inputs. The output response for input levels between 30 and 70 percent of V_{cc} is undefined.

In contrast to TTL thresholds, CMOS device threshold levels are a function of V_{cc} levels. Lowering or raising V_{cc} lowers or raises both *high* and *low* input thresholds. For standardization, input levels are specified with V_{cc} at 4.5 V for most optimized for 5-V V_{cc} CMOS parts. For example, AC parts are specified to have a minimum *high* input $V_{IH\ MIN}$ of 3.15 V, which is 70 percent of 4.5 V, and a maximum *low* input $V_{IL\ MAX}$ of 1.35 V, which is 30 percent of 4.5 V.

TTL compatible advanced CMOS and BiCMOS input voltage levels. Worst-case input level limits for CMOS and BiCMOS devices with TTL input levels (for example, ABT, ACT, BCT, and FCT) are specified as 0.8 V maximum for *low* inputs ($V_{IL\ MAX}$) and 2.0 V minimum for *high* inputs ($V_{IH\ MIN}$) (i.e., the same as those of Schottky TTL devices[10]). However, a subtle point often overlooked is that some CMOS and BiCMOS devices with CMOS input structures meet normal TTL input limits only when V_{cc} is equal to 4.5 V. At higher V_{cc} levels, $V_{IH\ MIN}$ may not meet 2.0 V. Both $V_{IL\ MAX}$ and $V_{IH\ MIN}$ tend to increase slightly with increased V_{cc}.

2.3.2 Input currents

Table 2.4 lists the input currents for NANDs and most standard parts for several of the more common advanced Schottky TTL, advanced CMOS, and BiCMOS logic families.

Table 2.5 lists the input currents for 54XX240 buffers for several of the more common advanced Schottky TTL, advanced CMOS, and BiCMOS logic families and bus interface logic families. Most bus interface devices in a given family will have similar input currents. Note that AC/ACT and AC11/ACT11 buffers have the same input specifications as NAND gates (in the respective family).

TABLE 2.4   54/74XX00 NAND Gate Input Current* at the *Low* and High Input Voltage Levels Listed

Family	I_{IL} @ V_{IL} (μA) (V)	I_{IH} @ V_{IH} (μA) (V)
AC	± 1 @ ground	± 1 @ V_{cc}
ACT	± 1 @ ground	± 1 @ V_{cc}
AC11	± 1 @ ground	± 1 @ V_{cc}
ACT11	± 1 @ ground	± 1 @ V_{cc}
ALS	-100 @ 0.5	$+20$ @ 2.7
AS	-500 @ 0.5	$+20$ @ 2.7
AC	± 1 @ ground	± 1 @ V_{cc}
BC†	± 1 @ ground	± 1 @ V_{cc}
FAST	-600 @ 0.5	$+20$ @ 2.7
LVQ	± 1 @ ground	± 1 @ V_{cc}

*Current out of a terminal is given a minus sign.
†Input current for 74BC00 is listed; 54BC00 data are not available.

TABLE 2.5   54/74XX240 Buffer Input Current* at the *Low* and *High* Input Voltage Levels Listed

Family	I_{IL} @ V_{IL} (μA) (V)	I_{IH} @ V_{IH} (μA) (V)
ABT	± 1 @ ground	± 1 @ V_{cc}
AC	± 1 @ ground	± 1 @ V_{cc}
ACT	± 1 @ ground	± 1 @ V_{cc}
AC11	± 1 @ ground	± 1 @ V_{cc}
ACT11	± 1 @ ground	± 1 @ V_{cc}
ALS	-100 @ 0.5	$+20$ @ 2.7
AS	-500 @ 0.5	$+20$ @ 2.7
FAST	-1000 @ 0.5	$+20$ @ 2.7
FCT	-5 @ ground	$+5$ @ V_{cc}
BCT	-1000 @ 0.5	$+20$ @ 2.7
LVQ	± 1 @ ground	± 1 @ V_{cc}

*Current out of a terminal is given a minus sign.

2.3.3 Output voltage levels

Advanced Schottky TTL output voltage levels. Output voltage level specifications for the F, AS, and ALS logic families are 0.5 V maximum for a logic *low* and 2.5 V minimum for a logic *high*. Actual logic *low* levels tend to be near 0.5 V regardless of load (see Chap. 3 for the reason). Actual logic *high* levels tend to be near 3.5 to 4.5 V unless a relatively heavy load referenced to ground is being driven.

Advanced CMOS output voltage levels. Output levels of advanced CMOS devices vary greatly with load conditions and temperature. Under static conditions, CMOS devices with complementary CMOS output structures go to V_{cc} or ground when driving high-impedance loads such as CMOS inputs. However, CMOS output levels are generally not specified with ground or V_{cc} output levels, but instead are typically specified with very light 50- or 100-μA loads. ACT and FCT device output levels are specified with currents that range from 1 to 24 mA for standard devices and up to 64 mA for bus interface devices. Thus, it is difficult to pick a standard set of conditions for defining advanced CMOS output levels. However, for the purposes of this book, and in most CMOS application information, CMOS output levels are typically specified as follows:

1. A worst-case true CMOS *high* output, for most 5-V optimized parts, is defined as being between V_{cc} and 0.1 V less than V_{cc} with V_{cc} at its minimum specified operating level (4.5 V for 5-V optimized parts); and a worst-case CMOS *low* output is between ground and 0.1 V above ground.[3,5] Output levels within 0.1 V of power or ground are possible only when devices are lightly loaded (100 μA or less), i.e., when high-impedance CMOS inputs are driven.

2. A worst-case TTL compatible ACT 5-V CMOS minimum *high* output is defined as 3.7 V, and a worst-case maximum *low* output is 0.5 V (in some cases 0.55 V) for a 54ACT device over the full range of military operating conditions.[3,5] In most cases, ACT devices, with TTL compatible inputs, have their output levels specified under load current conditions similar to those used to specify AS or FAST output levels (see Tables 2.6 and 2.7).

3. A worst-case TTL compatible FCT (including FCT-T) 5-V CMOS minimum *high* output is defined as 2.4 V, and a worst-case maximum *low* output is 0.55 V for a 54FCT device over the full range of military operating conditions.[8] In most cases, FCT devices have their output levels specified under load current conditions similar to those used to specify AS or FAST output levels (see Tables 2.6 and 2.7).

4. A worst-case LVC CMOS minimum *high* output is defined as being between V_{cc} and 0.2 V less than V_{cc} with V_{cc} at its minimum specified operating level (3.0 V); and a worst-case LVC CMOS *low* output is between ground and 0.2 V above ground for low output current conditions (100 μA or less). Worst-case output levels under 12-mA source and sink load conditions are $V_{cc}-0.6$ V for a worst-case minimum *high,* and a worst-case maximum *low* output is 0.4 V over the extended industrial operating conditions.[7] (See Tables 2.6 and 2.7.)

5. A worst-case TTL compatible LVQ CMOS minimum *high* output is defined as being between V_{cc} and 0.1 V less than V_{cc} with V_{cc} at its minimum specified operating level (3.0 V); and a worst-case LVQ CMOS *low* output is between ground and 0.1 V above ground for low output current conditions (50 μA or less). Worst-case output levels under 12-mA source or sink load conditions are $V_{cc}-0.6$ V for a worst-case minimum *high,* and a worst-case maximum *low* output is 0.5 V over the full range of military operating conditions.[12] (See Tables 2.6 and 2.7.)

TABLE 2.6   54XX00 NAND Gate Output Voltage at Load Currents* Shown and with $V_{cc} = 4.5$ V

Family	$V_{OL} @ I_{OL}$ (V) (mA)	$V_{OH} @ I_{OH}$ (V) (mA)
54AC00	0.1 @ 0.05	4.4 @ −0.05
	0.5 @ 24	3.7 @ −24
54ACT00	0.1 @ 0.05	4.4 @ −0.05
	0.5 @ 24	3.7 @ −24
54AC11000	0.1 @ 0.05	4.4 @ −0.05
	0.5 @ 24	3.7 @ −24
54ACT11000	0.1 @ 0.05	4.4 @ −0.05
	0.5 @ 24	3.7 @ −24
54ALS00	0.4 @ 4	2.5 @ −0.4
54AS00	0.5 @ 20	2.5 @ −2
74BC00†	0.5 @ 20	2.5 @ −1
54F00	0.5 @ 20	2.5 @ −1

*Current out of a terminal is given a minus sign.
†Parameters for 74BC00 are listed; 54BC00 data are not available.

TABLE 2.7   54XX240 or 54XX244 Buffer Output Voltage at Load Currents* Shown and with V_{cc} Equal to Recommended Minimum Operating Level

Family	$V_{OL} @ I_{OL}$ (V) (mA)	$V_{OH} @ I_{OH}$ (V) (mA)
54ABT240	0.55 @ 48	2.5 @ −3
54AC240	0.1 @ 0.05	4.4 @ −0.05
	0.5 @ 24	3.7 @ −24
54ACT00	0.1 @ 0.05	4.4 @ −0.05
	0.5 @ 24	3.7 @ −24
54AC11240	0.1 @ 0.05	4.4 @ −0.05
	0.5 @ 24	3.7 @ −24
54ACT11240	0.1 @ 0.05	4.4 @ −0.05
	0.5 @ 24	3.7 @ −24
54ALS00	0.4 @ 12	2.4 @ −3
54AS00	0.55 @ 48	2.4 @ −3
74BC240†	0.55 @ 48	2.4 @ −3
54BCT240	0.55 @ 48	2.4 @ −3
54F00	0.55 @ 48	2.4 @ −3
54FCT240	0.55 @ 48	2.4 @ −12
54FCT3244	0.5 @ 24	2.4 @ −3
54LVQ244	0.5 @ 12	2.4 @ −12
54LVT240	0.5 @ 24	2.4 @ −8

*Current out of a terminal is given a minus sign.
†Parameters for 74BC00 are listed; 54BC00 data are not available.

6. A worst-case TTL compatible FCT3 CMOS minimum *high* output is defined as being between V_{cc} and 0.2 V less than V_{cc} with V_{cc} at its minimum specified operating level (2.7 V); and a worst-case FCT3 CMOS *low* output is between ground and 0.2 V above ground for low output current conditions (100 μA or less). Worst-case output levels under 3-mA source load conditions are $V_{cc} - 0.6$ V for a worst-case minimum *high*; and a worst-case maximum *low* output when sinking 24 mA or less is 0.5 V over the full range of military operating conditions.[8] (See Tables 2.6 and 2.7.)

BiCMOS output voltage levels. Output levels of BiCMOS devices tend to be more stable with changing load conditions and temperature than CMOS outputs. BiCMOS outputs behave much the same as advanced Schottky TTL outputs. A worst-case BiCMOS minimum *high* output is typically 2.4 or 2.5 V for both 5- and 3.3-V optimized devices; and a worst-case maximum *low* output is 0.5 or 0.55 V for 5-V parts and 0.4, 0.5, or 0.55 V for 3.3-V LVT parts with the variation dependent on the output current level specification.[13,14] In most cases, BiCMOS devices have their output levels specified under load current conditions similar to those used to specify advanced Schottky output levels (see Tables 2.6 and 2.7).

Tables 2.6 and 2.7 list dc output voltage versus current for several of the more common advanced Schottky TTL, advanced CMOS, and BiCMOS logic families. Table 2.6 is for 54XX00 NAND gates and Table 2.7 for 54XX240 buffers. In general, the drive and output levels shown for each family's 54XX00 NAND gate are representative of all standard devices in that family. But caution must be exercised because some devices within a family may have different characteristics, and *drivers,* by definition, are expected to have more drive than NAND gates. But that is not always the case for the advanced CMOS logic families—they may have the same ratings. The drive and load levels shown for each family's 54XX240 buffers are representative of all buffers and bus interface devices in the family. But again caution must be exercised because some bus interface devices within a family may have different characteristics. The specifications for a given device should always be consulted and closely studied before the device is applied. Failure to read and understand device specifications remains one of the major sources of design error. Data sheet specifications should be read over and over. A great deal of attention should be given to the notes and fine print. For complex devices it is best to find and consult someone who has some experience with the part of interest. But having talked to someone about a part is not considered a very good excuse for not studying the data sheet when the part does not work as expected.

2.4   Compatibility of Logic Families

2.4.1   Common ground, common supply voltage, and TTL input and output levels

The various advanced Schottky TTL, advanced CMOS, and BiCMOS (including LVT) logic families *with TTL input levels* are input voltage level compatible and can be mixed as long as current drive specifications are not exceeded.[3] Advanced CMOS logic devices that have inputs compatible with TTL levels have logic family letter designators that end with T. For example, the ACT and FCT families have input thresholds that are designed to be compatible with TTL levels. No additional circuitry is required to transfer a signal from TTL or BiCMOS sources to ACT, BCT, FCT, or HCT devices (see Fig. 2.4). Current drive capabilities of TTL input compatible CMOS families are similar to those of advanced Schottky TTL and BiCMOS families, and CMOS input currents are of such a low magnitude that all TTL and BiCMOS families can source or sink several orders of magnitude more direct current than is needed to drive a very large number of CMOS inputs. In general, dc drive limits should never be exceeded when discrete advanced Schottky TTL, advanced CMOS, or BiCMOS devices are used, since input currents are typically only a few microamperes for CMOS and BiCMOS devices and typically under 1 mA for advanced Schottky TTL devices while output drive is typically 20 mA or more.

Caution: The BCT bus interface family has 1-mA input current sink requirements, and some octal FAST devices have 1- and 1.6-mA input currents. The dc drive is most likely to be an issue in systems where devices with high input current requirements are mixed with low drive LSI devices, ASICs, or some of the older logic families. Some present-day LSI devices including some 16-bit-wide memory devices have only 2 mA of drive. In all applications, an audit of signal loading

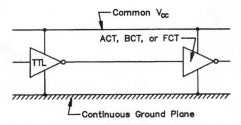

Figure 2.4   No additional circuitry is required to transfer signals from devices with TTL output levels to devices with TTL inputs such as ACT, ABT, or FCT.

should be performed as an ongoing task as well as one of the final design tasks.

2.4.2   Common ground, common supply voltage, CMOS inputs, and TTL outputs

The various TTL, CMOS, and BiCMOS families with TTL output levels and the 5-V CMOS families with CMOS input levels cannot be mixed without the use of additional interface circuitry for TTL to 5-V CMOS level signal transfers. The output voltage levels of all 5-V advanced CMOS devices are compatible with TTL input levels, but 5-V CMOS input levels are not compatible with TTL output levels. Thus, additional circuitry is required to transfer signals from TTL to 5-V CMOS voltage levels, but not in the other direction. Devices with 5-V CMOS input levels are TTL *low* level compatible, but are not TTL *high* level compatible. The minimum *high* output specification of TTL, CMOS, and BiCMOS devices with TTL level outputs is 2.4 or 2.5 V, and the minimum *high* input requirement for 5-V CMOS devices is 3.15 V (see Tables 2.6 and 2.7). Thus, when signals must be transferred from devices with TTL output levels to 5-V CMOS devices with CMOS thresholds, level shifters or pull-up resistors are required (see Fig. 2.5).[3] Pull-up resistors have a number of undesirable characteristics which include degraded rise times, extra power dissipation, and additional current sinking requirements for the drivers. The best means of transferring from TTL levels to 5-V CMOS level is to use ACT CMOS devices with TTL input levels and CMOS output levels.

2.4.3   Common ground, common supply voltage, TTL inputs, and CMOS outputs

Advanced CMOS logic devices have output levels that are compatible with TTL input levels when powered from a common source. *Low* CMOS output levels are approximately the same as TTL output *low*

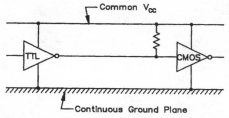

Figure 2.5   When signals must be transferred from devices with TTL output levels to CMOS devices with CMOS input levels, pull-up resistors or level-shifting circuits are required.

levels. *High* CMOS output levels from devices powered with 5 V are greater than normal TTL *high* levels, but do not exceed maximum TTL input limits. In many applications, higher *high* levels are of benefit. In noisy applications, they provide greater noise margin. Higher *high* levels do have some disadvantages. They generate more system noise due to larger signal transitions and increase *high*-to-*low* signal response times since they require more time to reach *low* switching thresholds. However, in most applications, transferring signals from 5-V CMOS devices to TTL devices requires no special circuitry, provided that all devices are powered with the same power supply (see Fig. 2.6).[3]

2.4.4 Common ground, different supply voltage levels

In general, the low-voltage BiCMOS LVT and CMOS LVC, LVQ, and FCT3 logic families are input and output signal level compatible with the 5-V logic families with TTL level inputs and outputs. However, there are a number of issues that may impact their overall system compatibility.[15] In most cases, transferring from low-voltage logic to 5-V devices with TTL input levels is not a problem if both supplies are active; the input and output levels are compatible. Transferring from 5-V TTL or CMOS devices to low-voltage devices may be a problem depending upon whether the low-voltage device has an input electrostatic protection network that includes a diode or diodes to V_{cc}. If such diodes are present, excessive input current may flow if the output level of the source exceeds a diode drop above V_{cc} of the low-voltage device.[16] In general, devices designed to have TTL output levels should not have sufficient current drive at the level of concern (e.g., above 3.3 V plus a diode drop for typical conditions) to cause an input overcurrent situation, but few if any parts are sufficiently specified to

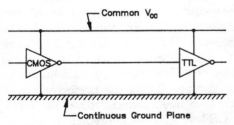

Figure 2.6. Transferring signals from CMOS devices with CMOS output levels to devices with TTL input levels requires no special circuitry provided that all devices are powered with the same power supply.

ensure trouble-free operation. Excessive input current is also a possibility at either interface if either supply lags the other supply at power turn-on, or turn-off, or if one supply fails. The solution to these input overcurrent issues at 3.3- to 5-V logic interfaces is to use devices without input diode clamps to V_{cc} at V_{cc} boundaries. Devices without V_{cc} clamps include all F, AS, and ALS TTL parts, LVT low-voltage parts, and a number of devices in several of the other logic families designed as translators between V_{cc} domains. Most low-voltage as well as 5-V CMOS and some BiCMOS devices have input diode clamps to V_{cc} and thus are unsuitable for use at 3.3- to 5-V or 5- to 3.3-V boundaries.

   Note: Low-voltage device output signal levels are not input signal level compatible with rail-to-rail 5-V CMOS inputs.

2.4.5   Dynamic interface issues

Dynamic as well as static interface compatibility must be considered when logic families are mixed. In general, no timing problems should be caused by mixing devices of approximately the same speed. However, mixing slow and fast devices can create timing problems. In such cases, the most common problem is hold-time violations. For example, in synchronous systems, signals originating from fast devices may go away before they can be captured by slow devices (see the hold-time requirements discussion in Chap. 10).

2.5   CMOS or TTL Levels?

In general, devices with TTL input and output levels are the best choice (low-voltage devices fall into this category since their voltage swings and input thresholds are approximately the same as the TTL levels); TTL output swings create less noise than 5-V CMOS rail-to-rail output swings and dissipate less dynamic power. As operating speed increases, there is less time for noise to die out, and dynamic power becomes more and more of a concern since it is a direct function of frequency (see Chap. 3). Other advantages of TTL are that (1) many 5-V LSI and VLSI parts, such as memories, PLDs, etc., are not available with CMOS inputs or output levels and (2) most standard test equipment is designed for TTL levels. Use of TTL levels allows a fallback to bipolar TTL parts if it is suddenly discovered that the preferred parts are not available. Only where maximum noise margin is needed, such as for clock signals, should 5-V CMOS levels be considered.

   Once either TTL or CMOS interface levels are selected, the system designer's task is to select devices or drivers with adequate drive. In general, the drive characteristic needed depends upon whether lightly loaded control signals or heavily loaded buses are being driven. Static (dc) drive is usually not an issue in advanced Schottky TTL, advanced CMOS, or BiCMOS systems. Input currents are relatively low and output drives relatively high. The direct input current for most advanced Schottky devices is under 1 mA, and for most CMOS and BiCMOS devices with CMOS input stage it is less than $\pm$ 10 μA. But caution must always be exercised—some BiCMOS bus interface parts have 1-mA input currents, and some advanced Schottky buffers have 1.6-mA input currents. Most advanced Schottky TTL, advanced CMOS, and BiCMOS logic functions such as gates, registers, and counters have *low* dc drive levels of 20 to 24 mA. Drivers and transceivers in these families typically have *low* dc drive levels of 48 to 64 mA. Thus, a large number of devices can be driven from a dc standpoint. However, ac drive is usually the issue in high-performance systems. Dynamic drive requirements (in high-performance systems) are a function of capacitive loading and transmission-line driving requirements and whether first incident wave switching is required (see Chaps. 6 and 7).

2.6 Noise Margins of Logic Families

The *noise margin* is the difference between the worst-case output level of a driving device and the worst-case input level at which the receiving device no longer recognizes the input as the intended *high* or *low* logic level. The difference between worst-case input and output levels is the tolerance that a given set of devices, or a given system built with a particular logic family, has for noise and other imperfections in the reference system and in the interconnection system. This built-in tolerance for noise is called the *noise margin*. Both static and dynamic noise margins are a concern in high-speed systems. Static noise margins define the low-frequency safety margins built into device input-output levels. The dynamic noise margin relates to the sensitivity of logic devices to noise spikes. For example, Fig. 2.7 illustrates static

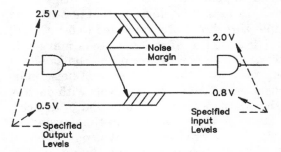

Figure 2.7. Static TTL input-output voltge level limits used to define static noise margins for most devices with TTL input and output levels.

input-output voltage level limits and static noise margins for most devices with TTL levels. Notice that *high* and *low* noise margins are different. Most devices with TTL input levels have more *high* than *low* noise margins. Most CMOS devices with true CMOS inputs have equal *high* and *low* noise margins. Advanced CMOS devices with true CMOS levels also have more noise margins than CMOS or BiCMOS devices with TTL levels, but they tend to need more noise margin since their wider, and in many cases faster, voltage swings generate more noise.

Device noise margin and system noise immunity are a great concern when today's devices are used; their fast edges generate much more noise than digital system designers are accustomed to dealing with. Yet, their static noise margins are approximately the same as those of older, slower bipolar and CMOS devices. Their dynamic noise margin tends to be less than that of the older logic families. They are more apt to react to narrow noise spikes because they are designed for high-speed operation.

An understanding of the static and dynamic noise margins of each device and each logic family used in a system is needed so that maximum advantage can be taken of the inherent noise margin. For example, most devices with TTL input and output levels have more *high*-level noise margin than *low*-level noise margin. That additional high-level noise margin should be taken advantage of by arranging the polarity of critical signals that have low-duty cycles so that they are in the *high* state most of the time. Thus, critical control signals, such as resets, should be *high* when inactive. Only devices that clock on *low*-to-*high* transitions should be used so that clock signals are *high* during the noisy time immediately following clock switching edges.

In general, systems using 5-V advanced CMOS devices with true CMOS input-output levels have greater noise margins than systems using TTL, CMOS, or BiCMOS devices with TTL input-output levels. However, it is not clear that there is any system advantage since advanced CMOS devices tend to generate more noise. Thus, CMOS devices need more noise margin than TTL devices. Where advanced CMOS devices with TTL input thresholds are connected to 5-V CMOS devices with CMOS output levels, the *high*-level noise margin is much greater than the TTL *high*-level noise margin and the *low*-level noise margin is slightly improved over the TTL *low*-level noise margin. Mixing 5-V CMOS devices with CMOS output levels with devices with TTL input levels is the worst possible combination of devices. The 5-V CMOS devices create a great deal of noise in the presence of devices designed for a more benign environment. Output levels of CMOS devices vary greatly with load conditions, and thus it is difficult to define generic CMOS noise margins (as can be done for TTL

TABLE 2.8   Specified Worst-Case Input-Output Voltage Levels for Typical Buffer

Family	Input levels, V		Output levels, V	
	$V_{IL\,MAX}$	$V_{IH\,MIN}$	$V_{OL\,MAX}$	$V_{OH\,MIN}$
ABT	0.8	2.0	0.55	2.5
AC	1.35	3.15	0.1	4.4
ACT	0.8	2.0	0.5	3.7
AC11	1.35	3.15	0.1	4.4
ACT11	0.8	2.0	0.5	3.7
ALS	0.8	2.0	0.5	2.4
AS	0.8	2.0	0.55	2.4
FAST	0.8	2.0	0.55	2.4
FCT	0.8	2.0	0.55	2.4
FCT3	0.8	2.0	0.5	2.4
BC*	0.8	2.0	0.5	2.5
BCT	0.8	2.0	0.55	2.4
LVQ	0.8	2.0	0.5	2.4
LVT	0.8	2.0	0.5	2.4

*Worst-case levels at +85°C.

circuits). Actual loaded input-output levels must be determined to establish the actual noise margin for a given application.

Table 2.8 shows the worst-case specified input and output voltage levels for typical buffers (such as octal 240s or 244s) for several of the more common logic families (output levels are for the load currents shown in Table 2.7). Buffer output levels are used because worst-case buffer output levels tend to be slightly poorer than gate output levels. Thus, noise margin is poorest at buffer interfaces.

2.6.1 Static noise margins of advanced Schottky TTL logic families

Worst-case noise margins over the military temperature range for the various advanced Schottky TTL families are listed in Table 2.9. The margins shown are based on the worst-case specified input and output voltage levels shown in Table 2.8. Note that the worst-case *high* and the worst-case *low* noise margins are different in each case. The *low* noise margin is either 0.25 or 0.3 V, and the *high* is 0.4 V. A 0.1- or 0.15-V difference between *high* and *low* noise margins may not seem

TABLE 2.9   Static Noise Margins of Advanced Schottky TTL Families

Family	*Low*-level noise margin, V	*High*-level noise margin, V
ALS	0.3	0.4
AS	0.25	0.4
F	0.25	0.4

significant, but advantage should be taken of the higher noise margin where it exists. In many applications, 0.1 or 0.15 V of additional noise margin will significantly enhance system reliability.

TTL noise margin change with temperature.   The threshold of TTL devices (i.e., the actual level where they switch states) is determined by the forward voltage drops across a combination of *pn* or metal-silicon diode or base-emitter junctions referenced to ground. The forward voltage drop across each of the junctions increases with lower operating temperatures and decreases with higher operating temperatures.* It follows that the threshold shifts in a similar manner. Thus, the actual noise margins, which are related to the actual input threshold level, shift with temperature.[6] *Low* noise margin increases with low temperature, and *high* noise margin decreases with low temperature. The opposite happens under high operating temperature conditions: *low* noise margin decreases and *high* increases. Data books show only worst-case *high* and *low* input limits, but designers should be aware of how the actual input threshold changes with temperature. In some cases, signal polarity can be arranged to take advantage of the actual (difference) noise margin.

2.6.2   Static noise margins of advanced CMOS logic families

Table 2.10 lists static *high* and *low* noise margins for various advanced CMOS logic families based on the input-output limits shown in Table 2.8.

TABLE 2.10   Static Noise Margins of Advanced CMOS Logic Families

Family	*Low*-level noise margin, V	*High*-level noise margin, V
AC	1.25	1.25
ACT	0.3	1.7
AC11	1.25	1.25
ACT11	0.3	1.7
FCT	0.25	0.4
LVQ	0.3	0.4

---

*The temperature coefficient for the forward voltage drop across a *pn* junction or a metal-silicon (Schottky) diode junction is approximately -2 mV/°C (see Chap. 3).

TABLE 2.11   Static Noise Margins of BiCMOS Logic Families

Family	*Low*-level noise margin, V	*High*-level noise margin, V
ABT	0.25	0.5
BC	0.3	0.5
BCT	0.25	0.5
LVT	0.3	0.4

2.6.3   Static noise margins of BiCMOS logic families

The BiCMOS logic families have TTL input-output levels and thus have static noise margins equivalent to TTL devices. Table 2.11 lists worst-case static noise margins for several BiCMOS logic families over the military temperature range and with V_{cc} equal to 4.5 V. The values listed in Table 2.11 can be derived from the specified worst-case input and output voltage levels listed in Table 2.8 (also see Refs. 8, 13, and 14). Note that the worst-case *high* and the worst-case *low* noise margins are different for all the families. For all the BiCMOS logic families, *low* noise margin is either 0.25 or 0.3 V, and *high* noise margin is either 0.4 or 0.5 V. A 0.15- or 0.2-V difference between the *high* and *low* noise margins may not seem significant, but advantage should be taken of the higher noise margin where it exists. In many applications, 0.15 or 0.2 V of additional noise margin may significantly enhance system reliability.

2.6.4   Dynamic noise immunity

Dynamic noise immunity refers to the sensitivity of logic devices to narrow pulses. Most of the older, slower logic families were insensitive to narrow pulses of only a few nanoseconds. That is not true with today's devices. They tend to react to pulses as narrow as 2 or 3 ns. Thus, narrow ground bounce and cross-coupling spikes caused by the fast edges of advanced Schottky TTL, advanced CMOS, and BiCMOS devices are a great concern from a system malfunction standpoint (see Chap. 4). Unfortunately, device sensitivity to spikes is typically not specified. Some manufacturers' data books contain some generic information on pulse rejection characteristics, but the information tends to be typical data on a logic family basis rather than worst-case data for specific devices. Figures 2.8, 2.9, and 2.10 are representative of the pulse rejection characteristics of today's high-speed parts. Most of today's devices with TTL level inputs have *low* level pulse rejection characteristics similar to those shown in Fig. 2.8. Most advanced CMOS devices with true CMOS input levels have pulse rejection characteristics similar to those shown in Figs. 2.9 and 2.10. As

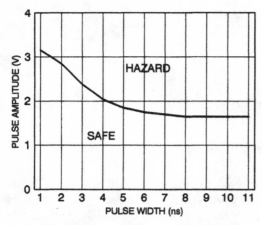

Figure 2.8 *Low* state pulse rejection characteristics of IDT FCT244 when operating with V_{cc} equal to 5 V. Pulse width measured at 50 percent amplitude. Most high-speed TTL, CMOS, and BiCMOS devices with TTL input thresholds have similar characteristics. (*Reprinted by permission of Integrated Device Technology, Inc.*)

Figs. 2.8, 2.9, and 2.10 show, most devices have some additional immunity to upset or output changes from very narrow input spikes, but keep in mind that most pulse rejection curves are typical data. Thus, pulse rejection curves should be viewed as general guidelines to expected performance—not as an absolute definition. Device pulse rejection characteristics are difficult to precisely define for all conditions. Clock circuits and asynchronous circuits should not rely on pulse rejection characteristics of devices to prevent malfunctions. Clock circuits and control signals to asynchronous inputs must be designed to be free of stray pulses.

2.6.5 Noise margin summary

In general, 5-V advanced CMOS devices with CMOS input thresholds have more noise margin than devices with TTL input and output levels or low-voltage CMOS devices. However, more noise margin is needed since the large voltage swings and fast edges of first-generation 5-V advanced CMOS devices with full rail-to-rail output swings generate more noise than advanced Schottky TTL, second-generation advanced CMOS, BiCMOS, or LV devices with TTL or near-TTL level output swings.

Because of the noise-generating characteristics of today's high-speed devices, system noise immunity must be optimized by selecting signal polarity with regard to optimum noise rejection. Most TTL,

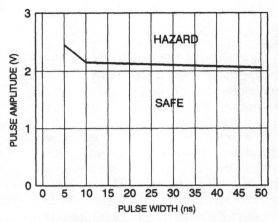

Figure 2.10 FACT AC family *low* level pulse noise margin with V_{cc} equal to 5 V. Pulse amplitude measured from ground. (*Reprinted by permission of National Semiconductor Corp.*)

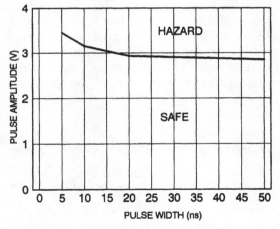

Figure 2.9 FACT AC family *high* level pulse noise margin with V_{cc} equal to 5 V. Pulse amplitude measured referenced to V_{cc}. (*Reprinted by permission of National Semiconductor Corp.*)

CMOS, and BiCMOS devices with TTL input-output levels have more *high* level signal noise margin than *low* level signal. Thus, in those systems that use devices with TTL input levels, critical signals that have low-duty cycles should be arranged so that they are in the *high* state most of the time. Only clocked devices that clock on *low*-to-*high* transitions should be used, so that clock signals are *high* when system noise is at a maximum (noise is a maximum immediately following clock switching edges). The same is true when CMOS devices with rail-to-rail outputs are used to drive devices with TTL inputs: *High* level noise margin is greater than *low* level noise margin by an even greater ratio (than when all devices have TTL levels). When CMOS or BiCMOS devices with TTL input levels are driven with TTL devices, *high* signals have maximum noise margin and the same considerations apply with regard to optimum signal polarity for maximum noise rejection.

Where CMOS devices with true CMOS input levels are used, *high* and *low* noise margin specifications are the same. Thus, either signal polarity is acceptable for critical low-duty cycle signals (i.e., reset signals). However, for commonality with parts with TTL levels, it is best to arrange critical low-duty cycle signals so that they are in the *high* state most of the time, since most systems will have a mix of devices with both TTL and CMOS levels.

When technologies are mixed, the actual noise margin may be a function of the power supply level. Input threshold levels of CMOS and BiCMOS devices (with CMOS input structures) are typically a function of V_{cc} whereas TTL device thresholds are a function of voltage drops across diodes or base-emitter junctions that are referenced to ground. Since input thresholds of devices with CMOS input structures change with changes in V_{cc}, where CMOS devices must interface with other devices (i.e., not other CMOS devices), extra care must be taken to ensure compatibility over worst-case V_{cc} levels.

2.7   References

1. Gary Tharalson, "Which Logic Family Is Best for You?" *Electronic Products,* May 1989, pp. 53–57.
2. Paul L. Matthews, *Choosing and Using ECL,* McGraw-Hill, New York, 1984.
3. *FACT Advanced CMOS Logic Databook,* National Semiconductor Corp., Santa Clara, Calif., 1993.
4. *IC MASTER,* Hearst Business Communications Inc., Garden City, N.Y., current year.
5. *Advanced CMOS Logic Data Book,* Texas Instruments Inc., Dallas, Tex., 1993.
6. Stan Baker, "Extending TTL," *Electronic Engineering Times,* October 16, 1989, pp. 41 and 52.
7. *Low-Voltage Logic Data Book,* Texas Instruments Inc., Dallas, Tex., 1993.
8. *High-Performance Logic Data Book Supplement,* Integrated Device Technology, Inc., Santa Clara, Calif., 1994.
9. *Bipolar Microprocessor Logic and Interface Data Book,* Advanced Micro Devices Inc., Sunnyvale, Calif., 1981.
10. *FAST Advanced Schottky TTL Logic Databook,* National Semiconductor Corp., Santa Clara, Calif., 1990.
11. *ALS/AS Logic Data Book,* Texas Instruments Inc., Dallas, Tex., 1986.
12. *Low Voltage Databook,* National Semiconductor Corp., Santa Clara, Calif., 1992.
13. *Bi-CMOS Logic Data,* Motorola Inc., Phoenix, Ariz., 1989.
14. *BiCMOS Bus Interface Logic Data Book,* Texas Instruments Inc., Dallas, Tex., 1989.

15. Brian C. Martin, "Tips for Straddling the 3-V to 5-V Fence," *Electronic Design,* April 4, 1994, pp. 67–73.
16. Kenneth M. Cuy, "Design Considerations Bring Unity to a Mixed-Voltage World," *EDN,* February 2, 1995, pp. 115–118.

2.8 Bibliography

Advanced CMOS Logic Designer's Handbook, Texas Instruments Inc., Dallas, Tex., 1988.

Alvarez, Antonio R.: *BiCMOS Technology and Applications,* Kluwer Academic Publishers, Norwell, Mass., 1989.

Bus Interface Products 1988 Data Book, Advanced Micro Devices Inc., Sunnyvale, Calif., 1987.

FCT—Fast, CMOS, TTL-Compatible Logic, Technical Note, Integrated Device Technology, Inc., Santa Clara, Calif., 1986.

Frederiksen, Thomas M.: *Intuitive CMOS Electronics,* McGraw-Hill, New York, 1989.

Funk, Dick: "Design Guidelines for CMOS Logic Systems," *Electronic Products,* March 28, 1984, pp. 75–79.

Tuck, Barbara: "TI's BiCMOS Bus Interface ICs Slash Standby Current," *Electronic Products,* June 15, 1987, pp. 17–19.

Wong, Thomas: "Not All BiCMOS Is Created Equal," *Electronic Engineering Times,* December 25, 1989, pp. 19, 22, and 24.

Advanced Schottky TTL, CMOS, and BiCMOS Logic Circuits

Management of system signal integrity requires insight into the operation of TTL, CMOS, and BiCMOS input and output circuits. High-speed digital devices cannot be applied successfully when the design effort is limited to functional logic considerations only. The electrical characteristics and the limitations of the devices being applied must be understood. Knowledge of the minute details of the internal structure of logic devices is not necessary, but an understanding of device interface circuitry is needed to comprehend the device and interconnection system interaction. An understanding of device and interconnection system interaction is needed to manage signal integrity. However, schematics and circuit details of today's logic devices, which are needed to understand interface operation, are not easy to come by. That has not always been the case; most small-scale integration (SSI) logic device data sheets included schematics that showed transistor-level device implementations, but current data sheets seldom include schematics. Sometimes schematics of basic SSIC devices, such as gates and drivers, can be found in the introductory section of data books. However, for medium-scale integration (MSI) devices, such as 4-bit counters, and for large-scale integration (LSI) devices, such as arithmetic logic units (ALUs), the most that is provided is a functional block-level representation. It would be impractical to show detailed internal schematics for MSI and LSI devices in data books, and detailed information on internal circuitry is of little use to system designers; but interface circuitry and interface parameter limits are needed.

3.1   Advanced Schottky TTL Circuits

Figure 3.1 is a schematic of a *F*airchild (now National) *a*dvanced *S*chottky *T*TL (FAST) two-input NAND gate. As would be expected, it is considerably more complex than an original TTL family NAND gate (for a comparison see Ref. 1). The advanced Schottky gate consists of a number of Schottky diodes (*D*3, *D*4, *D*5, *D*6, etc.), silicon *pn* diodes (*D*1 and *D*2), Schottky clamped bipolar transistors (*Q*1, *Q*2, *Q*3, *Q*4, etc.), and a bipolar transistor (*Q*6) where the original 54/7400 TTL NAND gate consisted of four bipolar transistors and a diode.[1] Both gates function identically from a logic standpoint. The difference is that the advanced Schottky gate performs the functions much faster and has interface characteristics that are optimized for control of signal integrity in high-speed systems. The input and output circuitry of the FAST NAND gate in Fig. 3.1 is typical of that used throughout the FAST family.

Input circuit.   FAST input circuits consist of diode and resistor networks, as shown in Fig. 3.1. The diode and resistor network performs the logic function (in this case an AND function which is followed by an inverter to get the NAND function) and important dynamic signal enhancement functions. The AND function is accomplished with diodes *D*1 and *D*2, which are conventional silicon diodes, and the 10-kΩ resistor tied between the anodes of *D*1 and *D*2 and V_{cc}. Diodes *D*5 and *D*6 are large-geometry Schottky diodes that provide high-speed clamping of input signal excursions below ground (a very important

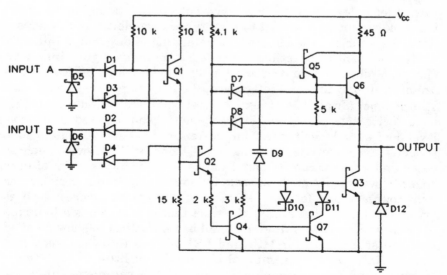

Figure 3.1   Advanced Schottky 54/74F00 NAND gate. (*Reprinted with permission of National Semiconductor Corp.*)

function for TTL signal integrity). Diodes $D3$ and $D4$ are used to remove stored charge from the base of $Q2$ on the negative transition of an input to help speed the internal response time of the gate. Note that the input impedance profile is typical of TTL circuits—a very high input impedance for *high*-level inputs with a somewhat lower impedance for *low* inputs. *High* signals see back-biased diodes. *Low* signal sources must sink a small amount of current sourced from the 10-kΩ resistor tied between the cathodes of $D1$ and $D2$ and V_{cc}.

Output circuit. The output is a conventional (for TTL circuits) totem-pole stage. Transistors $Q5$ and $Q6$ form a Darlington pair that supplies pull-up current for *low*-to-*high* transitions and static *high* signals. The 45-Ω resistor between the collectors of $Q5$ and $Q6$ and V_{cc} limits the output current drive during *low*-to-*high* transitions and thereby reduces *low*-to-*high* transient switching currents. The resistor also tends to match the *low*-to-*high* output impedance to that of the typical printed-circuit board characteristic impedance and thereby controls ringing and overshoot of *low*-to-*high* transitions. Transistor $Q3$ supplies pull-down current for *high*-to-*low* transitions and to maintain static *low* signals. Diode $D12$ on the output limits negative voltage excursions due to reflection caused by transmission-line effects.

For more information on the operation of FAST circuits, see Refs. 2 and 3.

3.1.1 Equivalent circuits for diodes and transistors

Analyzing and understanding TTL circuit functional operation are greatly simplified by substituting simple static equivalent circuits or models for the internal device diodes and transistors. The diode and transistor equivalent circuits, or models, shown and described below, are not exact, but they are adequate for most static analysis.

Diode equivalent circuits. Transistor-transistor logic (TTL) circuits use both standard silicon and metal-silicon diodes. Standard silicon diodes are formed by p- and n-type semiconductor material junctions, as shown in Fig. 3.2a.[4] Schottky or metal-silicon diodes are formed at metal-silicon junctions, as shown in Fig. 3.2b.[5] The schematic, or circuit

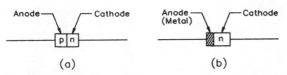

Figure 3.2 Semiconductor diodes. (a) pn junction diode; (b) metal-silicon junction diode.

diagram symbol, for standard silicon diodes is shown in Fig. 3.3*a*, and that for Schottky, or metal-silicon junction, diodes is found in Fig. 3.3*b*.

When diodes are forward-biased, i.e., when current is flowing in the direction shown in Fig. 3.3, a battery or direct-current (dc) voltage source along with a resistor is a useful static equivalent circuit (see Fig. 3.4).[6] In general, when one is dealing with TTL circuits, the resistor can be neglected since at the current levels of TTL circuits its effect is usually negligible. Typical diode *I-V* curves for silicon diodes and for metal-silicon diodes are shown in Fig. 3.5*a* and *b*.[7] As can be seen in Fig. 3.5, diodes do not have a sharp cut-on or cutoff *I-V* relationship, as is implied by a fixed battery equivalent circuit; but for most practical purposes, a fixed voltage source is an adequate representation of a forward-biased diode. Diodes in TTL circuits usually operate in the flat portion of the *I-V* curve. Forward voltage drop at room temperature (+25°C) flattens out for silicon diodes near 0.8 V and for Schottky diodes near 0.3 V (see Fig. 3.5). The exact value for any given diode depends upon a number of conditions such as temperature, current flow, and basic device parameters. For the purpose of understanding TTL device operation, the exact value is not very important. It is usually not critical whether 0.7, 0.8, or 0.9 V is used for silicon diodes, or 0.2, 0.3, or 0.4 V for Schottky diodes.

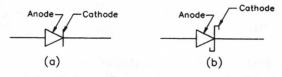

Figure 3.3 Diode symbols. (*a*) *pn* junction diode; (*b*) metal-silicon junction diode.

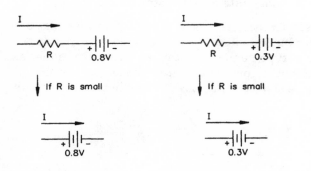

Figure 3.4 Forward-biased diode equivalent circuits. (*a*) *pn* junction diode; (*b*) metal-silicon junction diode.

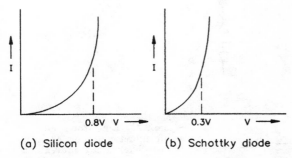

(a) Silicon diode   (b) Schottky diode

Figure 3.5   Diode V-I curves. (a) pn junction diode; (b) metal-silicon junction diode.

For forward currents within the designed operating current range, diode forward voltage drop does not change much with changing current levels, but forward drop does change as a function of temperature. The forward voltage drop across both silicon and Schottky diodes decreases by about 2 mV/°C increase in temperature (for currents in the normal operating range).[8]

**Silicon diode forward voltage
temperature coefficient is approximately
-2 mV/°C.**

In most TTL circuit applications, when diodes are reverse-biased, as shown in Fig. 3.6a, it is safe to treat them as open circuits with no current flow. However, reverse-biased diodes are more correctly modeled as current sources, as shown in Fig. 3.6b, where I is the leakage current. All diodes have some leakage. However, for a simplified functional analysis of digital circuits, it is safe to assume an open circuit.

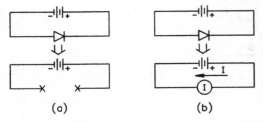

(a)   (b)

Figure 3.6   Reverse-biased diode equivalent circuits. (a) In most cases it is treated as an open circuit; (b) more exact case is a leakage current (source) path.

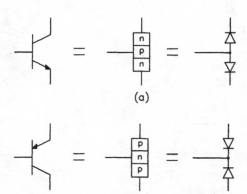

(a)

(b)

Figure 3.7 Transistor symbols, semiconductor properties, and back-to-back diode equivalent circuits. (a) *npn* transistor; (b) *pnp* transistor.

Transistor equivalent circuits. Some common graphical representations of transistors are shown in Fig. 3.7.[4,6] Note that under certain conditions transistors appear as back-to-back diodes, as shown in the right side of Fig. 3.7. For example, when isolated good transistors are checked for continuity between base and collector and between base and emitter, they appear as a pair of back-to-back diodes. In some cases, the back-to-back diode analogy of transistors helps in understanding the operation of TTL circuits.

The on, or conducting, and the off, or nonconducting, equivalent circuits for transistors are shown in Figs. 3.8 and 3.9. When one is dealing with digital circuits, the linear operation of transistors is of little concern. Digital designers are mainly concerned with transistors in

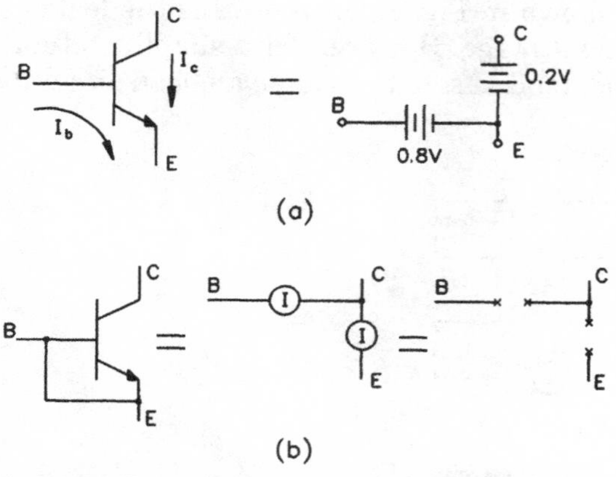

(a)

(b)

Figure 3.8 Equivalent circuits for transistors. (a) For an on *npn* transistor; (b) for an off *pnp* transistor.

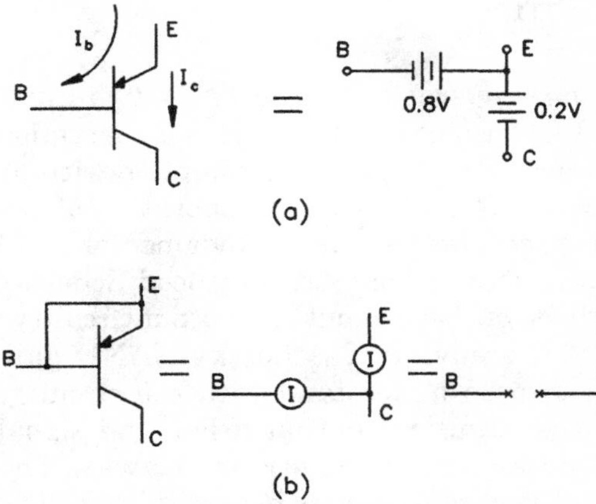

(a)

(b)

Figure 3.9 Equivalent circuits for *pnp* transistors. (*a*) For an on *pnp* transistor; (*b*) for an off *npn* transistor.

the on or off states. Figure 3.7 shows the equivalent circuit for an on and an off *npn* transistor, and Fig. 3.8 shows the same for an on and an off *pnp* transistor. The values shown for the battery or dc voltage sources are typical numbers. Whether 0.6 or 1.0 V is used for the base-emitter drop makes little difference. Likewise, whether 0.3, 0.4, or 0.5 V is used for the on value of collector-to-emitter drops is not of great significance for simple functional analysis.

The Schottky TTL families use Schottky diode clamps connected between the base and the collector of most transistors to speed up turnoff. Schottky diode clamps keep clamped transistors from going into saturation by diverting current from the base.[6] A nonsaturated transistor turns off faster than a saturated transistor.[9] Schottky diode clamps greatly enhanced the viability of TTL technology. Schottky diode clamps were the key that led to an economical manufacturing process for high-speed, low-power TTL devices.

An on Schottky *npn* transistor and its equivalent circuit are shown in Fig. 3.10. The off condition is the same as for a conventional silicon transistor and is shown in Fig. 3.8*b*.

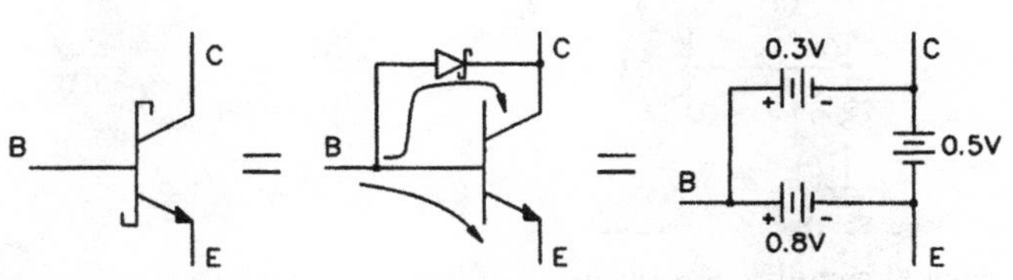

Figure 3.10 Schottky clamped *npn* transistor.

3.1.2 Functional operation of the TTL NAND gate

An examination of the functional operation of the FAST two-input NAND gate in Fig. 3.1 is useful for insight into the functional operation of all TTL circuits.[9,10] A two-input NAND gate is a simple device by today's MSI and LSI TTL devices. Nonetheless, the operation of the input, output, and internal phase-splitter circuits is fundamental to all TTL circuit operation. More functionally complex advanced Schottky devices are structured around the same basic input and output circuitry.[2]

The functional operation of the advanced Schottky NAND gate (shown in Fig. 3.1) is much easier to understand with the circuitry used to enhance switching speed, transient output drive, and signal quality in a transmission-line environment stripped away. The remaining functional portion of the gate is shown in Fig. 3.11. The removal of the enhancement diodes and transistors unclutters the circuit, but does not affect the static functional action of the primary devices that make up the functional portion of the gate.

The basic gate is composed of three functional areas (see Fig. 3.11): an input section, a phase-splitter section, and an output section. Most TTL devices have similar functional areas. More complex functions have additional circuitry, but similar or equivalent input, output, and phase-splitter circuitry is used. For example, a register or latch must contain some additional circuitry to store information, but the input and output circuitry will be similar to that of a basic gate.

> *The following analysis is not rigorous, but the approach and results are useful for understanding basic digital circuit operation.*

Equivalent circuit with a *low* input. Figure 3.12 shows the basic gate (Fig. 3.11) with diode and transistor equivalent circuits substituted

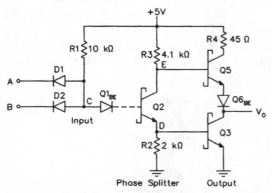

Figure 3.11 Basic functional circuitry of a two-input TTL NAND gate.

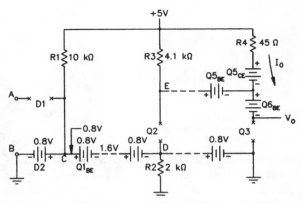

Figure 3.12 Basic two-input TTL NAND gate equivalent circuit for a *low* input.

for normal diode and transistor schematic representations. When input *B* is grounded as shown in Fig. 3.12, the associated diode is forward-biased and current flows out of the device and into ground. Currents flowing out of TTL devices are defined as negative. Thus, *low* input currents $I_{\text{in low}}$ or I_{IL} and *high* output currents $I_{\text{out high}}$ or I_{OH} are given minus signs. It is perhaps awkward for some to think of a current coming out of a device as negative, but the sign given to current flow has little functional consequence. For example, current flow changes direction each one-half cycle in alternating-current (ac) devices. Input-output current flow for TTL devices is somewhat analogous; it changes direction with the state of the signal. If a signal is *low*, current flows out of the driven devices and into the source. If it is *high*, it flows out of the source and into the load.

Low current I_{IL} is calculated using the portion of the gate equivalent circuit shown in Fig. 3.13 and Eq. (3.1).

$$|I_{IL}| = \frac{V_{cc} - V_f(D2)}{R_1} \tag{3.1}$$

$$= \frac{5\text{ V} - 0.8\text{ V}}{10\text{ k}\Omega} = 0.42\text{ mA}$$

The older TTL families have different values of resistors in the input section. Schematics for the original standard TTL family typically show 4 kΩ, and 20 kΩ is a typical value for the LS family. However, regardless of the value of the input section resistor, the same general method can be used to calculate the typical *low* input current for the other families. The calculation will not result in the exact input current values specified in a manufacturer's data books, and exact values should not be expected. The

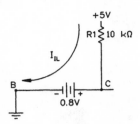

Figure 3.13 Input current path equivalent circuit with a grounded input.

manufacturer's device specification must allow for all worst-case conditions. The models produce typical values since typical parameter values are used. If worst-case internal component parameters are used in the models, the models will yield worst-case currents. Some might ask, Why bother looking at input currents, etc., if the derived parameter values are not exact numbers? One reason is to understand the nature of the current flow. If the operation of a circuit is understood, special or unusual interface conditions can be better addressed.

The next step in the overall gate analysis is to determine whether the phase-splitter transistor $Q2$ is turned on or off. If $Q2$ is on, it must have base-emitter current flow. For $Q2$ to have base current, the voltage at node C must be greater than 2.4 V (the base-emitter drops of $Q1$ plus $Q2$ plus $Q3$), but the voltage is only 0.8 V at node C with an input grounded; thus $Q2$ must be off. It does not matter which input is grounded, or if both are grounded—the voltage at node C is 0.8 V for either case. Two 0.8-V voltage sources in parallel or one 0.8-V voltage source between node C and ground results in the same voltage at node C. With $Q2$ in a nonconducting, or off, state, its collector-to-emitter nodes E to D are drawn open. The next step is to determine whether $Q3$ is on or off. Node D is at 0 V when $Q2$ is off. With node D at 0 V, there is no source of base current for $Q3$; hence $Q3$ is off also. Such a result should be expected, since the device is a NAND gate, and a NAND with a *low* input should have a *high* output (which requires $Q3$ to be off). However, at this point, it has been established only that the circuit does not have a *low* output. It has not been shown that the circuit has a *high* output, i.e., that the Darlington pair $Q5$ and $Q6$ are on.

To show that $Q5$ and $Q6$ are on and that the circuit has a *high* output, it must be shown that $Q5$ and $Q6$ have base-emitter current flow. From inspection of Fig. 3.12 it can be seen that $Q5$ and $Q6$ have a source of base current from node E as long as the output voltage V_o is less than two diode drops below V_{cc}. The two diode drops are those of the base-emitter (junction) drops of $Q5$ and $Q6$.

Most TTL output pull-up circuitry is structured so that a source of base current is available to quickly drive the output to a *high* level. Once an output reaches a *high* level, very little output current is needed to maintain a *high* when normal TTL inputs are driven. Power is saved by reducing the drive once a static *high* condition is achieved.

Output *high* voltage levels.   The above analysis of the basic gate, with a low input, shows that a *low* input on any of, or all, the inputs turns on $Q5$ and $Q6$ and pulls the output V_o *high*. The magnitude of V_o *high* depends on the value of the load and the output current. There are two sources of output *high* current: I_c through the collector emitters of $Q5$ and $Q6$ and I_b through the base emitters of $Q5$ and $Q6$, as shown in Fig. 3.14. The current I_b, which must exist for $Q5$ and $Q6$ to be on, establishes one limiting value for the output voltage V_o, which is

$$V_o = V_{cc} - V_{BE}(Q5) - V_{BE}(Q6) - I_b R3 \qquad (3.2)$$

However, the load resistance R_L must be known to determine I_b. For the example circuit, V_o as a function of I_b, by using Eq. (3.2), is

$$V_o = 5 \text{ V} - 0.8 \text{ V} - 0.8 \text{ V} - I_b (4.1 \text{ k}\Omega)$$

Notice that the upper limit for a *high* output is 3.4 V (5 V − 1.6 V) when $I_b = 0$ (infinite load impedance).

In high-current situations, the collector-emitter current path I_c through $Q5$ and $Q6$ may establish the output *high* level rather than the current path through the base I_b. The conditions of both paths must be calculated to establish which path is dominant. To determine V_o in the collector path-limited case, the current I_o through $R4$, the collector emitter of $Q6$, and R_L are calculated, and the output voltage V_o is determined by using I_o times the load resistance R_L. Alternately, a simple voltage divider calculation can be done thus:

$$V_o = \frac{R_L}{R_L + 45 \ \Omega} [5 \text{ V} - V_{CE}(Q5)] \qquad (3.3)$$

In most actual applications, when a gate is driving a load to ground, the load is a low enough impedance for some amount of base

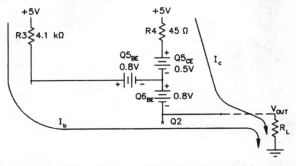

Figure 3.14   Basic two-input TTL NAND gate *high*-output equivalent circuit.

current to flow in $Q5$ and $Q6$, but not so low that the conditions of Eq. (3.3) are met. Thus, in most grounded load cases, Eq. (3.2), which includes the I_b term, should be used to determine the output level. Grounded loads are not the normal TTL static load configuration; but when an output switches from a *low* to a *high* level, the transient load current flow is to ground (see Sec. 4.2.2).

Most TTL signals observed in the laboratory have *high* levels that are above 3.4 V and are often in the range of 4.0 to 4.7 V. Yet, Eq. (3.2) indicates that the *high* limit is 3.4 V. Why the discrepancy? The inconsistency is due to the use of a load connected to ground in the model (Fig. 3.14); normal TTL loads (inputs) tend to pull signals up rather than down. The actual load when TTL devices are driving other TTL devices is shown in Fig. 3.15.

The load—in the normal case, the input of another TTL device— pulls V_o up to the supply level (5 V) less one diode forward-voltage drop (0.8 V). The actual worst-case input-output current and voltage specifications for the various TTL families are shown in Chap. 2. Note that an output *high* level, under all circumstances, is a function of its load.

Equivalent circuit with *high* inputs. The equivalent circuit for the case where both inputs are at a high level, where a normal static input *high* level can range between 2.5 V and slightly above the plus supply rail (input levels and limits are listed in Chap. 2), is shown in Fig. 3.16. Both inputs must be at a *high* level to initiate the NAND action, i.e., a *low* output. With both inputs within the specified *high* input level range, both input diodes $D1$ and $D2$ are reversed-biased and act as open circuits. Since the diodes act as open circuits, input levels have no influence on the voltage at node C. Node C attempts to go toward $+ 5$ V, but it is clamped by the base-emitter junctions of $Q1$, $Q2$, and $Q3$. Node C attempting to go positive provides $Q2$ with a source of base current from the $+ 5$-V supply through the 10-kΩ resistor. With base current, $Q2$ turns on and provides $Q3$ with base cur-

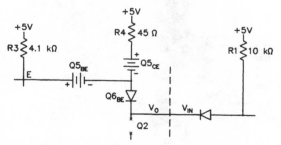

Figure 3.15 Equivalent circuit for a TTL output connected to a TTL input.

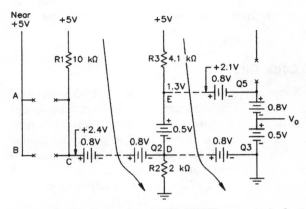

Figure 3.16 Basic two-input TTL NAND gate equivalent circuit for both inputs *high*.

rent, which turns it on (a small amount of current is diverted from the base of $Q3$ by the 2-kΩ resistor between the emitter of $Q2$ and ground, but not enough to prevent $Q3$ from turning on). With $Q3$ on, the output V_o is pulled down to a level equal to the saturation voltage of $Q3$, which is typically near 0.5 V for Schottky clamped transistors. Thus, the output is in a *low* state. A NAND gate with both inputs *high* is expected to have a *low* output.

The final step is to establish that $Q5$ and $Q6$ are off and are not trying to pull the output *high* at the same time as it is being pulled *low* by $Q3$. Totem-pole TTL output stages are not designed to have the pull-up section (the Darlington pair $Q5$ and $Q6$) on at the same time as the pull-down section ($Q3$). Having both pull-up and pull-down sections on at the same time would cause a potentially destructive high-current condition in the output stage. Establishing that $Q5$ and $Q6$ are off is best accomplished by assuming the conditions required for $Q5$ and $Q6$ to be on. For $Q5$ and $Q6$ to be on, they need base current, which means node E must be greater than V_{CE} of $Q3$ plus V_{BE} of $Q6$ plus V_{BE} of $Q5$ (see Fig. 3.16). That is, assume current is flowing through the base emitter of $Q5$ which results in a forward voltage drop of 0.8 V, and that current is flowing through the base-emitter junction of $Q6$ so that its base-emitter drop is 0.8 V and the collector-emitter voltage of $Q3$ is 0.5 V. If that is the case, the sum of the voltage drops from the base of $Q5$ to ground is 2.1 V. Thus, node E, which is the same as the base of $Q5$, must be at 2.1 V for the Darlington pair $Q5$ and $Q6$ to be on. However, one of the conditions for having $Q3$, the pull-down output transistor, on was that $Q2$ was on. With $Q2$ and $Q3$ on, node E is 1.3 V (V_{CE} of $Q2$ plus V_{EB} of $Q3$) which is less than 2.1 V, so this means that $Q5$ and $Q6$ must be off. Therefore, the pull-up output stage transistors are not on and are not in conflict with the pull-down output transistor.

3.2 Advanced CMOS Logic Circuits

Advanced CMOS logic devices are built with n-channel and p-channel enhancement-mode metal-oxide semiconductor field-effect transistors (MOSFETs). The symbols and terminal nomenclature for enhancement-mode field-effect transistors are shown in Fig. 3.17.[7] Enhancement-mode n-channel MOSFETs operate somewhat analogously to npn bipolar transistors, and enhancement-mode p-channel MOSFETs operate somewhat analogously to pnp bipolar transistors (see Figs. 3.18 and 3.19).

Gate ─│   Drain   Gate ─│   Source
       │   Source   │   Drain
    n–channel p–channel

Figure 3.17 MOSFET schematic symbols.

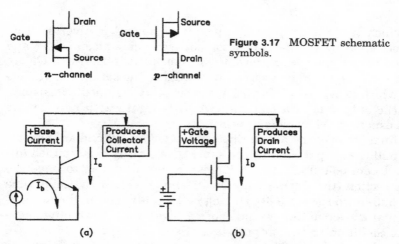

(a)   (b)

Figure 3.18 (a) Bipolar npn and (b) n-channel MOSFET equivalency.

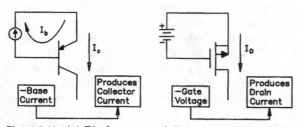

Figure 3.19 (a) Bipolar pnp and (b) p-channel MOSFET equivalency.

Analyzing and understanding CMOS circuit operation are greatly simplified by substituting simple static equivalent circuits or models for the internal MOSFETs. The equivalent circuits or models shown and described below are not exact, but they are adequate for most static analysis. The equivalent circuit for an on MOSFET is a resistor between the drain and source and an open circuit for the gate connection (see Fig. 3.20). The equivalent circuit for an off MOSFET is an open circuit between all terminals. The typical on resistance of the MOSFETs used in advanced CMOS devices is near 10 Ω. The off impedance of most MOSFETs is extremely high; off MOSFETs have some leakage current, but in most digital applications off leakage currents are of such a low magnitude that off MOSFETs can be considered open circuits. The same is true of the gate input impedance; in most cases it is extremely high.

Most advanced CMOS logic devices, both LV and 5-V, are made with MOSFET circuits arranged in complementary n-channel and p-channel pairs.[10] The complementary pairs use p-channel MOSFETs for pull-ups and n-channel MOSFETs for pull-downs. Logic devices

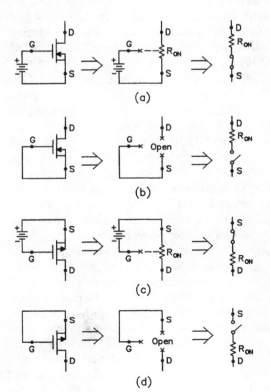

(a)

(b)

(c)

(d)

Figure 3.20 Equivalent circuits for on and off MOSFETs. (a) on n channel; (b) off n channel; (c) on p channel; (d) off p channel.

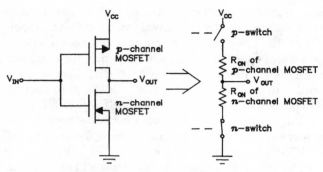

Figure 3.21 CMOS inverter and equivalent circuit.

implemented with complementary pairs have no dc paths between V_{cc} and ground; one MOSFET in each complementary pair is on and the other is off at all times. Hence, CMOS devices dissipate little dc power. A typical complementary inverter stage and its equivalent circuit[10] are shown in Fig. 3.21. The equivalent circuit for the inverter consists of two resistors and two ideal switches in series between V_{cc} and ground. In the equivalent circuit, the switching action of the MOSFETs is represented by the ideal p switch and n switch. The two resistors represent the on resistance of the two MOSFETs. A CMOS inverter functions as follows: When the input level is near V_{cc}, the p-channel pull-up MOSFET is off and the n-channel pull-down MOSFET is on. When the input level is near ground, the n-channel pull-down MOSFET is off and the p-channel pull-up MOSFET is on. When the n-channel pull-down MOSFET is on, the output level is near ground. When the p-channel pull-up MOSFET is on, the output level is near V_{cc}. Most first-generation advanced CMOS logic devices (see Chap. 2 for the definition of first-generation devices) have complementary outputs that operate in a similar fashion and have signal levels that switch between ground and V_{cc}. Signals that switch between ground and V_{cc} are sometimes described as *rail-to-rail levels.*

Advanced CMOS technology's chief selling point has been low power consumption and cool system operation, but at system operating speeds above 30 MHz, first-generation 5-V advanced CMOS with its wide, fast rail-to-rail voltage swings may dissipate more power than advanced Schottky TTL devices. In addition, 5-V rail-to-rail voltage swings intensify most of the problems associated with high-speed logic applications, such as crosstalk, ground bounce, and transmission-line effects. Thus, some second-generation 5-V advanced CMOS logic families, notably the FCT-T family, have returned to TTL-level output voltages. These lower-output voltage swing devices typically use source-follower pull-up circuits in their output stages (see Fig. 3.22).

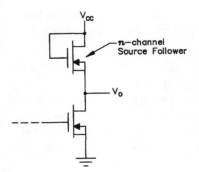

Figure 3.22 CMOS output stage with a source-follower pull-up resistor.

Source-follower pull-up circuits cut off when the voltage across the pull-up MOSFET is approximately equal to the threshold voltage of the MOSFET. And MOSFETs used in advanced CMOS logic circuits tend to have threshold voltages of 1 V or less. Thus, source-follower outputs tend to cut off (i.e., cease to supply current) at about 4 V under typical conditions, which means devices with source-follower outputs typically have *high* outputs that are near 4 V. Thus, advanced CMOS devices with source-follower pull-up output stages have output levels approximately the same as those of advanced Schottky TTL devices. Limiting signal swings to TTL levels reduces dynamic power dissipation, crosstalk, and ground bounce and greatly simplifies the system designer's overall signal integrity management task. Logic families with source-follower outputs by necessity have TTL-level input thresholds since under worst-case conditions *high*-output levels may not meet true 5-V CMOS *high*-input level requirements. Low-voltage CMOS has all the advantages of reduced-voltage-swing 5-V CMOS by virtue of its inherent lower-voltage signal swing.

The input impedance of advanced CMOS logic devices is very high when signals are between V_{cc} and ground (i.e., within the rails). MOSFETs have very high gate input impedance, which is ideal from a signal loading standpoint, but MOSFET gate impedance is so high that all inputs must have some form of electrostatic damage (ESD) protection circuitry. The typical ESD protection network consists of diodes connected between signal lines and power and ground (see Sec. 3.6). Some inputs may also have high-speed clamp diodes to limit signal overshoots and to improve signal quality in transmission-line environments (see Chap. 7). Under normal signal conditions, these ESD and signal clamp diodes are reverse-biased; they come into play only when signals exceed the rails.

Input threshold levels are typically set by controlling the relative sizes of the complementary input MOSFETs. If they are equal, the threshold is centered between power and ground. If one device is larger than the other, the threshold shifts in that direction. From a schematic standpoint, advanced CMOS devices with TTL input levels look the same as CMOS devices with CMOS input levels; they have the same input circuit structure.

CMOS logic structures. Logic functions, such as NORs and NANDs, are implemented by using multiple complementary structures.[7,10] For example, two-input CMOS NOR gates are implemented with two series pull-up and two parallel pull-down MOSFETs, as shown in Fig. 3.23. The opposite arrangement—parallel pull-up and series pull-down—is used to implement CMOS NAND gates. For example, two-input NAND gates are implemented as shown in Fig. 3.24.

To implement logic functions with multiple inputs, the number of complementary pairs of series and parallel MOSFETs can be increased as needed (up to some practical limit). However, as the number of series and parallel devices increases, output *high* and *low* impedances become increasingly more unbalanced. For example, the variable output impedance of an unbuffered two-input NOR gate (Fig. 3.23) is shown in Fig. 3.25. Advanced CMOS devices use output buffers to isolate internal logic function structures from line and load capacitances (which tend to be much larger than internal device node capacitances) to balance output drive and response.

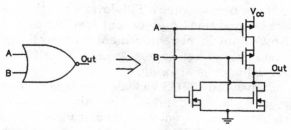

Figure 3.23   Two-input CMOS NOR gate.

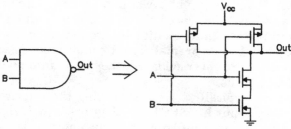

Figure 3.24   Two-input CMOS NAND gate.

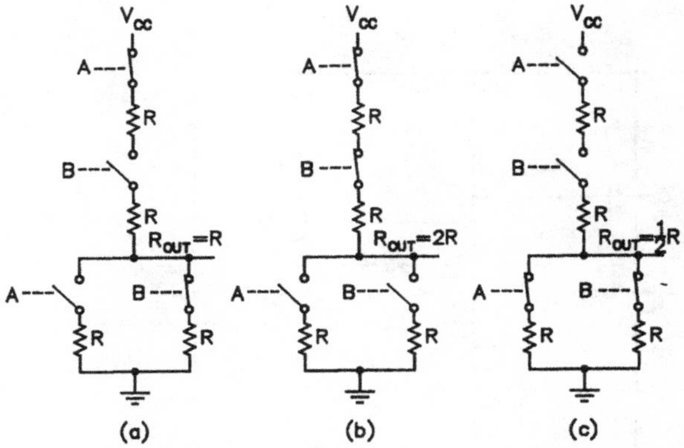

Figure 3.25 Variable output impedance of a CMOS two-input NOR gate.

3.3 BiCMOS Logic Circuits

BiCMOS logic circuits are built with a semiconductor technology that combines CMOS and bipolar transistors on the same chip. Most discrete BiCMOS logic devices are built with CMOS cores and bipolar output circuits, although some discrete BiCMOS devices also have bipolar input structures. Some BiCMOS LSI and ASIC devices use bipolar transistors in the core as well as on external interfaces.[11] Bipolar outputs and internal drive stages provide higher drive and more stable drive characteristics than can be achieved with CMOS technology alone. BiCMOS technology can provide either ECL or TTL interfaces. However, the discussion of BiCMOS circuits in this chapter is limited to those with TTL-level interfaces. BiCMOS logic devices, with TTL levels and interface circuitry coupled to a CMOS core, offer the best of both CMOS and bipolar advanced Schottky TTL technology. BiCMOS has the following advantages over CMOS: improved signal quality, less crosstalk, less dynamic power dissipation, and less transient-current generation which means less ground bounce. The advantage of BiCMOS over bipolar TTL is the reduced static power dissipation.

Figure 3.26 shows the internal circuitry of a BiCMOS logic device.[12] Typically, the input and core logic of BiCMOS logic devices (those that operate with TTL levels) are implemented by using advanced CMOS technology and conventional CMOS circuit techniques. Output stages are implemented by using bipolar technology. Most outputs are implemented with conventional totem-pole output stages (as shown in Fig. 3.27) that are similar in structure and operation to those used in advanced Schottky TTL devices.[13]

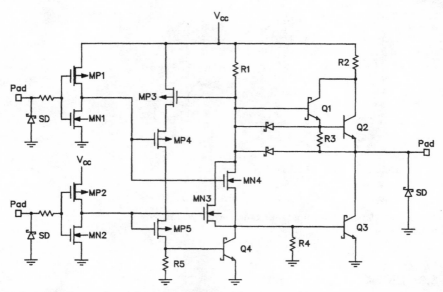

Figure 3.26 Internal circuitry of a BiCMOS 74BC08 AND gate. MP1 and MP2 are high-threshold *p*-channel MOSFETs; MP3, MP4, and MP5 are *p*-channel MOSFETs; and MN1, MN2, MN3, and MN4 are *n*-channel MOSFETs. (*Reprinted by permission of Toshiba Inc.*)

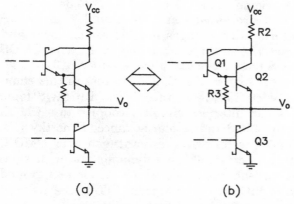

(a)   (b)

Figure 3.27 (*a*) Schottky TTL totem-pole output stage; (*b*) BiCMOS totem-pole output stage.

Bipolar totem-pole output stages have several system advantages:

1. Totem-pole stage output voltage (signal) swing is typically about 3.4 V instead of near 5 V, as is the case for normal 5-V CMOS outputs. Less output voltage swing means less dynamic power (see Sec. A.4 in the Appendix), less crosstalk, and less transient switching current.

Less transient switching current means fewer signal and power integrity problems, such as ground bounce and power and reference level corruption, that come with large transient currents (see Chap. 4).

2. The resistor between the pull-up transistor and V_{cc} in a totem-pole output stage limits the output current drive during *low*-to-*high* transitions and thereby reduces *low*-to-*high* transient switching currents. The resistor also tends to match the *low*-to-*high* output impedance to that of the typical printed-circuit board characteristic impedance and thereby controls ringing and overshoot of *low*-to-*high* transitions.

3. Bipolar transistor drive characteristics tend to be more stable with temperature than MOSFETs. Thus, bipolar output stage drive characteristics can be optimized for a given application and will remain optimized over the entire operating temperature range. In contrast, the MOSFETs' on impedance changes by a factor of approximately 0.6 percent per degree Celsius which translates to an approximate 0.3 percent per degree Celsius change in speed. Thus, CMOS devices slow down significantly at high temperature and speed up significantly at low temperature. This large variability in output impedance with temperature, approximately 4-to-1 when process and power supply effects are added, makes it impossible to optimize CMOS output impedance for wide-temperature-range operation. Devices that barely have adequate drive at 125°C have excessive drive at −55°C and cause severe ringing unless special precautions are taken. BiCMOS devices do not have such a large variability in drive and speed with temperature. Thus, BiCMOS parts can be made that maintain high drive at high temperature without having excessive drive at low temperature.

Totem-pole output stage voltage swing is limited to approximately 3.4 V because the Darlington pull-up output transistor no longer has drive above approximately 3.4 V. Darlington transistors require about 1.6 V of base-emitter voltage for base current. Without base current, the output (emitter) can no longer supply load current which causes the output *high* level to stabilize at approximately 3.4 V with V_{cc} equal to 5 V. The actual magnitude of V_{out} *high* depends on the value of the load and the output current. There are two sources of output *high* current: I_c through the collector emitter of $Q2$ and I_b through the base emitters of $Q1$ and $Q2$, as shown in Fig. 3.28. Base current I_b must exist for the Darlington pair $Q1$ and $Q2$ to be on. Thus, the voltage drop across $R1$ due to I_b establishes a limiting value for V_{out} *high* which is (assuming I_c is very small)

$$V_{out} = V_{cc} - V_{BE}(Q1) - V_{BE}(Q2) - I_b(R1) \tag{3.4}$$

As I_b goes to zero (infinite load impedance), V_{out} approaches 3.4 V:

$$V_{out} = 5\ \text{V} - 0.8\ \text{V} - 0.8\ \text{V} - (0)(R1) = 3.4\ \text{V}$$

assuming V_{cc} equal to 5 V and V_{BE} equal to 0.8 V for $Q1$ and $Q2$.

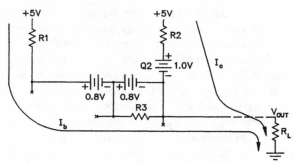

Figure 3.28 BiCMOS totem-pole output stage equivalent circuit for a *high* output.

In high-load current situations, such as when an output is switching from *low* to *high,* the collector-emitter current path I_c through $Q2$ may establish the output *high* level rather than the current path through the base I_b. The output voltage V_{out} in the collector-path-limited case can be determined by using a simple voltage-divider calculation such as shown here:

$$V_{out} = \frac{R_L}{R_L+R2} [5 \text{ V} - V_{CE}(Q2)] \tag{3.5}$$

In most static situations, the devices being driven have such high impedances that little output current flows, which means little base or collector current flows. Thus, in most static situations the conditions of Eq. (3.4) are met, which means that most *high* outputs reach their theoretical limit of about 3.4 V when V_{cc} is equal to 5 V. Yet, most BiCMOS signals observed in the laboratory have *high* levels above 3.4 V and are often in the range of 4.0 to 4.7 V. Why are they higher than the theoretical limit? Because signals typically overshoot when they switch and often stabilize above the theoretical limit. Leakage currents may also pull signals up beyond the theoretical limit.

3.4   No Opens or Intermediate Logic Levels on CMOS or BiCMOS Inputs

Most CMOS and BiCMOS device input circuits cannot tolerate intermediate logic levels. Intermediate logic levels in the region between valid logic *lows* and logic *highs* cause excessive current in CMOS and BiCMOS complementary MOSFET input structures (see Fig. 3.29a). Under normal operating conditions, input signals are near ground or V_{cc}, and one or the other of the complementary MOSFETs is on while the other is off. Thus, under normal conditions no current flows between V_{cc} and ground except for short-duration transient switching

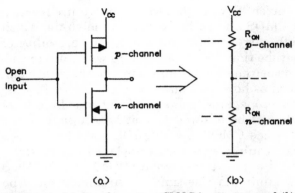

Figure 3.29 (*a*) Complementary CMOS input stage and (*b*) equivalent circuit when the input voltage is in the intermediate range between a valid logic *high* and valid logic *low*.

currents. In contrast, under abnormal input signal level conditions when input levels are in the intermediate or indeterminate logic level region, both MOSFETs may turn on. When both input transistors are on, I_{cc} may go up to a dangerous level. The typical profile for supply current versus input voltage for a CMOS or BiCMOS input stage is shown in Fig. 3.30.[14,15] The equivalent circuit for a complementary stage with an intermediate-level input is two resistors between V_{cc} and ground (see Fig. 3.29*b*). The two resistors represent the on impedance of the two MOSFETs. Since the on impedance of the MOSFETs used in advanced CMOS and BiCMOS devices is relatively low,[16] internal paths initiated by open or intermediate-level inputs can cause excessive internal device currents. Excessive internal current as a result of intermediate-level inputs can cause overheating and destruction of parts. Even if the intermediate-level input condition lasts for only a very short time, the device temperature is

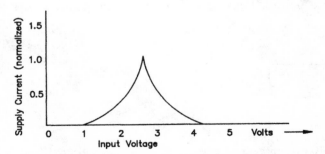

Figure 3.30 Typical profile of supply current versus input voltage for CMOS complementary input stages.

increased due to extra current flow. High device temperature increases the susceptibility of CMOS and BiCMOS parts to latch-up, which leads to additional high current flow and a greater possibility of device destruction. The time that a part can endure with an intermediate-level input depends on the internal impedance of the device and other considerations, such as how deep into the internal circuitry the intermediate logic level propagates. In general, intermediate-level input conditions should not be allowed to last longer than a few microseconds. However, some CMOS and BiCMOS parts have specified minimum rise-time requirements that translate to more stringent requirements. In all applications, when CMOS and BiCMOS logic devices are used, minimum rise-time requirements must be established and adhered to in the design.[17]

3.5 Latch-up and Latch-up Prevention

All CMOS and BiCMOS devices are intrinsically susceptible to latch-up.[18] *Latch-up* occurs when internal parasitic silicon controlled rectifier (SCR) structures that are inherent in CMOS (and the CMOS portion of BiCMOS) integrated circuits are triggered on.[19] When triggered on, parasitic SCRs cause low-impedance paths between V_{cc} and ground that remain on until either V_{cc} is removed or the part is destroyed. Latch-up usually disrupts the functional operation of a part and in many cases will cause permanent damage, even though some parts may return to normal operation after power is cycled off and then back on. Latch-up may be initiated by voltage overshoots or undershoots which cause substrate currents that exceed device ratings at one or combinations of device inputs, outputs, or supply terminals. Thus, latch-up can be prevented by limiting both static and transient input and output currents.

All CMOS and BiCMOS integrated circuits have parasitic four-layer *pnpn* structures, as shown in Fig. 3.31, that can be triggered into a regenerative switching mode if sufficient current is injected into the appropriate points. Four-layer structures associated with

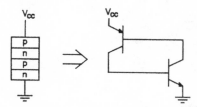

Figure 3.31 Four-layer *pnpn* SCR structures found in CMOS and BiCMOS integrated circuits.

input-output circuits are most exposed to transient currents and are most likely to latch up. Manufacturers use a number of techniques to minimize the chance of latch-up—increased spacing between parasitic devices to reduce gain, guard rings around diffusion areas,[20] low-impedance substrates,[21] and special doping[22] to prevent injected currents from developing sufficient potential to trigger parasitic structures, to name a few. However, all CMOS integrated circuits have parasitic SCR structures that can be triggered on if sufficient current is injected. Most advanced CMOS and BiCMOS logic devices have latch-up immunity for injected current levels of 100 to 200 mA depending upon the device and device manufacturer. Latch-up immunity above 100 mA is usually sufficient for most applications without the addition of external control techniques such as current-limiting resistors. Where extreme transient conditions exist, 100-mA immunity is usually not sufficient; external current limiting is required. Some of the older devices may latch up with injected current levels as low as 10 mA.

Military specification MIL-M-38510/606A[23] attempts to bring some standardization to CMOS and BiCMOS device latch-up immunity definition and testing, but the scope of the testing required by MIL-M-38510/606A is very limited. For example, it only requires that one of each input and output circuit type on a given chip be tested.

The basic MIL-M-38510 latch-up test for a 5-V part consists of injecting a current pulse of ± 150 mA for a duration of 500 ms with the part V_{cc} at 5.5 V and the part at an ambient temperature of $+125°C$. Device I_{cc} is monitored to ensure that latch-up does not occur. The test implies that parts which meet the specification (i.e., MIL-M-38510) should not latch up under worst-case environmental conditions with ± 150 mA injected into inputs or outputs. However, there is no assurance that all inputs and outputs on a chip will have the same latch-up immunity or that there is not some accumulative effect if more than one input or output is subjected to injected currents at the same time. Simultaneously injecting current into more than one input or output is a very real possibility in bus driver-receiver applications. Bus signals may ring and overshoot and inject current into multiple inputs or outputs on byte-wide drivers and receivers. Since MIL-M-38510 does not require a test for that condition and in general manufacturers do not test more than one input at a time, there is no assurance that a part will not latch up at lower current when current is injected into multiple inputs. Thus, when CMOS and BiCMOS parts are used, it is best to limit injected current where possible and practical. For example, unused CMOS inputs should not be connected directly to V_{cc} or ground to prevent transient noise spikes on power or ground or fast power supply turn-on from injecting sufficient current to trigger parasitic structures associated with the tied-off inputs.

The fact that a system is latch-up-free at room temperature does not guarantee that it will be latch-up-free at high temperature. High temperature increases the susceptibility of CMOS devices to latch-up. Thus, extra precautions must be taken to limit injected substrate currents at high temperature, and conditions that unnecessarily increase chip temperature must be avoided. Inputs must not be allowed to float or have slow transitions since floating inputs or inputs with slow transitions increase the device operating temperature and increase the chance for latch-up.

Where signals cross board or system unit boundaries, which is where they are most exposed to transient conditions, current limiting should be provided to ensure that the device's input and output current ratings are not exceeded. Where CMOS or BiCMOS sources and loads are not powered by the same source, interconnecting signal lines must be current-limited or clamped to prevent injected substrate currents in unpowered parts. Unpowered parts with substrate currents caused by powered input signals may latch up when local V_{cc} is applied.

Series resistors provide the simplest means of current-limiting CMOS or BiCMOS interfaces. Current-limiting resistors should be as large as possible, but resistor size must be balanced against excessive speed degradation. Under most board-to-board and other internal system conditions, special current limiting is not required when advanced CMOS or BiCMOS devices are used. However, if long external lines with a high probability of being exposed to abnormal conditions connect directly to CMOS or BiCMOS devices, or if some of the older CMOS logic families or special custom devices are being used, then great care must be taken to limit interface currents.

3.6 Electrostatic Discharge Protection

Oxide-isolated gate field-effect transistors (MOSFETs), such as used in CMOS and BiCMOS integrated-circuit logic devices, have extremely large gate-to-drain and gate-to-source impedances—100 MΩ or more.[24] Unless bypassed, such high impedances would allow significant electrostatic buildup. Thus, standard practice today is to add some form of low-impedance bypass circuitry to exposed external device terminals to prevent damage from electrostatic buildup.[25] Gate-to-drain and gate-to-source voltages (due to electrostatic charge) must be limited to less than the dielectric breakdown voltage of the gate oxide.

Various combinations of diodes, transistors, and zener diodes are used to implement low-impedance clamp or discharge paths for input

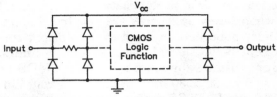

Figure 3.32 Typical electrostatic protection networks used on CMOS and BiCMOS logic device inputs and outputs.

and output terminals. Most input-output protection networks implemented with diodes are similar to the network shown in Fig. 3.32. The diodes are arranged to clamp either positive or negative electrostatic voltage excursions to levels below MOSFET gate oxide breakdown limits. In addition to diodes or transistors, most input protection networks include some resistance[26] to limit current to protect the diodes; but most output clamps do not have current-limiting resistors (see Fig. 3.32). Series output resistance would impact normal operation, and ideally protection networks protect against electrostatic damage without interfering with normal operation when signal levels are between V_{cc} and ground. However, when signal levels exceed V_{cc} or ground due to overshoots caused by transmission-line effects, some clamping action may occur depending on the speed of response of the diodes or transistors used in the protection networks. In some cases, input protection networks provide effective dynamic clamping, but input or output protection diodes should not be relied upon to provide effective clamping of high-frequency signals. In most instances, input protection network impedance is too high and diode response too slow for effective dynamic signal clamping. Different manufacturers use different protection networks for the same generic part, so care must be exercised if dynamic response is important. Each manufacturer's parts must be evaluated for the particular application at hand (see Chap. 7). Protection networks reduce—but do not eliminate—the susceptibility of parts to ESD. Also, the effectiveness of protection circuitry varies from manufacturer to manufacturer, so that the ESD sensitivity of the same generic part can be different.

In all applications, large static and dynamic currents must be prevented from flowing in input and output ESD protection networks to prevent possible latch-up of parasitic SCRs that are inherent in CMOS integrated circuits (see Sec. 3.5). Even normal signals that overshoot or undershoot V_{cc} or ground can induce latch-up if they have excessive energy. Series current-limiting resistors offer the best means of controlling static and transient currents injected into protection networks. Series resistors should be used at system interfaces to limit current in protection networks in applications where signal sources may be powered when receiving devices are not. In all applications, input currents under abnormal or worst-case transient-current conditions must be kept below actual specified device limits. Absolute maximum dc input limits for most advanced CMOS or BiCMOS logic devices range from 20 to 30 mA. Transient-current limits for most advanced CMOS and BiCMOS devices are typically above 100 mA; but caution must be exercised, for some CMOS devices may latch up with injected currents as low as 10 mA and output circuits are often more susceptible to latch-up than input circuits are. Thus, all inputs and outputs should have series current-limiting resistors to prevent excessive input or output currents.

Isolated system interface signals that connect directly to CMOS inputs or outputs are an invitation to ESD problems.[27] All external system signals that connect to CMOS inputs should have shunt resistors to V_{cc} or ground and series current-limiting resistors (see Fig. 3.33).[28] Shunt resistors help prevent electrostatic buildup when input lines are disconnected and prevent open inputs from floating (and perhaps overheating—see Sec. 3.4). In applications where high-speed signals must cross external unit boundaries, series current-limiting resistors may cause excessive RC delays. However, if it is not possible to use series current-limiting resistors, and the possibility of excessive static or transient input currents exists, then other steps must be taken to control the situation.

Good low-impedance chassis grounds are essential for ESD control. The chassis of electronic equipment must be solidly connected to ground with a rugged low-impedance ground line.[27] Green lines in power cords should not be relied on to provide chassis ground. Likewise, green lines in power cords should not be relied on to ensure that units under test and test equipment are at the same potential. Units under test and test equipment must be grounded together and to earth ground with visible ground cables before test probes or other test connections are made to the unit under test. Not only must the chassis be grounded, but also it must provide good shielding and internal circuitry must be solidly referenced to chassis ground (generally at one point to prevent ground loops) to prevent electrostatic dif-

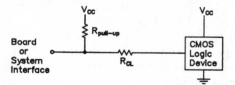

Figure 3.33 ESD and latch-up protection network for exposed CMOS and BiCMOS inputs.

ferences between the internal electronic components and the chassis. Ideally all printed-circuit boards and motherboards are built with multiple power and ground planes so that all signal lines are enclosed by power and ground planes, to provide ESD shielding of signal interconnections. Ground planes must extend to all areas of printed-circuit boards to maximize the ESD shielding.

Electrostatic stress damage to integrated circuits (ICs) is responsible for a good share of system failures.[29] A U.S. Department of Defense analysis of field failures of ICs indicates that over 50 percent are due to ESD.[30] It seems safe to assume that ESD is responsible for even a larger percentage of IC failures in commercial equipment since perhaps more care is taken to prevent ESD damage in military systems than in commercial equipment. Because of mounting evidence of widespread failures of ICs occurring as a result of ESD damage, the Department of Defense requires semiconductor manufacturers to classify military ICs according to the electrostatic discharge tolerance. The three classifications are

Class 1:   Sensitivity range 0 to 1999 V

Class 2:   Sensitivity range 2000 to 3999 V

Class 3:   Sensitivity range 4000 to 15,999 V

Semiconductor manufacturers must indicate the ESD rating of military ICs on the packages. The ESD rating is indicated by

Class 1:   A single triangle

Class 2:   Two triangles

Class 3:   No triangle marking

When parts are available from multiple sources, builders of military equipment are required to buy the parts with the highest ESD classification. Most advanced CMOS and BiCMOS parts are rated as class 2 devices. Most advanced Schottky parts are rated as class 3 devices. Table 3.1 lists ESD ratings for several advanced CMOS logic families.

ESD is a serious concern when advanced CMOS and BiCMOS devices are used. Smaller-geometry devices are inherently more sus-

TABLE 3.1   ESD Ratings of Some Representative Logic Families

Manufacturer	Logic family	ESD rating,* V
National	FACT	>2000
Motorola	FACT	>2000
Texas Instruments	BCT	>2000
National	FAST	>4000

*See respective data book for current ESD specifications.

ceptible to ESD, and smaller geometries make it more difficult to build in robust input and output ESD protection networks.[31] In most cases, ESD ratings of ASICs and LSI devices are less than those of SSI devices. Many ASICs fall into the class 1 category.

For comprehensive coverage of ESD and ESD control issues, see Ref. 32 by Owen McAteer.

3.7 References

1. James E. Buchanan, *CMOS/TTL Digital Systems Design,* McGraw-Hill, New York, 1990.
2. *FAST Advanced Schottky TTL Logic Databook,* National Semiconductor Corp., Santa Clara, Calif., 1990.
3. *FAST Logic Applications Handbook,* National Semiconductor Corp., Santa Clara, Calif., 1990.
4. A. S. Grove, *Physics and Technology of Semiconductor Devices,* Wiley, New York, 1967.
5. Aldert van der Ziel, *Solid State Physical Electronics,* Prentice-Hall Inc., Englewood Cliffs, N.J., 1968.
6. Jacob Millman, *Microelectronics, Digital and Analog Circuits and Systems,* McGraw-Hill, New York, 1979.
7. Jacob Millman and Herbert Taub, *Pulse, Digital, and Switching Waveforms,* McGraw-Hill, New York, 1965.
8. H. C. Lin, *Integrated Electronics,* Holden-Day, San Francisco, 1967.
9. Charles A. Holt, *Electronic Circuits Digital and Analog,* Wiley, New York, 1978.
10. M. Morris Mano, *Digital Design,* Prentice-Hall Inc., Englewood Cliffs, N.J., 1984.
11. Liang-Tsai Lin and Richard Spehn, "Fast, Low-Powered Logic Array Unites CMOS and Bipolar," *Electronic Design,* April 16, 1987, pp. 82–88.
12. *Toshiba Bi-CMOS Logic TD 74BC Series Data Book,* Toshiba Corp., Tokyo, Japan, 1989.
13. James E. Buchanan, *BiCMOS/CMOS Systems Design,* McGraw-Hill, New York, 1991.
14. *Advanced CMOS Logic Designer's Handbook,* Texas Instruments Inc., Dallas, Tex., 1988.
15. *FACT Advanced CMOS Logic Databook,* National Semiconductor Corp., Santa Clara, Calif., 1993.
16. Gerald C. Cox, "Impedance Matching Tweaks Advanced CMOS IC Testing," *Electronic Design,* April 1987, pp. 71–74.
17. Nathan O. Sokal, "Check Lists Help You Avoid Trouble with MOS and Memory ICs," *EDN,* November 27, 1986, pp. 229–235.
18. Larry Wakeman, "Closing in on CMOS Latch-up," *Integrated Circuits Magazine,* April 1985, pp. 38–44.
19. Ronald R. Troutman, *Latchup in CMOS Technology,* Kluwer Academic Publishers, Hingham, Mass., 1986.
20. R. R. Troutman, "Epitaxial Layer Enhancement of n-Well Guard Rings for CMOS Circuits," *IEEE Electronic Device Letters,* vol. ELD-4, no. 12, December 1983, pp. 438–440.
21. J. E. Schroder, A. Ochoa, Jr., and P. V. Dressendorfer, "Latch-up Elimination in Bulk CMOS LSI Circuits," *IEEE Transactions on Nuclear Science,* vol. NS-27, no. 6, December 1980, pp. 1735–1738.
22. W. R. Dawes, Jr., and G. F. Derbenwick, "Prevention of CMOS Latch-up by Gold-Doping," *IEEE Transactions on Nuclear Science,* vol. Ns-23, no. 6, December 1976, pp. 2027–2030.
23. MIL-M-38510/606A, *General Specification for Microcircuits,* Navy Publications Center, Philadelphia, March 8, 1988.
24. Ed Oxner, *Designing with Field-Effect Transistors,* 2d ed., Siliconix Inc., McGraw-Hill, New York, 1989.

25. *Electrostatic Discharge Control Handbook for Protection of Electrical and Electronic Parts, Assemblies and Equipment (Excluding Electrically Initiated Explosive Devices),* DOD-HDBK-263, Department of Defense, Washington, May 1980.
26. Thomas M. Frederiksen, *Intuitive CMOS Electronics,* McGraw-Hill, New York, 1989.
27. *Electrostatic Discharge and Electronic Equipment: A Practical Guide for Designing to Prevent ESD Problems,* Institute of Electrical and Electronics Engineers Press, New York, 1989.
28. M. J. Walsh, *Choosing and Using CMOS,* McGraw-Hill, New York, 1985.
29. Warren Yates, "Department of Defense Orders ESD Protection Guarantees for ICs," *Electronic Products,* October 1989, pp. 13–14.
30. Stan Baker, "National Guarantees FAST ESD Protection," *Electronic Engineering Times,* September 4, 1989, pp. 87 and 94.
31. Sean Gold and Gary Maulding, "Electrostatic Self-Defense," *EDN Products Edition,* June 20, 1994, pp. 36–37.
32. Owen J. McAteer, *Electrostatic Discharge Control,* McGraw-Hill, New York, 1990.

Inductance and Transient Switching Currents

4.1 Inductance

Signal and power distribution system inductance is responsible for many of the signal integrity difficulties encountered in high-speed digital systems. However, many designers continue to ignore interconnection inductance. The general impression seems to be that inductance and inductive effects are not significant in digital applications. Perhaps that was the case with the older, slower logic families, but that is no longer true. When today's high-speed logic devices are used, interconnection inductance is a major cause of signal integrity problems. Very short connections have significant inductance and voltage loss when devices have switching transient currents with frequency components greater than 100 MHz, which is the case when advanced Schottky TTL, advanced CMOS, or BiCMOS devices are used (see Chap. 1).

Inductance is a measure of the ability of a circuit to convert electromagnetic energy to a magnetic field. In certain applications, it is desirable to create a strong magnetic field, but creating strong magnetic fields is not important in digital applications. In digital systems, signal energy loss must be minimized to minimize signal degradation, which means the inductance (and generation of magnetic fields) must be minimized. Yet, most texts that deal with the subject of inductance describe means for increasing rather than decreasing inductance. They describe inductors that consist of numerous turns of wire and leave the reader with the general impression that a number of turns of wire are needed to achieve significant inductance. Even the symbol for an inductor implies that a number of turns of wire are needed for a useful inductor; and that may be the case at 60 Hz, but that is not the case at 100 MHz. Since voltage loss across an inductor is proportional to frequency, at 100 MHz a very small inductor can cause significant loss. Thus, for the successful application of high-speed logic devices, power and signal interconnection inductance must be minimized.

Inductance can be minimized by package design, printed-circuit (PC) board design, layout techniques (the shorter and closer to ground, the better), and the use of special techniques for interconnection wiring. However, even when the best possible techniques are applied, transient-voltage spikes due to inductive effects will be significant with respect to TTL signal levels (LV and BiCMOS device signal levels are similar to TTL) or CMOS signal levels and noise margins. Thus, system design approaches, such as synchronous design practices, must be followed that minimize system susceptibility to transient-voltage spikes (see Chap. 10).

4.1.1 Physical and electrical factors that influence inductance

Inductance is associated with a closed loop. However, it is possible to uniquely ascribe an inductance to portions of a closed loop with the concept of self-inductance.[1] The *self-inductance L,* often simply called *inductance,* of a current-carrying circuit is defined as the flux linkage per unit current.[2] That is,

$$L = \frac{\phi}{i} \tag{4.1}$$

where ϕ is the magnetic flux and i is the current. Equation (4.1) is generally shown as

$$L = \frac{N\phi}{i} \tag{4.2}$$

where N is the number of turns of wire in an inductor. The more common equation for self-inductance, Eq. (4.2), reinforces the idea that an inductor must be composed of numerous turns of a conductor, but note that 1 is an acceptable number for N in Eq. (4.2).

Equations (4.1) and (4.2) show that the inductance L is directly proportional to the flux linkage. Since low inductance is desired for digital interconnections, it is important to understand what flux linkage is and how to minimize it. Flux density (flux linkage per unit area) is a measure of the ease with which flux can link with itself. The more concentrated the flux is, the greater the magnetic field and the inductance. Flux does not need to link with other sources of flux; but flux, like current, must have a complete path. To decrease inductance, *the ease with which flux can link with itself* must be impeded. The two variables that determine *the ease of linkage,* and thus the inductance, are the geometry of the circuit and the permeability of the magnetic medium. An iron core or other high-permeability μ material near a coil of wire increases the ease at which flux can link with itself and thus increases the inductance. Likewise, nearby low-permeability material reduces inductance. The permeability of the insulating material of PC boards and of most insulating material is low; it is near that of air. Thus, when one is dealing with conventional interconnection systems, little reduction in inductance can be effected by changing the material adjacent to signals.

However, digital designers have some control over circuit geometry. Circuit inductance can be decreased by decreasing the length of the circuit (coil) or by arranging the circuit so that the flux linkage is not enhanced (i.e., by arranging the circuit topology so that flux cancels rather than enhances—coiling enhances flux linkage, and thus coiling is to be avoided).

Equations for calculating the inductance of various physical arrangements of conductive elements can be found in numerous references. For many configurations the equations are quite complex. However, in all cases, flux linkage and inductance are proportional to the area enclosed by the circuit (current) path.[3] That is,

$$L = K \times \text{area enclosed by current path} \qquad (4.3)$$

$$L \propto \text{area enclosed by current path}$$

where K is a constant related to conductor geometry and the permeability of the surrounding material. Thus, even though the two current paths shown in Fig. 4.1 are the same length, the current path in Fig. 4.1a has less inductance than the current path in Fig. 4.1b, because the enclosed area of Fig. 4.1a is less than that of Fig. 4.1b. Since there is often little flexibility in the choice of insulating material permeability or conductor size, minimum inductance is achieved by minimizing the area enclosed by the current path. To minimize area, signal lines and current return paths must be in close proximity.[4] That is, signal lines need to be

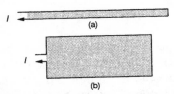

Figure 4.1 Inductance is minimized by keeping lines short and by minimizing the area enclosed by the current path. (*a*) Low-inductance path; (*b*) high-inductance path, even though the lines are the same length.

run close to ground planes (which serve as a return path), and signal lines in cables need to be twisted with a return line.

4.1.2 Transient voltage drop across inductors

The effect of changing the magnetic field $d(\phi)$ on an electric circuit is an induced voltage. The effect is described by Faraday's law, which states that the induced voltage v is

$$v = \frac{d(\phi)}{dt} \tag{4.4}$$

for a single-turn inductor, which is the case for most digital circuits.

However, the change in voltage across an inductor due to a changing current is of greater interest to digital designers. By using Eqs. (4.1) and (4.4), it can be shown that a change of current i with time causes a corresponding change in the magnetic flux ϕ and induces a voltage v in the circuit.

First rearranging Eq. (4.1) to

$$Li = \phi \tag{4.5}$$

and then differentiating both sides with respect to time t give

$$L\frac{di}{dt} = \frac{d(\phi)}{dt} \tag{4.6}$$

From Faraday's law the induced voltage is

$$v(t) = \frac{d(\phi)}{dt} \tag{4.7}$$

and it follows that

$$v(t) = \frac{d(\phi)}{dt} = L\frac{di}{dt} \tag{4.8}$$

and

$$v(t) = L\frac{di}{dt} \tag{4.9}$$

is the familiar equation for the time-varying voltage across an inductor. Equation (4.9) shows that either, or both, L or di/dt must be minimized to lessen undesirable transient voltages in signal and power connections. Inductance is minimized as described in Sec. 4.1.1. Transient switching currents di/dt are controlled by keeping loads as small as possible and by the use of components that inherently generate less transient current (see Sec. 4.2).

4.2   Transient Switching Currents

The fast edges of today's TTL, CMOS, and BiCMOS devices rapidly charge and discharge signal line and load capacitances and in the process cause large transient currents.[5] First-generation advanced CMOS logic devices with rail-to-rail voltage swings and no control of output slew rates are notorious noise generators and are very difficult devices to use successfully in systems. For that reason, some of the newer advanced CMOS logic families have returned to TTL-level output swings (e.g., the FCT-T family), and most second-generation advanced CMOS devices have incorporated some control of output slew rates. However, output slew rates can only be reduced a certain amount without reducing potential system operating speeds. Signals must switch relatively fast to support 20-MHz or greater operation, and fast edges inherently cause large load switching transient currents. Most TTL, LV CMOS, and LV or 5-V BiCMOS devices have TTL-level output swings, which means lower output transient currents compared to first-generation 5-V advanced CMOS devices.

Load switching transient currents are not the only source of transients in digital systems; most TTL, CMOS, and BiCMOS logic devices are built with internal circuits that have transient internal feedthrough currents when switched. Unless proper high-frequency interconnection and power distribution techniques are used, these load and internal transient switching currents will cause significant shifts in reference levels, large drops in local V_{cc} levels, and crosstalk or coupling into other signals, any one of which can lead to intermittent or total system failure.

4.2.1   Transient internal switching currents

Most advanced CMOS logic devices and the core of most BiCMOS logic devices are built with complementary circuit structures that use p-channel MOSFETs for pull-up switches and n-channel MOSFETs for pull-down switches.[6,7] Complementary circuits have no dc paths, other than leakage paths, between V_{cc} and ground. Yet, under dynamic conditions, complementary circuits have the potential for significant internal transient feedthrough switching currents; both pull-up and pull-down MOSFETs may be on for short overlapping times during switching.[8,9] The bipolar totem-pole output stages[10] used in TTL and BiCMOS devices have some feedthrough current flow during switching.

Most CMOS and BiCMOS memory devices [e.g., dynamic RAM (DRAM), static RAM (SRAM), ROM, first-in first-out (FIFO) memory devices] have large internal current demands when accessed. To save power, most such devices power down the peripheral circuitry except when they are being accessed, which means when accessed large currents are required to quickly power up the peripheral circuitry to minimize the access time. The various circuit mechanizations used to power down memory devices are not covered since they are very device-specific. But system designers must be aware that most memory devices have large transient-current demands when accessed.

Transient internal switching currents in TTL and BiCMOS devices. Each time a TTL or BiCMOS device switches, internal transient currents flow between V_{cc} and ground in the complementary stages in the core of the device and in the bipolar totem-pole output stages. In SSI and MSI devices, most of this internal device transient switching current is the result of feedthrough in the totem-pole output stages.[11,12] Feedthrough occurs because both pull-up and pull-down totem-pole transistors are on for a short time whenever outputs switch. Device designers attempt to minimize totem-pole feedthrough currents, but it is difficult to match the turn-on and turn off characteristics of transistors or the timing of the separate drive signals. Most totem-pole outputs have added circuitry to help match the turn-on and turn off of output stage transistors, but a perfect match is never achieved. Figure 4.2 shows a bipolar TTL or BiCMOS totem-pole output stage and the equivalent circuit for a totem-pole output when both output transistors are on at the same time. In the equivalent circuit (Fig. 4.2b), the 0.5-V voltage source represents the lower output transistor $Q2$ (on V_{CE} for Schottky clamped transistors is near 0.5 V), and the 1.0-V voltage source represents the forward drop across the pull-up Darlington transistor $Q1$.

The upper limit for the internal peak transient feedthrough current I_p is a function of the output-stage current-limiting pull-up resistor

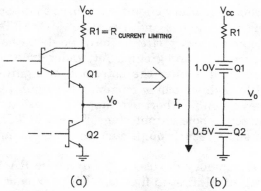

Figure 4.2 (a) Totem-pole output stage; (b) simplified equivalent circuit during switching.

($R1$ in Fig. 4.2) and the collector-to-emitter voltage drop V_{CE} of the two output transistors. That is,

$$I_p = \frac{V_{cc} - V_{CE(\text{sat})}(Q1) - V_{CE(\text{sat})}(Q2)}{R1 \text{ (current limiting resistor)}} \qquad (4.10)$$

Data sheets never list a value for $R1$, but from output short-circuit current ratings, the value of $R1$ can be estimated. For standard advanced Schottky TTL elements, NANDs, NORs, etc., in National Semiconductor's 54/74F logic family,[13] the short-circuit rating (to ground or 0 V) is typically listed as 60 to 180 mA and for drivers, such as 240s, 244s, etc., 100 to 225 mA at a V_{cc} of 5.5 V.

When the output of a device is short-circuited to ground, the output short-circuit current I_{OS} is

$$I_{OS} = \frac{V_{cc} - V_{CE(\text{sat})}(Q1)}{R1} \qquad (4.11)$$

If I_{OS} is specified, $R1$ can be found by rearranging Eq. (4.11) to get

$$R1 = \frac{V_{cc} - V_{CE(\text{sat})}(Q1)}{I_{OS}} \qquad (4.12)$$

Using the worst-case output short-circuit current rating for drivers of 225 mA, we find that $R1$ is

$$R1 = \frac{5.5 \text{ V} - 1 \text{ V}}{225 \text{ mA}} = 20\Omega$$

Given a value of 20 Ω for the current-limiting resistor and V_{cc} at 5 V, the peak feedthrough current I_p could be as large as [from Eq. (4.10)]

$$I_p = \frac{5 \text{ V} - 1.0 \text{ V} - 0.5 \text{ V}}{20 \ \Omega} = \frac{5 \text{ V} - 1.5 \text{ V}}{20 \ \Omega} = 175 \text{ mA}$$

which is near the value of the short-circuit current used to derive $R1$, as expected.

Actual peak output-stage feedthrough currents will be much lower than 175 mA for several reasons. It is unlikely that both transistors will be fully on during a significant portion of the switching period. Furthermore, simple static transistor models, as used, are not sufficient for ac or transient analysis. In addition, inductance, which is not addressed in the equivalent circuit, tends to have a significant limiting effect at the switching speeds of today's devices. The purpose of the above discussion is to illustrate the basic mechanism that causes internal feedthrough switching currents and to show that they can have significant magnitude, not to determine exact values.

The duration of feedthrough currents is short. Fast logic devices must have close matching of the on-off characteristics of the totem-pole output transistors to prevent power dissipation from being excessive at high data rates. The overlap time in today's devices is very short since they typically switch in 1 to 3 ns.

Output-stage transient feedthrough switching currents will vary with the device, logic family, load, and operating temperature. Thus, systems with poor power and ground distribution networks that operate correctly at one given temperature and set of conditions may not operate at another temperature or under another set of conditions. Changing conditions may change transient feedthrough currents, which may cause different noise or reference-level disturbances. Changing parts may also change feedthrough currents and operating margins.

Transient internal switching currents in CMOS devices.   Figure 4.3*a* shows a simple CMOS inverter with one complementary stage. During switching, both the pull-up MOSFET $Q1$ and the pull-down MOSFET $Q2$ may be on for a short time. Hence, the switching transition equivalent circuit is two resistors between V_{cc} and ground, as shown in Fig. 4.3*b*. Gates and other CMOS logic devices have more complicated equivalent circuits than the inverter shown in Fig. 4.3 (see Sec. 3.2), but they have analogous dynamic current paths.

One approach to estimating the feedthrough current for a simple inverting buffer is to divide the supply voltage V_{cc} level by the sum of the on impedances (resistances) of the two MOSFETs. Typical on resistance R_{on} of advanced CMOS output-stage MOSFETs is near 10 Ω; thus the peak internal transient switching current I_p could approach

$$I_p = \frac{V_{cc}}{2R_{on}} = \frac{5\,V}{2(10\,\Omega)} = 0.25\,A \qquad (4.13)$$

Actual transient feedthrough currents do not reach levels of 0.25 A. Both MOSFETs are not fully on at the same time, and most output-

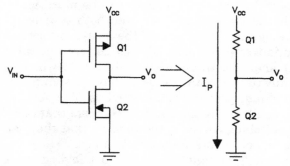

Figure 4.3   Inverting CMOS buffer and simplified equivalent circuit during switching.

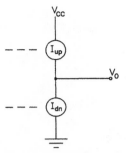

Figure 4.4 More exact switching transition equivalent circuit for complementary CMOS stage.

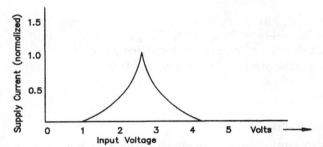

Figure 4.5 Typical profile of supply current versus input voltage for advanced CMOS logic devices.

stage MOSFETs go into current limit below 0.25 A. Advanced CMOS outputs with 24-mA worst-case static output drive ratings typically have a dynamic current limit of approximately 150 mA (typical value). Thus, a more exact CMOS complementary stage equivalent circuit (during switching) consists of two current sources in series, as shown in Fig. 4.4. The pull-up current source I_{up} represents the pull-up MOSFET in current limit, and the pull-down current source I_{dn} represents the pull-down MOSFET in current limit.

The more exact equivalent circuit is conceptually correct, but it is of limited use in predicting peak transient feedthrough currents since current source limits are not specified on data sheets or other manufacturers' literature. The device output short-circuit current rating may be appropriate in certain cases, but in general, feedthrough current will not reach short-circuit current magnitudes. Both devices will not be fully on at the same time. The peak transient feedthrough current magnitude is difficult to establish with simple models, but the simple models do show the basic cause of feedthrough currents. Curves of supply current versus input voltage clearly show feedthrough current occurring when input voltage is in the intermediate region (see Fig. 4.5). Plots,

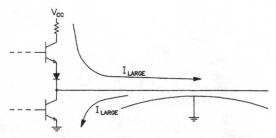

Figure 4.6 Signals with fast rise and fall times have large charging and discharging currents when driving large-capacitance loads.

such as Fig. 4.5, showing supply current versus input voltage can be found in most CMOS logic device data books.[8,9] Figure 4.5 is normalized since the plot is not intended to represent a particular device. Its purpose is to show the typical profile of feedthrough current versus input voltage.

4.2.2 Transient load currents

Each time a digital signal changes levels, its line and load capacitances must be charged or discharged, as shown in Fig. 4.6, and the faster the rise or fall time, the larger the charging or discharging current. Large charging currents increase the possibility of system upset due to noise. For example, when large charging currents flow in high-impedance signal, power, or ground connections, they may cause voltage transients in excess of logic device noise margins. Also, large switching currents increase the possibility of cross-coupling to nearby signal lines. The potential for system upset is greatest when 5-V advanced CMOS is used; 5-V CMOS output voltage swings are larger than TTL or LV logic levels, and as a result, 5-V CMOS transient switching currents are larger.

The magnitude of transient load currents must be known (determined) so that the signal and power distribution systems can be designed to keep the noise level down to an acceptable level. To aid in that task, the following discussion briefly describes how to calculate transient load currents under several typical system conditions.

Switching currents for driving lumped capacitance loads. When a load can be treated as a lumped load, i.e., when the load is very near the source, simple RC network calculations can be used to determine peak charging currents if the output resistance R_o of the driving

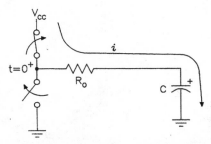

Figure 4.7 Equivalent circuit of a logic device charging a lumped capacitance with the output stage modeled as two ideal switches and a fixed resistance.

device is known.[6,14] The charging current i for the lumped capacitance load in Fig. 4.7 is

$$i = \frac{V_{cc}}{R_o}\varepsilon^{-t/(R_oC)} \qquad\qquad (4.14)$$

and the peak transient current I_L at time $t = 0 +$ is

$$I_L = \frac{V_{cc}}{R_o} \qquad \text{at } t = 0^+ \qquad\qquad (4.15)$$

However, the output dynamic resistance R_o in Fig. 4.7 and in Eqs. (4.14) and (4.15) is not specified, so Eqs. (4.14) and (4.15) have limited practical value for load current calculations. Static (i.e., dc) output resistance can be derived from the worst-case output voltage levels, V_{OL} or V_{OH}, which are specified at a given output current on most data sheets. In most cases, R_o is different for *high*- and *low*-level outputs. Even if R_o is known, the charging current does not build to its full value instantaneously, as implied by Eq. (4.15), due to circuit inductance and other effects.

In most applications, TTL, CMOS, or BiCMOS driver output transistors are in current limit during most of each switching transition interval. Thus, during signal transitions, outputs should be treated as current sources,[15] as shown in Fig. 4.8, and device output short-circuit current I_{OS} should be used to estimate the peak output current. The output short-circuit current is listed on most data sheets. If the short-circuit current is not listed on the data sheet of interest, sometimes it can be found in the general logic family specifications typically located in one of the front sections of data books.

Current when lumped loads are driven with a constant rate of change of voltage. The rate of change of voltage with time when a capacitor is charged with a constant current I is

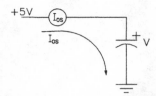

Figure 4.8 Equivalent circuit of a logic device charging a lumped capacitance with the output stage modeled as a current source.

$$\frac{dv}{dt} = \frac{I}{C} \tag{4.16}$$

When Eq. (4.16) is rearranged,

$$I = C\,\frac{dv}{dt} \approx C\,\frac{\Delta V}{\Delta t} \tag{4.17}$$

For a typical TTL-level change of 3.5 V in 2 ns and a 50-pF load, assuming a constant current output and substituting I_L for I in Eq. (4.17), the resulting peak transient load current I_L is

$$I_L = (50 \text{ pF})\left(\frac{3.5\text{V}}{2\text{ ns}}\right) = 87.5 \text{ mA}$$

which is a significant transient current. Large digital systems will have a large number of similar signals switching at any given clock time. A large number of signals demanding 87.5 mA at one time obviously places a burden on the power source and distribution system. However, much larger transient load currents are to be expected when 5-V CMOS devices are used. Many 5-V advanced CMOS devices have signal transitions of 5 V in 2 ns. When a signal transitions 5 V in 2 ns while driving a 50-pF load, the peak transient load current I_L is

$$I_L = (50 \text{ pF})\left(\frac{5 \text{ V}}{2\text{ ns}}\right) = 125 \text{ mA}$$

A system using 5-V CMOS devices will have many signals with similar transient load currents at any given time. Some signals will cause even larger switching currents (than above), since some first-generation advanced CMOS devices switch in 1 ns. Switching currents increase at cold temperatures since MOSFET on impedance decreases as temperature decreases. Lower on resistance increases drive capability and reduces the rise time. The larger the transient load currents, the greater the demands placed on the power and signal interconnections.[5]

It is much easier to apply devices with lower nominal switching currents such as TTL, LV CMOS, or BiCMOS than 5-V CMOS. Lower switching currents mean less noise and fewer system disruptions. Furthermore, device switching characteristics and system timing tend to be more constant over temperature when devices with bipolar output stages are used. The output impedance of devices with bipolar output stages does not change as much as the output impedance of CMOS devices with temperature changes.

In all high-speed systems, the magnitude of transient feedthrough and load capacitance charging currents must be factored into the design of the power and reference distribution system and into the sizing and placement of local decoupling capacitors. When one is using advanced Schottky TTL, advanced CMOS, or BiCMOS technology, to design a power distribution and signal interconnection system that can tolerate such high levels of transient currents is a challenge. Great care must be taken to ensure low dynamic impedances.

Load capacitance. The dynamic performance of most of today's SSI and MSI devices is specified and tested with 50-pF loads. However, in many very typical applications, the actual load capacitance will exceed the standard 50-pF test load, which means the actual device performance will be different from that specified and transient load currents will be higher than those present during test. Thus, load capacitance is an important power distribution design parameter. Load capacitance is the sum of the interconnection capacitance and the input or output capacitance of all devices connected to the interconnection. Buses in particular connect to a large number of loads, and those loads are typically bidirectional ports with approximately twice the load capacitance of unidirectional ports.

To aid in the calculation of load capacitance, typical device input-output and typical interconnection capacitances are listed in Table 4.1. The data in Table 4.1 are useful for quick estimates of load capacitance or as a general guide when actual data are unavailable. However, the actual specified device capacitance and interconnection capacitance, when available, should be used in transient load current calculations.

TABLE 4.1   Typical Device and Interconnection Capacitance

SSI or MSI inputs, 5 pF
SSI or MSI outputs, 7 pF
SSI or MSI bidirectional ports, 15 pF
LSI devices in large packages, 10 to 15 pF
PC board traces, 2 to 4 pF/in
Wire-wrap wires, 1 to 2 pF/in
Welded-wire wires, 1 to 2 pF/in

Switching currents for driving distributed loads. Distributed loads differ from lumped loads in that a finite time is required for the signal to propagate along the signal path. The driving source does not instantaneously see the entire load. Transmission lines are distributed loads. When devices are driving transmission lines (see Chap. 7 for the definition of a transmission line), the transient load current I_L is equal to the magnitude of the signal change ΔV divided by the transmission-line characteristic impedance Z_o (see Fig. 4.9):

$$I_L = \frac{\Delta V}{Z_o} \qquad (4.18)$$

Transient load currents, as defined by Eq. (4.18), exist until steady-state conditions are established on the transmission line, i.e., until all ringing and reflections have subsided.

In most applications where advanced Schottky TTL, advanced CMOS, and BiCMOS devices are used, the dynamic load should be viewed as a transmission line. Most lines have propagation delays that are long relative to the rise time of the signal. When lines are long, it is incorrect to treat the total line capacitance as a lumped load. The line impedance isolates the driver from the more remote capacitance of the line and loads. Thus, in *long*-line cases, the Z_o of the line should be used to calculate the transient driver and load currents, and transmission-line analysis must be used to determine the transient signal response to determine ΔV (see Chap. 7).

It is desirable to have the interconnection impedance as high as possible to reduce transient switching currents, but high line impedance increases the chances for crosstalk. Thus, no ideal circuit board or motherboard interconnection impedance exists. When the conflicting requirements are weighed and balanced, line impedances near 60 Ω provide the optimal balance between switching current levels and crosstalk. However, most manufacturers of high-density multilayer

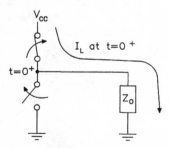

Figure 4.9 When a transmission line is driven, the transient load current is equal to the voltage change divided by the transmission-line impedance.

PC boards have difficulty achieving a line impedance of 60 Ω or greater. Thus, when PC boards are used, the main concern is to ensure that the line impedance is high enough that the signal line impedance does not cause excessive dynamic loading. To limit signal degradation, the unloaded signal line impedance should be greater than 40 Ω (see Chaps. 6 and 7).

4.3   Ground Bounce

The fast edges of today's logic devices cause large, high-frequency transient load currents. Large load currents mean large currents in the ground and power connections of the switching devices. These large currents in the ground and power connections in combination with the inductance of the package leads, bond wires, and chip metallization cause large shifts in chip reference and power supply levels.[16] These level shifts are called *ground bounce* and *power supply droop*. If the level shifts are large enough, they may cause

1. Logic errors in the switched device or at the inputs of devices connected to signals that originate from the switched device

2. Nonmonotonic transitions on outputs, which can cause double clocking if the outputs are used as clock signals

3. Degradation of propagation delays due to the supply voltage across the switched device being reduced, which reduces drive

Many first-generation advanced CMOS devices have severe ground bounce, particularly at cold temperatures, where output impedance is lowest. To reduce ground bounce, some manufacturers change to center ground pins on some parts.[8] Center power and ground pins lower the average and worst-case inductance between internal points on a chip and external ground or supply voltage levels, since average and maximum distances to external connections are reduced. Center ground (or power) pins reduce the ground connection inductance to near 5 nH where conventional dual in-line packages (DIPs) with end ground (or power) pins have from 10 to 15 nH of inductance. One of the advantages of the lower and more controlled output voltage swings of advanced Schottky TTL and BiCMOS (when compared to advanced CMOS) is less ground bounce or power supply droop, which allows most 20-pin and under TTL and BiCMOS parts to have their ground pin in the conventional location (i.e., at one end of the package).

   Table 4.2 shows the range of typical pin inductances for several common packages.[17,18] The two values listed in Table 4.2 are representative of the inductance of the longer and the shorter signal paths (pins) into or out of a given package style. Twenty-pin plastic leaded

TABLE 4.2   Package-Pin Inductance

Package	Self-inductance, nH	
	Upper value	Lower value
14-pin DIP	10	3
20-pin DIP	15	3
20-pin PLCC	5	4
28-pin DIP	17	5
44-pin PLCC	6	5
100-pin PLCC	15	12

chip carriers (PLCCs) are nearly symmetric. Hence, there is little difference in the length, or inductance, of the pins. The actual worst-case pin inductance for the various listed package styles may vary considerably from that shown in Table 4.2, so actual package specifications should always be consulted. Note that surface-mounted packages such as LCCs and PLCCs have less lead inductance then DIP packages and offer an advantage where they can be used.

Ground-bounce (or power supply droop) problems are compounded when several heavily loaded drivers in a common package switch simultaneously.[19] One observable manifestation of ground bounce or power supply droop is the appearance of transient-voltage spikes on stable outputs when other heavily loaded devices in the (same) package switch.[20]

Figure 4.10 shows a common situation where ground-bounce spikes will be observable on a stable output of an octal driver (power supply droop will occur for the opposite switching conditions). A ground-

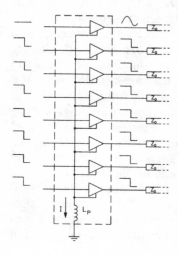

Figure 4.10   Ground-bounce spike on a static output (the top buffer) when other buffers in the package switch.

bounce spike will occur on the stable output when the other drivers switch from a *high* to a *low* level. *High*-to-*low* switching causes a large transient current to flow from the loads to ground through the package ground pin. The inductance of the pin and the large transient current cause a transient-voltage drop (spike) across the ground pin. The transient-voltage spike causes the reference level of the internal chip to shift in the positive direction, causing a positive voltage spike on the stable output, as shown in Fig. 4.10. The magnitude of the spike depends on the total load of the switched outputs. In many common situations, the magnitude of the spike will exceed the noise margin of the receiving device.

To find the magnitude of a transient ground-bounce voltage spike for a given application, first the change in current di/dt in the package ground pin must be determined. For example, the total package di/dt for the octal driver application shown in Fig. 4.10 is found as follows: In this case, seven buffers driving lines with a characteristic impedance Z_o of 50 Ω simultaneously switch. Assuming that all outputs transition 3.5 V, which is typical for TTL-level outputs, the change in current ΔI [use Eq. (4.18) times 7] is

$$\Delta I = 7\left(\frac{\Delta V}{Z_o}\right) = 7\left(\frac{3.5 \text{ V}}{50 \text{ }\Omega}\right) = 490 \text{ mA} \tag{4.19}$$

Once ΔI is known, the transient ground-bounce voltage is calculated from Eq. (4.20):

$$v(t) = L \frac{di}{dt} \tag{4.20}$$

which is approximated by

$$\Delta V = L \frac{\Delta I}{\Delta t} \tag{4.21}$$

For a ΔI of 490 mA, a signal transition of 3 ns, and a ground pin inductance of 15 nH (15 nH is representative of the inductance of a typical 20-pin dual-in-line package with an end ground pin—see Table 4.2), the ground-bounce spike ΔV is

$$\Delta V = (15 \text{ nH})\left(\frac{490 \text{ mA}}{3 \text{ ns}}\right) = 2.45 \text{ V}$$

but a spike of 2.45 V will not occur because of self-limiting. As ground bounce lifts the device's reference, the device's output drive capability is reduced and it slows down, which reduces the current which produces ground bounce. If a ground-bounce spike of 2.45 V were to occur, it would greatly exceed the static or dynamic *low*-level noise margin of devices with TTL-level inputs and would exceed the static noise margin of CMOS devices with CMOS input levels (see Chap. 2 for noise margin specifications). Yet, 50-Ω dynamic loads and the other conditions are not unusual. In many cases, much lower board impedances must be driven and PC boards may have effective impedances Z_o as low as 20 or 30 Ω. Large lumped capacitance loads have very low dynamic impedances and when switched, they may cause very large currents which in turn cause very large ground-bounce spikes.

Repeating the above ground-bounce calculation for a 5-V CMOS octal driver with 5-V output swings (the other conditions the same), we see that the change in current ΔI when 7 CMOS driver switch is

$$\Delta I = 7\left(\frac{5.0 \text{ V}}{50\Omega}\right) = 700 \text{ mA}$$

and the ground-bounce spike ΔV is

$$\Delta V = (15 \text{ nH})\left(\frac{700 \text{ mA}}{3 \text{ ns}}\right) = 3.5 \text{ V}$$

which exceeds the CMOS *low*-level static noise margin (1.5 V in this case where V_{cc} is 5 V) and greatly exceeds the static *low* noise margin of TTL, CMOS, or BiCMOS devices with TTL input levels. Ground-bounce spikes are particularly troublesome when CMOS devices with TTL input levels are used. Most CMOS devices with TTL inputs still have full rail-to-rail output voltage swings and the accompanying large ground-bounce spikes. To reduce ground bounce, some of the newer CMOS logic families have less than rail-to-rail output swings[21] and a number of other ground-bounce reducing features such as slew rate control.[22]

Techniques for minimizing ground-bounce effects. All devices have some ground bounce, even the new, improved second-generation advanced CMOS and BiCMOS devices.[23] Even when all external connections are ideal, i.e., zero impedance, some package-pin inductance remains, which may cause significant ground bounce depending upon the load and output slew rate.[24] Ground bounce can be controlled on critical clock and strobe signals by carefully following the design practices that limit ground bounce, but it is impractical to follow those design practices for all signals. To bound the magnitude of the signal integrity design task, some implementation technique is needed that is tolerant of ground-bounce spikes on most signals.[25] Synchronous design (Chap. 10) is one such technique. Synchronous logic is insensitive to spikes on most control and data lines except at active clock edges since a fundamental principle of synchronous design is that all control and data inputs are clock-activated. Synchronous design prohibits the use of spike-sensitive asynchronous inputs on storage elements (flip-flops) or cross-coupled gates for performing operational logic functions. Thus, short ground-bounce spikes on control or data signals (that are not in time phase with the clock—which they should not be in a properly designed synchronous system) do not upset synchronous systems.

To further limit the possible detrimental effects of ground bounce or power supply droop, the buffers used to drive critical signals, such as clocks and signals that go to asynchronous inputs, such as resets and presets, must be segregated into separate packages. The purpose is to prevent ground bounce caused by one group of buffers switching from causing spikes on the unswitched (at that time) buffers in the common package. For example, different-frequency clock signals should not be buffered with buffers that reside in a common package. As an additional precaution in waveshape-critical applications, all buffers in an octal package should not be used if all are driving heavily loaded lines and all switch at once; the output waveshape may be degraded. Clock signal fan-out buffers are a typical example of a case where all buffers would switch at the same time. When the number of buffers used in an octal package is limited due to ground-bounce considerations, those used should be the buffers nearest the ground pin or pins.

4.4 Guidelines for Reducing Inductance and Transient-Current Effects

> Internal device and load-related transient switching currents are a major source of noise and signal integrity problems in today's digital systems. Their presence and nature must be understood and the power distribution system designed to minimize them, or else there is little chance of success. It is essential that high-speed systems have low-impedance power distribution systems and local decoupling capacitors to replenish local transient-current demands.[26]

The following guidelines will help reduce the adverse effects of inductance and transient switching currents when high-speed advanced Schottky TTL, advanced CMOS, or BiCMOS devices are used in high-performance systems:

1. Use low-impedance planes to distribute power and ground.

2. Use a high-frequency decoupling capacitor located as directly as possible between the power and ground pin of each advanced CMOS or BiCMOS device, and use one for each advanced Schottky TTL driver or MSI device and one for every two advanced Schottky TTL SSI devices or gates.

3. In critical applications where ground bounce or power supply droop must be minimized, use packages with lower pin inductance such as leaded or leadless chip carriers (LCCs, PLCC, etc.).

4. The use of sockets or device carriers must be avoided (or their use carefully evaluated) since they add inductance and increase ground bounce and power supply droop.

5. Signal lines must run near ground (reference) planes to minimize inductance. When signals cannot be routed near a ground plane (such as between separate racks, cabinets, etc.), signals should be sent via twisted-pair lines.

6. When one is using prototyping boards (such as wire-wrap, welded-wire, etc.), the power and ground planes must be continuous through the package, and connector-pin fields and package (or socket) ground and power pins must be soldered directly to the planes by using solder washers or clips.

7. Limit loading to reduce transient load currents.

8. Limit loading of signals with critical waveshape requirements originating from a common package, to reduce total package power and ground-pin currents.

9. Limit the number of devices (drivers) used in a package when signals are driven with waveshape critical requirements such as clock signals.

10. Use only those drivers nearest the package ground pin in critical applications (particularly where signals have TTL level).

11. Do not mix asynchronous control signals such as clears, presets, etc., in packages with other heavily loaded signals.

12. The loading and the number of outputs that can switch simultaneously must be limited on devices that drive sensitive inputs such as clocks, clock or latch enables, and asynchronous sets, resets, etc., to reduce ground bounce and power supply droop.

13. Critical signals such as clocks of different frequency or phase, clock or latch enables, and asynchronous sets, resets, etc., must be segregated into separate packages to prevent ground bounce or power supply droop interference.

14. Do not mix critical signals, such as clocks and clock enables, in PLDs that have other signals which are not phase-aligned or are not the same frequency or duty cycle.

15. Be careful to limit the load on byte-wide (or wider) devices to limit ground bounce if the waveshape or spikes are an issue.

16. Synchronous design practices, which prohibit the use of asynchronous inputs on storage elements (flip-flops) or cross-coupled gates for performing operational logic functions, should be followed to prevent short spikes, such as might be generated by ground bounce, from upsetting the system.

17. Use devices with TTL-level output swings where possible.

18. Use second-generation advanced CMOS devices with slew rate control and other improvements that reduce switching transients where devices with CMOS output levels must be used.

19. Never use devices or logic families that have more drive or that are faster than required, and where possible, add series-damping

resistors (or use devices with them built in) to slow down transitions and reduce transient-current effects.

4.5 References

1. R. Paul Clayton, *Introduction to Electromagnetic Compatibility*, Wiley, New York, 1992.
2. A. H. Fitzgerald and D. E. Higginbotham, *Basic Electrical Engineering*, 5th ed., McGraw-Hill, New York, 1981.
3. *High-Speed Board Design Techniques*, Publication 16356, Advanced Micro Devices, Inc., Sunnyvale, Calif., 1992.
4. Reuben Lee, Leo Wilson, and Charles E. Carter, *Electronic Transformers and Circuits*, Wiley, New York, 1988.
5. H. B. Bakoglu, *Circuits, Interconnections, and Packaging for VLSI*, Addison-Wesley, New York, 1990.
6. Jacob Millman, *Microelectronics, Digital and Analog Circuits and Systems*, McGraw-Hill, New York, 1979.
7. Liang-Tsai Lin and Richard Spehn, "Fast, Low-Power Logic Array Unites CMOS and Bipolar," *Electronic Design*, April 16, 1987, pp. 82–88.
8. *Advanced CMOS Logic Designer's Handbook*, Texas Instruments Inc., Dallas, Tex., 1988.
9. *FACT Advanced CMOS Logic Databook*, National Semiconductor Corp., Santa Clara, Calif., 1993.
10. Barbara Tuck, "TI's BiCMOS Bus Interface ICs Slash Standby Current," *Electronic Products*, June 1987, pp. 17–19.
11. Morris M. Mano, *Digital Design*, Prentice-Hall, Englewood Cliffs, N.J., 1984.
12. Charles A. Holt, *Electronic Circuits Digital and Analog*, Wiley, New York, 1978.
13. *FAST Advanced Schottky TTL Logic Databook*, National Semiconductor Corp., Santa Clara, Calif., 1990.
14. Jacob Millman and Herbert Taub, *Pulse, Digital and Switching Waveforms*, McGraw-Hill, New York, 1965.
15. R. T. Maniwa, "Low-Power: An Overview," *Integrated System Design*, March 1995, pp. 20–30.
16. David Shear, "EDN's Advanced CMOS Logic Ground-Bounce Tests," *EDN*, March 2, 1989, pp. 88–97.
17. *Advanced CMOS Logic Design Considerations*, SCLA004, Texas Instruments Inc., Dallas, Tex., 1986.
18. *FAST Logic Applications Handbook*, National Semiconductor Corp., Santa Clara, Calif., 1990.
19. *Simultaneous Switching Evaluation and Testing*, Texas Instruments Inc., Dallas, Tex., 1987.
20. *FCT—Fast, CMOS, TTL—Compatible Logic Technical Note*, Integrated Device Technology Inc., Santa Clara, Calif., December 1986.
21. *1994 High-Performance Logic Data Book*, Integrated Device Technology Inc., Santa Clara, Calif., 1994.
22. Lisa Gunn, "Output Control Quiets Noise Usually Found in Advanced CMOS Logic," *Electronic Design*, October 12, 1989, pp. 30–32.
23. David Shear, "EDN Ground-Bounce Tests Revisited," *EDN*, April 15, 1993, pp. 120–151.
24. Richard A. Quinnell, "Ignore Packaging Effects at Your Peril," *EDN*, June 9, 1994, pp. 47–52.
25. Richard Funk and James Nadolski, "Advanced CMOS—Pinouts Are Not the Crucial Factor," *Electronic Engineering Times*, August 4, 1986, p. 33.
26. Isidor Straus, "Designing for Compliance, Part 1: Designing PC Boards for EMC Compliance," *Compliance Engineering 1994 Reference Guide*, vol. 11, no. 2, Compliance Engineering, Boxborough, Mass., 1994.

5

Power Distribution

The electrical and mechanical design of power distribution systems for equipment using high-speed advanced Schottky TTL, advanced CMOS, or BiCMOS devices is a difficult task. Today's high-speed TTL, CMOS, and BiCMOS devices have severe transient-current demands. Unless the best design practices are followed, power distribution systems will be plagued with inductance that will degrade the quality of the delivered power, which in turn will degrade system operation. The design objective is to ensure that the inductance and overall impedance of the power distribution system do not degrade the distributed voltages below the operating limits of the logic devices being used nor introduce intolerable noise. Of primary importance in high-speed digital systems is the use of very low-impedance planes throughout the distribution systems and the use of decoupling capacitors located very close to each device.[1]

In the typical large digital system, the power distribution system designer must address possible voltage loss at each of the following power system interfaces:

1. Component power and ground connections to board power and ground planes

2. Circuit board power and ground planes

3. Circuit-board-to-motherboard power and ground connections

4. Motherboard power and ground planes

5. Motherboard power and ground plane connections to power and ground feeder lines or buses

6. Power and ground lines or buses between motherboard and power supplies

Both ac and dc losses are of concern at each interface, but power distribution problems are most often caused by ac losses when high-speed TTL, CMOS, or BiCMOS devices are used.[2] Their large transient switching currents will cause severe voltage loss and degrade or prevent system operation unless power system inductance is minimized. Guidance for dealing with each of the above cases is given in the following sections.

5.1 Component Power and Ground-Pin Connections to Power and Ground Planes

The connections between component power and ground pins to power and ground planes must be direct to minimize ground bounce or power supply droop—no wiring or long printed-circuit (PC) board tracks. When components that have leads which project through PC boards are used, e.g., dual-in-line packages, then power and ground leads should connect directly to the respective plane. When surface-mounted packages are used, power and ground connections to the respective planes must be as short as possible. Long tracts to feedthrough vias must be avoided. Wired power and ground connections must not be used when wire-wrap or welded-wire universal boards are used.

Often during the developmental phase of a project, there is the temptation to wire ground and power connections. Yet, simple calculations of voltage loss as a function of transient switching currents (that are to be expected when high-speed TTL, CMOS, or BiCMOS devices are used) show the inappropriateness of wired power or ground connections. On wire-wrap boards, it is difficult to achieve connections that are much less than 1 in. Various references show the inductance of a 1-in length of no. 30 wire to be in the range of 15 to 50 nH, depending upon how close the wire is to a ground plane or other return path.[3,4] The transient voltage drop ΔV across a 1-in wire with an inductance of 20 nH, and the same load and switching conditions as used for the TTL or BiCMOS package-pin ground-bounce calculations in Chap. 4 (seven outputs switching in 3 ns with level changes of 3.5 V and 50-Ω loads), is from Eq. (4.21):

$$\Delta V = L \frac{\Delta I}{\Delta t} = (20 \text{ nH}) \left(\frac{490 \text{ mA}}{3 \text{ ns}} \right) = 3.26 \text{ V}$$

Even with a 50 percent allowance for self-regulation, ground bounce due to ground wire and package ground-pin inductance (which must be added to the above) is in excess of TTL- or CMOS-level static or dynamic noise margins.

The inductance of wired power or ground connections cannot be tolerated when high-speed logic components are used. Power and ground connections must be made directly to power and ground planes. When prototyping boards (such as wire-wrap or welded-wire) are used, the package (or socket) power and ground pins must be connected directly to the power and ground planes by solder washers or clips.[5] Even sockets must be avoided in most applications, since they add inductance and increase ground bounce and power supply droop.

5.2 Voltage Loss across Planes

Low-impedance planes must be used to distribute power and ground on circuit boards and motherboards in high-performance TTL, CMOS, or BiCMOS systems. Planes are needed to keep the dc resistance and the ac impedance as low as possible to supply high direct and pulse currents with minimum voltage loss. There should be no interruptions in the planes except clearance holes for vias (feedthroughs).

5.2.1 DC loss

In LV or in 5-V TTL, CMOS, or BiCMOS systems, dc losses in the ground or reference distribution interconnections should be kept to negligible levels on circuit boards and motherboards. Slightly greater loss can usually be tolerated in the V_{cc} side of the power system, especially if all devices have TTL input levels. A typical design goal for circuit boards or motherboards is to keep the total dc loss on both V_{cc} and ground to less than 1 percent of the nominal supply level (which is 50 mV in a 5-V system).

The dc drop across a circuit board or motherboard plane is difficult to calculate since currents in planes are not confined to known paths. One useful approach for estimating dc voltage drops across a plane is to segment the plane into squares, as shown in Fig. 5.1, and sum the more manageable and more easily determined drops across the individual squares. First, determine the current requirements of each square (i.e., the supply current requirements of components or circuit board connector pins located in that portion of the plane). Second, average the current for each row of squares, and make the assump-

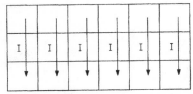

Figure 5.1 Divide ground or voltage planes into squares to make *IR* loss calculations.

tion that the current density is uniform in each square in a given row across the plane (i.e., from left to right in Fig. 5.1). Third, determine the cumulative current in each square in a column of the squares, working from the top of the plane to the bottom. Use the sheet resistance of the plane and the current in a given square to calculate the *IR* drop across each square. Sum the drops across the square to arrive at the drop across the plane or to points of interest.

Resistance of a section of a plane.   For a section of a plane, with dimensions as shown in Fig. 5.2, the resistance is [6]

$$R = \rho \, \frac{l}{wt} = \rho \, \frac{l}{\text{area of cross section}} \tag{5.1}$$

where ρ is the resistivity of the plane. For a square section ($l = w$), the resistance is

$$R = \frac{\rho}{t} = \frac{\rho}{\text{thickness}} = \text{sheet resistance} = \rho_s \tag{5.2}$$

The approximate sheet resistance for three common weights of copper PC board conductive layers is [7]

0.5-oz copper plane ≈ 1.0 mΩ per square

1.0-oz copper plane ≈ 0.5 mΩ per square

2.0-oz copper plane ≈ 0.25 mΩ per square

Today most multilayer printed backplane and circuit boards are built with 1-oz copper signal and power planes; but as signal density increases and signal line widths move to 5 mils and below, $\frac{1}{2}$-oz signal planes are used. Very high-current applications, such as backplane power and ground layers in systems that use many ECL devices or other high-powered devices, often use 2-oz or heavier material.

The sheet resistance used to calculate the drop across a plane should be derated from the solid plane based on the number and location of voids. In many applications, voids due to clearance holes for vias and package or connector pins will result in cross-sectional area losses in excess of 50 percent, and in some cases as much as 70 percent. The cross-sectional loss must be determined and sheet resis-

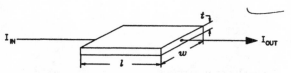

Figure 5.2   Square section of a plane showing dimensions used to define sheet resistance.

tance adjusted appropriately. Alternatively, the number of power and ground layers can be increased. In most TTL, CMOS, or BiCMOS circuit board applications, dc loss in power or ground planes is not significant when 1-oz or heavier copper planes are used. However, in backplane or motherboard applications, several 1-oz or 2-oz layers may be required to keep dc losses from being significant.

5.2.2 AC loss

The ac voltage loss in power and ground planes due to inductance is typically of much greater concern than dc loss in high-speed TTL, CMOS, or BiCMOS systems.[3] The inductance of power and ground planes is kept low by using continuous planes with no cutouts except for feedthroughs (vias) and by keeping the power and ground planes as close together as possible. The basic equation for the inductance of two parallel plates or planes of equal width w, where the width is much greater than the separation b, is given by Matick[8] as

$$L = 4\pi\mu_r \times 10^{-7} \frac{b}{w} \text{ with units of } \frac{\text{H}}{\text{m}} \qquad (5.3)$$

The relative permeability μ_r is approximately 1 for nonconducting materials[9] such as the epoxy glass used to separate planes in multilayer PC boards. Thus, by using a parallel-plate model, the inductance of closely spaced power and ground planes on PC boards is given by (with the unit changes to nanohenrys per centimeter)

$$L = 4\pi \frac{b}{w} \text{ with units of } \frac{\text{nH}}{\text{cm}} \qquad (5.4)$$

The parallel-plate model assumes uniform current density which is not the actual case in most local situations on a PC board. On a PC board the current is typically flowing to or from a point (the power or ground pin of a package). However, it seems reasonable to assume that most of the transient-current flow, when a device switches, follows a relatively direct path between the nearest decoupling capacitor and the power and ground pins of the device. If that is the case, then the question is, How wide is the path in which the current flows relative to the separation of the power and ground planes? From Eq. (5.4) we can see that if the width-to-separation ratio is on the order of 10 to 1, the inductance per centimeter is on the order of 1 to 2 nH. However, if the power and ground path is very long, then 1 or 2 nH/cm quickly becomes significant at today's TTL, CMOS, or BiCMOS edge speeds and transient load currents (see ground-bounce calculations in Chap. 4). To minimize the transient-current path in power distribution networks, each high-speed device needs a nearby decoupling capacitor to supply the nearly instantaneous change in current that occurs when high-speed devices switch. Decoupling capacitors are needed because it is generally impractical to get the impedance of planes much below 1 or 2 nH/cm, and 1 or 2 nH/cm is significant at the high-pulse currents demanded by today's advanced Schottky TTL, advanced CMOS, and BiCMOS devices. The voltage loss in planes due to inductance is calculated by using the basic equation for the voltage drop across an inductor, which is

$$v(t) = L \frac{di}{dt} \approx L \frac{\Delta I}{\Delta t} \tag{5.5}$$

where ΔI is the change in current when a device switches from one level to the other and Δt is the rise or fall time of the signal.

It is important when high-speed TTL, CMOS, or BiCMOS devices are used that the board power and ground planes be continuous throughout all device and connector-pin fields, as shown in Fig. 5.3. Boards with ground cutouts for pin rows should not be used with today's high-speed digital devices. Some board manufacturers' catalogs describe universal boards with the required continuous planes as "Schottky" boards.

Figure 5.3 High-speed Schottky circuit board showing ground plane connections between each socket. (*Courtesy of Stitch Wire Systems Corp. Reprinted with permission of Stitch Wire Systems Corp.*)

5.3 Circuit-Board-to-Motherboard Connections

Device-to-PC-board interfaces are not the only system interfaces where ground bounce or power supply droop is a concern (see Chap. 4). Any circuitry not connected to its ground or supply voltage by a continuous plane can experience ground bounce or power supply droop. For example, circuit-board-to-motherboard or backplane connections by necessity (so that boards can be removed) are not continuous. To keep ground bounce and power supply droop within limits that allow reliable transmission of single-ended signals, circuit-board-to-motherboard connectors must have a sufficient and well-distributed number of ground and power connections. Circuit-board-to-motherboard ground integrity is essential. The circuit board reference must be very close to that of the motherboard and the other boards in the system. If a good ground level is maintained and circuit boards have sufficient decoupling (see Sec. 5.4), the number of circuit-board-to-motherboard power connections is not as critical as the number of ground connections.

The number of ground (or voltage) pins needed in a circuit-board-to-motherboard connector (or in any connector) should be calculated based on an overall system noise budget[10] that defines the allowable ground bounce at the connector (see Fig. 5.4). The parallel inductance L_p of the ground or power pins,

$$\frac{1}{L_p} = \frac{1}{L_1} + \frac{1}{L_2} + \cdots + \frac{1}{L_N} \tag{5.6}$$

must be small enough that the transient voltage drop $v(t)$ across the connector,

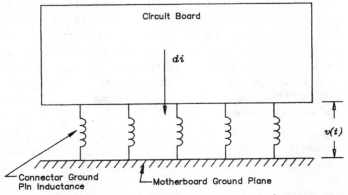

Figure 5.4 Circuit-board-to-motherboard connector inductance must be low so that transient interface signal currents do not shift the board reference level a significant amount.

$$v(t) = L_p \frac{di}{dt} \tag{5.7}$$

for the worst-case number of simultaneous switching outputs does not cause a transient voltage shift greater than that allowed in the error budget. As a rule of thumb, there should be a ground pin for every four to eight outputs (the faster the edge speed of the signals, the more pins required), and the ground pins must be evenly distributed across the connector.[11] For example, for a typical two-row connector, as a minimum a ground pin is needed for every 0.5 to 1 in of connector.

Static dc voltage loss across connectors is generally not a problem in TTL, CMOS, or BiCMOS systems, but dc loss must be carefully evaluated. Some high-density connectors have relatively high resistance and are not rated for very high currents. As a general guideline in high-reliability applications, connector-pin currents should be limited to 50 percent of the manufacturer's rating.

5.4   Power-Supply-to-Motherboard Connections

Advanced Schottky TTL, advanced CMOS, and BiCMOS systems require low-impedance power-source-to-load connections to meet the high-dc and high-pulse-current requirements of today's systems. It is essential to minimize the inductance L of the power supply to load conductors and connections, in order to control undesirable transient voltage drops. Minimum inductance is achieved by minimizing the area enclosed by the current path and by keeping the current path as short as possible. In low-current applications, the dc resistance of the power connections is seldom significant. In high-current applications (e.g., greater than 50 A), the dc resistance of power connections can be a major issue. A great effort should be made to minimize the length of V_{cc} and ground conductors between power supply and power and ground planes in backpanels or motherboards. The optimum arrangement is a dedicated power supply for each motherboard, with the supply located as close as possible to the motherboard (i.e., plugged into the motherboard). A local power supply for each unit keeps V_{cc} and ground connections as short as possible and minimizes the chance of circulating ground-loop currents.

Remote power supply connections.   If it is not possible to connect the power supply directly to the load (e.g., motherboard) power and ground planes, then the connections must be made by using some very low-impedance connection technique such as twisted-pair lines or low-impedance closely coupled bus bars.[12] Minimizing the inductance of remote power connections is as important as minimizing the resistance due to the pulsed-current demands of advanced Schottky or advanced CMOS systems. To help supply peak current demands and to reduce radiated noise, some bulk capacitance should be located near where power connects to the motherboard. In remote applications with very high transient-current demands, motherboards should have bulk capacitors distributed around the perimeter. The value of the bulk capacitance should be in the range of 50 to 100 times the value of the worst-case simultaneously switched load capacitance. Bulk capacitors must be chosen carefully. Many large-value capacitors are sensitive to surge current, ripple current, reverse voltage, and overvoltage. The best solution is to design the power distribution system so that bulk decoupling capacitors are not needed. A local power supply with short low-impedance connections to low-impedance power planes achieves that purpose. However, in those cases where power supplies cannot be located near the load, they should be connected as shown in Fig. 5.5. Independent low-impedance source and return paths (such as twisted pairs) are used for each supply so that return current from one supply does not modulate the voltage level of the other supply.

When the power supply cannot be located near the load, overshoot at turn-on and undershoot at turnoff are common occurrences. Power supply overshoot and undershoot are enhanced by the amount of inductance in the supply path. Thus, it is essential to minimize the inductance of the power conductors to control overshoot and undershoot, as well as to ensure a low-impedance path for transient load

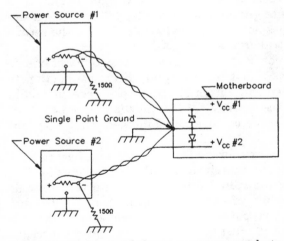

Figure 5.5 Recommended remote power supply to motherboard connection and proper system grounding scheme.

demands. Where line inductance between the supply and the load is significant, the possibility of overshooting at turn-on (because the line inductance isolates the source from the load) can be minimized by mounting a small resistor (for example, 10 to 100 Ω) directly across the power supply terminals to provide a real (noninductive) load. A resistor at the source has additional benefits, for it tends to reduce reflected noise by matching (terminating) the power lines. A power supply may have very low dc output impedance and may be capable of sourcing or sinking large direct currents, yet the output may reflect incident ac noise due to transmission-line effects (see Chap. 7). If the supply output impedance does not match the line impedance, noise pulses or other load-related disturbances may persist for some time before their energy is dissipated.

In general, power supply return or reference outputs should not be connected to the chassis ground at the supplies. From a signal integrity standpoint, the power supplies' output return lines, backpanels (or motherboards), ground planes, chassis, racks, etc., should be connected to earth, or chassis, ground at only one central point.[13] (However, there are safety issues with single-point grounds; see Sec. 5.9). In most applications, the best location for the central ground point is where the ground lines connect to the motherboard or backpanel. A single system ground point prevents circulating ground currents. Circulating ground currents introduce noise that can upset system operation; thus extraneous ground currents must be avoided.[4] To ensure that power supplies have a reference at all times, remote power supply return or reference outputs should be connected to earth ground through a resistor, such as a 150-Ω one, as shown in Fig. 5.5. A resistor prevents ground-loop currents, yet provides a reference so that a supply does not go to some harmful level if the return (reference) line to the central ground point is disconnected.

Systems or units must not float, to prevent the possibility of unsafe voltage levels. All systems must have a solid, direct connection to earth ground to protect personnel from electric shock hazards and to prevent damage to interface devices.[14,15] If a unit is allowed to float, then even if input-output devices are not damaged, they may not operate correctly.

Use of a single power source for multiple units, e.g., backpanels, motherboards, chassis, etc., is undesirable. With a single unit feeding multiple units, grounding individual units creates multiple grounds and introduces the possibility of large circulating ground currents. When multiple units must be powered from a single source, the single-point ground (see Sec. 5.9) must be located at the power source, as shown in Fig. 5.6. Figure 5.6 shows the correct way to connect multiple units to a single power source. Separate power and return lines

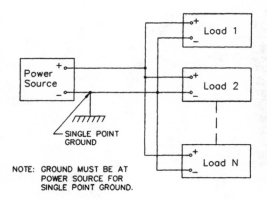

Figure 5.6 Typical power connections and single-point ground connection for single power source to multiple loads (not a recommended arrangement—it is usually best to have loads grounded locally).

(twisted pairs or closely coupled bus bars) should be used to connect each unit to the supply. Ground lines should not be serially connected to limit unit-to-unit interference. A single supply for multiple units is not a desirable arrangement and should be avoided if at all possible.

5.5   Voltage Loss in Power Conductors

When you calculate power conductor loss, be sure to include both power and ground return lines.

Many of today's digital systems have power supply current requirements of 100 A or more. In such applications, power conductors must be carefully designed to minimize voltage loss; very small resistances are significant in high-current applications. Even in low-current applications, power conductor loss is often underestimated. In all applications, dc voltage loss in power wiring or bus bars must be evaluated. Power conductors must be sized so that the loss in the power leads, when added to the voltage tolerance of the power supply, plus an allowance for noise and other losses, does not result in a voltage at the components that is below their minimum specified operating level. The minimum operating level for most 5-V TTL devices is 4.5 V for military temperature-rated devices and 4.75 V for commercial rated devices. The minimum operating level for 5-V CMOS devices varies widely; many AC devices are rated to operate down to 2 V, but their speed decreases significantly at reduced supply voltages. Most TTL-level compatible CMOS devices (that is, ACT and FCT) are specified for operation down to 4.5 V. Low-voltage (3.3-V) devices are typically specified for operation down to 2.7 or 3 V depending on the vendor. In all cases, vendor specifications should be checked.[16,17]

When the power conductor loss is calculated, the conductor manufacturer's resistance specifications should be consulted for actual

TABLE 5.1   Resistance of Stranded Copper Conductor

AWG no.	mΩ/ft
4	0.27
6	0.43
8	0.67
10	1.2
12	1.8
14	2.9
16	4.5
18	5.9
20	9.5
22	15
24	24
26	40
28	64
30	100
32	160
34	260
36	410

resistance data. However, if stranded copper wire is used, the voltage drop can be estimated from the data listed in Table 5.1. Table 5.1 lists the approximate resistance (in milliohms per foot) for several common sizes of stranded copper conductor.[18,19]

5.6   Voltage Loss in Power Connections

Voltage loss at power connectors or other power-line junctions such as at bolted terminals is a serious problem in high-power systems. Large high-speed digital processing systems often require supply currents that range from 100 to 200 A. In such applications, a small connector or junction resistance can result in large voltage losses. To minimize the voltage loss, the power connections must be tight and clean and must have sufficient contact area (to limit the current density).[20] In most large-current applications (greater than 100 A), it is not practical to use a quick-disconnect power connector; bolted junctions are required.

Determining the resistance of power connections under all conditions is a difficult task. Contact pressure, oxidation of mating surfaces, and actual mating surface area (there may be high or low spots) are all critical parameters that are difficult to establish initially and with aging. To compensate for these uncertainties, power connections should be designed with a generous safety margin.

Multiple power and ground connections to backpanel planes (backplanes) may be required in high-current applications to limit the current density and voltage loss in backplanes in the vicinity of power connections. When multilayer PC motherboards with thin planes are used in high-current applications, the current density in the vicinity of power connections is of special concern. In such applications, the voltage loss in the plane in the vicinity of connections must be evaluated and corrective measures (such as multiple connections) taken if the loss is significant.

Radial resistance of a thin plane from a point. The radial change in resistance dR of a thin plane as a function of distance r from a point or circular void (see Fig. 5.7) is[6]

$$dR = \rho_s \frac{dr}{2\pi r} \qquad (5.8)$$

where ρ_s is the sheet resistance and dR between two points r_1 and r_2 in a thin plane is

$$dR = \frac{\rho_s}{2\pi} \int_r^{r_2} \frac{dr}{r} \qquad (5.9)$$

and the resistance R between r_1 and r_2 is

$$R = \frac{\rho_s}{2\pi} \ln \frac{r_2}{r_1} \qquad (5.10)$$

Where multilayer PC motherboards with thin planes are used in high-current applications, Eq. (5.10) should be used to calculate the resistance in the vicinity of power and ground connections, and the results should be used to calculate possible voltage loss.

Example calculations. The voltage drop in the vicinity of a 10-A and a 200-A connection to a 1-oz copper plane is determined to illustrate the

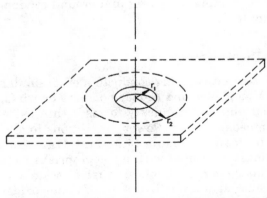

Figure 5.7 Variables used to determine the radial resistance of a plane.

possible voltage loss at the power or ground plane to power conductor junctions. A 10-A connection is typical of circuit board current requirements. Many large systems have motherboards with 200-A or greater requirements.[21]

For 10-A connection. For the 10-A case, a 0.030-in diameter hole is used as a starting point. A 0.030-in diameter hole ($r_1 = 0.015$ in) is consistent with the mounting needs of a 10-A connector. From Eq. (5.10), the radial resistance of a 1-oz copper plane at 2 in, starting from a 0.030-in-diameter hole, is approximately 0.4 mΩ.

The voltage loss V_{loss} across 2 in of plane is

$$V_{loss} = (10\text{ A})(0.4 \times 10^{-3}\text{ Ω}) = 4\text{ mV}$$

Four millivolts is not a significant loss. Thus, similar low-current connections to 1-oz copper planes should not be a concern in most applications.

For 200-A connection. A 0.375-in-diameter hole is typical of the bolt or stud size that might be used to connect a 200-A power conductor terminal to a motherboard. The radial resistance of a 1-oz plane at 2 in, starting from a 0.375-in-diameter hole, is about 0.2 mΩ, and the voltage loss V_{loss} with 200 A of current flow is

$$V_{loss} = (200\text{ A})(0.2 \times 10^{-3}\text{ Ω}) = 40\text{ mV}$$

A 40-mV loss at both the power and ground connections to a motherboard must be evaluated in conjunction with other possible voltage losses in the power system. Such a large loss, coupled with other unavoidable junction and line losses in the power-supply-to-motherboard power feeder system, may impact the system operating margin. Where high-current connections must be made to a plane, connection losses can be minimized by connecting the power and ground conductors to the motherboard at multiple points.

5.7 Connections between Dissimilar Metals

Direct connections between current-carrying conductors of dissimilar metals, such as aluminum backplanes and copper bus bars or wires, must be avoided. Untreated aluminum quickly forms a thin oxide film, which causes a high-impedance joint. Power connections to aluminum backplanes must be made by using bimetallic transition joints, or contact surfaces must be coated with an appropriate joint compound.[22,23] Joint compounds contain chemicals that dissolve surface oxide films and seal joints against moisture and further oxidation. A joint compound, such as Alcoa No. 2 Electrical Joint

Compound, or an equivalent compound, should be used on all untreated aluminum-to-aluminum or aluminum-to-copper electrical connections. Transition joints are formed by creating a metallic bond between an aluminum backplane and some other metal, such as copper, that does not form a high-impedance oxide film. The metallic bond between the aluminum and copper prevents an oxide layer from forming at the aluminum-copper junction, and the copper outer layer provides a low-impedance surface for power connections.[24]

5.8   Overvoltage Protection

Power supply overshoots at turn-on or failures to a higher than normal output level must be guarded against.[25,26] For long-term system reliability, power supplies must be limited to levels that will not instantly destroy devices or stress devices so that their useful life is reduced. The typical goal is to keep all steady-state and transient supply voltage levels for 5-V parts below 7 V, since 7 V is the absolute maximum rating for most 5-V TTL, CMOS, and BiCMOS logic components. *Caution:* Some 5-V parts have a 6-V absolute maximum rating which makes them very difficult to protect. Low-voltage (3.3-V) devices typically have an absolute maximum rating of 4.6 V.[16,17] It is not uncommon for power supplies to fail in such a manner that the output voltage goes to a higher level than normal. Yet, it is usually carelessness in the adjustment or connection of the supply to the load or overshoot at turn-on that creates an overvoltage problem. Whatever the reason, it is very discouraging to have an entire system destroyed due to some overvoltage condition on the power supply (and it most assuredly will be a very unpleasant task to explain the situation to your supervisors).

Thus, to ensure that supply voltages do not exceed device limits, all power supplies should be equipped with overvoltage shutdown circuits (often called *crowbars*). In addition, all systems should have passive clamping devices (ones not dependent on other sources of power) for each power input source located directly and permanently at the load (so that the devices will not be neglected or improperly connected).[27] In most applications, passive clamps should be located where power is connected to motherboards or backpanels, as shown in Fig. 5.8. Zener diodes can be used, but power transient suppressors have better characterization for transient voltage suppression applications than zener diodes. The passive clamping device must have the transient power-handling capability to last long enough to trip the circuit breaker or primary fuse in the power supply. Removing the primary source of power from the supply ensures that the faulty or improperly adjusted supply is taken off line and that it will remain off until cor-

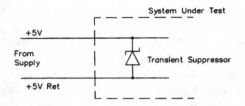

Figure 5.8 Overvoltage protection clamp.

rective action is taken. Zener diodes and silicon transient suppressors tend to fail short-circuited when exposed to excess voltage, which also helps safeguard the circuitry being protected.

5.9 System Grounding

System grounding must address power distribution, signal integrity, personnel safety, lightning protection, electromagnetic interference (EMI), and ESD issues.[28] These issues are not mutually exclusive; what is good for one may be bad for another. In general, none of these issues can be ignored. Most certainly, personnel safety cannot be ignored. If these issues are not addressed in the initial design, it may be impossible to adequately address them all at a later date.

Safety ground.   Cabinets, racks, or any conductive enclosures or structures receiving or generating potentially lethal voltages or currents are required by product safety agencies and electrical wiring codes to be connected to earth ground (earth ground for stationary equipment and vehicle frame for equipment inside a vehicle). The safety ground connection must have a steady-state current/voltage capacity equal to or greater than the largest current/voltage source connected to the equipment.

Lightning ground.   Antennas and equipment connected directly to external antennas must have a low-impedance path to earth ground (or vehicle frame) that can handle upward of 100,000 A for a few milliseconds. Lightning grounds are typically made with no. 2 AWG or larger copper conductor run in the most direct route possible (no sharp turns) to ground (or vehicle frame).

Power grounds.   Power grounds serve as return paths for primary power (to a system). In most electronic systems, primary power returns are not connected to ground at the load or loads. Primary power returns are connected to ground at their source or at distribution points (e.g., at breaker boxes). Primary power returns are not connected at the load to prevent power currents from flowing in and modulating signal ground; but even when primary power returns are not physically connected to ground at the loads, some primary power current will flow in signal ground due to parasitic coupling. These parasitic currents *will modulate single-ended interface signals*. Primary power coupling to signal ground is minimized by the use of primary power sources with low harmonic distortion, isolation transformers and inductor input filters (terminated back to the power source), and careful component layout and shielding to reduce capacitive coupling.

Signal ground. Electronic components must be connected to a common reference level to communicate, unless special translation techniques are used (e.g., opto-isolators). This common reference level is typically called *signal ground*. Signal ground is often further divided into analog and digital (signal) ground (treatment of analog and digital ground within a system is not covered here—the discussion here applies to either or both). Signal ground is typically referenced (connected) to earth ground or the vehicle frame ground. Ideally, no current flows from signal ground into the reference (earth or frame ground). If current does flow to the reference, then the signal ground potential will be modulated depending upon the impedance of the connection and the magnitude of the stray current(s). This modulation may not disturb internal system signals, but most certainly will disturb interface signals not transmitted or received in a manner that will negate the effects of the modulation. To ensure that internal (system) signals are not disturbed by signal ground currents, the impedance of signal ground (within a system) must be low enough that internal or external signal and power return currents do not cause a significant difference in potential from one point to any other point. Continuous ground planes are the only practical means of achieving sufficiently low impedance for today's high-speed analog or digital systems. Where devices are not referenced to a common plane, it is to be expected that their reference levels will be different. They will be different due to voltage modulation caused by parasitic signal and power currents returning to their source through the signal ground reference connections. To minimize the consequences of parasitic current flow from signal ground to earth or frame ground, digital signal ground (planes) and low-frequency analog (usually defined as below 10 kHz) are connected to their enclosure at one point only. This approach is commonly known as a *single-point ground system*. To minimize possible detrimental effects of the parasitic return currents that will exist in all cases, even when great care has been taken, it is important that the one connection to earth or frame ground be a very low-impedance connection (i.e., a wide strap)—not a long wire. Where high-frequency analog signals are present, standard procedure is to connect the analog signal ground to the enclosure in as many places as possible—ideally continuously. The reason is that at high frequencies, parasitic coupling defeats any attempt to form a single-point ground.

EMI grounds. In general, to meet EMI requirements, today's high-speed electronic devices must be enclosed in conductive enclosures tied to earth or frame ground. Interconnections between electronic device housings must be enclosed in metallic conduit or braided conductive shields that are connected at both ends (in the most direct manner possible to the source and receiving unit's enclosures). Connecting shields at both ends means that reference level differences (between source and receiving units) will cause parasitic currents to flow in interconnecting conduits or shields, which in turn will cause current flow in the signal and safety grounds (of both units). These parasitic currents, in turn, *will modulate single-ended interface signals.*

ESD ground. Electronic devices, boards, or backplanes within cabinets or racks must be connected to earth or frame ground to prevent unsafe levels of static charge buildup (which can cause ESD damage). Cabinets, racks, heat sinks, etc., must likewise be connected to ground to prevent static buildup that might discharge to a sensitive node of a nearby electronic device. It is very important that all circuit grounds internal to a metallic enclosure be connected to the enclosure, to prevent the circuit reference potential from differing from that of the enclosure.[29] System enclosures and cables properly configured to meet EMI requirements and signal and safety ground issues also address most system-level ESD issues.

Grounding and power distribution summary for electronic equipment racks or cabinets. Figure 5.9 shows *good*-practice grounding and power distribution connections for electronic equipment racks or cabinets. Numbers enclosed in carrots in Fig. 5.9 cue to a pertinent practice listed below.

1. Racks or other overall system enclosures are connected to earth ground by the input power cable green line and by a visible conductor with a current capacity equal to or greater than that of the input power source.

2. All backplanes within a rack are solidly connected to the rack (chassis) and to each other with a low-impedance conductor such as a copper bus bar.

3. The analog ground system within a rack is solidly connected (referenced) to the chassis wherever possible.

4. The digital grounds (backpanel or motherboard ground planes) are isolated from the rack (chassis) except at one point.

5. Modules (circuit boards) within a rack that have both analog and digital circuitry maintain physically separate areas for analog and

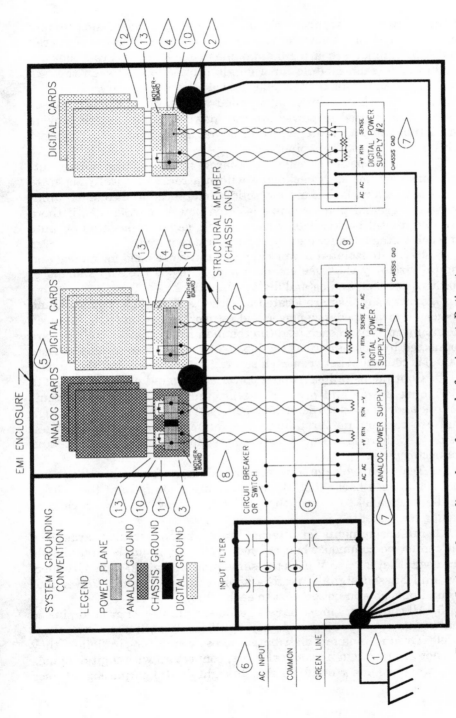

Figure 5.9 Power distribution and grounding scheme for a rack of equipment. Pertinent points are numbered, keyed, and summarized in text. (*Drawing courtesy of Larry Gorsky.*)

111

digital circuits and separate ground reference systems. Analog circuits are referenced to a separate (analog) ground plane that is referenced to the digital motherboard ground plane in one location. Provisions are made inside each module for a single connection between the two ground systems. This connection is added later if necessary.

6. Each rack or cabinet is supplied with a single primary power source that is used to power internal power supplies which provide the actual working voltages. Working voltage sources are not shared with multiple racks or cabinets.

7. Separate power supplies or separate isolated power supply outputs are used for each backplane within a rack. Physically separate units within a rack that are not solidly referenced to a common uninterrupted ground plane require isolated power sources (i.e., if there are two digital backpanels within a rack, separate isolated outputs for each voltage and for each backpanel are required).

8. Separate isolated power supply outputs are used for analog and digital circuitry that use common supply levels (i.e., no sharing of voltages between analog and digital circuits).

9. Power supplies are located as close as possible to the load, and dedicated low-impedance power and return lines or bus bars are used to supply current to each load (no common return paths). Returns are connected to ground only at the load. A 100-Ω resistor (or appropriate value) is connected between each return line and ground at the supply.

10. Continuous uninterrupted power and ground planes are used to distribute power and provide the ground reference for all circuit boards and motherboards or backpanels. The planes extend through and are continuous throughout the connector- and component-pin fields (i.e., there are ground plane connections between all device and connector pins).

11. Transient-voltage suppressors (clamps) for each voltage are located on each backpanel. Suppressors are sized to limit the voltage at the backpanel to a level that will not destroy the logic devices or analog components.

12. Pin assignments for internal units (such as circuit boards) in a rack must be common when common voltages, grounds, and signals are used (that is, $+ 5$ V uses the same pins on a given type of connector, and bussed signals use the same connector pins). Power and ground pins should not be next to each other.

13. All connectors must have a sufficient number of ground pins so that signal return currents do not significantly shift signal reference levels. Ground pins are distributed across connector-pin fields—they are not grouped. On a practical basis, connectors with digital signals typically have one ground per four to eight digital output signals (see Sec. 5.3).

5.10   Decoupling Capacitors

Advanced Schottky TTL, advanced CMOS, and BiCMOS devices require decoupling (also called *bypass*) capacitors to provide a local source of load-switching current to compensate for power and ground system inductance. *Local* decoupling capacitors are needed to supply a nearby source for the large high-frequency pulse-switching currents, and *bulk* capacitors are needed to provide circuit boards with enough capacitance to support longer-term, lower-frequency board transient-current demands.

5.10.1   Local decoupling

All high-speed logic devices need local decoupling capacitors to supply the current demanded during switching intervals (i.e., when changing states).[30] The fast edge rates of today's TTL, CMOS, and BiCMOS devices exacerbate the requirement for local decoupling. Local decoupling capacitors compensate for power distribution system inductance and prevent large transient shifts in local power or reference levels when large loads are quickly charged.[31] Even when low-impedance power and ground planes are used, they have significant inductance at today's TTL, CMOS, and BiCMOS edge rates. Planes, just as discrete wires, require a finite time for current to flow from one point to another. When several devices in a given area switch at once, significant instantaneous current must be available to prevent large shifts in local power or ground levels. Planes alone, even when closely spaced, do not provide sufficient local storage of energy, i.e., charge (they are not good capacitors), to supply the instantaneous current (charge) demanded when a large number of devices in a given area switch at the same time.[32] Thus, even well-designed power and ground distribution systems may have local transient excursions of V_{cc} and ground that violate device power supply levels, unless local decoupling is present. With low supply voltage, devices slow down, signal transitions slow down, and the potential system operating speed is reduced. Decoupling capacitors located near the power terminals of devices limit local power-level transient excursions to harmless levels.

Guidelines for sizing local decoupling capacitors.   When advanced Schottky TTL, advanced CMOS, or BiCMOS devices are used, it is extremely important to provide an adequate amount of local decoupling for octal drivers or for parts driving large amounts of capacitance. A general guideline for the amount and placement of decoupling capacitors for TTL, CMOS, or BiCMOS devices mounted on conventional PC, high-speed wire-wrap, or welded-wire board is as follows:

Guidelines for Sizing Local Decoupling Capacitors

1. For advanced Schottky TTL, one 0.1-μF high-frequency decoupling capacitor mounted as close as possible to the V_{cc} pin of each high-current driver, MSI, or LSI device package and one decoupling capacitor for every two packages of SSI logic functions[10]

2. For advanced CMOS or BiCMOS devices, one 0.1-μF high-frequency decoupling capacitor mounted as close as possible to the V_{cc} pin of each SSI or MSI device.[1,32,33]

In all applications, the manufacturer's decoupling recommendation must be followed. In many cases, larger values such as 0.22 μF are recommended for LSI devices, e.g., dynamic memories and programmable devices. Devices in large packages with multiple power and ground pins have special decoupling requirements; again, the manufacturer's recommendations must be closely followed. Some manufacturers recommend a parallel combination of a large-value and a small-value capacitor to increase the frequency range, e.g., a 0.1-μF and a 0.01-μF. However, in general, such a scheme is not significantly more effective than using the larger-value capacitor alone[34] and is not used unless the device manufacturer recommends such a configuration.

A typical design goal is to provide enough local decoupling capacitance to keep (support) the local dc supply voltage level within 1 percent of the nominal dc supply level under worst-case switching current demands. To meet that goal, the local decoupling capacitance C_d must be at least 100 times the maximum possible simultaneously switched load capacitance C_{load} for the worst-case combination of simultaneously switched signals within a package. That is,

$$C_d \geq 100 \, C_{load}$$

where C_{load} is the signal track capacitance plus the input or output capacitance of the devices connected to the line.

The benefit of local decoupling capacitors can be illustrated by using the principle of equality or charge. For example, Fig. 5.10 represents the output stage of a gate or buffer along with the power source and load circuitry that typically surrounds a logic device. When $S1$ closes ($S1$ closing represents a gate switching from a *low* level to a *high* level), the nearby 0.1-μF decoupling capacitor $C1$ supports the local supply V_{cc} level and provides the transient current demanded by the 100-pF load $C2$. Without the nearby decoupling capacitor, the V_{cc} level at the gate is reduced by the voltage drop across the power source inductance L_s. A reduction in V_{cc} may upset other gates in the package. For example, other outputs may shift to incorrect levels. In addition, the gate responsible for the change in V_{cc} (i.e., the gate that switched) may not respond as expected owing to an out-of-specification V_{cc} level.

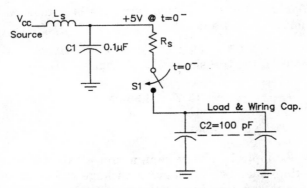

Figure 5.10 Idealized equivalent circuit when a logic device
with a nearby decoupling capacitor switches from *low* to
high (capacitor and logic device lead inductance are not
shown.)

For the circuit shown in Fig. 5.10, the final steady-state charge Q_f
on $C1$ and $C2$, reached sometime after switch $S1$ is closed, is equal to
the initial charge Q_i on $C1$ and $C2$ before $S1$ is closed (see Fig. 5.11).
That is,

$$Q_i = Q_f \qquad (5.11)$$

It is assumed the initial charge on $C2$ is zero since the device is
switching from a *low* level to a *high* level. Thus,

$$Q_i = (C1)V_{cc} \qquad (5.12)$$
$$Q_f = (C1)V_f + (C2)V_f \qquad (5.13)$$
$$C1(V_{cc}) = (C1 + C2)V_f \qquad (5.14)$$

$$V_f = \frac{C1}{C1 + C2} \, V_{cc} \qquad (5.15)$$

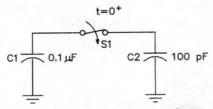

Figure 5.11 Decoupling capacitor $C1$ serves as a
reservoir of charge for quickly charging the load
capacitance $C2$.

The results, Eq. (5.15), show that the voltage excursion is a function of the voltage divider formed by $C1$ and $C2$.

Example with $C1 = 0.1~\mu\text{F}$ and $C2 = 100$ pF. For the circuit values shown in Figs. 5.10 and 5.11, the transient-voltage excursion is

$$V_f = \frac{01~\mu\text{F}}{0.1~\mu\text{F} + 100~\text{pF}}~(5~\text{V}) = 4.995~\text{V}$$

$$\Delta V_{cc} = 5~\text{mV}$$

However, the above example is a very benign and ideal case. In most situations, more than one device in a given package will change at the same time. All eight outputs of an octal driver or register may switch at once, resulting in transient switching current levels eight times those of the above example. In addition, in all real applications there is significant inductance between the decoupling capacitor and the device that is switching, which will cause the transient-voltage excursion to be significantly more than the 5-mV value calculated above. Even the best capacitors have significant effective series inductance (ESL) and effective series resistance (ESR) at advanced Schottky TTL, advanced CMOS, and BiCMOS edge speeds (see Fig. 5.12). Thus, it is important to select capacitors with good high-frequency performance. In most applications, ceramic capacitors are the best choice, when size, cost, and frequency response are all considered. Aluminum electrolytic and the various tantalum capacitors do not have adequate frequency response for local decoupling. Where very high-frequency response is required, 0.01-μF ceramic capacitors are generally superior to larger-value ceramic capacitors. Because capacitors behave as RLC networks, they have a resonant frequency above which they look more like an inductor than a capacitor. Typically as the capacitance goes down, the inductance goes down also, which means the resonant frequency goes up. Unfortunately, the series resistance typically goes up as the capacitance goes down.[35] Capacitor manufacturers' catalogs often list ESR but typically do not list ESL. However, ESR is frequency-dependent, and the ESR data given are normally low-frequency data (ESR decreases at higher frequencies). Sometimes graphs of impedance versus frequency are provided or can be obtained from the manufacturer, from which high-frequency ESR and ESL can be extracted.

Figure 5.12 High-frequency equivalent circuit for capacitors.

Decoupling capacitor leads need to be as short as possible to minimize the inductance between the capacitor and the device being decoupled.[36] Either surface-mounted or radial-leaded devices are best, but dual-in-line package (DIP) profile capacitors made especially for decoupling have reasonable high-frequency characteristics. Axially leaded capacitors should not be used since in most mounting arrangements their leads must be relatively long, which means higher inductance.[37]

The actual transient supply voltage excursion seen by a switching device is a function of the total inductance and resistance between the decoupling capacitor and the device plus the decrease in local supply level due to charge transfer to the load (see above). The inductance includes the ESL and lead inductance of the decoupling capacitor and the inductance of the power and ground plane and the package power and ground pins. In the typical application, the only significant resistance in the path is the ESR of the decoupling capacitor. The transient-voltage excursion due to inductance in the current path is determined by the basic equation for the voltage loss across an inductor

$$v(t) = L \frac{di}{dt} \approx L \frac{\Delta I}{\Delta t} \qquad (5.16)$$

where ΔI = change in current when device switches from one level to
    another
Δt = rise or fall time of signal
L = sum of capacitor ESL and lead inductance and power and
    ground plane and switching device power lead inductance

The loss due to ESR is simply

$$v(t) = \Delta I \, (\text{ESR}) \qquad (5.17)$$

A reasonable design goal is to keep the transient supply voltage excursions seen by the switching device due to inductance, resistance, and charge transfer below 0.2 V.

Local decoupling summary. Local decoupling capacitors supply local transient-current needs and prevent local degradation of V_{cc}. To serve that function, they must have good high-frequency response and must be located as close as possible to the power pins of the package being decoupled, to minimize the interconnection inductance.

5.10.2 Bulk decoupling

Bulk decoupling capacitors help compensate for inadequate power or ground connections between circuit boards and motherboards or between motherboards and power supplies. Large bulk capacitors provide low-frequency replenishment of charge to local decoupling capacitors to help maintain V_{cc} at the proper level.[38] In addition,

1. Circuit board bulk capacitors reduce the transmission of board-generated nose to the motherboard.
2. Motherboard bulk capacitors help eliminate low-frequency ripple and ringing due to power supply conductor inductance.
3. Circuit board and motherboard bulk capacitors help reduce the transmission of digital switching noise back to the power source; thus bulk capacitors help to meet emission requirements.

Bulk decoupling capacitors must be sized for worst-case low-frequency charge replenishment.[39] A good rule of thumb to follow is this: The value should be approximately 50 to 100 times the total worst-case simultaneous switched load capacitance. The simultaneous switched load capacitance is the total signal track capacitance plus the total device load for the worst-case combination of signals, within a unit, that could switch at one time. In circuit board bulk decoupling applications, solid-tantalum capacitors in the 10-μF, or greater, range are used. In backplane or motherboard applications, 10,000-μF bulk capacitors are often used.

Caution. Tantalum capacitors, or other large-value capacitors, tend to be less reliable than most other devices used in digital systems. Hence, the use of tantalum capacitors should be minimized. It is much more preferable to reduce the inductance of the power distribution system than to try to compensate for a poor distribution system with bulk capacitors. If the impedance of the power distribution system can be kept low enough, high-value (0.1-μF or larger) ceramic capacitors, which are more rugged and have a superior high-frequency response, can suffice for bulk decoupling as well as local decoupling.

In cases where bulk tantalum capacitors are required, careful attention must be paid to the application so as to limit ripple currents, transient-voltage spikes, in-rush currents, and polarity reversals. Tantalum capacitors can be destroyed or degraded unless precautions are taken to ensure that the voltage ratings are not exceeded. Care must be taken to keep tantalum capacitors as cool as possible since voltage ratings decrease at high temperature. When tantalum capacitors are used for decoupling, they should be selected so that the maximum applied voltage during normal operation is close to the derated maximum rated voltage. Tantalum capacitors should not be excessively derated. However, the worst-case operating voltage (including transient conditions) must never exceed the maximum voltage rating at the maximum operating temperature (tantalum capacitors are rated for lower voltage at high temperature).

Tantalum capacitors are polarized, so care must be taken to not reverse leads during installation. Tantalum capacitors, as well as the location where they are to be installed, should be clearly marked to reduce the opportunity for incorrect installation. Extra care must be taken to ensure that the polarity of input power is never reversed. Small power supply reversals at turn-on or turnoff, which often occur, will damage certain types of tantalum capacitors.[40,41] Many of the capacitor styles available in the size range needed for bulk decoupling are only rated for 0.5 V of reverse voltage. Ensuring that power supply undershoots will not exceed 0.5 V is a difficult task. Use of a normally reverse-biased silicon diode in parallel with a bulk capacitor is not a solution since high-current silicon diodes clamp at 0.8 to 1.2 V, depending upon the temperature and the current. However, there are large-value tantalum-cased tantalum capacitors available (military type CLR-79) with reverse-voltage tolerance up to 3 V, but they are expensive.

Meeting surge current limits is usually less of a problem than meeting reverse-voltage requirements. Slow turn-on of supplies, plus power conductor impedance, is often sufficient to limit surge currents to acceptable levels.

The application of large bulk capacitors presents both mechanical and electrical problems. The coefficients of expansion of the case, lead frame, and tantalum slug of solid-tantalum capacitors are all radically different. Thus, wide operating temperature ranges and temperature excursions during installation (soldering) can degrade devices.

For maximum decoupling capacitor reliability, the largest-value capacitor for a given case size and voltage should not be used. Compromises may have been made to pack a little more into a little less.

5.11 Summary of Power Distribution Requirements

Internal device and load-related transient switching currents in advanced Schottky TTL, advanced CMOS, or BiCMOS systems offer the potential for serious ruination of power distribution system integrity. The nature and presence of high-frequency pulse currents in today's high-speed TTL, CMOS, or BiCMOS systems must be understood and the power distribution system designed to accommodate them, or else there is little chance of success. It is essential that high-speed systems have low-impedance power distribution systems and local decoupling capacitors to replenish local transient-current demands. For minimum inductance, power and its return current paths must be in close proximity and as short as possible. Low-inductance power and ground interconnections are needed to ensure that switching transients generated by active devices driving large-capacitance loads do not upset other nearby devices. The inductance of real-world power connections cannot be ignored when systems are built with today's TTL, CMOS, or BiCMOS devices.

5.12   Summary of Techniques for Minimizing Inductance and Transient-Current Effects in Power Distribution Networks

For minimum inductance, power and ground planes must be continuous and in close proximity.

Techniques for minimizing the inductance and the detrimental transient-current effects in power distribution systems include the following:

1. Planes must be used to distribute power and ground on PC boards and motherboards or backplanes. Continuous planes or very fine grids that are effectively planes are essential for high-speed systems; never use point-to-point wiring.

2. Continuous ground planes with no avoidance areas in component package- or connector-pin fields are required for circuit boards and motherboards.

3. Local and bulk decoupling capacitance for digital circuits should be equal to or greater than 100 times the worst-case local simultaneous switched capacitive load. Analog circuit bypassing should be such that the circuit will meet the system performance and noise requirements.

4. Manufacturer's recommended decoupling for advanced CMOS and BiCMOS devices is one decoupling capacitor for each device. Recommended practice for advanced Schottky SSI gates is one decoupling capacitor for two gates and one for each advanced Schottky TTL driver. Standard values used are 0.1 µF for the SSI or MSI device and 0.22 µF for large-memory devices or other VLSI devices. Decoupling capacitors should be located as close as possible to the V_{cc} pin of the decoupled device.

5. Decoupling capacitors must be referenced to the appropriate ground or return (that is, V_{cc} decoupling capacitors for digital circuits must be referenced to V_{cc} return, which is usually called *digital ground*).

6. Power supplies should be located as close as possible to the powered circuitry, and twisted-pair lines (to minimize the area between the lines and hence the inductance) should be used to bring power to local-power planes when the power supply cannot be connected directly to the power and ground planes. When the power supply cannot be

directly connected to the motherboard planes, local bulk decoupling may be needed at the power entry point.

7. Ground pins must be evenly distributed across all connector-pin fields, including custom chip or multiple-chip packages. The number of connector ground pins required to minimize the effects of transient load currents must be determined based on a system ground upset error budget. A rule of thumb for the number of connectors ground pins is a minimum of one ground pin per four to six outputs.

8. When one is using prototyping boards (such as wire-wrap, welded-wire, etc.), the power and ground planes must be continuous through the package- and connector-pin fields, and package (or socket) ground and power pins must be soldered directly to the respective planes by solder washers or clips on universal boards. Wiring of power and ground connections with discrete wires is not an acceptable practice due to excessive inductance.

9. The use of sockets or device carriers must be avoided (or their use carefully evaluated) since they add inductance and increase ground bounce and power-supply droop. Sockets with built-in decoupling capacitors are a better choice where sockets must be used.

5.13 References

1. *FACT Advanced CMOS Logic Databook,* National Semiconductor Corp., Santa Clara, Calif., 1993.
2. James E. Buchanan, *CMOS/TTL Digital Systems Design,* McGraw-Hill, New York, 1990.
3. Henry W. Ott, *Noise Reduction Techniques in Electronic Systems,* 2d ed., Wiley, New York, 1988.
4. Ralph Morrison, *Grounding and Shielding Techniques in Instrumentation,* 3d ed., Wiley, New York, 1986.
5. Anthony P. Visco, "Coaxing Top Bipolar Speeds from Prototyping Boards," *Electronic Products,* September 1, 1987, pp. 55–58.
6. H. C. Lin, *Integrated Electronics,* Holden-Day, San Francisco, 1967.
7. William R. Blood, Jr., *MECL System Design Handbook,* 4th ed., Motorola Semiconductor Products Inc., Phoenix, Ariz., 1988.
8. Richard E. Matick, *Transmission Lines for Digital and Communication Networks,* McGraw-Hill, New York, 1969.
9. John C. Truxal, *Control Engineers' Handbook,* McGraw-Hill, New York, 1958, p. 7-4.
10. *FAST Logic Application Handbook,* National Semiconductor Corp., Santa Clara, Calif., 1990.
11. *High-Speed-Board Design Techniques,* Publication 16356, Advanced Micro Devices, Inc., Sunnyvale, Calif., 1992.
12. *F100K ECL User's Handbook,* Fairchild Camera and Instruments Corp., Puyallup, Wash., 1985.
13. Edward R. Oates, "Good Grounding and Shielding Practices," *Electronic Design,* no. 1, January 4, 1977, pp. 110–112.
14. *1993 National Electrical Safety Code,* Institute of Electrical and Electronics Engineers, New York, 1992.
15. Mark W. Earley, Richard H. Murry, and John M. Caloggero, *National Electric Code 1990 Handbook,* 5th ed., National Fire Protection Association, Quincy, Mass., 1989.

16. *ABT Advanced BiCMOS Technology Data Book,* Texas Instruments, Dallas, Tex., 1993.
17. *High-Performance Logic 1994 Data Book,* Integrated Device Technology, Inc., Santa Clara, Calif., 1994.
18. Charles A. Harper, *Handbook of Electronic Packaging,* McGraw-Hill, New York, 1969.
19. Douglas Varney, "Determine Wire Size with Nomograms," *Electronic Design,* no. 20, September 27, 1977, pp. 90–93.
20. Charles A. Harper, *Handbook of Wiring, Cabling and Interconnections for Electronics,* McGraw-Hill, New York, 1972.
21. Tom Ormond, "Backplanes Play a Crucial Role in High-Speed Systems," *EDN,* July 10, 1986, pp. 222–228.
22. *Aluminum Building Wire Installation Manual,* The Aluminum Association, New York, 19XX.
23. *Bimetallic Electrical Transition Joints,* Aluminum Company of America, Pittsburgh, Penn.
24. Charles A. Harper, *Handbook of Materials and Processes for Electronics,* McGraw-Hill, New York, 1970.
25. Richard Klein, "Protecting Circuits from Over and Under Voltages, *The Electronic Engineer,* March 1969, pp. 59–61.
26. Richard W. Fox, "Six Ways to Control Transients," *Electronic Design,* no. 11, May 24, 1974, pp. 52–57.
27. *Cypress Application Handbook,* Cypress Semiconductor, San Jose, Calif., 1994.
28. Daryl Gerke and Bill Kimmel, "The Designer's Guide to Electromagnetic Compatibility, Ch. 10, Grounding...Facts and Fallacies," *Supplement to EDN,* January 20, 1994, pp. S91–S100.
29. R. Paul Clayton, *Introduction to Electromagnetic Compatibility,* Wiley, New York, 1992.
30. Ramzi Ammar, "The Bypass Capacitor in High-Speed Environments," *ABT Advanced BiCMOS Technology Data Book,* Texas Instruments, Dallas, Tex., 1993.
31. Bill Travis, "Use Local Bypass Capacitors to Meet Rigorous High-Speed-System Demands," *EDN,* January 5, 1995, pp. 63–70.
32. Jock Tomlinson, "Avoid the Pitfalls of High-Speed Logic Design," *Electronic Design,* November 9, 1989, pp. 75–84.
33. William Hall, "Advanced CMOS Design Guidelines: Understanding and Addressing Noise," *National Anthem,* (a publication of National Semiconductor Corp.), Santa Clara, Calif., November/December 1989, pp. A6–A8.
34. R. Paul Clayton, "Effectiveness of Multiple Decoupling Capacitors," *IEEE Transactions on Electromagnetic Compatibility,* vol. 34, no. 2, May 1992, pp. 130–133.
35. *A Guide to Backplane Electrical Performance Measurements,* Standard P1194.0/D2, Institute of Electrical and Electronics Engineers, New York, 1989.
36. Robert B. Cowdell, "Bypass and Feedthrough Filters," *Electronic Design,* no. 17, August 16, 1975, pp. 62–67.
37. *ATMEL Data Book 1989,* ATMEL Corp., San Jose, Calif., 1989.
38. Arch G. Martin and R. Kenneth Keenan, "Neater Decoupling on Surface-Mount Boards," *Electronic Products,* August 15, 1987, pp. 47–49.
39. Laudie Doubrava, "Bypass Supply Loads with Care for Optimum Transient Response," *EDN,* September 20, 1979, pp. 113–117.
40. Arthur F. Upham, "Failure Analyses and Testing Yield Reliable Products," *EDN,* August 8, 1985, pp. 165–174.
41. Jack Blaugrund, "Application Requirements Have Profoundly Influenced Capacitor Design," *Electronic Design,* May 28, 1992, pp. 71–76.

6

Signal Interconnections

Each distinct class of digital system or subsystem has specific interconnection requirements, with some being much more critical than others. However, when today's high-speed digital devices are used to implement a system, the interconnection system and the signal routing, at any of the system levels or boundaries, cannot be left to chance or based on purely mechanical concerns. Signal path electrical requirements, which determine the signal integrity, must be given high priority for the system operating speed to approach the intrinsic speed of the logic devices used. Until recently, system operating speed was limited by the digital components, but that is no longer true in high-performance systems. Delays in the interconnections are responsible for a major portion of signal delays in systems operating at 50 MHz and higher.[1]

When today's advanced Schottky TTL, advanced CMOS, or BiCMOS devices, which may have edge speeds as fast as 1 ns, are used, the functional design and the signal interconnection system can no longer be treated as separate entities. They must be viewed as an integral portion of the overall functional system design. Time delays through interconnections cannot be ignored since they may be a significant part of most signal delays. Likewise, waveform distortion due to reflections and resonance phenomena and signal attenuation due to imperfect transmission media cannot be ignored. To further complicate matters, the loading, load placement, conductor topology, and conducting and insulating media all influence the waveform quality. Also, crosstalk between adjacent signals cannot be ignored, since it becomes more severe with higher edge speeds and with higher clock frequencies there is less time for it to dampen out.

6.1 Signal Interconnection Categories

Signal interconnections fall into three basic categories in most large digital systems:

1. Interconnections within a circuit card (component-to-component)
2. Interconnections between circuit cards that are mounted on a common motherboard (board-to-board)
3. Interconnections between separate units such as boxes, chassis, racks, and cabinets (unit-to-unit)

Each category has specific physical and electrical design and implementation requirements that must be addressed to ensure signal integrity. These special requirements must be understood so that the proper interface devices and physical interconnections can be selected. Fundamental signal integrity issues that must be addressed at each interconnection level include signal dynamic response requirements, interconnection and device propagation delays, transmission-line effects, and crosstalk.[2]

The fast edge transitions of today's devices will cause severe cross-coupling (crosstalk) between signals, noise in the power and ground distribution system, and degraded signals due to transmission-line effects (all of which will impair correct system operation) unless the physical interconnection system is designed to limit the side effects of fast edges.[3] When devices have fast edges, the physical routing of all signals is critical.

In the past, interconnection design did not require much effort. Interconnection delays and transmission-line effects are not significant when low-speed devices are used in low-speed systems, but that is no longer the case. Most systems using advanced Schottky TTL, advanced CMOS, or BiCMOS devices are expected to operate near the limits of technology. Operating near the limits of technology does not come easy. A great deal of design time is necessary to optimize interconnection networks for most signals, particularly clocks and other critical signals, such as memory data and address lines.

6.2 Physical Means of Interconnecting Signals

Large high-speed digital systems typically use the following means of physical interconnection for the three interconnection categories:[4-6]

1. Multilayer PC wiring boards for component-to-component connections

2. Multilayer PC or wire-wrap backpanels for board-to-board connections

3. Shielded twisted-pair cables, twin axial cables, or coaxial cables for unit-to-unit connections

Minimizing signal line length is a fundamental requirement in all three categories. Reducing signal line length reduces the capacitance load, minimizes the chance for crosstalk, and reduces transmission-line effects and signal interconnection propagation delays.

Continuous ground planes are essential and are a fundamental requirement for circuit boards, motherboards, backpanels, etc., when advanced Schottky TTL, advanced CMOS, or BiCMOS devices are used.[7] Ground planes must not be broken or interrupted by device and connector-pin fields.[7] Ground planes must be arranged so they are below (or above) all signal runs, including signal traces going to connector-pin fields. Ground planes are needed near each signal trace to provide low-impedance return paths for transient load currents and to reduce cross-coupling between signals. A nearby plane provides a shielding effect. Voltage planes are important, but not as important as ground planes. Voltage planes must be continuous where boards are populated with circuits, but voltage planes do not have to be continuous in all pin fields.

6.2.1 Component-to-component connections

Multilayer PC boards with multiple voltage and ground planes are required for most of today's component-to-component connections because of signal density and electrical requirements.[7] Multilayer PC boards with multiple signal layers provide high signal density, and multilayer PC boards with multiple ground and voltage planes provide good signal isolation. It is usually impossible to interconnect high-performance circuits without multiple signal layers. Multiple voltage and ground planes are required for isolation because high signal density and fast signal edges increase the probability of coupled noise.

6.2.2 Board-to-board connections

Board-to-board connections are typically implemented by using one of the following methods:

1. Multilayer PC motherboards with multiple signal layers and ground and voltage planes

2. Wire-wrap signal connections above a multilayer backpanel with ground and voltage planes

3. Wire-wrap signal connections, bus bars for voltage connections, and a backpanel that serves as a ground plane

With attention to the basic concerns of a high-performance signal distribution system, any of the above structures can be used successfully for most high-speed digital applications. Very high-speed applications, in the hundreds of megahertz, require multilayer mother-daughter PC boards with controlled impedance signal layers (instead of standard printed wiring interconnections that do not have controlled impedances), so that the response of signals can be accurately predicted and controlled. In all cases, daughterboard-to-motherboard connections must have sufficient ground pins that transient load currents do not cause significant shifts in the reference level of daughterboards[3,8] (see Chap. 5).

At the board-to-board level, signal connections tend to be dominated by bus structures that have an increased probability of crosstalk due to long runs across backpanels or motherboards. Care should be taken in the assignment of daughterboard connector signal pins so as to minimize the length of signal lines. Also, care must be taken to isolate signals that could be upset by cross-coupling (Sec. 6.8 discusses cross-croupling and its control). In general, buses should be grouped together rather than intermingled.

6.2.3 Unit-to-unit connections

Unit-to-unit connections in high-speed digital systems are typically implemented by using some type of twisted-shielded pair connections. For very high-performance applications, controlled-impedance twisted-shielded pair, twin axial, or coaxial cable interconnections are used so that terminations can be closely matched to the cable impedance.[9] In all cable interconnections, the cable impedance, propagation delay, dispersion, and shielding factor must be considered.[10] Knowledge of cable impedance is needed so that proper terminations can be selected; the propagation delay must be known to predict the transport delay. Dispersion characteristics are important in long cables with high data rates; if dispersion is excessive, data and controls may be skewed sufficiently to cause errors. Sufficient shielding is needed to maintain data integrity and prevent excessive radiation. Cable manufacturers' data books and Refs. 11 and 12 are recommended for guidance on these issues.

All unit-to-unit signal cables must include ground lines for signal return currents. When single-ended high-level interunit communica-

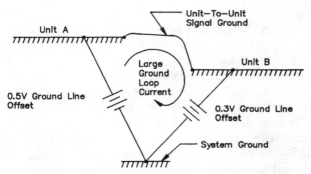

Figure 6.1 Large ground-loop currents may flow in unit-to-unit ground connections because of reference-level offsets.

tion is used (low-level single-ended signals should never be used—see Chap. 9), ideally there should be one ground line per signal line. When balanced differential interunit communication is used, one ground line per four to eight signal pairs is a good rule of thumb. If differential signals are perfectly balanced, no return ground lines are needed—but differential signals are never perfectly balanced. Thus, some grounds are needed to provide a direct return path for the unbalanced portion of the signal currents. However, direct unit-to-unit ground connections offer the potential for large ground-loop currents, as shown in Fig. 6.1. Thus, when unit-to-unit signal grounds are required to ensure a low-impedance path for signal return currents, care must be taken to ensure that all units have low-impedance ground connections, in order to prevent large interunit reference voltage offsets and large ground-loop currents. If large offset voltages exist between units, the ground current in the signal return lines can be of such a magnitude as to disrupt system operation by introducing noise[13] and in severe cases overheat and burn out the signal return lines.

6.3 Interconnection Impedance

The interconnection characteristic impedance Z_o is the key parameter that interrelates many aspects of high-speed system signal integrity and performance. An optimum range of Z_o exists that is a function of the electrical characteristics of the logic family used and of mechanical limitations and requirements. This optimum range of Z_o is the best compromise among noise, delay, crosstalk, and mechanical constraints.[14] Lines with high Z_o are easier to drive, but high Z_o increases crosstalk (coupled signals are attenuated less), RC delays, and transmission-line ringing (TTL, CMOS, and BiCMOS devices tend to have low output impedance so there is greater mismatch). Mechanical constraints, such as board thickness limits, make it difficult to achieve high Z_o in high-density multilayer PC boards. Most mechanical issues tend to push Z_o low, but low Z_o attenuates signals which reduces signal-to-noise margins, increases delay (signals, take longer to reach switching thresholds—first incident switching may not occur), and increases transient switching currents, which increases system noise. When the cumulative effects are considered, 50 to 60 Ω tends to be the optimum impedance for advanced Schottky TTL, advanced CMOS, and BiCMOS systems and a practical range of Z_o to achieve from a mechanical standpoint.

The *characteristic impedance* Z_o of an ideal transmission line is defined as[15,16]

$$Z_o = \sqrt{\frac{L}{C}} \tag{6.1}$$

and the *propagation delay* t_{pd} as

$$t_{pd} = \sqrt{LC} \tag{6.2}$$

where L and C are as shown in Fig. 6.2. At a sufficiently high frequency, which is exceeded by the frequency components in the switching edges of advanced Schottky TTL, advanced CMOS, and BiCMOS devices, the inductive and capacitive effects cancel and a transmission line appears to the source and load as a pure resistance.[15]

Advanced Schottky TTL, advanced CMOS, and BiCMOS circuits do not require precise control of line impedance for waveshape control, as do ECL circuits. In some but not all cases, TTL, CMOS, and BiCMOS circuits have input clamps for waveshape control (see Chap. 7). Input clamps are less sensitive to variations in line impedance, but input dynamic clamping characteristics are seldom specified and many parts do not have effective clamps, which means that predicting the signal response in TTL, CMOS, or BiCMOS systems is difficult, if not impossible. Practical experience has shown that a 2-to-1 line impedance range can be tolerated on signal lines that require wave-

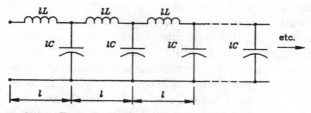

Figure 6.2 Equivalent circuit for an ideal transmission line.

shape control, such as clocks, and even more on lines that do not require waveshape control (assuming the settling time is available). Thus, precise control of the impedance of the signal line is not a major issue vis-à-vis waveshape control. The main issues relative to PC board characteristics are minimum line impedance and control of crosstalk.

The impedance of signal lines must be high enough that the driving devices can drive the signal lines in a timely manner. If the line impedance is too low, signals require too long a time to reach the final value and system operating speed is reduced. It is essential that certain signals, such as clocks, reach a level that exceeds the switching threshold of the receiving devices on the first trip down the line (this is called *first incident switching*).[17]

Real TTL, CMOS, and BiCMOS devices have some finite amount of output impedance; when they switch, the output impedance forms a divider with the line impedance until the line is charged to the new state.[18] Hence, signals tend to step to new levels, as shown in Fig. 6.3. If the line impedance is too low, it may take a number of steps for the signal to reach the final value.[19] In low-speed applications, stepping waveforms may not cause problems. For example, data and control signals with steps are not disruptive in synchronous systems if time is available for signals to reach valid logic levels (see Chap. 10). However, the extra time that a stepping signal requires to reach a valid logic level reduces the potential system operating speed. In a few cases, a waveform with a step can cause secondary problems. If a step happened to be near the threshold level of a receiver, the receiver input circuitry might oscillate during the time that the signal dwells in the threshold region. In some cases, the oscillation may generate enough noise to upset nearby circuits. But in most cases, the time that signals dwell in the intermediate region is relatively short, and

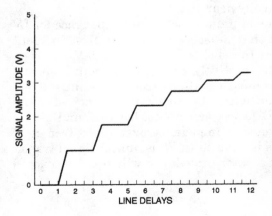

Figure 6.3 Interconnection impedance forms a divider with device output impedance that causes signal transitions to step up or down.

as a result no ill effects are caused. However, signals with steps must not be used to clock devices; multiple clocking may occur. For example, signals with steps are inherent near the source of TTL- or CMOS-driven line. To prevent steps from causing multiple clocking, clock lines must be routed so that the devices being clocked are located near the ends of the lines (see Chap. 8 for clock distribution guidelines). Alternately, the line impedance must be high enough that any steps are well above the threshold of the clocked devices.

In TTL and BiCMOS applications, minimum line impedance requirements are established by dynamic *high*-state output impedance. Dynamic *high*-state output impedance is higher than *low*-state output impedance because TTL and BiCMOS totem-pole output stages have a resistor in the pull-up circuit, but not in the pull-down circuit (see Figs. 3.1 and 3.11). The output impedance for advanced Schottky devices is typically near 20 Ω for drivers and near 45 Ω for standard logic function. BiCMOS data books do not list *high*-state output impedance, but it is reasonable to assume that BiCMOS devices have output impedances in the same range as those of advanced Schottky TTL devices. For first incident wave switching and to prevent multiple clocking from steps dwelling in the threshold region, clock lines or other lines where wave edge shape is important must have an effective line impedance on the same order as the device output impedance. The voltage divider formed by the device output impedance and the line impedance must not attenuate the signal so much that the signal does not exceed the switching threshold of the receiving devices (the switching threshold for 5-V TTL and BiCMOS devices and LV CMOS devices or 5-V CMOS devices with TTL levels is near 1.5 V). If the interconnection system minimum line impedance meets the needs of *high*-going signals, it will be more than adequate for *high*-to-*low* TTL or BiCMOS transitions, since *low* TTL or BiCMOS device output impedance tends to be much less than *high*-state output impedance (typically near 10 Ω).

Forty ohms is also near the minimum usable line impedance for LV or 5-V CMOS-level signals that must switch on the first incident wave. Advanced CMOS input thresholds, both LV and 5-V, are typically at 30 and 70 percent, respectively, of V_{cc}. Thus, both *high* and *low* initial signal transitions must equal or exceed two-thirds of V_{cc}. Under nominal + 25°C conditions, the output impedance of many advanced CMOS SSI or MSI logic components, both LV and 5-V, is near 10 Ω. The worst-case output impedance over the extremes of military operating conditions is near 20 Ω. Thus, initial signal transitions on lines with 40-Ω or greater impedance will equal or exceed two-thirds of V_{cc}.

6.3.1 Loaded transmission-line impedance

Distributed lumped loading on lines lowers the effective impedance and increases the propagation delay. The effective characteristic impedance Z_o' and effective propagation time t_{pd}' of a line are a function of the total lumped load capacitance C_{LOAD} and the total intrinsic line capacitance C_{LINE}. The expressions for effective characteristic impedance and effective propagation delay of loaded lines are[4]

$$Z_o' = \frac{Z_o}{\sqrt{1 + C_{LOAD}/C_{LINE}}} \tag{6.3}$$

$$t_{pd}' = t_{pd}\sqrt{1 + \frac{C_{LOAD}}{C_{LINE}}} \tag{6.4}$$

where C_{LOAD} is the total lumped capacitance (inputs and outputs) of each device connected to the line and C_{LINE} is the total line capacitance. Determination of C_{LOAD} is straightforward; C_{LOAD} is the sum of the input, or output, capacitances, as the case may be, of all the devices connected to the line. Determining C_{LINE} requires that per-unit-length line capacitance C be known ($C_{LINE} = C$ per unit length $\times$ line length). However, deriving C (per unit length) is not a straightforward process. One approach is to use the basic equation for Z_o, Eq. (6.1),

$$Z_0 = \sqrt{\frac{L}{C}}$$

rearrange it to the form

$$C = \frac{L}{Z_o^2} \tag{6.5}$$

to calculate C per unit length of line. The characteristic impedance Z_o used in Eq. (6.5) can be calculated from equations such as (6.12), (6.14), and (6.16), or it may be available from the manufacturer's specifications; but L in Eq. (6.5) is not readily available and is difficult to calculate.

The most practical means of determining the capacitance per unit length of a line C is to measure the propagation delay of an actual unloaded PC board track of the configuration of interest and to use the measured time (t_{pd} measured) and the calculated Z_o [from Eqs. (6.12), (6.14), or (6.16)] in Eq. (6.8). Equation (6.8) is derived from Eqs. (6.6) and (6.7), which are specific cases of Eqs. (6.1) and (6.2). Thus,

$$t_{pd}(\text{measured}) = \sqrt{LC} \qquad (6.6)$$

$$Z_o(\text{calculated}) = \sqrt{\frac{L}{C}} \qquad (6.7)$$

$$C = \frac{t_{pd}(\text{measured})}{Z_o(\text{calculated})} \qquad (6.8)$$

and the total capacitance of the line C_{LINE} is

$$C_{\text{LINE}} = C \times \text{line length} \qquad (6.9)$$

where the line length is in the same units as C.

It is important to note that lines with a number of loads will have an effective Z_o' much less than the unloaded Z_o and that the effective t_{pd}' will be much greater. It is not unusual for the effective impedance of bussed lines, or other lines that connect to numerous locations, to be reduced to one-half the intrinsic unloaded impedance. It is not uncommon for the effective Z_o' of a loaded PC track to be as low as 20 Ω, and the actual propagation delay as large as 3.5 ns/ft.

The use of uncontrolled-impedance PC boards or motherboards introduces the risk of very low effective impedance lines. However, high-impedance multilayer boards are difficult and expensive to build. To keep the impedance up, lines must be very narrow or else the separation between lines and reference planes needs to be large, which may increase the thickness of the board beyond practical limits. Also, higher board impedance increases the possibility of crosstalk. Thus, when all issues are considered, the optimal unloaded line impedance tends to be from 50 to 60 Ω.

6.4 High-Density Multilayer PC Boards

As system performance goes up, so do the interconnection requirements. Each succeeding generation of systems requires devices with more pins packed more closely together. More package-pin connections in a given area mean less room for signal interconnections because feedthrough holes for package pins or vias to surface-mounted packages take away signal interconnection area. Yet, at the same time, interconnection requirements continue to increase. The only solution is finer lines with closer spacing and more signal layers, both of which increase mechanical complexity and cost. To meet the high signal density and electrical requirements of today's high-performance systems, the typical high-density PC board is built with several signal layers with 4- to 8-mil lines with similar line-to-line spacing. Signal layers or pairs of signal layers are normally sandwiched between voltage and ground planes to limit crosstalk. Signal layer to voltage or ground plane spacing is typically 4 to 8 mil.

6.5   Characteristic Impedance of Some Common Interconnection Structures

From a practical standpoint, the basic equations for characteristic impedance and propagation time, Eqs. (6.1) and (6.2), respectively, are of limited value since L and C are difficult to determine. However, most texts that deal with transmission lines show empirically derived equations for determining the characteristic impedance and propagation delay time for most common physical interconnection structures. *Caution:* These empirical equations are valid only for a very limited range of parameters. They have been fitted to the dimensions of typical backpanel wiring and PC board interconnection structures. For dimensions that are extreme, equations may be very inaccurate. Where highly accurate results are needed, one or more of the signal integrity tools with conductor impedance calculation capability should be used (see Refs. 20 and 21 for listings of signal integrity tools).

For wire-wrap or welded-wire boards, the basic physical interconnection structure is a wire over a ground or voltage plane (voltage planes serves as ac references), as shown in Fig. 6.4.

For a wire above a reference plane, Z_o is[22]

$$Z_o = \frac{60}{\varepsilon_r \, (\text{eff})} \ln \frac{4h}{d} \qquad (6.10)$$

where d is the wire diameter, h is the distance from ground to the center of the wire, and t_{pd} is

$$t_{pd} = 1.017 \sqrt{\varepsilon_r \, (\text{eff})} \qquad (6.11)$$

and the constant 1.017 is the reciprocal of the velocity of light in free space.[15] In both Eqs. (6.10) and (6.11), ε_r is the effective dielectric constant of the material in the separation between the reference plane

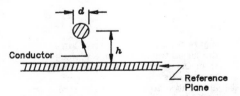

Figure 6.4   Wire over a reference plane with variables used to calculate the line impedance and propagation delay.

and the wire. For a wire in air, the dielectric constant is 1, but the case of a wire in air holds little interest. For an actual wire-wrap, or welded-wire, board, the separation consists of air, the insulation on the wire, and other conductors. Thus, the effective dielectric constant is difficult to determine, and Z_o and t_{pd} calculations are quite complex. Actual measurements of wire-wrap and welded-wire boards show Z_o to be in the range of 80 to 200 Ω and t_{pd} to be on the order of 1.5 ns/ft. The value of Z_o is dependent upon the distance between the wires and the reference plane. If the wires are not kept close to the reference plane, then Z_o values higher than 200 Ω are possible.

For PC board interconnections, two basic physical arrangements of conductors relative to reference planes are possible:

1. Conductors may be located above a reference plane.

2. Conductors may be enclosed between two reference planes.

Printed-circuit board connections above a reference plane are called *microstrip conductors* (see Fig. 6.5). A microstrip conductor can be on the surface of a PC board as shown in Fig. 6.5*a*, or buried in a board, as shown in Fig. 6.5*b*. Configuration (*a*) corresponds to conductors on uncovered surface layers of PC boards, and configuration (*b*) to conductors on internal layers of multilayer PC boards (that are not enclosed by reference planes). Figure 6.5*b* is more common today. Most present-day high-performance systems are built with multilayer PC boards with buried signal layers.

The equation for Z_o (in ohms) for a microstrip transmission line on the surface of a dielectric is

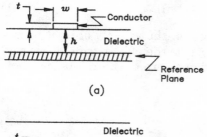

(a)

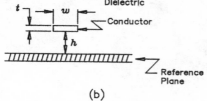

(b)

Figure 6.5 (*a*) Microstrip conductor on the surface of a dielectric; (*b*) microstrip conductor buried in a dielectric with variables used to calculate the line impedance and propagation delay.

$$Z_o = \frac{60}{\sqrt{0.475\varepsilon_r + 0.67}} \ln\left(\frac{5.98h}{0.8w + t}\right) \qquad (6.12)$$

which is usually shown as[23,24]

$$Z_o = \frac{87}{\sqrt{\varepsilon_r + 1.41}} \ln\left(\frac{5.98h}{0.8w + t}\right)$$

and t_{pd} for a surface microstrip conductor (in nanoseconds per foot) is

$$t_{pd} = 1.017 \sqrt{0.475\varepsilon_r + 0.67} \qquad (6.13)$$

where h, t, and w are in inches and are as shown in Fig. 6.5 and ε_r is the dielectric constant of the material between the conductor and the reference plane.

The equation for Z_o (in ohms) for a buried microstrip transmission line is

$$Z_o = \frac{60}{\sqrt{\varepsilon_r}} \ln \frac{5.98h}{0.8w + t} \qquad (6.14)$$

and t_{pd} for a buried microstrip (in nanoseconds per foot) is

$$t_{pd} = 1.017\sqrt{\varepsilon_r} \qquad (6.15)$$

(the variables are as defined above).

Printed-circuit board connections with a reference plane above and below conductors are called *stripline conductors* (see Fig. 6.6).

The equation for Z_o (in ohms) for a centered stripline conductor is[24]

$$Z_o = \frac{60}{\sqrt{\varepsilon_r}} \ln \frac{4b}{0.67\pi(0.8w + t)} \qquad (6.16)$$

$$t_{pd} = 1.017\sqrt{\varepsilon_r} \qquad (6.17)$$

where b, h, t, and w are in inches and are as shown in Fig. 6.6.

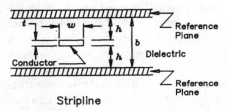

Stripline

Figure 6.6 Centered stripline conductor with variables used to calculate the line impedance and propagation delay.

Equations exist for Z_o for off-center stripline conductors (i.e., where the two h dimensions in Fig. 6.6 are not equal), but they tend to be a good deal more complicated than Eqs. (6.16) and (6.17) and as yet there is no industrywide standard equation for off-center stripline (see Ref. 25). Off-center stripline conductors are sometimes called *off-set stripline* when there is only one layer of conductors between a set of planes or *dual stripline* when there are two layers of conductors between a set of planes. For Z_o analysis purposes, each offset stripline or dual stripline conductor layer can be treated as follows: For most engineering estimates of Z_o for offset or dual stripline, Eq. (6.16) can be used to calculate two values of Z_o by using $2h_1 + t$ and $2h_2 + t$ for b for the two cases and averaging the two results (where h_1 and h_2 are the two unequal h dimensions for a given conductor layer). Where more accurate results are needed, one or more of the signal integrity tools with conductor impedance calculation capability should be used (see Refs. 20 and 21 for a list of signal integrity tools).

The dielectric constant ε_r for epoxy glass PC board typically ranges from 4 to 5. For interconnection layers on most present-day multilayer PC boards, 1-oz copper plating is used. Conductor thickness t in Eqs. (6.12), (6.14), and (6.16) for 1-oz copper is approximately 0.0014 in (the t of 2-oz copper is 0.0028 in). Today it is not uncommon to see production boards with 4- to 8-mil-wide conductors w with similar line-to-line spacing and similar line-to-adjacent-voltage or line-to-ground-plane spacing h. Such boards typically have Z_o values in the range of 30 to 70 Ω and t_{pd} in the range of 1.8 to 2.2 ns/ft (see Figs. 6.7 and 6.8).

The Z_o curves shown in Fig. 6.7 for buried microstrip and in Fig. 6.8 for centered stripline were generated by using Eqs. (6.14) and (6.16), respectively. The curves are not exact because the equations used to generate them are not exact, and the curves are even less exact as the parameters become more extreme. Furthermore, they do not take into account effects of other nearby signal lines which will be present in most applications. However, the equations are accurate enough for most engineering purposes and are useful for quick estimates of Z_o versus line width and dielectric thickness. Figure 6.7 shows the characteristic impedance Z_o of microstrip conductors in epoxy glass PC boards ($\varepsilon_r = 4.5$) as a function of conductor width w and height h above a reference plane. Figure 6.8 shows the characteristic impedance of centered stripline conductors in epoxy glass PC boards ($\varepsilon_r = 4.5$) as a function of conductor width w and distance h from the two reference planes.

In addition to wires over grounds, microstrip, and stripline conductor configurations, digital designers must often deal with coaxial cables and twisted-pair interconnections. Cable parameters, such as Z_o and t_{pd}, are supplied in cable manufacturers' catalogs (which

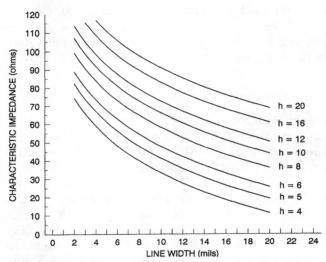

Figure 6.7 Characteristic impedance Z_o of microstrip conductors in epoxy glass PC boards ($\varepsilon_r = 4.5$) as a function of conductor width w and height h above a reference plane (see Fig. 6.5 for definition of w and h).

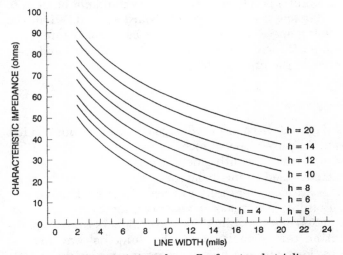

Figure 6.8 Characteristic impedance Z_o of centered stripline conductors in epoxy glass PC boards ($\varepsilon_r = 4.5$) as a function of conductor width w and distance h from the two reference planes (see Fig. 6.6 for definition of w and h).

should be consulted when such interconnections are used). Coaxial cables are available with various Z_o values; typical values range from 50 to 90 Ω.[26] Twisted-pair lines have Z_o in the neighborhood of 120 to 150 Ω, and shielded twisted-pair lines are in the 70- to 120-Ω range.[9]

6.6   Breadboard Interconnections

Often during the breadboard phase of a project, welded-wire or wire-wrap interconnections are used at both the component-to-component and motherboard levels to expedite the completion of the initial breadboard unit and so that corrections or modifications can be easily incorporated.

When one is breadboarding with off-the-shelf welded-wire or wire-wrap boards, only those boards that are described as Schottky boards should be used when high-speed devices are being applied. Schottky boards have ground and voltage planes that are interconnected between all device and connector pins (see Chap. 5 and Fig. 5.3) and provide low-impedance return paths for signals.

When high-speed devices are interconnected with wired boards, the signal response characteristics will not be representative of the final PC board system. Thus, wired breadboards should be used only to establish the functionality of a logic design; they should *not* be used to forecast the operating speed of the final PC board system. When the limits of the operating speed of a system must be demonstrated, the breadboard system must have the same physical dimensions and electrical characteristics as the final product.

6.7   Routing Guidelines

When high-speed digital devices are used, signal routing cannot be left to chance or based on purely mechanical concerns. Specific routing instructions must be given to drafting departments or routing houses. Generalized statements lead to misunderstandings. Electrical (digital) designers and PC board designers tend to speak different languages.[26] Electrical designers think in terms of impedances, inductances, capacitances, and propagation delays, while PC board designers think in physical implementation terms such as widths, lengths, and layers. Statements such as "keep all clock lines as short as possible" have little meaning to drafting departments or routing houses. Specific physical routing instructions with specific signal names must be called out.

To simplify the task of routing boards, signals should be grouped into categories based on waveshape control requirements, crosstalk limits, or other special requirements. For example, clocks, strobes, buses, memory address, data, chip-select, and write lines, and asynchronous signals, ECL signals, and analog signals have special routing requirements. Analog and ECL signals require special care when they are mixed with TTL- or CMOS-level signals (see paragraph on ECL and analog signals below).

Clock signals.   Clock signals have waveshape, skew, and crosstalk control requirements.

To meet clock signal waveshape requirements, clock signals must be routed on layers with reasonably controlled impedance. Clock lines must not branch or have long stubs. Termination networks must be properly located. The location of the source and the locations of the loads must be controlled (see Chap. 8).

To control clock skew, clock lines may need defined maximum and minimum lengths.

To meet crosstalk limits, clock signals must be isolated and confined between reference layers. Other signals must not be mixed with clocks. Clock signals on a given layer must have extra spacing between lines. Clock signals of different frequencies must have extrawide spacing, as must clock signals and other signals if they are to be mixed.

Strobes.   Strobes typically have the same requirements as clocks (see above paragraph).

Buses.   Signals common to a given bus can run next to other signals in the bus (which may save space), but not with other buses or signals.

Output enables and other asynchronous controls.   Output enables and other non-clock-activated signals have the same isolation requirements as clock signals (see clock signals paragraph above).

Asynchronous reset and initialization signals.   Asynchronous resets and initialization signals have the same isolation requirements as clock signals (see clock signals paragraph above).

Memory address and data lines.   High-speed memory address and data signals need to be isolated by reference planes to prevent feedback. For a given memory, address signals can run next to other address lines and data lines can run next to other data lines as bused signals (see buses paragraph above; also see Chap. 13 for more details).

Memory chip-select lines.   Asynchronous memory chip-select lines have the same routing requirements as clocks or strobes (see clock signals paragraph above).

Memory write lines.   Memory write lines require the highest possible degree of isolation from crosstalk. They must be isolated by reference planes and by extrawide line-to-line spacing from other signals, particularly other memory chip-selects, address line, and data buses.

ECL and analog.   ECL and analog signals require a high degree of isolation from TTL- or CMOS-level signals. They must be physically isolated in separate board areas with separate ground and voltage planes that are isolated from TTL or CMOS switching currents.

Once the electrical designer has established the electrical requirements or limits of each signal category based on system performance requirements and error budgets, the requirements must be translated to specific mechanical requirements for the PC board designer or routing house.

Routing order.   Most PC board routers route signals from point to point and thus do not cause branches. However, when the order of the loads and sources (i.e., their relative position along their interconnecting line) is important, their locations must be defined and relayed to the routing house. In general, in lower-performance applications, the locations of loads and sources on a signal line are not critical. As performance increases, the physical relationship of loads and sources becomes more important. The routing order must be specified in high-speed applications. Routing order is of particular importance for clocks and other signals, such as strobes, that have waveshape requirements or settling-time requirements. Typically, when waveshape control or minimum settling time is required, the source is located at one end of the line and any parallel termination or clamping at the other end, with the loads grouped near the termination or clamped end of the line. Alternately, if series-terminated is used (see Chap. 7), the series termination network must be located very near the source.

In some applications where minimum settling time is needed, lines are often center-driven or made into loops. Center-driving lines or looping lines (back to the source) reduces the effective line impedance[27] seen by the driver to $\frac{1}{2}Z_o$ and more nearly matches the line impedance to the output impedance of the typical TTL, CMOS, or BiCMOS drivers, which in turn reduces ringing and signal settling times. Looping lines back to the source also has an additional benefit: It typically reduces the worst-case distance between the source and the most remote load and thus reduces the worst-case propagation time. Center-driving and looping techniques are often used on clock and memory address lines to improve waveshape and reduce settling time. Loops may also be useful in some bus applications to reduce the settling time. The line impedance can be further lowered by connecting additional lines between loops to form grids. However, grids, loops, etc., are beneficial only where the effective line impedance (before being looped or gridded) is much greater than the driver output impedance (which is the typical situation when advanced Schottky TTL, advanced CMOS, or BiCMOS bus drivers are used). If the basic line impedance is much less than the driver worst-case output impedance, then grids and loops are not beneficial. Lines may require numerous reflections to step up to the final value, and thus such an arrangement might degrade the response time. If such arrangements are considered, caution must be exercised since CMOS device output impedance may change by a factor of 2 to 1 from nominal with process variations and the extremes of the military operating conditions (see Chap. 2). An additional complication, since most routers will not automatically connect loops or grids, is that manual intervention and layout is required.

6.8   Crosstalk

Crosstalk is the noise voltage developed on signal lines when nearby lines change state. Crosstalk occurs due to capacitive and inductive coupling between adjacent or nearby lines. It is a function of the separation between signal lines, the linear distance that signals lines run parallel with each other, and the height above a ground, or other reference, plane.

The faster (relative to older logic families) edge rates of today's logic devices greatly increase the possibility of coupling or crosstalk between signals.[7] Increased coupling, plus faster device response, greatly increases the possibility that system operation will be degraded by crosstalk. Synchronous design practices reduce the possibility of crosstalk's disrupting system operation (see Chap. 10) if time can be allotted for crosstalk to subside. But when advanced Schottky TTL, advanced CMOS, or BiCMOS devices are applied, the goal is usually to achieve high operating speed. To maximize speed, crosstalk must be reduced to levels where no extra time is required for the signal to stabilize.

Multilayer PC boards with multiple voltage and ground planes are needed to achieve the isolation required for critical signals in high-performance systems.[28] In less critical applications, it is usually possible to use dual stripline stack-ups to route related signals at right angles on adjacent layers. But in very critical applications, voltage and ground planes should be used to isolate all signal layers. For example, when very high-speed memory devices are used, address and data signals should be isolated by reference planes. Other techniques of isolating critical signals include using extrawide spacing between signal lines and running ground traces on each side of critical signals. When signals are not isolated by planes, care must be taken to ensure that noisy signals are not run directly above or below a critical signal for some length.

On welded-wire or wire-wrap boards or backpanels, the wiring should be as direct as possible between points so as to randomize the routing, and the wiring should be kept as close as possible to the ground (or voltage) plane. Care must be taken to ensure that wiring is not channelized. Particular care must be taken to ensure that the critical signals, such as clocks, do not get channelized with noisy signals.

On welded-wire or wire-wrap boards or backpanels, critical single-ended signals should be run twisted with a ground wire connected to ground at the source and at the load, as shown in Fig. 6.9. Twisting signal lines with ground lines provides the most direct path possible for return currents and offers some shielding effect. Return currents tend to flow in the nearby twisted ground line and not in the power or ground planes (see Fig. 6.10). Thus, transient-current flow and noise are reduced in the power and ground system. In addition, twisted-pair signal lines provide better control of line impedance, which allows more accurate terminations, which in turn helps control ringing and line reflections. Twisted-pair lines also tend to confine the magnetic fields of the two twisted conductors, which minimizes the chance for coupling into adjacent wiring.

In all but the most trivial systems, some signal line inevitably must run close to and parallel to other signals. Where signals are close and parallel, two forms of crosstalk exist: forward and backward. *Forward crosstalk* is present on coupled lines in time coincidence with an active wavefront on a nearby driven line and exists for the duration of

Figure 6.9 Twist signal lines with ground lines to reduce crosstalk.

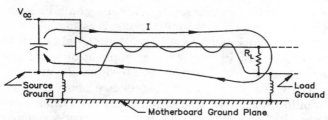

Figure 6.10 Twisted-pair lines provide a direct low-impedance return current path.

the edge transition of the driven line. *Backward crosstalk* on coupled lines flows away from the wavefront on the nearby active line and exists for twice the propagation delay of the coupled line length.[29] Both forms of crosstalk can cause circuit malfunctions. Backward crosstalk tends to be more detrimental, since it tends to be of a higher amplitude and lasts longer, but either form can cause logic errors. The extent of possible upset of a coupled-to line is dependent upon the polarity and amplitude of the coupled noise relative to the logic level of the signal that is disturbed and the physical topology of the lines. The signal flow may be such that the coupling is of little concern. For example, backward crosstalk is of no concern at output node C in Fig. 6.11. However, backward crosstalk could be a major problem for a circuit with the topology shown in Fig. 6.12.

In the case shown in Fig. 6.12, backward crosstalk may or may not cause a problem depending upon the polarity of the coupled signal. If the coupling adds to or subtracts from the existing level so that the resulting composite signal has more margin, then the coupling is of little concern (assuming that the coupled signal does not cause excessive ringing). Since it may be impractical to analyze all possible combinations, the safest approach is to assume that there will be some combinations of active and inactive signals such that some inactive signals will be degraded by crosstalk.

In those cases where the interconnect topology and the polarity of the coupling are in the harmful direction, crosstalk may or may not be harmful depending on the amplitude and duration of the coupled voltage. If the amplitude of the coupled voltage is less than the noise

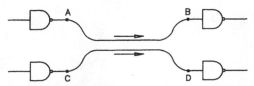

Figure 6.11 Coupled lines with the signal flow in the same direction.

Figure 6.12 Coupled lines with the signal flow in the opposite direction.

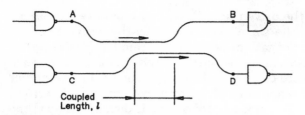

Figure 6.13 Coupling occurs where signal lines are in close proximity, which may be only a small portion of the total signal length.

margin of the logic components used, then the coupling may not be detrimental. Likewise, if the duration of the coupled pulse is short enough, then even though it exceeds the noise margin of the receiving devices, the receiving devices may not react to a narrow pulse. Some device manufacturers are specifying the pulse immunity of their devices to help designers evaluate the possible detrimental effects of ground-bounce transients (see Chap. 2). Such data are also useful for determining the sensitivity of devices to coupled pulses.

These are the general expressions for crosstalk voltage amplitude between two lines with coupled length l (see Fig. 6.13) for the two types of crosstalk:[30,31]
Backward crosstalk V_B

$$V_B = \frac{K_C + K_L}{4} \frac{2t_p}{t_r} (\Delta V_S) \tag{6.18}$$

for coupled line lengths from $l = 0$ to $l = t_r (2t'_{pd})$ and

$$V_B = \frac{K_C + K_L}{4} (\Delta V_S) \tag{6.19}$$

for coupled line lengths of $l = t_r (2t'_{pd})$ or greater.
Forward crosstalk V_F

$$V_F = \frac{K_C - K_L}{2} \frac{t_p}{t_r} (\Delta V_S) \tag{6.20}$$

For Eqs. (6.18), (6.19), and (6.20)

ΔV_S = driving signal transition amplitude
K_C = capacitive coupling coefficient
K_L = inductive coupling coefficient
t'_{pd} = effective propagation delay of media
t_p = propagation delay of coupled length ($l \times t_{pd}$)

t_r = rise time of driving signal
l = coupled length

and

$$K_C = \frac{C_m}{C}$$

$$K_L = \frac{L_m}{L}$$

where C_m = mutual capacitance between lines
C = capacitance between lines and ground
L_m = mutual inductance between lines
L = inductance of each line

In a homogeneous material, K_C and K_L are equal and no forward crosstalk exists.[31] However, conductors in typical digital applications are nor surrounded by a pure homogeneous material. Welded-wire or wire-wrap interconnections, as well as PC board interconnections, are surrounded by a conglomerate of materials, other conductors, insulation, etc. Yet, for practical engineering purposes, forward crosstalk is of little concern in welded-wire or wire-wrap circuit board or motherboard interconnections or in embedded conductors in multilayer PC boards. The exception occurs when two lines have a long coupled length (relative to the active signal rise time); in those cases, the t_p/t_r term in the forward crosstalk equation becomes significant. Where forward crosstalk exists, it consists of a pulse with width equal to the rise time t_r of the driving source. The amplitude is proportional to the coupled length.

Equation (6.18) shows that the backward crosstalk magnitude is a function of coupled line length for coupled line lengths from $l = 0$ to $l = t_r/2t_{pd}$. At $l = t_r/2t_{pd}$ (which is the *critical line length*[4]—see Chap. 1), backward crosstalk reaches a maximum amplitude; for longer coupled lengths, it increases in width but does not increase in amplitude[32] [see Eq. (6.19)]. The duration of backward crosstalk is equal to the two-way delay of the coupled length l.

> Backward crosstalk reaches a maximum amplitude where the propagation delay t_p of the coupled length of line is equal to one-half the rise time t_r of the active signal, i.e., when the coupled line length is equal to the critical line length.[4]

It is apparent from the limits of Eq. (6.18) that the coupled line length needed for maximum amplitude coupling is reduced as the signal rise time decreases. A signal trace adjacent to a trace driven with a signal with a 2-ns edge transition requires one-half the coupled length to achieve the limiting value of crosstalk, as is required for a signal with a 4-ns edge transition. It therefore follows that systems with signals with fast rise times will have significantly more crosstalk than systems with signals with slow rise times.

To calculate crosstalk from Eqs. (6.18), (6.19), and (6.20), the line capacitance C, inductance L, and propagation delay t_p, as well as the mutual capacitance C_m and inductance L_m between lines, are needed. All are difficult to determine manually. Fortunately, today there are programs available, such as Quad Design's XTK crosstalk program,[33-35] that calculate crosstalk based on conductor topology and driver-receiver input-output characteristics.[36]

When crosstalk calculation tools are not available, the family of crosstalk plots for microstrip, dual stripline, and centered stripline conductors (see Fig. 6.14) shown in Figs. 6.15 to 6.17 allows a quick estimation of the approximate amplitude of backward crosstalk [which is usually of greatest concern since it tends to be larger than forward crosstalk, except where lines are very long—see Eq. (6.20)]. The backward crosstalk curves shown in Figs. 6.15 to 6.17 are for

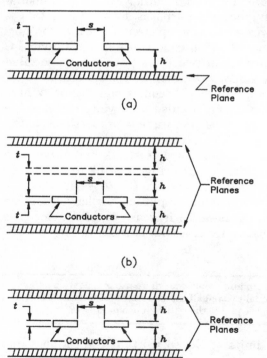

Figure 6.14 Typical PC board interconnection structures. (a) Microstrip; (b) dual stripline; (c) stripline.

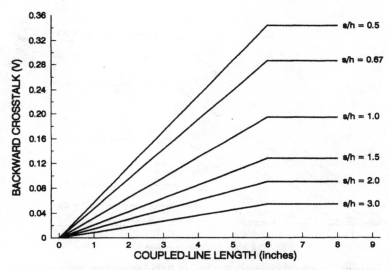

Figure 6.15 Buried mircostrip backward crosstalk per volt of signal transition in 2 ns versus coupled line length l, spacing s, and height h above a reference plane for conductors in epoxy glass PC boards with a dielectric constant ε_r of 4.5 (data calculated by using Quad Design XTK crosstalk simulation program). (See Fig. 6.14 for definition of dimensions.)

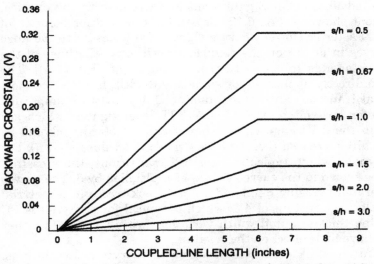

Figure 6.16 Dual stripline backward crosstalk per volt of signal transition in 2 ns versus coupled line length l, spacing s, and distance h from reference planes for conductors in epoxy glass PC boards with a dielectric constant ε_r of 4.5 (data calculated by using Quad Design XTK crosstalk simulation program). (See Fig. 6.14 for definition of dimensions.)

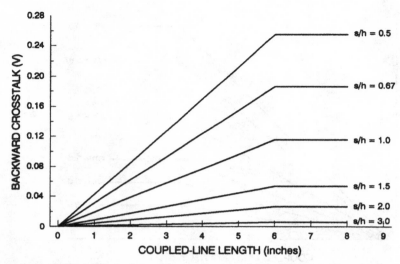

Figure 6.17 Stripline backward crosstalk per volt of signal transition in 2 ns versus coupled line length l, spacing s, and distance h from reference planes for conductors in epoxy glass PC boards with a dielectric constant ε_r of 4.5 (data calculated by using Quad Design XTK crosstalk simulation program). (See Fig. 6.14 for definition of dimensions.)

unit-level (1-V) signal transitions with 2-ns transition times (on the driven line). They were developed by using an advanced CMOS gate driving an advanced CMOS gate input in a circuit with the physical arrangement shown in Fig. 6.12. Crosstalk is plotted for point C (of Fig. 6.12). Faster or slower (driving signal) rise times move the knee of the curves in or out on the coupled length axis—the knee of the curves corresponds to the critical line length [see Eq. (7.1)]. The curves are directly applicable for signals with ECL levels since most ECL signal transitions are approximately 1 V. Crosstalk amplitude estimates for low-voltage CMOS- and TTL-level signals, which are typically in the 3-V range unless they overshoot or ring, should be proportionally increased (i.e., by 3 to 4 times the values shown). For CMOS signals, which typically have 5-V transitions, the crosstalk amplitudes shown in the curves should be multiplied by 5. The curves were generated by using 8-mil-wide, 2-mil-thick traces in a material with a dielectric constant of 4.5, which is typical for epoxy glass PC boards. Line thickness and width variation, within 2 to 1 in either direction, have little effect on the results.

Backward crosstalk estimates based on the curves shown in Figs. 6.15 to 6.17 should be accurate enough for most engineering purposes, but sight must not be lost of the fact that crosstalk is usually not a simple phenomenon. In most cases, it is the result of complex interactions between a number of signals and their reflections. Actual measurements are the most reliable source for determining crosstalk, but the practicing engineer seldom has the time or resources to make controlled measurements on final production configuration boards, and measurements "after the fact" are of little benefit except for educational purposes. Crosstalk is a major problem when high-speed digital devices are used; it will cause problems unless the interconnection system is designed to minimize it.[37]

6.9   Signal Interconnection Summary

1. Circuit boards and motherboards must have continuous power and ground planes (except for clearance holes for feedthroughs and vias).

2. Signals that are highly susceptible to crosstalk should be run at right angles to one another or isolated by reference planes (when multilayer PC boards are used). For example, memory address lines must run at right angles to memory data lines as a minimum safeguard. In most applications, memory address and data lines should be isolated by reference planes.

3. Signals, such as clocks, that are highly sensitive to crosstalk should be isolated by reference planes from signals on other layers and by extrawide line-to-line spacing (see Figs. 6.15 to 6.17).

4. Interconnection line impedance should be greater than 40 Ω so as to not excessively degrade TTL- or CMOS-level signals.

5. Signal lines must run near reference planes (either power or ground) to minimize cross-coupling. When signals cannot be positioned near a reference plane (such as between separate units), signals should be sent via differential twisted-pair lines (the need for differential signals between units not referenced to a common ground plane is described in Chap. 9).

6.10   References

1. Mike Meredith, "Analyzing Interconnect Timing," *Electronic Engineering Times,* September 11, 1989, p. T6.
2. Robert Cutler, "Your Logic Simulation Is Only as Good as Your Board Layout," *VLSI System Design,* July 1987, pp. 40–42.
3. Tim Tripp and Bill Hall, "Good Design Methods Quiet High-Speed CMOS Noise Problems," *EDN,* October 29, 1987, pp. 229–236.
4. Robert K. Southard, "High-Speed Signal Pathways from Board to Board," in 1981 WESCON Electronic Show & Convention, Rec., Session 18, San Francisco, September 1981, paper 2.

5. Charles A. Harper, *Handbook of Electronic Packaging,* McGraw-Hill, New York, 1969.
6. Charles A. Harper, *Handbook of Wiring, Cabling and Interconnections for Electronics,* McGraw-Hill, New York, 1972.
7. Jock Tomlinson, "Avoid the Pitfalls of High-Speed Logic Design," *Electronic Design,* November 9, 1989, pp. 75–84.
8. Joseph DiCerto, "Poor Packaging Produces Problems," *The Electronic Engineer,* September 1970, pp. 91–93.
9. Ronald A. Crouch, "Choose Cable with Care to Optimize System Design," *EDN,* November 5, 1978, pp. 113–116.
10. Frank Timmons, "Wire or Cable Has Many Faces, Know Them All before Choosing, Part II," *EDN,* March 1, 1970, pp. 49–55.
11. Henry W. Ott, *Noise Reduction Techniques in Electronic Systems,* 2d ed., Wiley, New York, 1988.
12. Ralph Morrison, *Grounding and Shielding Techniques in Instrumentation,* 3d ed., Wiley, New York, 1986.
13. H. C. Brown, "Get Rid of Ground-Loop Noise," *Electronic Design,* no. 15, July 19, 1969, pp. 84–87.
14. N. C. Arvanitakis and J. J. Zara, "Design Considerations of Printed Circuit Transmission Lines for High Performance Circuits," in 1981 WESCON Electronic Show & Convention, Rec., Session 18, San Francisco, September 1981, paper 4.
15. Richard E. Matick, *Transmission Lines for Digital and Communications Networks,* McGraw-Hill, New York, 1969.
16. H. R. Kaupp, "Characteristics of Microstrip Transmission Lines," *IEEE Transactions on Electronic Computers,* vol. EC-16, no. 2, April 1967, pp. 185–193.
17. *FACT Advanced CMOS Logic Databook,* National Semiconductor Corp., Santa Clara, Calif., 1993.
18. William Heniford, "Muffling Noise in TTL," *The Electronic Engineer,* July 1969, pp. 63–69.
19. Joseph L. DeClue, "Wiring for High-Speed Circuits," *Electronic Design,* no. 11, May 24, 1976, pp. 84–86.
20. "Analog/Mixed-Signal Simulation Tools," *Integrated System Design,* March 1995, pp. 82–87.
21. "Signal Integrity—Tools," *Computer Design,* special report, April 1995, pp. 57–72.
22. William K. Springfield, "Designing Transmission Lines into Multilayer Circuit Boards," *Electronics,* November 1, 1965, pp. 90–96.
23. *Applications Handbook,* Cypress Semiconductor Corp., San Jose, Calif., 1994.
24. William R. Blood, Jr., *MECL System Design Handbook,* 4th ed., Motorola Semiconductor Products Inc., Phoenix, Ariz., 1988.
25. Robert E. Canright, "A Simple Formula for Dual Stripline Characteristic Impedance," *IEEE SOUTHEASTCON 1990 Proceedings,* vol. 3, pp. 903–905.
26. Shiv C. Tasker, "Making the Best Use of On-Board Interconnections," *Electronic Engineering Times,* December 4, 1989, pp. 41 and 66.
27. *A Guide to Backpanel Performance Measurements,* Standard P1194.0/D2, Institute of Electrical and Electronics Engineers, New York, 1989.
28. Ivor Catt, "Crosstalk (Noise) in Digital Systems," *IEEE Transactions on Electronic Computers,* vol. EC-16, no. 6, December 1967, pp. 743–768.
29. John A. DeFalco, "Predicting Crosstalk in Digital Systems," *Computer Design,* June 1973, pp. 69–75.
30. Tushar Gheewala and David MacMillan, "High-Speed GaAs Logic Systems Require Special Packaging," *EDN,* May 17, 1984, pp. 8–14.
31. John J. Kozuch, "A High Speed Approach to Controlled Impedance Packaging," Multiwire Div., Kollmorgen Corp., Melville, N.Y., January 1987.
32. John A. DeFalco, "Reflection and Crosstalk in Logic Circuit Interconnections," *IEEE Spectrum,* July 1970, pp. 44–50.
33. Richard Nass, "PC-Board Speeds Skyrocket," *Electronic Design,* September 28, 1989, pp. 31–32 and 37–38.
34. Ravender Goyal, "Managing Signal Integrity," *IEEE Spectrum,* March 1994, pp. 54–58.

35. Richard A. Quinnell, "CAD Tools Help Cure Transmission-Line Woes," *EDN*, March 1, 1991, pp. 47–52.
36. Roderic Beresford, 'How to Tame High-Speed Design," *High Performance Systems*, September 1989, pp. 78–82.
37. Lee W. Ritchey, "What's Good Enough?" *ASIC & EDA*, February 1994, pp. 12–18.

6.11 Bibliography

Frost, John: "Backplane-Design Basics Help Avert System-Design Problems," *EDN*, July 8, 1993, pp. 122–130.
Kumar, Girish: "The Impact of Design Parameters on Signal Integrity," *ASIC & EDA*, April 1993, pp. 33–49.

Transmission-Line Effects

Transmission-line effects were of little concern when the older, slower TTL or CMOS logic families were used. However, when advanced Schottky TTL, advanced CMOS, or BiCMOS devices are used, transmission-line effects are a concern at all interconnection levels. Transmission-line effects begin to appear when signal rise or fall times are near the propagation delays of the interconnecting lines. As rise or fall times decrease relative to line propagation delays, transmission-line effects become more pronounced. For all practical purposes, all signal lines are transmission lines when today's high-speed logic components are used because of their fast rise and fall times.

The common criterion for the line length, called the *critical line length,* for the onset of significant transmission-line effects is as follows: The *critical line length* occurs when the effective per-unit propagation delay of the line t'_{pd} is equal to one-half the rise time t_r of the signal (typically measured between 20 and 80 percent)[1,2], i.e.,

$$\text{Critical line length} = \frac{1}{2} \frac{t_r}{t'_{pd}} \qquad (7.1)$$

More conservative versions of the rule cut the ratio to one-fourth or one-fifth of the signal rise time relative to the per-unit line propagation delay.[3]

Effective per-unit line propagation delays for typical PC boards range from 2 to 4 ns/ft. For a signal with a rise time of 2 ns on a board with a 2 ns/ft line propagation delay, the critical line length is

$$\text{Critical line length} = \frac{1}{2} \left(\frac{2 \text{ ns}}{2 \text{ ns/ft}} \right) = 0.5 \text{ ft}$$

Since many of today's devices have rise times of 2 ns or less, transmission-line effects must be considered in most applications where they are used, since most signal runs, even on small PC boards, exceed 0.5 ft.

7.1 Basic Transmission-Line Theory

The following discussion is a basic introduction to transmission-line theory and its applications as they relate to high-speed advanced Schottky TTL, advanced CMOS, and BiCMOS devices and systems. A thorough discussion of transmission lines is beyond the scope of this book. A number of good references on the subject of transmission lines exist (see references listed at the end of the chapter). All designers involved in the application of high-speed logic devices should quickly procure (if they do not already have) some of the listed reference material and undertake a thorough study of transmission lines, if they are not currently conversant on the subject. A basic understanding of transmission lines and transmission-line effects is essential to the successful application of high-speed logic devices.

Signals are well behaved when the signal source impedance, signal line impedance, and load impedance are very closely matched (i.e., almost equal) and the line has only one source and one load with no discontinuities, branches, or stubs. In such cases, one line propagation delay (approximately 2 ns/ft if the line is in a PC board) after a signal is launched into a line at the source, a signal very much like the signal launched at the source can be observed at the load. If the signal source, line, and load are not matched, or if the circuit topology does not consist of the ideal case of one source and one load, then the signal quality will degrade due to transmission-line ringing and other effects. Signal sources, loads, and lines are not matched on a typical PC board or a welded-wire or wire-wrap circuit board or motherboard. Thus, when signal runs are greater than the critical line length [see Eq. (7.1) for the definition], the signal quality will degrade due to transmission-line effects, and additional time, beyond the one-way propagation delay of the lines, will be required for signals to settle.

As unterminated signal lines increase in length beyond the critical line length, the signal quality progressively degrades and takes longer to stabilize. Depending upon where along a line a signal is observed, transmission-line effects will be apparent on lines longer than the critical line length under most conditions, even when lines are properly terminated. When signal lines are not significantly longer than the critical length, transmission-line effects may not be severe enough to impact normal operation but are present and observable.

Certain logic families incorporate features that help control transmission-line effects. Most TTL and BiCMOS components are built with current-limiting pull-up resistors in their totem-pole output stages and input clamp diodes (see Chap. 3), both of which help control transmission-line response. Some CMOS components have effective input clamps that help control transmission-line effects, but there is little uniformity in CMOS input-output circuitry or in the response of CMOS input-output circuits. Thus, when CMOS logic components are used to drive lines longer than the critical length, additional time beyond the one-way line propagation time must be allowed for signals to settle, unless some form of termination is added. However, it is impractical to terminate all signals in most digital systems since terminations require additional components and may dissipate additional power (depending upon the method of termination used). Thus, in most applications where advanced CMOS devices are used, additional time beyond the one-way line propagation time must be allowed for signals to settle.

7.1.1 Ideal transmission-line response

A long transmission line,[4] as shown in Fig. 7.1, with a one-way delay greater than the signal rise time, with one source and one load, responds to signal transitions approximately as follows:

1. A signal transition is initiated at the source.

2. The signal travels along the transmission line with a delay time depending on the dielectric constant of the surrounding material.

3. The signal arrives as the first incident wave at the load after a delay that is a function of the line length and the dielectric constant of the material adjacent to the line.

4. Part of the energy of the first incident wave is absorbed by the load in establishing the initial signal level at the load.

5. The part of the energy of the first incident wave not absorbed due to mismatch between the line and the load impedance is reflected back toward the source.

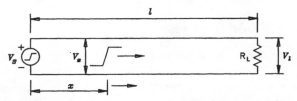

Figure 7.1 Ideal representation of a long transmission line with one source and one load.

6. When the reflection of the first incident wave arrives at the source, part of it may be absorbed by the source in establishing a new signal level; any mismatch is reflected back toward the load.

7. When the second incident wave arrives at the load, part of the energy is absorbed in establishing a new signal level; any mismatch is reflected back to the source as in 5 above.

8. The cycles of reflections between load and source are repeated with part of the energy absorbed in each cycle; after some time, depending upon the characteristics of the source, line, and load, the reflected transient levels are so small that they are negligible.

Reflections. The voltage reflected when an incident wave arrives at a load is determined by the mismatch between the impedance of the line and the load (or source). If a transmission line is terminated with an impedance that is equal to the characteristic impedance Z_o of the line, then there will be no reflection from the end of the line and the only signal appearing on the line will be the incident wave. If some other value of termination is used, a portion of the incident wave will be reflected, and the signal appearing on the line will be the sum of the incident and reflected waves. The magnitude and polarity of the reflection from a load or a source is quantitatively described by the reflection coefficient ρ.

The equation for the reflection coefficient ρ_L for the load end of a line is[5,6]

$$\rho_L = \frac{R_L - Z_o}{R_L + Z_o} \qquad (7.2)$$

and the reflection coefficient ρ_S for the source end of the line is

$$\rho_S = \frac{R_S - Z_o}{R_S + Z_o} \qquad (7.3)$$

If either end of the line is exactly matched to Z_o, that is, if $R_S = Z_o$ or $R_L = Z_o$, then the reflection coefficient is zero, the incident wave is completely absorbed, and no reflection occurs.

The action of a transmission line with nonzero reflection coefficients is shown diagrammatically in Fig. 7.2 (the dimensions x and l are as shown in Fig. 7.1).

A couple of cases of ρ hold special interest:

1. $\rho = +1$ when $R_L = \infty$ or $R_S = \infty$ (an open circuit at the ends of the line)

When $\rho = +1$, the signal doubles when the incident wave arrives at the end of the line.

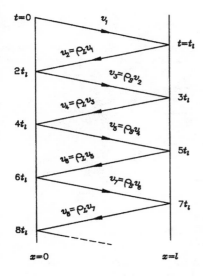

Figure 7.2 Lattice diagram for a long transmission line with one source and one load.

2. $\rho = -1$ when $R_L = 0$ or $R_S = 0$ (a short circuit at the ends of the line)

When $\rho = -1$, the incident wave reverses its polarity and subtracts an amount equal to the incident wave from the existing voltage at the load (or source), and the new voltage level is reflected back toward the other end of the line. The energy in an incident wave is *not* absorbed by a short circuit.

Case 1 above is the typical situation for TTL, CMOS, or BiCMOS logic circuits; inputs are sensitive to voltage (not power) and require only a small portion of the energy in the incident wave arriving from the transmission line to maintain steady-state operation (i.e., the load impedance is very large with respect to the line impedance). Therefore, the voltage at the load device is increased (up to double) compared to the incident wave, and a significant portion of the energy is reflected back toward the source.

Case 2 above is approximated by typical CMOS *high* and *low* outputs and TTL and BiCMOS *low* outputs; their effective output impedance is not zero, but it is much less than the normal line impedance. Thus, *low* TTL or BiCMOS outputs, or CMOS *high* or *low* outputs, have negative reflection coefficients. Energy is reflected with a reversal of voltage polarity. A negative reflection coefficient at the source of a line will cause overshoot that may have occurred at the load end of the line to be converted to undershoot on alternate reflection cycles. The undershoot, when it arrives at the load, may cause the signal level to transition to the threshold region of the receiving device,

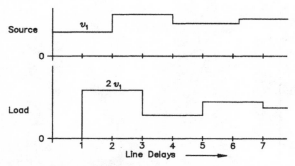

Figure 7.3 Typical response of a long transmission line with one source and one load.

upsetting the logic sense of the signal. Under such conditions, which are typical of advanced Schottky TTL, advanced CMOS, and BiCMOS devices, a number of round trips may be required for the excess energy in the signal to be absorbed and for the signal to achieve a steady-state value. Figure 7.3 illustrates the classical response of a line with a low-impedance source and a single high-impedance load.[4,6,7] Figure 7.3 is drawn for a load reflection coefficient of $+1$ and a source reflection coefficient of -0.5, which are typical of today's TTL, CMOS, and BiCMOS devices.

In the case illustrated in Fig. 7.3, the waveform at the load end does not undershoot (on the second incident wave) below V_1. But in many actual cases the signal will undershoot back into the threshold region of the receiving device and will remain there until the signal travels back to the source and back to the load. Thus, for most lines that are not terminated, five line delays must be allowed for signals to settle. After five line delays, most of the energy in a wavefront will have been absorbed and the undershoot will have effectively dampened out in most cases. However, it is difficult to generalize a very complex phenomenon. For example, devices with very low-impedance clamp diodes on their inputs may extend the settling time to seven or nine line delays. Time-critical situations must be carefully analyzed with transmission-line tools or with reflection diagrams, as described in Sec. 7.2.

A rule of thumb for most timing analysis: *Allow five line delays for unterminated lines to settle.*

7.1.2 Transmission-line termination

There are two basic means of terminating transmission lines: series (source) termination and load termination. Either method can be used to achieve a stable signal at the far (load) end of a line after one line delay. However, the response at the source and at intermediate points is different for the two methods of termination. Series-terminated lines required at least two line delays for signals to stabilize at the source end of a line; properly designed load-terminated lines reach steady-state conditions at the most remote point after one line delay.

Load termination.   A line is defined as *load-terminated* when the load at the end of the line is matched to the impedance of the line. Figure 7.4a, b, c, and d shows various means of load termination.[8,9] The same dynamic results are achieved with each of the configurations.

When a line is load-terminated with a matching impedance (R_L of the load = Z_o of the line), regardless of the dc circuit configuration of the terminating network, the signal at the source, at intermediate points, and at the load should appear as a well-behaved signal, as shown in Fig. 7.5. In such a case, the signal is launched into the line and at some later time (equal to the propagation time of the line t_{LINE}) arrives at the load. The energy in the wavefront is absorbed, and a steady-state level is established upon arrival of the incident wave at

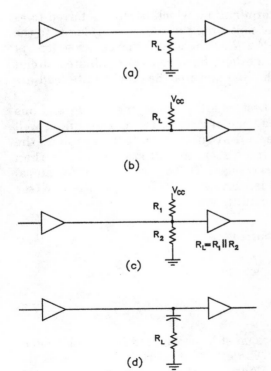

(a)

(b)

(c)

(d)

Figure 7.4 Load termination R_L. (a) Termination to ground; (b) termination to V_{cc}; (c) split termination; (d) ac termination.

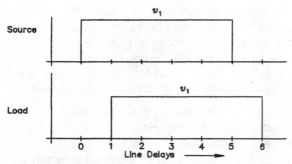

Figure 7.5 Idealized source and load waveforms in a load-terminated line.

the load (see Fig. 7.5). In Fig. 7.4 it is implied that the receivers have infinite impedance, and for all practical purposes, that is the case for TTL, CMOS, and BiCMOS device inputs, as long as the signal levels remain between ground and V_{cc}. Thus, load termination resistors (networks) do not need to be adjusted to compensate for receiver input impedance.

Source termination. Source termination, which is often referred to as *series termination,* consists of matching the source impedance to the line impedance, as shown in Fig. 7.6. The waveforms at the source, at intermediate points, and at the load for a source-terminated circuit that is exactly matched to the line and that has an infinite load are shown in Fig. 7.7.

Series termination works best where there is one source and one load. The waveform at the load end of a series-terminated line is well behaved, but at the source and at intermediate points near the source, the leading edge of the waveform will step up rather than make a smooth transition (see Fig. 7.7). The initial step (or steps) occurs as a result of the divider formed by R_S and Z_o of the line (see Fig. 7.8). The amplitude of the initial step is

$$V_{t=0} \text{ (at source)} = \frac{Z_0}{R_s + Z_0} \, Vcc \tag{7.4}$$

When R_S is matched to Z_o, the amplitude of the initial step is

$$V_{t=0} \text{ (at source)} = \frac{1}{2} \, V_{cc} \quad \text{when } R_S = Z_o \tag{7.5}$$

The driver output impedance must be considered in the selection of series termination resistors. The effective source impedance is the sum of the driver output impedance and the source termination resis-

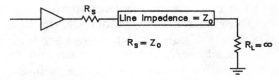

Figure 7.6 Source termination R_S.

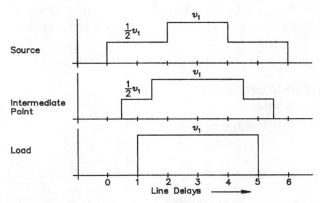

Figure 7.7 Waveforms in a source-terminated line.

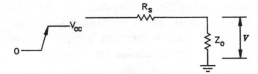

Figure 7.8 Series termination resistance and line impedance form a divider that causes a step in the initial waveform launched into a series-terminated line.

tor. Hence, for an exact match to a line, a source termination resistor must have a value equal to Z_o less the driver output impedance. In TTL and BiCMOS applications, it is impossible to exactly match the line impedance for both *high*- and *low*-going signals since the output impedances of totem-pole output stages are different for the two states (see Chap. 3).

One advantage of series termination is that no additional dc power is dissipated due to the termination. However, care must be taken to ensure that the noise margin is not significantly reduced by voltage dropped across series termination resistors due to static load currents. Advanced Schottky TTL input currents are low relative to some of the older TTL logic families, but they are large enough to cause significant voltage drop across series resistors. Most CMOS and BiCMOS devices have CMOS input circuits which have very high input impedance. Thus, CMOS load currents are very low, and dc voltage drops across series-terminating resistors are not significant when CMOS loads are driven. As a rule of thumb, to minimize noise margin loss and to provide slightly underdamped signals (which reach valid logic levels faster), series termination resistors should be approximately one-third to one-half the line characteristic impedance Z_o. A value in the range of 22 to 33 Ω is appropriate for most applications.

7.2 TTL, CMOS, and BiCMOS Device Transmission-Line Response

The response of advanced Schottky TTL, advanced CMOS, and BiCMOS logic devices in a transmission-line environment cannot be determined by using simple ideal transmission-line theory. Ideal transmission-line theory is based on fixed linear source and load impedances. The input-output current-voltage relationships of TTL, CMOS, and BiCMOS devices are nonlinear. Graphical techniques or transmission-line analysis programs that incorporate nonlinear models are needed to predict their response.

A graphical technique, sometimes called *Bergeron plots,* is useful to predict the response of TTL, CMOS, and BiCMOS devices.[10] Bergeron plots predict signal response by combining nonlinear device input-output I/V characteristics with the interconnection impedance. The succession of changes in voltage and current at the source and load is predicted by intersections of the input-output I/V characteristics and the load lines that represent the transmission-line impedance. Bergeron plots assume that quasi-steady-state conditions are achieved at each end of the transmission line before any reflection from the other end alters those conditions (this condition is met if the two-way delay is greater than the rise time). Losses, distortions, and source switching transients are neglected. Common dielectrics and conductors do not result in significant signal losses for rise times of 1 ns or greater and line lengths less than 1 m.

The basic obstacle to using Bergeron plots to predict signal response is that dynamic V/I interface specifications are not listed or shown on most TTL, CMOS, or BiCMOS device data sheets; or if they are supplied, they are typical values without minimum and maximum limits. Without worst-case dynamic limits, system designers cannot accurately predict worst-case dynamic performance. Parts from different lots or from different manufacturers may behave much differently. If the worst-case dynamic response cannot be predicted, potential performance must go unrealized; extra and wasted time must be allocated for signals to settle.

7.2.1 Typical advanced CMOS device transmission-line response

The output impedance of advanced CMOS devices is low relative to typical printed-circuit board line impedance, and the input impedance is much greater than the line impedance for normal signal levels.[11,12] For signal levels beyond the static operating range (transient levels greater than the supply or reference), the input impedance of CMOS devices may remain very high or may change drastically. Inputs may have parasitic diodes, electrostatic protection diodes, and in some cases signal clamping diodes that begin to conduct as signals exceed the power rails.[12] When clamping circuits have an effective high-frequency impedance near or less than the interconnection impedance and the breakpoint is near or within a diode drop of V_{cc} or ground, input clamps control transmission-line ringing in most applications. However, if receiving devices do not have clamps or if the clamps are not effective at high frequencies, then severe ringing may occur.

Typical clamped input line response.   The typical source-load response for CMOS devices where the input is clamped by a low-impedance diode beyond the power rails* is as follows:

1. The source launches excess energy into the line.[13,14]

2. The load presents a high impedance to the line in the normal signal range, which causes overshoot into the clamping region where most of the signal energy is absorbed, but some is reflected back to the source.

3. The source converts the reflected overshoot to undershoot and reflects the excess energy back to the load. If most of the excess

---

*The following nomenclature and definitions are used. *Overdamped signals* occur when the source impedance or termination impedance is higher than the transmission-line impedance; *underdamped signals* occur when the source or termination impedance is lower than the transmission-line impedance. *Overshoot* is a signal transition beyond the steady-state level (i.e., below the normal *low* state—above the normal *high* state). *Undershoot* is a signal excursion between steady-state *high* and *low* levels (undershoot usually occurs after the nominal signal level has been reached the first time). The *rise time* is the time required for a signal to switch from its previous steady-state level to a new steady-state level. To reduce ambiguity, rise time is usually measured for only a central portion of the interval between steady-state signal levels, such as 20 to 80 percent levels.

energy in the first incident wave is absorbed at the load, the undershoot is small and does not impact operation.

4. The alternate overshoot-undershoot cycles quickly subside.

The above sequence of events for a FACT advanced CMOS gate driving a 50-Ω line is shown in the reflection diagram in Fig. 7.9.[15] The reflection diagram for a *low*-to-*high* transition is constructed by first drawing a 50-Ω load line from the V_{OL} quiescent point to the point where it intersects with the V_{OH}/I_{OH} curve,* as shown by line 1. The voltage at the intersection, approximately 4 V, is the amplitude of the first step at the source and of the first incident wave launched down the line. Next a line is drawn at a −50-Ω slope from the intersection to the V_{IN}/I_{IN} curve (see line 2). The voltage at this second intersection represents the amplitude of the initial signal seen at the load and the first reflection back from the load. The process of drawing lines is continued until they converge at the V_{OH} quiescent voltage. The reflec-

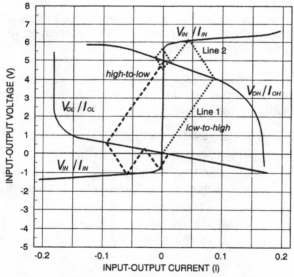

Figure 7.9 Reflection diagram for FACT CMOS gates with a 50-Ω interconnection. (*Reprinted with permission of National Semiconductor Corp.*)

---

*Load lines terminating on V_{OH}/I_{OH} and V_{OL}/I_{OL} curves have positive slopes, and lines terminating on V_{IN}/I_{IN} curves have negative slopes. The transmission line acts as a load to the source; thus changes at the source have a positive Z_o slope. Likewise, the transmission line acts as a source to the load; thus changes at the load have a negative Z_o slope.

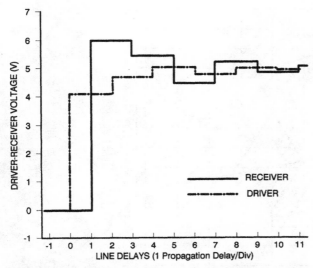

Figure 7.10 *Low*-to-*high* source and load waveforms predicted by the reflection diagram shown in Fig. 7.9. (*Reprinted
with permission of National Semiconductor Corp.*)

tion diagram for a *high*-to-*low* transition is constructed in a similar
manner (see Fig. 7.9). Figure 7.10 shows the theoretical waveforms
(for the *low*-to-*high* transition) at the source and load based on the
results of the reflection diagram of Fig. 7.9.

Note that the low-impedance input clamps at the load limit the
overshoot for both *low*-to-*high* and *high*-to-*low* transitions to near 1 V.
The low source impedance relative to the line characteristic impedance then converts the reflected 1-V overshoot to about a 1-V undershoot. Several reflection cycles are required before steady-state conditions are reached, but the signal never undershoots into the critical
region near the threshold.

Typical unclamped input line response.   The typical source-load
response for CMOS devices where the input remains a high impedance beyond the power rails is as follows:

1. The source launches excess energy into the line.

2. The load presents a high impedance to the line which causes overshoot and reflection of most of the signal energy back to the source.

3. The source converts the overshoot to undershoot and reflects the
   excess energy back to the load.

4. The alternate overshoot-undershoot cycles repeat as damped ringing.

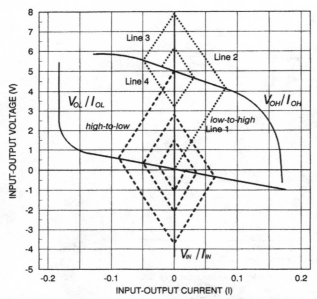

Figure 7.11 Typical reflection diagram for advanced CMOS input-output circuits without input clamps for signals below ground or above V_{cc} when interconnected with a 50-Ω transmission line.

The above sequence of events is shown in the reflection diagram of Fig. 7.11. The sequence is the same as for Fig. 7.9 except since the load does not have input clamps, line 2 is drawn to the zero-current axis (the V_{IN}/I_{IN} relationship is a vertical line at zero current). The voltage at the intersection of the zero-current axis is approximately 8 V, which is the amplitude of the reflection of the first incident wave from the load. Note that the unclamped load results in more than a 3-V overshoot. When the 3-V overshoot returns to the source—the intersection of line 3 and the V_{OH}/I_{OH} curve—the low output impedance of the source converts the 3-V overshoot to a 2-V undershoot (line 4). An undershoot of 2 V results in a signal level that is nearly midway between the *low* state and the *high* state. Several reflection cycles will be required before steady-state conditions are reached. Settling times are notably prolonged when devices do not have effective high-frequency input clamps.

7.2.2 Typical TTL and BiCMOS device transmission-line response

Reflection diagrams for advanced Schottky TTL and for BiCMOS devices look very much the same since both device families have simi-

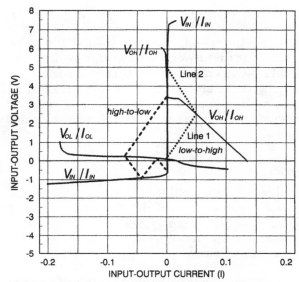

Figure 7.12 Typical reflection diagram for advanced Schottky TTL or BiCMOS input-output circuits with input clamps for signals below ground but not above V_{cc} when interconnected with 50-Ω transmission line.

lar totem-pole output circuits and both tend to have good dynamic clamps to ground on their inputs.[10] Figure 7.12 is a reflection diagram for an advanced Schottky TTL octal buffer based on the output V/I curves shown in the *FAST Advanced Schottky TTL Logic Databook*[16] and an assumed input V_{IN}/I_{IN} curve for signal excursions above and below ground when it is interconnected with a 50-Ω transmission line. Note that signals quickly stabilize and do not have dangerous undershoot levels. *High*-to-*low* transitions overshoot (in the negative direction), but do not ring back into the dangerous region. *Low*-to-*high* transitions do not overshoot V_{cc} or ring back. They stabilize at about 5 V where line 2 intersects the vertical (high-impedance) V_{IN}/I_{IN} curve. At that point, both V_{OH}/I_{OH} and V_{IN}/I_{IN} are vertical on the zero-current axis, which precludes drawing additional reflection diagram lines (i.e., the diagram converges at that point).

The starting point for *high*-to-*low* transitions depends upon load and leakage currents and signal frequency. In low-frequency applications, *high* signals that dynamically stabilize above the level where the output can supply current tend to drift down to the point where the output can supply current—the intersection of the V_{OH}/I_{OH} curve with the zero-current axis. In high-frequency applications, *high* signals in the region of zero output current may not have time to drift to the stable static level. Hence, in certain circumstances, signal characteristics are not constant but are a function of recent signal history. In Fig. 7.12, the *high*-to-*low* transition starts from the point where the V_{OH}/I_{OH} curve intersects the zero-current axis (i.e., at the point where *high*-level drive current is first available). Depending upon circumstances, a *high*-to-*low* reflection diagram starting at the intersection of line 2 with the V_{IN}/I_{IN} curve should also be constructed. Note that more reflection cycles are required to reach a stable *low* state if the *high*-to-*low* transition reflection diagram is started from the point where line 2 intersects the V_{IN}/I_{IN} curve.

7.2.3 Controlling undershoot

Undershoot may impact circuit operation if it is of such a magnitude that signal levels degrade to near or beyond the threshold levels of the receiving devices. Thus, undershoot is the most important condition to avoid[2] in networks that behave as transmission lines. Undershoot can be controlled as follows:[7]

1. The source can be designed to control the amount of energy launched into the transmission line.
2. The load response can be designed to absorb some of the overshoot to control the amount of energy reflected back to the source.
3. The source can be designed to absorb some of the reflected overshoot from the load and to control the conversion to undershoot.

The benefits of limiting the amount of energy launched into interconnections include less transient current, less crosstalk, and less overshoot energy to be absorbed or reflected. However, a moderate degree of overshoot is beneficial. The benefits include the increased first incident signal amplitude to improve initial noise margin, reduced rise-time degradation due to discrete capacitance loads, and compensation for line losses. If the source impedance is greater than the line impedance, then not enough energy is sent down the line and the initial signal amplitude is reduced at the load. The signal may not have sufficient amplitude for first incident wave switching, which slows the response of the line. Reduced signal amplitude causes loss of signal-to-noise margin at the load. To evaluate these effects for devices of interest, both maximum and minimum dynamic output characteristics are needed; but they are usually not available for advanced Schottky TTL, advanced CMOS, and BiCMOS devices. In contrast, ECL (which is intended for high-performance applications) data sheets specify both minimum and maximum dynamic output values.

High-load impedance minimizes steady-state power consumption and maximizes signal levels and noise margins. However, excess energy in incident waves will cause signals to overshoot, and transient disturbances (such as crosstalk) are reflected with increased amplitude. Thus, it is advantageous for the load to absorb a reasonable portion of any excess energy to minimize overshoot and ringing. Overshoot response should be well matched to the lowest transmission-line impedance for relatively low currents. For large currents, a dynamic impedance less than the line impedance will reduce overshoot and the overshoot recovery time. A low-impedance clamp diode provides the desired response.[5]

The effect of source impedance on reflected waves is often overlooked. However, source impedance is very critical because it is usually responsible for the conversion of reflected overshoot to undershoot. Source response to overshoot should be either nearly matched or overdamped, to prevent conversion of overshoot to undershoot and loss of signal noise margin. However, the overdamping should be limited so that steady-state conditions are approached quickly (if steady-state conditions are not achieved before the next clock interval, the response is a function of the previous signal history). Therefore, minimum and maximum specifications are necessary to characterize source response to reflected overshoot.

7.2.4   Optimum source-load impedance characteristics

For optimum high-speed performance of advanced Schottky TTL, advanced CMOS, or BiCMOS devices in a transmission-line environment, with no external terminating resistors, the ideal source-load impedance characteristics are as follows:

1. The source output response at high currents, i.e., for the initial step, must be underdamped (lower impedance) with respect to the minimum transmission-line impedance to ensure first incident wave switching. However, the amount of underdamping must be minimized to limit the initial voltage and current and the resultant crosstalk and power source and reference-level transient upset.

2. The load input impedance between the power rails should be very high to minimize power dissipation and maximize steady-state signal levels.

3. The load response to overshoots at high currents must be underdamped (lower impedance) with respect to the minimum transmission-line impedance to minimize the first incident wave overshoot and the amplitude of the reflected wave. However, the amount of underdamping must be minimized to limit the time required to achieve a steady state.

4. The source response to reflected overshoots must be overdamped (higher impedance) with respect to the maximum transmission-line impedance, to ensure that conversion to undershoot does not occur. However, the amount of overdamping must be minimized to limit the time required to approach steady-state conditions.

7.3 Driver-Receiver Response Test Circuit

Since the dynamic characteristics of advanced Schottky TTL, advanced CMOS, and BiCMOS devices in transmission-line environments are not specified, system designers need some means of establishing how candidate devices may react in a transmission-line environment. A simple test setup that is useful for observing signal response is easily implemented as follows: Connect the output of a driver (e.g., an AC240) to the input of a device of interest, using 3 or 4 ft of 50-Ω coaxial cable; apply a clock to the input of the driver driving the coaxial cable, and observe the output of the coaxial cable at the receiving device (see Fig. 7.13). The purpose of the coaxial cable is to simulate the 50-Ω impedance of a typical multilayer PC board (75- or 90-Ω coaxial cable can be used if it is more appropriate for a given application). The longer the length of coaxial cable used, the more pronounced will be the transmission-line effects. A 3- to 4-ft length is usually sufficient for most observations. A test as described will quickly establish the effectiveness of the clamps and other techniques for controlling transmission-line effects that the manufacturer may have incorporated in the device under test. However, a test of one device does not establish that all devices of that type or of that logic family will behave in a similar manner. They more than likely will not. Not all devices in a logic family have the same input-output circuitry. Manufacturers are constantly updating and changing devices to increase producibility, but that does not mean the transmission-line characteristics are always improved. There are wide variations in the transmission-line response characteristics of the same generic part from different manufacturers. Response characteristics change significantly with temperature, power supply voltage, and process limits. Thus,

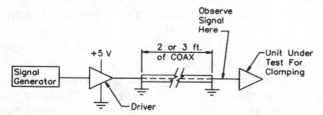

Figure 7.13 Circuit for observing transmission-line response and input clamping circuit efficiency.

device response needs to be checked at the extremes of the operating temperature and power supply voltage range. Yet, no matter how many tests are performed, there is no guarantee that production lots of a given device or devices will behave in a similar fashion. With all the variables, the best that can be hoped for in testing devices is to identify logic families and LSI devices built with a given technology or by a given manufacturer that tend to behave well in a transmission-line environment. Until manufacturers start specifying advanced Schottky TTL, advanced CMOS, and BiCMOS devices in a manner that allows a determination of their worst-case dynamic performance in transmission-line environments, the system designer is left with little solid information to predict performance.

7.4   Summary of Techniques for Dealing with Transmission-Line Effects

1. Signal lines with waveshape requirements (such as clocks) must be terminated.
   a. Series termination is best for most single-source to single-load applications.
   b. Load termination is best for single-source to multiple-load applications.
   c. Terminations that result in slightly underdamped lines provide optimum response.
2. When signals are sent between circuit boards, allowance must be made for possible signal degradation due to transmission-line effects since most board-to-board interconnections will be long. Worst-case board-to-board signal propagation time budgets must allow for possible added signal length due to extender boards, since most digital systems must function with boards extended for troubleshooting. Unterminated board-to-board and unit-to-unit signal interconnections must allow five line delays for ringing and reflections to subside.
3. Interconnection line impedance should be greater than 40 Ω (unloaded) so as to not excessively degrade initial signal levels.
4. Signals routed to test points should be buffered to prevent test equipment and transmission-line effects caused by interconnecting lines from interfering with normal system operation.
5. Signals that are used internally and externally to a board or unit should have external lines buffered to isolate internal signals from transmission-line reflections or other external disturbances such as short circuits.
6. Input signals to boards, racks, or systems should be received at one place with a device with effective input clamps so as to minimize load-induced transmission-line effects.

7. *Caution:* Many LSI and VLSI parts, such as PLDs, FIFOs, etc., do not have input clamps or do not have effective high-speed signal input clamps. If that is the case, signals will ring severely.

7.5   References

1. William R. Blood, Jr., *MECL System Design Handbook,* 4th ed., Motorola Semiconductor Products Inc., Phoenix, Ariz., 1988.
2. Thomas Balph, "Implementing High Speed Logic on Printed Circuit Boards," in 1981 WESCON Electronic Show & Convention Records, Session 18, San Francisco, September 1981, paper no. 1.
3. David Royle, "Transmission Lines and Interconnections, Part Three," *EDN,* June 23, 1988, pp. 155–160.
4. Jacob Millman and Herbert Taub, *Pulse, Digital and Switching Waveforms,* McGraw-Hill, New York, 1965.
5. R. G. Saenz and E. M. Fulcher, "An Approach to Logic Circuit Noise Problems in Computer Design," *Computer Design,* April 1969, pp. 84–91.
6. Joseph L. DeClue, "Wiring for High-Speed Circuits," *Electronic Design,* no. 11, May 24, 1976, pp. 84–86.
7. Anh Nguyen-huu, "An Analysis of the Ringing Phenomenon in Digital Systems," *Computer Design,* July 1971, pp. 39–45.
8. *FAST Logic Applications Handbook,* National Semiconductor Corp., Santa Clara, Calif., 1990.
9. David Royle, "Transmission Lines and Interconnections, Part Two," *EDN,* June 23, 1988, pp. 143–148.
10. R. A. Stehlin, "Bergeron Plots Predict Delays in High-Speed TTL Circuits," *EDN,* November 15, 1984, pp. 293–298.
11. Robert K. Southard, "High-Speed Signal Pathways from Board to Board," in 1981 WESCON Electronic Show & Convention Records, Session 18, San Francisco, September 1981, paper no. 2.
12. *Advanced CMOS Logic Designer's Handbook,* Texas Instruments Inc., Dallas, Tex., 1988.
13. K. Leung, "Controlled Slew Rate Output Buffer," *IEEE 1988 Custom Integrated Circuits Conference CH2584-1/88,* Rochester, NY, 1988, pp. 5.5.1–4.
14. "Electronic Design Report," *Electronic Design,* May 12, 1988, pp. 77–79.
15. *FACT Advanced CMOS Logic Databook,* National Semiconductor Corp., Santa Clara, Calif., 1993.
16. *FAST Advanced Schottky TTL Logic Databook,* National Semiconductor Corp., Santa Clara, Calif., 1990.
17. E. A. Burton, "Transmission-Line Methods Aid Memory-Board Design," *Electronic Design,* December 8, 1988, pp. 87–91.

7.6   Bibliography

Applications Handbook, Cypress Semiconductor Corp., San Jose, Calif., 1994.
Divekar, Dileep, Raj Raghuram, and Paul K. U. Wang: "Simulate Transmission-Line Effects in High-Speed PCB and MCM Systems," *Electronic Design—PCB CAD Designers' Guide,* April 11, 1991, pp. 113–122.
Matick, Richard E.: *Transmission Lines for Digital and Communications Networks,* McGraw-Hill, New York, 1969.
Quinnell, Richard A.: "High-Speed Bus Interfaces," *EDN,* September 30, 1993, pp. 43–50.
"Signal-Integrity Tools," *Computer Design,* special report, April 1995, pp. 57–72.
Skilling, Hugh H.: *Electric Transmission Lines,* McGraw-Hill, New York, 1951.

8

Clock Distribution

Clock signal quality is a critical matter that must not be neglected in the design of high-speed digital systems. Clock signals must be as nearly perfect as possible, which means clock distribution networks and clock generation circuitry must be paid a great deal of attention.

8.1 Universal Clock Distribution Guidelines

Clock signals require an optimal electrical environment. Transmission-line effects, crosstalk, ground bounce, and skew must be tightly controlled. In advanced Schottky TTL, advanced CMOS, and BiCMOS systems, clock distribution circuitry must incorporate some form of line termination for waveshape control to limit undesirable transmission-line effects.[1] If it is not properly terminated, ringing and other transmission-line effects may cause extra clocking. To allow proper termination, clock signals must be routed to their destinations via reasonably well-controlled impedance paths and clock signal wiring (routing) topology must be controlled to control transmission-line effects. Serial connections are the simplest and easiest topology to control, but other arrangements such as loops and stars can be used if they are fully analyzed (which usually requires signal integrity software tools). A serial connection means that the clock signal is routed from the source to the load or loads with no branches or stubs. Branches and long stubs complicate or defeat most termination techniques.

Clock lines must be physically arranged so as to minimize cross-coupling or other adverse interference that could cause extra clocking. Parallel runs adjacent to other signals or other clocks must be kept as short as possible to minimize the opportunities for cross-coupling. When multilayer printed-circuit boards are used, clock signals should be isolated and shielded from other signals by locating clock traces between reference planes. On welded-wire or wire-wrap circuit boards or backpanels where it is practical (i.e., where the runs are long enough), special wiring techniques that provide some shielding and control of impedance should be used. For example, wire-wrappable coaxial cables, shielded twisted pairs, or twisted pairs can be used (ground is used with the clock in twisted pairs). As a minimum, long clock lines should be twisted with a ground line to provide some control of line impedance and to minimize radiated energy. Care must be taken to ensure that wired clock lines which are not shielded do not get bundled with other signals.

Clock distribution networks (trees) must be designed to minimize skew between clock signals. Skew reduces the potential system operating speed by decreasing the time that signals have to settle and may cause logic malfunctions if the skew is sufficient to cause hold-time violations. To accomplish the needed alignment, clock distribution circuitry must be standardized. Low-skew drivers, such as those designed specifically for clock buffer application, must be used for all clock drivers. Clock drivers at each level in distribution networks must be identical generic devices of the same logic family so that propagation delays are matched. Where possible, all drivers in a given level should be located in a common package. Drivers and loads must be arranged so that loads are equalized. Clock lines must be very short so that wiring propagation delays are insignificant, or lines must be of near-equal length in each distribution level to equalize physical propagation delays.

Clock driver loading must be limited to much less than the specified dc rating to prevent loading effects from corrupting clock signals. In high-speed systems, static (dc) loading is usually not an issue. Dynamic (ac) loading is the greatest concern and has the greatest effect on clock signal quality. In most standard applications, where advanced Schottky TTL, advanced CMOS, or BiCMOS devices are used, dc drive limits are seldom exceeded, but actual ac loading often exceeds the standard test load capacitances, which means that ac characteristics will be degraded from those specified (the standard test load used to specify most dynamic switching characteristics is 50 pF). Capacitance loading effects include increased signal rise time and driver ground bounce. Clock signals with slow rise times are prone to double clocking because of noise riding on slowly rising or falling edges. Slow rise times make it more difficult to control skew since the switching threshold of the next level of clock buffers (or final clocked device) may be crossed at slightly different times. Excessive loading also causes ground bounce to increase, which adds to clock signal corruption. To minimize ground bounce and power supply droop, the capacitance loading of individual drivers and of groups of drivers in a common package must be limited to minimize the switching currents in package power and ground pins. For example, if octal parts such as 240s or 244s are used, no more than six of the eight drivers should be used. Those used should be the six nearest the ground pin (or pins) of the package. The two spare drivers should not be used for other purposes. Furthermore, as a rule of thumb, the number of loads driven by any one of the 240 or 244 buffers should be limited to 6 and the total package load limited to 36. Even with limitations on the loading of the active drivers such as described, six drivers switching six loads at once can generate significant ground bounce (or power supply droop) which may degrade clock signal quality and may appear as spikes on the outputs of the other drivers in the package if frequencies or phases are mixed in a package (see Chap. 4).

Because of ground-bounce issues, different clock frequencies or phases should not be mixed in a common package. If two different frequencies are mixed in a common package, spikes due to ground bounce or power supply droop may appear on the lower frequency when the higher frequency switches. Figure 8.1 shows the possible results (ground-bounce spikes on the lower-frequency signal) of using buffers in a common package for two different clock frequencies.[2] The do-not-mix guideline applies for other signals. Other signals may corrupt the clock, or the clock may corrupt the other signals.

To supply the transient-current needs of clock drivers, local decoupling capacitors and circuit boards with continuous low-impedance power and ground planes are a necessity.[3,4] Each clock driver package should be decoupled with a high-frequency capacitor (typically 0.1 μF) located as close as possible to the package (see Chap. 5 for guidelines on selecting the value). The clock driver package power and ground pins must connect directly to the respective circuit board power and ground planes. When universal welded-wire or wire-wrap prototyping boards are used, solder clips or washers must be used for clock driver package power and ground-pin connections to power and ground planes.[5] Actual welded-wire or wire-wrap wiring should never

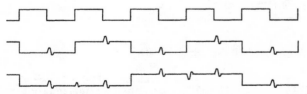

Figure 8.1 Low-frequency clock signals may have noise spikes when higher-frequency clocks switch, if different clock frequencies are mixed in a package.

be used to make clock driver power or ground connections; the inductance is too large.

To minimize the effects of cross-coupling, all clocked devices with TTL input thresholds should be selected so that they change states on the *low*-to-*high* transition of the clock. The goal is to have all local clock signals in the *high* state, which has maximum noise immunity, when the majority of system signals are switching and generating noise (see Fig. 8.2).

When devices with TTL input levels are used for clock distribution, clock signal phasing at all major distribution levels (i.e., at all major interfaces) should be such that all interface clock signals are in phase with component level clock signals (i.e., all clock signals should switch from a *low*-to-*high* level at the same time). The design objective is to ensure that long clock lines which have a high probability of being exposed to noise, such as the clock lines that traverse backpanels or motherboards, are in the maximum noise immunity state during the time of peak system noise (Fig. 8.2).

When devices with TTL input levels are used, low-frequency clocks (10 MHz or less) should be shaped so that the *low* state is as short as possible, to optimize clock signal noise immunity (see Fig. 8.2). Such an arrangement keeps clock signals in the maximum noise margin state for a longer time, allowing a longer time for system signals to transition and a longer time for noise due to delayed transitions to die out before clock signals go to the *low* state, which has less noise margin than the *high* state. Above 10 MHz, a nonsymmetric clock signal is usually not practical, but for systems with slower clock rates such a configuration should be considered. If clock pulses are narrowed, care must be taken to ensure that the clock pulse width is adequate for the slowest logic family or device that might be used in the system.

When clock sources and loads are not solidly referenced to a common uninterrupted ground plane, clock signals must be transmitted by some means that provides a high degree of noise margin. The noise margin of single-ended devices with either TTL or CMOS levels is not adequate for clock distribution when the transmitting and receiving

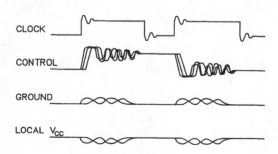

CLOCK

CONTROL

GROUND

LOCAL V_{CC}

Figure 8.2 TTL-level clock signal phasing for maximum noise margin.

devices are not directly referenced to a low-impedance common ground plane. When an adequate low noise reference system does not exist, clock signals are typically distributed by using some form of balanced differential transmission that has a high level of common-mode noise rejection capability.

There are three distinct categories of clock distribution in the typical large digital system:

1. Component-to-component connections (i.e., circuit board clock distribution)

2. Board-to-board connections (i.e., motherboard clock distribution)

3. Unit-to-unit connections (i.e., between chassis, racks, cabinets, etc.)

Interconnection categories 1 and 2 are present in most systems. The need for category 3 depends upon the system size and the functional relationship of separate units. Small self-contained systems have no need for unit-to-unit connections. Likewise, many large systems are composed of separate autonomous functional units, with each separate unit having its own internal clock source.

8.2 Board Level Clock Distribution

To optimize noise immunity, circuit boards, and where possible entire systems, should be designed to operate using only a single clock frequency and phase. In many cases, this ideal single frequency and phase will not be possible, but it should be the goal. The clock source for small systems with only one circuit board is typically an on-board oscillator. Large systems with multiple circuit boards typically have a central clock source (board) that provides clock signals to each board. Regardless of whether an external source or an on-board oscillator is the source for the board clock signals, a standard clock tree, such as that shown in Fig. 8.3, should be used to buffer and fan out clock signals. The clock tree should be the same on all boards in a given system. If boards have an external source, each board clock input signal (or signals) should be received with a single receiver and then fanned out to the loads, as shown in Fig. 8.3. If load termination is used, it should be at the end of the incoming clock line and located reasonably close to the receiver. The receiver and termination should be located at a central point on the board. The goal of the placement is to minimize the lengths of the secondary (i.e., board) clock signals. Note that load termination works best with TTL-level signals (see Sec. 8.3).

A board level clock tree such as shown in Fig. 8.3 provides a means of fanning out to multiple loads on a board without presenting a large

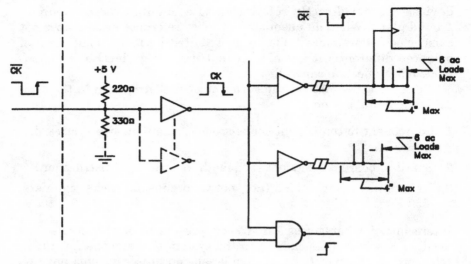

Figure 8.3 Typical circuit board clock tree.

load to the clock source. Ideally, only one receiver is used to receive the input clock signal, to minimize load capacitance and optimize clock signal integrity. However, requiring that board clock inputs be limited to one load may force board clock trees to extra levels on large boards with many clocked devices. Extra levels are always undesirable in clock trees. Extra levels add uncertainty to clock edge phasing because of the added variability of the additional components in the tree. Thus, in applications where boards are very large, adding receiving devices is usually a better solution than increasing the clock tree depth. Up to six receivers can be used when split terminations appropriately matching the line impedance are used, but the number should be kept as small as possible and the distance between them must be small (all the receivers should be in the same package, which will inherently limit the distance). When source termination is used, only one receiver is preferred; but more can be used if the source termination is customized to the load.

Clock alignment

Optimal system operation is dependent on tight clock alignment.

Alignment of board clock signals is essential in all but trivial applications, and it may be essential even in trivial cases if two or more flip-flops or registers must exchange data. Proper data transfers between digital storage elements (flip-flops, counters, registers, memories, etc.)

are contingent upon the system active clock edges being closely aligned and remaining so over time and for all environmental conditions. Clock misalignment reduces the effective clock period and thus reduces the usable setup time available for signals, which becomes a greater concern as the frequency of operation goes up. Close alignment is needed to prevent hold-time violations when register-to-register transfers must be made. Alignment of clock signals in advanced Schottky TTL, advanced CMOS, or BiCMOS systems typically needs to be near 1 ns or less. As a general rule, the higher the clock speed, the tighter are the alignment requirements; but tight clock alignment is required regardless of frequency from a hold-time violation standpoint.

Clock alignment is a function of the physical routing of the clock signals and propagation delay variations of the clock buffers. Variations in delays due to signal routing can be controlled by equalizing the length and loading of the various clock interconnection networks in each level of the clock tree. Buffer delay variations are minimized by using specially designed low-skew clock buffers, which are available from most of the major IC manufacturers (coverage of the various clock drivers is beyond the scope of this book—see the bibliography in Sec. 8.7). The specially designed low-skew clock buffers have specified skew limits whereas most standard buffers in the various logic families do not. Where one of the customized clock drivers cannot be used, to minimize skew, all board clock buffers in a given level of the clock tree should be of the same generic type from the same logic family.

To optimize alignment of board clock signals, the following steps should be taken:

1. The final level of the board clock tree buffers should be centrally located.

2. Low-skew clock drivers, or at least identical generic devices, should be used in each given level.

3. Clock buffers should all be in the same package where possible.

4. Loading for each level should be balanced.

5. Line lengths should be minimized and similar in each level. For very large boards, definite minimum and maximum clock line lengths should be established to limit possible skew.

Ground bounce in clock buffers.   Ground bounce can be a severe problem in clock buffer packages, since all drivers in clock buffer packages switch at the same time. When all devices in a package switch simultaneously, load and totem-pole feedthrough currents combine to exacerbate ground bounce. To minimize the potential for ground-bounce disturbances, the number of clock buffer loads should be limited to well below dc fan-out ratings. For example, 54F240s have a dc drive rating of 48 mA and thus can drive forty-eight 54F240 inputs (I_{IL} = 1 mA). However, 48 loads at 5 pF per load result in a 240-pF load (with no allowance for the wiring capacitance), which is well above the 50-pF load at which the ac parameters are specified. In addition, if all eight devices in an octal driver package (such as a 240 or 244) were used with each buffer driving 48 loads, the total ac load that would have to be charged or discharged at each clock edge transition would be 1920 pF (240 pF×8). Such a large ac load would result in severe ground bounce. Ground bounce, when an octal buffer package is used as a clock driver, is further aggravated by the totem-pole transient feedthrough current of eight simultaneously switching buffers (see Chap. 4). Using all eight buffers, with each fully loaded, is a somewhat extreme example, but it illustrates the need to limit ac loading of clock buffer packages. If octal devices are used as clock buffers, then it is best to use no more than six of the drivers in the package and the six used should be the six nearest the ground pin (or pins). A good rule of thumb for the use of advanced Schottky TTL, advanced CMOS, or BiCMOS SSI gates, hex inverters, or octal buffers is the following: Limit the ac load to no more than 6 loads per driver and no more than 36 loads per package. The extra drivers in clock buffer packages should not be used for other purposes, since they may exhibit severe ground-bounce spikes during clock transitions. It is important that the extra drivers not be used for signals that might go to asynchronous inputs, such as flip-flop sets or resets, which are sensitive to spikes. In cases where multiple clock frequencies or phases must be used on a board, they should not be mixed in common buffer packages. Ground bounce from the higher-clock-frequency transitions may appear as spikes on the lower-frequency clock signals (see Fig. 8.1).

Waveshape control. When advanced Schottky TTL, advanced CMOS, or BiCMOS devices are used on boards of any significant size, some means of waveshape control must be used for clock lines. When actual routed line lengths are considered, clock signal lines on most boards will have propagation delays that will exceed one-half the rise time of the clock signal at its source (which is the common criterion for the beginning of significant transmission-line effects). Thus, on most boards some means of termination must be used to ensure clock waveshape control. The common board clock termination techniques are

Load termination

Source termination

Diode clamp termination

On circuit boards, it is impractical to limit clock lines to a single source and single load, which is the optimum configuration for terminating lines; multiple loads must be driven by drivers in all but the most trivial designs. A typical circuit board is populated with numerous clocked devices, such as flip-flops, counters, registers, shift registers, etc., all of which require clock signals. When synchronous design practices are followed, as they should be in most cases, all clocked devices on a board require the board clock signal. Thus, in most cases, board level clock distribution needs are such that a driver per load is not practical. The physical arrangement of the interconnections between clock sources and their multiple loads is important from a signal quality standpoint and must not be left to chance. Control of transmission-line effects requires an appropriate arrangement (from a transmission-line standpoint) of clock signal interconnections. In most cases, clock signal wiring must be connected serially from the source to the loads with no branches or stubs. Branches and long stubs complicate or defeat all transmission-line termination techniques.

Load termination. Load termination works best in most multiple-load situations, but in most board clock distribution applications it is impractical to load-terminate each clock line on a board. Load termination dissipates a great deal of power, and split load termination increases the system parts count. There are ac coupling schemes for load-terminating lines that reduce power dissipation, but these schemes require even more discrete components than normal direct-coupled load termination networks. Where board clock lines are load-terminated, they should be terminated so that they are slightly underdamped for optimum edge speed but not so underdamped that excessive ringing occurs. Underdamped signals have faster rise times and thus reach threshold levels faster than critical damped or overdamped signals do. A suggested range for termination impedance is 1.2 to 2 times the characteristic impedance Z_o of the line being terminated.

Source termination. Source or series termination is the most practical method of terminating board clock lines. Series or source termination works best when there is only one source and one load, and for that reason it would not seem suitable for board clock termination; but when all the issues are considered, the disadvantages of load termination outweigh the disadvantages of series termination at the board level. Series termination requires care in the physical placement of the loads; but when the placement requirements are understood, series termination works well.

Either ferrite shield beads or small-value resistors located near the driving source can be used to series- or source-terminated clock lines. Ferrite beads work best in most applications. Ferrite beads (see

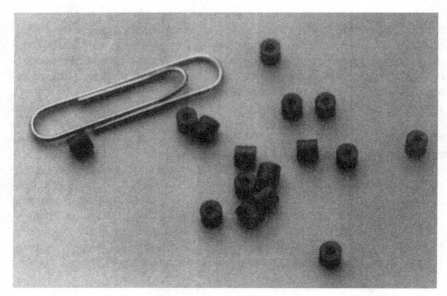

Figure 8.4 Ferrite shield beads of the type used for series-terminating clock lines.

Fig. 8.4), which are made of a lossy ferrite material, present little impedance to clock signals at low frequencies, but at high frequencies they act as small lossy impedances. When a shield bead is used for source termination, the terminated line must pass through the bead and the bead must be located very near the driver (as a rule of thumb, within 1 in). Beads with impedances from a few ohms to near 50 Ω at 100 MHz are available. Figure 8.5 shows a typical impedance-frequency profile for a shield bead. The bead impedance needed in a

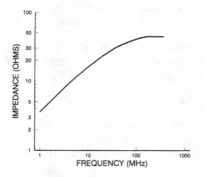

Figure 8.5 Impedance versus frequency for a ferrite bead of the type used for series-terminating clock lines (based on catalog data for Fair-Rite Products Corp. part number 2743019446). (*Reprinted with permission.*)

given application is set by the clock driver edge rates and circuit board characteristic impedance. When welded-wire or wire-wrap boards, which tend to have a characteristic impedance on the order of 100 Ω, are used, beads with an impedance near 50 Ω at 100 MHz should be selected. For clocks on printed-circuit boards, which typically have a characteristic impedance near 50 Ω, a 25-Ω bead at 100 MHz should be used. The desire is to not overdampen clock signals and thus not slow down edges too much. The goal is to remove enough energy to prevent excessive overshooting, which in turn will prevent undershooting of clock signals.

The disadvantage of series resistor termination of board clock lines is the reduced dc noise margin when TTL devices or devices with significant input current are driven. However, the reduction is generally very minimal for advanced CMOS or BiCMOS devices with CMOS inputs since most devices with CMOS inputs have very low direct input current (typically on the order of ± 10 μA or less), but caution must be exercised. The noise margin of clock lines can be compromised unless care is taken to evaluate the actual load in each given situation. For example, the *low*-level input current specification for BCT BiCMOS bus interface logic is 1.0 mA. Assuming six loads, the total dc load is 6 mA. If a 51-Ω series resistor is used, the drop across the resistor is 306 mV (6 mA × 51 Ω). A drop of 306 mV exceeds the *low* noise margin of all logic families with TTL levels (see Chap. 2) and cannot be tolerated. Thus, series resistors cannot be used in such an application, or much lower-value resistors must be used.

Series termination, with either shield beads or resistors, has the advantage of requiring only one discrete component per line and does not dissipate any extra dc power. Series termination does present one problem: When long lines are driven, signal transitions near the source will step up (or down), as shown in Fig. 8.6. Steps are caused by the voltage divider formed by the series termination and the line impedance. Thus, clock waveforms with steps are inherent near the source when long lines are source-terminated (see Chap. 7). The result

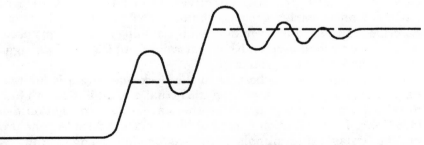

Figure 8.6 Source-terminated lines have an inherent step near the source that may ring and cause extra clocking.

is that signals may dwell for some time in the threshold region of receiving devices. When a step dwells in the threshold region of a device, double clocking of the receiving clocked device may occur due to ringing or noise riding on the intermediate logic level of the step. To avoid extraneous clocking, clock lines must be kept very short or loads must be grouped very closely at the end of lines (within 4 in is good).

Diode clamp termination.   If the clocked devices have high-speed diode clamps on their clock inputs, diode clamp termination is the simplest technique for terminating clock lines. No extra parts are required. Diode clamps or clamps constructed with other devices, such as transistors connected as diodes, control waveshape (when signals exceed the rails, that is, V_{cc} or ground) by removing the excess energy in the wavefront that causes the signal to exceed the rail. Without excess energy in the wavefronts, transmission-line ringing quickly subsides. However, not all devices have effective high-frequency clamps for signal levels beyond the normal static input operating range (transient levels greater than the supply or reference). Many parts have inputs with low-frequency parasitic diodes and electrostatic protection diodes, but low-frequency clamps are not effective at the frequencies in the wavefronts of interest. Effective clamping requires high-frequency diode or transistor networks that begin to conduct as signals exceed the power rails. When clamping circuits have an effective high-frequency impedance near or slightly less (but not much less) than the interconnection impedance and the breakpoint is near or within a diode drop of V_{cc} or ground, then input clamps control transmission-line ringing in most applications (see Chap. 7). However, if receiving devices do not have clamps or if the clamps are not effective at high frequencies, then severe ringing may occur. The problem for designers is that the transmission-line clamping effectiveness of the input diodes is usually not specified and some parts have good clamps and others do not. Most advanced Schottky TTL parts have effective clamps to ground but do not have clamps to V_{cc}. Clamps to V_{cc} are not needed for TTL-level signals since the signals typically do not swing to V_{cc}. The input clamping effectiveness of advanced CMOS and BiCMOS parts varies greatly. Clamping effectiveness testing as described in Chap. 7 is recommended if clamping is the means used to control clock signal quality. Note that rail-to-rail CMOS clock signals require clamps to both ground and V_{cc}.

Diode clamping works best when the clock line length is limited to near or only slightly greater than the actual critical line length [actual critical line length is based on the loaded-line propagation delay (see Chap. 7 for definition of critical line length and loaded-line propagation delay)]. For signals with 2-ns or slower edges, Table 8.1 shows the maximum usable clock line lengths for conventional PC

TABLE 8.1   Clock Signal Maximum Line
Length versus Number of Loads for Typical
PC Board Applications

Maximum length, in	Number of loads
7.5	1
7	2
6.5	3
6	4
5.5	5
5	6

boards for a usable range of ac loads (a load is defined as 5 pF). If the clock source has faster than 2-ns edges, the overall lengths should be reduced accordingly, but 2 ns is a reasonable value for most advanced Schottky TTL, advanced CMOS, and BiCMOS devices. Not all loads on a clock line have to have a clamp, but the last load on the line must have an effective clamp. The actual as-routed PC board track length from the first load (the one nearest the source) to the last load must meet the 4-in rule described for series termination.

Clock board power distribution.   Power distribution to board clock circuitry must conform to the best possible design standards. Each clock driver package should be decoupled with a high-frequency decoupling capacitor, such as a 0.1-μF ceramic, located as close as possible to the package and as directly as possible between the power and ground pins of the package. Clock drivers must be connected as directly as possible to the power and ground planes or grids of the host board. When welded-wire or wire-wrap boards are used, the clock driver package power and ground connections and decoupling capacitor connections must be made directly to the power and ground planes with solder clips or washers. Wiring should never be used for power or ground connections of clock circuitry; the inductance of wire connections aggravates ground-bounce problems.[6]

When board-to-motherboard connectors do not contain an adequate number of ground pins, or under other noisy reference conditions, some form of balanced differential connection to the clock source must be used to ensure a clean, noise-free board clock source. An inadequate number of grounds in board-to-motherboard connectors may cause board ground bounce (see Chap. 5), which may cause ground-bounce noise on the clock signals which may appear as extra clock pulses. Thus, where standard TTL-level or CMOS-level single-ended clock signals are used, a low-impedance reference path must exist between board reference planes and the motherboard reference plane, to prevent reference level shift in excess of single-ended TTL-level or CMOS-level noise margins when large load currents are switched.

Clock gating. Gating of board clocks should be avoided where possible, since gating the clock places severe restrictions on the timing of the gating signals relative to the clock. It is more desirable to gate a clocked element's control signals than the clock itself. However, when gating is required, two-level clock trees as shown in Fig. 8.3 provide a safe means of gating clocks. The intermediate level (CLK) can be safely gated with signals that originate from devices clocked with the final stage ($\overline{\text{CLK}}$) of the clock tree (see Fig. 8.7). No spiking occurs on the gated clock line since the control signal safely brackets the intermediate clock signal (CLK in Fig. 8.7). If boards are built with only one level of clock signal buffers, there are no easy means of ensuring that gated signals have the proper time relationship to nongated clock signals (gated signals will lag), nor are there means of ensuring that gate control signals bracket clock signals. Thus, gated clocks tend to spike.

Summary of board level clock distribution techniques

1. Use only a single clock frequency and single phase.
2. Use at least a two-level clock tree so that clocks can be safely gated where necessary.
3. Use the same type of devices (preferably devices in the same package) in each level of a clock tree.
4. Balance clock signal loads.
5. Centralize the distribution point for board clock lines.

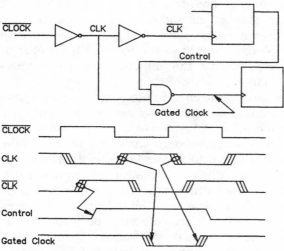

Figure 8.7 Two-level clock trees provide a safe means of gating clocks.

6. Keep clock lines short, or balance clock line lengths.

7. Limit the number of ac loads per clock driver package, to keep ground bounce within limits.

8. Do not mix clock frequencies, phases, or other signals in clock driver packages.

9. Provide a decoupling capacitor for each clock driver package as near as possible to the package power pins.

10. Directly connect power and ground pins of clock driver packages to board power and ground planes (no wiring).

11. Terminate all clock lines, to ensure high-quality clock signals.

12. Closely group all loads near the end of clock lines, to prevent false triggering due to edge steps near series-terminated board clock sources.

13. Isolate clock signal lines to minimize cross-coupling.

14. When devices with TTL input levels are used, use only those devices that clock on *low*-to-*high* transitions.

15. Avoid gating of clocks where possible, but if it is necessary, be certain that the phasing of the clock and the control signal is such that the gated clock will not spike.

8.3   Board-to-Board Clock Distribution

Board-to-board clock signal interconnections, where the individual circuit boards are referenced to a common backpanel or motherboard ground plane, are generally transmitted and received via single-ended devices. Single-ended interconnections are used for economical and practical reasons. Single-ended drivers are readily available at low cost, and single-ended interconnections use the minimum number of connector pins. However, providing the electrical environment needed for single-ended clock signals requires a great deal of effort. Single-ended advanced Schottky TTL, advanced CMOS, or BiCMOS devices do not have a great deal of noise margin, and board-to-board clock lines tend to be long runs that pass through noisy areas. When single-ended interconnections are used, it is essential that circuit board-to-motherboard connectors have an adequate number of properly distributed ground pins, to ensure low-impedance board-to-motherboard ground connections (see Chap. 5). Single-ended board-to-board clock signal lines must be properly terminated, and care must be taken in their routing to reduce the possibility of coupled noise. Noise on clock lines that run between boards is an all too common problem.

Clock signals for boards common to a backpanel or motherboard should all originate from a central source. In the typical application, the central source consists of a clock board that houses a master oscillator and a clock buffer tree to drive clocks to other boards on the common motherboard. In some applications, instead of housing an oscillator, the central clock board receives an externally generated clock and redistributes it to the local boards. In either case, an individual clock signal should be sent to each circuit board on the backpanel via a dedicated clock driver and receiver for each board in the unit, as shown in Fig. 8.8.

Clock signals should never be run to multiple boards when advanced Schottky TTL, advanced CMOS, or BiCMOS devices are used, owing to the difficulty of properly terminating multiple-board loads. If a clock signal is sent to multiple boards, when one or more boards (loads) are not present or when a board is extended out of the housing for troubleshooting purposes, then the physical arrangement is changed and the termination may no longer be effective. To achieve the clock signal quality needed for proper system operation, board-to-board clock lines must be properly terminated at all times when high-speed devices are used. Likewise, all systems must be designed so that they will operate when boards are absent or when extender boards are in use. All systems will have component failures or other faults, and therefore they must be able to operate with some number of circuit boards extended out of the housing for troubleshooting. The only practical way to achieve such a design is to send an individual clock line to each board. Each board should receive its clock signal with a single receiver that can be used to buffer and redrive the clock within the circuit board. Clock lines from the central source should

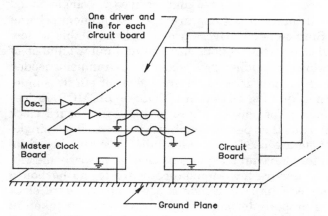

Figure 8.8 When clock signals are distributed to multiple boards, each board should have a dedicated driver and interconnecting line to prevent transmission-line effects from corrupting clock signals.

never be used to directly drive devices on circuit boards; such an arrangement is certain to degrade the clock signal and result in improper system functioning.

Great care must be taken in the routing of clock signal lines on backpanels or motherboards. Clock interconnections must be implemented with controlled impedance lines so that lines can be properly terminated and crosstalk can be controlled. On wire-wrap backpanels, clock lines should be run via coaxial cables, shielded twisted pairs, or at the very minimum twisted pairs with a ground wire, as shown in Fig. 8.9. The ground line in a twisted pair and the shield of a coaxial cable or shielded-twisted pair should be connected to ground at both the source and the load, as close as possible to the actual driver and receiver, to provide a direct return current path. However, in most applications it is not practical to run ground lines to the actual drivers and receivers on the circuit boards. A ground pin on the source and load circuit board-to-motherboard connectors near where the active clock line exits the source board and enters the load board is close enough for most applications. Coaxial cable, shielded twisted-pair, or twisted-pair interconnections provide a known and controlled characteristic impedance. Wire-wrap coaxial cable is available with a Z_o of 50 and 100 Ω, shielded-twisted pair with a Z_o of 75 to 100 Ω, and twisted-pair lines typically have Z_o in the range of 100 to 120 Ω. Where clock lines are not shielded, care must be taken to ensure that clock lines do not get bundled with other signals.

Care must be taken that board-to-board clock signal interconnections do not have significant discontinuities (in characteristic impedance) or large branches or stubs (which there should not be, since there should be only one source and one load). Large discontinuities, branches, or stubs can cause severe reflections which may degrade clock signal edges to the extent that false clocking occurs.

To control crosstalk, clock signal traces on printed-circuit motherboards must be physically isolated from other signals. If possible, they should be isolated in the vertical dimension by reference planes. In the horizontal dimension, line-to-line spacing between traces with different-frequency clock signals or between clock signals and other signals must be such that little coupling occurs. As a rule of thumb, the line spacing should be such that the coupling does not exceed 50 percent of the worst-case noise margin of the clock receivers. A clock

Figure 8.9 Twist clock lines with ground lines when wire-wrap backpanels are used to reduce interference and control impedance.

signal noise budget should be established for each design that includes an allowance for crosstalk.[7]

In all cases, board-to-board clock lines should be as short as possible, but where clock lines cannot be kept very short, all lines should be made equal physical lengths so as to match line propagation delays. To minimize the length of board-to-board clock lines, the clock source board should be located near the center of the motherboard or card cage. To minimize skew in active clock edges, all drivers and receivers should be of the same generic type and logic family, and the terminations and effective load at each receiving board should be the same.

When advanced Schottky TTL, advanced CMOS, or BiCMOS devices are used, clock lines that transition backpanels must be terminated to ensure clock quality. Such lines generally have two-way propagation delays that are long relative to the rise (or fall) times of the signals and hence must be treated as transmission lines. Either source or destination termination may be used for TTL-level clock signals. Each method has advantages and disadvantages, but destination termination as shown in Fig. 8.10 is recommended for most TTL-level applications. When CMOS devices with true CMOS input threshold levels are used, split termination can be used only if the driver has sufficient *high* output current to drive the split termination to the proper *high* CMOS input levels. Most CMOS board-to-board clock signals are source-terminated, as shown in Fig. 8.11.

Source termination can be implemented with small-value series

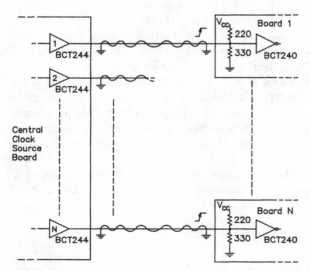

Figure 8.10 Recommended board-to-board clock distribution scheme when clock signals have TTL levels.

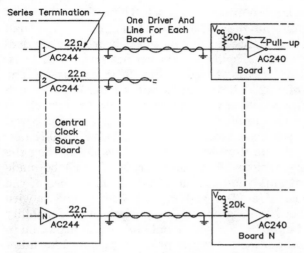

Figure 8.11 Recommended board-to-board clock distribution scheme when clock signals have CMOS levels.

resistors or ferrite shield beads located very near the driver. One advantage of series termination is that no additional dc power is dissipated due to the termination. However, in TTL-level applications, care must be taken to ensure that the *low*-level noise margin is not significantly reduced by series termination resistors. In applications where CMOS or BiCMOS devices with CMOS inputs are used, the dc drop across series-terminating resistors is not significant since CMOS inputs source or sink very little current. To minimize TTL-level noise margin loss and to provide underdamped signals, series termination resistors should be approximately one-third to one-half the line characteristic impedance Z_o. A value from 22 to 33 Ω is appropriate for most applications. The value should be low enough that the *low* state noise margin is not reduced by more than 50 to 100 mV. When the response of a source-terminated transmission is determined, the driver output impedance must be considered. The effective source impedance is the sum of the driver output impedance and the external series-terminating resistor.

Ferrite beads are recommended when TTL or other devices with bipolar inputs that have significant *low*-level input current are used and must be series-terminated.[8] Ferrite beads, with zero static (dc) impedance, eliminate possible dc offset problems, yet provide the needed amount of impedance at high frequencies.[6] They also help suppress electromagnetic interference.[9]

Destination termination of TTL-level backpanel clock lines is customarily implemented with split terminations (sometimes described as

Thevenin's terminations). For optimum response, Thevenin's equivalent impedance of split-termination networks should be slightly higher than the line characteristic impedance Z_o. For most PC board and welded-wire or wire-wrap applications, split-termination networks with resistor values of 220 and 330 Ω, as shown in Fig. 8.10, are used.[1] The equivalent impedance of a 220/330 Ω split termination is 132 Ω, which provides a near match for welded-wire or wire-wrap interconnections and approximately a 2-to-1 underdamped termination for PC board interconnections (which is acceptable in most cases); 220/330-Ω networks are available in standard multiple-resistor packages. When the impedance of split terminations is chosen, a tradeoff must be made between driver current sink requirements and the closeness of the match to line impedance. Most TTL, CMOS, or BiCMOS devices with TTL-level outputs do not have a great deal of current drive capability (i.e., *high* state drive), but do have high current sink capability when in the *low* state. Thus, termination networks must be optimized for minimum loading of the driver in the *high* state. Split termination accomplishes that purpose. No *high*-level static drive current is required when split-termination resistor values are properly selected. The divider effect of the split-termination network establishes the *high* level. In the *low* state the driver must sink a current equal to V_{cc} divided by the value of the termination network resistor connected to V_{cc} (220 Ω in the case of a 220/330-Ω network). When 220/330-Ω networks are used, the sink current is about 22 mA under nominal conditions. Since most standard CMOS or BiCMOS logic devices (NANDs, NORs, etc.) are only rated to sink 20 to 24 mA (depending on the logic family), drivers with high current capability, such as 240s or 244s, must be used to meet the current sink requirements of 220/330-Ω split terminations. The advantages of destination termination include these:

1. Coupled noise and crosstalk tend to be damped more quickly.

2. Edge rates do not degrade as much as they would under similar circumstances (line and load impedance) with source termination.

3. More than one device can be used to receive the signal (on the receiving board), which helps minimize board clock tree depth on large boards.

The disadvantages of destination termination include

1. Increased power dissipation

2. Higher current drive requirements placed on the driver

In most applications, the advantages outweigh the disadvantages. Thus, destination termination is commonly used for most board-to-board applications with TTL-level interfaces. Destination termination can be used on CMOS-level interfaces, but series termination is best in most cases.

With either source or destination termination, clock lines should be terminated so that they are slightly underdamped for optimum edge speed, but not so underdamped that excessive ringing occurs. Underdamped signals have faster rise times and thus reach threshold levels faster than critical damped or overdamped signals. A suggested range for termination impedance is 1.2 to 2 times the characteristic impedance Z_o of the line being terminated.

The phasing of TTL-level clock signals that traverse backpanels or motherboards should be such that the *low*-to-*high* transition of the clock signal is the system's active clock edge. Such a phasing will ensure that the clock lines are in the *high* state with maximum noise margin when the majority of system signals are switching. Systems with clock rates that are relatively slow, with respect to the minimum clock pulse-width requirements of the devices being clocked, should shape clock signals so that the logic *low* state is as short as possible, to further enhance the noise margin. Such an arrangement keeps clock signals in the maximum-noise-margin state for a longer time, thus allowing a longer time for system signals to transition and a longer time for noise due to delayed transitions to die out before clock signals go to the *low* state, which has less noise margin than the *high* state.

The need for a large number of well-distributed grounds in board-to-motherboard connectors is an issue that is often overlooked. It is important that the clock distribution board be solidly referenced to the motherboard ground plane, to ensure that the clock distribution board does not experience excessive ground bounce when all the clock drivers switch simultaneously. An admirable design goal is to provide an adjacent board-to-motherboard ground pin for each clock signal pin in the connector. In most cases that is not practical; connector-pin limitations often force a compromise in the number of ground pins. If a ground pin for each clock signal is not possible, a careful analysis must be performed to determine the number of ground pins required to keep board ground bounce within limits. The requirement is to keep clock distribution board transient reference level shifts due to ground bounce below the threshold level of the clock receiver (on the clock distribution board) and below the threshold of the most sensitive clock receiver or receiving devices on the boards receiving the distributed clock signals.

When board-to-motherboard connectors do not contain an adequate number of ground pins, or under other noisy reference conditions, some form of balanced differential connection to the clock source (if it is not on the central clock board) and loads must be used to ensure clean, noise-free clock signals. If standard TTL-level or CMOS-level interfaces are used, when board-to-motherboard connectors do not contain an adequate number of ground pins, noise may be injected into the clock signals and appear as extra clock edges. Thus, if single-ended clocks are used, a low-impedance reference path must exist between board reference planes and the motherboard reference plane to prevent reference level shift in excess of single-ended TTL or CMOS noise margins.

Summary of board-to-board clock distribution techniques

1. Centralize the source and distribution point for board-to-board clock signals.

2. Use a separate clock driver and clock line for each board.

3. Terminate all clock lines to ensure clock signal quality.

4. Use very short lines or make all lines equal to keep line propagation delays equal.

5. Use coaxial cable or shielded twisted-pair, or at the minimum twist each clock line with a ground line to control impedance and reduce coupling when wired backpanels are used.

6. To optimize noise margin, phase TTL-level board-to-board clock signals so that *low*-to-*high* transitions are in phase with the active edge of the clock at the component level.

7. Use the same type of device for all drivers to match propagation delays.

8. Use the same type of device for all receivers to match propagation delays.

9. Limit the number of drivers or receivers used in octal packages to keep ground bounce within limits.

10. Do not mix clock frequencies, phases, or other signals in clock driver or receiver packages, to prevent clock signal corruption due to ground bounce.

11. Provide a decoupling capacitor for each clock driver and receiver.

12. Directly connect power and ground pins of clock drivers and receivers to circuit board power and ground planes (no wiring).

8.4   Unit-to-Unit Clock Distribution

The interconnection of high-frequency clocks between physically separate units (i.e., between units that do not have a common backplane, backpanel, or motherboard) is one of the most difficult clock distribution tasks. When clocks must be sent between components not directly referenced to a common ground plane, the clocks must be transmitted by some means that provides a sufficient amount of noise tolerance for the application. In Chap. 4, high-frequency transient switching currents are shown to result in the generation of significant voltage transients across the inductance of a 1-in wire. It follows that the inductance of several feet of wire, as is generally required to interconnect separate units, will result in very large transient-voltage shifts that will exceed the noise margin of LV or 5-V single-ended advanced Schottky TTL, advanced CMOS, or BiCMOS devices with either CMOS or TTL levels. Thus, to prevent noise from corrupting clock signals transmitted between units, some form of transmission is needed that has a high level of noise rejection. Differential line drivers connected to differential line receivers with shielded twisted-pair cable, as shown in Fig. 8.12, are the common solution (see Chap. 9).

Most unit-to-unit interconnections are long transmission lines (see Chap. 7) and thus must be properly terminated to ensure clock signal quality. To allow proper termination, unit-to-unit clock signals must be transmitted via dedicated driver-receiver pairs connected with controlled-impedance twisted-pair lines. Unit-to-unit clock lines should be terminated so that they are slightly underdamped for optimum edge speed, but not so underdamped that excessive ringing occurs. Underdamped signals have faster rise times and thus reach threshold levels faster than critical damped or overdamped signals. A suggested range for termination impedance is 1.2 to 2 times the characteristic impedance Z_o of the line being terminated. Series termination is recommended for most unit-to-unit clock connections. Series termination provides short-circuit protection for drivers, dissipates less power than load termination, and reduces unit-to-unit current flow.

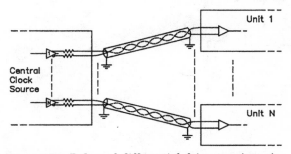

Figure 8.12 Balanced differential driver-receiver circuits are required for unit-to-unit clock distribution.

Summary of unit-to-unit clock distribution techniques

1. Centralize the source and distribution point for system clock signals.

2. Use balanced differential driver-receiver interconnections for noise immunity (single-ended interconnections are not adequate).

3. Use a separate driver and shielded twisted-pair line for each unit-to-unit clock.

4. Use a single receiver at the load.

5. Terminate all lines to ensure clock signal quality.

6. Use equal line lengths to balance propagation delays.

7. Use the same type of device for all drivers to balance propagation delays.

8. Use the same type of device for all receivers to balance propagation delays.

8.5   Test Clock Input Port

High-speed digital systems need some means of varying the clock frequency or frequencies during initial design verification and during test. A lower-frequency clock is often needed during initial checkout. A lower-speed clock allows fundamental logic errors to be separated from errors caused by transmission-line effects and from other complications caused by full-speed operation. A variable higher-frequency clock signal is needed to check for operating-frequency margin once a system is operational.

A circuit for injecting a test clock is shown in Fig. 8.13. The test port is activated when the control input is jumpered. Many other con-

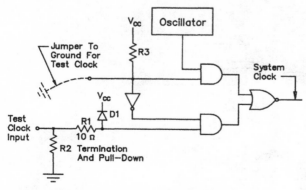

Figure 8.13 Typical test clock input circuit.

figurations are possible. A multiplexer will serve equally well. In all cases, clock switching circuit inputs connected to external test clock sources must be voltage- and current-limited to protect the clock switching circuit from overvoltage conditions likely to occur in test environments. For example, the test input port must be protected so that excess input current does not flow when the system V_{cc} is off and the test clock source is still on, or when the clock source signal amplitude is not properly adjusted. In the circuit in Fig. 8.13, resistor $R1$ limits the input current and diode $D1$ shunts current to V_{cc} in case of excessive signal amplitude or if the clock source is turned on when the system V_{cc} is not present. Test clock input ports must not float when the test clock is not present; a pull-up or pull-down resistor is required which can also serve as a termination for the external clock signal ($R2$ in Fig. 8.13).

8.6 References

1. David Royle, "Designer's Guide to Transmission Lines and Interconnections, Part Two," *EDN*, June 23, 1988, pp. 143–148.
2. S. Abramson, C. Hefner, and D. Powers, *Simultaneous Switching Evaluation and Testing Design Considerations*, Texas Instruments Inc., Dallas, Tex., 1987.
3. Robert B. Cowdell, "Bypass and Feedthrough Filters," *Electronic Design*, no. 17, August 16, 1975, pp. 62–67.
4. Tom Ormond, "Backplanes Play a Crucial Role in High-Speed Systems," *EDN*, July 10, 1986, pp. 222–228.
5. P. Anthony Visco, "Coaxing Top Bipolar Speeds from Prototyping Boards," *Electronic Products*, September 1, 1987, pp. 55–58.
6. Isidor Straus, "Designing for Compliance, Part 1: Design of the PC Board," *Compliance Engineering 1994 Reference Guide*, vol. 11, no. 2, Compliance Engineering, Boxborough, Mass., 1994, pp. 127–135.
7. *FAST Logic Applications Handbook*, National Semiconductor Corp., Santa Clara, Calif., 1990.
8. C. Parker, B. Tolen, and R. Parker, "Prayer Beads Solve Many of Your EMI Problems," *EMC Technology & Interference Control News*, vol. 4, no. 2, April–July 1985.
9. Ronald W. Brewer, "Suppress EMI/RFI from the Ground up," *Electronic Design*, PIPS special edition feature, March 28, 1991, pp. 73–86.

8.7 Bibliography

Bursky, Dave: "Eliminate Signal Skews with GaAs Clock Chips," *Electronic Design*, August 9, 1990, pp. 39–42.
CDC Clock-Distribution Circuits Data Book, Texas Instruments Inc., Dallas, Tex., 1994.
Clock and Timing Products Data Book, Applied Micro Circuits Corp., San Diego, Calif., 1992.
"GaAS Clock Drivers from Two Companies," *Electronic Products*, July 1992, p. 89.
Hanke, Chris, and Gary Tharalson: "Low-Skew Clock Drivers Maximize MPU Systems," *Electronic Design*, August 9, 1990, pp. 86–89.
Low Skew Clock Drivers and Programmable Delay Circuits, Motorola Inc., Phoenix, Ariz., 1993.

Swager, Anne W.: "Timing Techniques Help Signals Stay in Sync," *EDN,* February 17, 1992, pp. 81–88.

Tharalson, Gary: "Low-Skew Clock Drivers: Which Type Is Best?" *Electronic Products,* May 1992, pp. 85–92.

Timing Solutions, Rev. 4, Motorola Inc., Phoenix, Ariz., 1994.

Timing Technology Products Data Book, Cypress Semiconductor Corp., San Jose, Calif., 1993.

1994 High-Performance Logic Data Book, Integrated Device Technology Inc., Santa Clara, Calif., 1994, chap. 9.

Device, Board, and Unit Interfaces

Interface signal level requirements and interface circuit operating characteristics are linked to the stability of the ground reference system. If a low-impedance reference can be maintained between devices, single-ended interfaces are possible. If a low-impedance reference cannot be maintained, differential or high-level signal interfaces are required. In most systems, it is possible to maintain a solid ground reference at the component-to-component and board-to-board levels, but not at the unit-to-unit level. In most large systems, the physical spacing between units or other practical limitations prevent implementation of high-frequency low-impedance reference paths between units. Thus, the typical high-performance systems built with advanced Schottky TTL, advanced CMOS, or BiCMOS components uses the following electrical interfaces:

1. Single-ended TTL or CMOS levels for component-to-component and board-to-board communication

2. Balanced differential line drivers and receivers for high-speed unit-to-unit communication

3. High-level single-ended drivers and receivers for low-speed unit-to-unit communication

Noise is a particular concern for interconnections between physically separate units. Unit-to-unit interface circuitry must have the capability of operating properly in the presence of high levels of noise and dc reference offsets.

Single-ended interfaces. Most component-to-component and board-to-board connections are implemented with single-ended signal interconnections. Single-ended interconnections require the minimum possible number of interconnections (one), and single-ended driver-receivers are as simple as possible; thus single-ended communication minimizes complexity and cost. However, single-ended TTL- or CMOS-level communication is possible only when the interconnected components are referenced to a common solid ground plane (see Fig. 9.1). Thus, circuits and motherboards must have continuous ground planes with no cutout areas, and circuit board-to-motherboard connectors must have a sufficient number of evenly distributed ground connections that the circuit board ground plane appears as an extension of the motherboard ground plane.[1,2] Circuit board-to-motherboard ground connection inductance must be low enough that transient return currents do not shift the reference level of circuit boards beyond single-ended threshold limits.

> Single-ended TTL, CMOS, or BiCMOS signals must be referenced to a *solid common ground plane* for reliable communication.

The basic interface levels of advanced Schottky TTL, advanced CMOS, and BiCMOS devices are bounded by established standards, and there are only two basic standards in common use: TTL and CMOS levels (3.3-V device levels are approximately the same as TTL levels). In general, devices with TTL input and output levels are the best choice; TTL output swings create less noise than CMOS 5-V rail-to-rail output swings and dissipate less dynamic power. As the operating speed increases, there is less time for noise to die out and dynamic power becomes more and more of a concern, since it is a direct function of frequency. Other advantages of TTL levels include these: Many LSI and VLSI parts, such as memories, PLDs, etc., are not available with CMOS input or output levels. Much of the standard test equipment is designed for TTL levels. Use of TTL levels greatly increases the chances of finding an alternate part if the initially selected part is not available. Only where extra noise margin is needed, such as in clock signals, are CMOS levels a viable option.

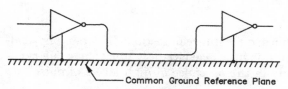

Common Ground Reference Plane

Figure 9.1 Single-ended TTL- or CMOS-level circuits must be referenced to a common ground plane.

9.1   Component-to-Component Interfaces

Once either TTL or CMOS interface levels are selected, the next task is to select devices with adequate drive. In general, static (dc) drive is usually not an issue in systems using advanced Schottky TTL, advanced CMOS, or BiCMOS components since dc input values for devices in these logic families are typically very small (less than ± 10 μA for CMOS and BiCMOS and less than 0.6 mA for advanced Schottky TTL). But caution must always be exercised—some advanced Schottky TTL and BiCMOS bus interface parts have 1-mA and greater input currents. However, ac drive requirements in high-performance systems are a complicated function of dynamic loading and transmission-line driving requirements and whether first incident wave switching is required (see Chap. 7).

9.1.1   Input level requirements

Failure to provide proper input voltage levels to TTL, CMOS, or BiCMOS devices may result in destructions of parts as well as logic malfunctions. Input levels that fall between logic *high* and *low* input limits and inputs that exceed V_{cc} or ground are both classified as improper inputs, and both can be destructive. In general, advanced CMOS parts with true CMOS inputs require inputs to have levels between ground and 30 percent of V_{cc} or between 70 percent of V_{cc} and V_{cc}, to ensure that one or the other of the MOSFETs in the input complementary structure is off. Advanced CMOS devices with TTL-level inputs (those designated ACT, FCT, etc.) and BiCMOS devices with CMOS input stages require inputs to have levels between ground and 0.8 V or between 2.0 V and V_{cc}, to ensure that one or the other of the MOSFETs in the input complementary structure is off. When input levels fall in the intermediate region, both MOSFETs in the input complementary structure may turn on and current flow from V_{cc} to ground through the input complementary structure can result in overheating of parts and possible eventual failure. For example, such a condition may exist when a device with TTL output levels is used to drive a device with CMOS input levels. A worst-case TTL minimum *high* output level, which is 2.5 V, does not fall between V_{cc} and 70 percent of V_{cc}. Hence, pull-ups or other circuitry are required on TTL-to-CMOS-level interfaces to ensure that inputs do not dwell in the danger zone. See Chap. 2 for interface level specifications.

When input levels exceed V_{cc} or go below ground by more than 0.5 V, even for a very short time or by a very small amount, some CMOS and BiCMOS devices can be damaged. When inputs or outputs exceed V_{cc} or ground, parasitic SCRs in electrostatic protection circuits can be triggered on, which can result in excessive V_{cc}-to-ground currents and destruction of parts. If input (or output) levels can exceed V_{cc} or ground when devices are powered, then some means of current limiting must be provided so that the current levels needed for SCR triggering are not reached (see Chap. 3). It is also important to limit current at interfaces where one side of the interface may be powered before the other side is. If current is allowed to flow into input (or output) protection networks of unpowered devices, those devices may latch up when power is applied. It is good practice to have some series resistance in circuit board or system interfaces to low-impedance sources or loads, to ensure that input or output current ratings are not exceeded.

9.1.2 Unused inputs

Unused TTL inputs. Unused TTL inputs fall into two basic categories:

1. Unused TTL inputs requiring a logic *low* should be tied directly to ground. The use of a pull-down resistor may shift the input level above a logic *low* level. If a pull-down resistor must be used for some reason, such as testability, then it must be sized to ensure that minimum *low* input level requirements are not exceeded.[3] *Don't-care* inputs are generally tied to a logic *low* level for simplicity of wiring.
2. Unused TTL inputs that require a logic *high:*
   a. Those that can be tied directly to V_{cc}. Unused inputs on AS, LS, ALS, and FAST devices, or other TTL devices that have real diode inputs, can be tied directly to the local $+V_{cc}$ supply voltage. No fundamental circuit principles are violated in doing so. However, current-limited static *high* input levels are safer than direct connections to V_{cc}. Current-limited *high* levels reduce the chance for damage due to accidental short circuits and enhance testability. Pull-up (current-limiting) resistors or inverters that have their inputs tied to ground can serve as sources of current-limited static *high* levels (normal loading limits apply). Pull-up resistors are used in most cases.
   b. Those that require current limiting. Standard TTL and S logic families that have multiple-emitter inputs require the use of a current-limited source of a static *high* input level. Pull-up resistors connected between the supply and the unused inputs needing to be pulled up can serve as a current-limited logic *high,* or a *high* output from an inverter with its input grounded can be used.

Input pull-up resistors are required for certain TTL families and not for others, depending upon whether the input structure consists of real diodes or multiple-emitter transistors. If the input circuitry consists of a multiple-emitter transistor, a current-limiting resistor is required. If the input network consists of real diodes, current limiting is not needed.

The advanced Schottky TTL logic families (AS, ALS, and FAST) as well as the older LS logic family have input circuits implemented with real diodes. An example of a diode input structure (that of a two-input FAST NAND gate) is shown in Fig. 3.1. Either standard silicon diodes or combinations of silicon and metal-silicon diodes are used, but in either case the diodes used are real diodes that do not interact with one another in unexpected ways.

When devices with real diode inputs are used, there is no reason from an electric circuit standpoint to use an external current-limiting pull-up resistor (there are reasons for doing so from a test standpoint and to decrease the chance for accidental V_{cc} short circuits to ground). Devices with real diode inputs have a maximum *high* input voltage limit equal to the V_{cc} supply voltage limit (7 V for most 5-V TTL devices). Thus, the power supply voltage range is not restricted when diode inputs are connected directly to the power supply. However, that is not the case with multiple-emitter inputs which are used on some of the older logic families. For example, most standard TTL and S TTL devices have multiple-emitter inputs. Multiple-emitter inputs are only specified for an absolute maximum input level of 5.5 V. If multiple-emitter inputs are connected directly to the supply, positive power supply voltage excursions must be limited to a maximum of 5.5 V. However, it is difficult to limit power supply excursions to 5.5 V. Thus, when standard TTL or S devices with multiple-emitter inputs are used, the safest approach is to current-limit inputs. Under no circumstance should production hardware using standard TTL or S logic devices be designed without some form of input current limiting.

Unused CMOS or BiCMOS inputs. Unused inputs on powered CMOS or BiCMOS devices must never be left open or floating; a valid *high-* or *low* logic level is required at all times.[4] Valid input logic levels are required

1. To ensure that input circuits do not oscillate and upset device operation or increase system noise levels
2. To ensure that inputs do not float into the undefined input region between a valid *high* and *low* logic level where both the pull-up *p*-channel and the pull-down *n*-channel complementary MOSFETs in the input stage both turn on, creating a low-impedance path between V_{cc} and ground that causes the device to overheat and be destroyed

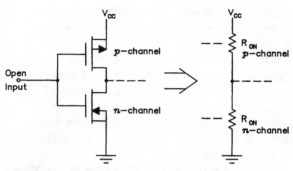

Figure 9.2 CMOS input stage and open input equivalent circuit.

Figure 9.2*a* shows a CMOS or BiCMOS input stage with an open input, and Fig. 9.2*b* shows the resulting equivalent circuit. The open input equivalent circuit is two resistors between V_{cc} and ground. The resistors represent the on impedance of the two MOSFETs. Since the on impedance of the MOSFETs used in advanced CMOS and BiCMOS devices is relatively low,[5] internal V_{cc}-to-ground paths initiated by open inputs can cause excessive internal device currents. Excessive internal current as a result of open inputs can cause overheating and destruction of parts. Even if the open input condition only lasts for a very short time, the device temperature is increased due to extra current flow. High device temperature increases the susceptibility of CMOS and BiCMOS parts to latch-up, which leads to additional high current flow and a greater possibility of device destruction. The time that a part can endure with an open input depends on the internal impedance of the device and other considerations, such as how deep into the internal circuitry the intermediate logic level propagates. In general, floating input conditions should not be allowed to last longer than a few microseconds. However, some CMOS and BiCMOS parts have specified minimum rise-time requirements that translate to more stringent requirements. In all applications, when CMOS and BiCMOS logic devices are used, minimum rise-time requirements must be determined and adhered to in the design. The typical profile for CMOS and BiCMOS device supply current versus input voltage is shown in Fig. 9.3.[6,7]

Unused inputs on used CMOS and BiCMOS devices should be pulled *high* or *low* as required for proper logic device operation. Unused inputs on unused devices can be connected to the most convenient level. Theoretically all advanced CMOS and BiCMOS device inputs can be connected directly to V_{cc} or ground; no current limiting is required from an input circuit operation standpoint. However, it is

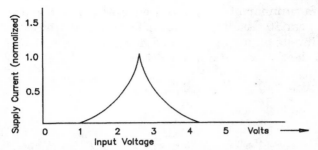

Figure 9.3   CMOS input stage supply current versus input voltage.

best to use a pull-up or pull-down resistor to facilitate test (a *high* or *low* input level can be injected) and to prevent the possibility of latch-up due to transient input current injection during power turn-on or under other transient supply conditions. Latch-up due to transient currents in inputs connected to low-impedance sources (such as V_{cc} or ground) is a known possibility with some of the older CMOS logic families. Latch-up should not be a problem when advanced CMOS or BiCMOS devices are used, but it is safer to current-limit connections to unused inputs.

Unused inputs that are often overlooked and are not pulled up or down include bidirectional ports, unused PAL or PLD inputs, and PAL outputs that serve as feedback paths. CMOS input structures must not float, not even for a short time, no matter what the terminal is called.

CMOS or BiCMOS inputs that connect directly to external sources must have pull-up or pull-down resistors so that they do not float in the absence of the normal source. Often during board or system test, not all input sources are present, and without pull-ups or pull-downs those CMOS or BiCMOS devices with open input lines will be damaged.

Techniques for tying off unused inputs

Pull-up or pull-down resistors.   A resistor tied to V_{cc} (hence, a pull-up) or a resistor tied to ground (hence, a pull-down) provides the simplest means of tying off unused inputs. A great number of inputs can be connected (tied off) with one pull-up or pull-down resistor without violating minimum *high* or *low* input level requirements, since input currents are very low, 1 to 10 μA, for most CMOS and BiCMOS devices. However, it is generally not wise, or practical, to tie too many points together. Troubleshooting a short-circuited line tied to a great number of points can be very difficult, and the longer the line, the greater the chance for coupled noise. Thus, for practical considerations, the maximum number of inputs pulled up by one resistor should be limited to near 10. Loading of pull-up or pull-down resistors (i.e., the number of inputs pulled up or pulled down by each resistor) should not approach the theoretical limit, which is

$$V_{cc\ min} - I_{in\ total} R_{pull-up} \geq V_{in\ high\ min}$$

for pull-up resistors and is

$$I_{in\ total} R_{pull-down} \leq V_{in\ low\ max}$$

for pull-down resistors. In most pull-up or pull-down applications, for either advanced CMOS or BiCMOS devices, 1-kΩ resistors are used. Higher values increase the chances for noise pickup (due to higher source impedance) and problems due to board leakage currents or defective devices with excessive input current.

Current-limited pull-up or pull-down voltages. Other connections that can be used to tie off unused inputs include these:

1. Tie unused inputs that require a *high* input to the *high* output of an inverter that has its input tied to ground.

2. When a current-limited *low* level is required, use the output of an inverter or a noninverting buffer that has its inputs tied to the appropriate level.

3. Tie unused inputs to used inputs that are functionally the same (on the same device), i.e., parallel inputs.

Paralleling inputs. When unused inputs are tied to used inputs (on the same device) that are functionally the same, the logical operation of the device is not affected and the unused inputs are prevented from floating. However, paralleling inputs can degrade dynamic performance. The capacitance load is increased, which can adversely affect high-frequency performance, and the noise margin may be reduced. Paralleling inputs parallels the capacitance associated with each input and increases the capacitance between the external signal source and the internal structure of the device. The increased capacitance increases the possibility of noise being injected into the internal circuitry of the device and upsetting it. Thus, paralleling inputs is not a good practice for high-speed devices.

9.1.3   Derating current drive specifications

In most applications where advanced Schottky TTL, advanced CMOS, or BiCMOS logic families are used in high-performance systems, the ac drive capability limits system operation rather than the dc drive considerations. However, care must be taken to not exceed specified device dc drive limits. In very critical high-reliability applications, manufacturers' dc output drive specifications should be derated and dc drive-limited accordingly. The input-output voltage levels and current load and drive ratings shown on most logic device data sheets are defined and tested under static conditions. It cannot be assumed that static ratings are adequate for all dynamic situations. If a part is not tested in a configuration exactly as the part is used, there is always some uncertainty as to how it may function. Drive derating is one method used to compensate for that uncertainty. Drive derating also helps compensate for device degradation with aging and worst-case combinations of electrical and environmental stress.

In benign applications, not exceeding manufacturers' ratings may be adequate to ensure a reliable design. However, in high-performance applications, it is best to not fully load devices so as to leave some margin for uncertainties. In critical applications, such as military or space applications, an extra allowance is needed to ensure that parts will function at the extremes of the operating voltage, frequency, and temperature ranges and with long-term aging and other degenerative effects. The typical derating criterion used for systems that must operate over the full military temperature range of -55 to $+125°C$ is to limit *fan-out,* or the actual load current of devices, to no more than 70 percent of the manufacturer's specified value. For space applications a derating factor of 50 percent is often used.

Circumstances where dc drive limits are often inadvertently violated include those where signals are load-terminated or where the load includes a large number of TTL or BiCMOS devices with bipolar inputs.

9.1.4 Increasing drive capability

When more drive is needed, either ac or dc, the most obvious technique is to split a heavily loaded signal into segments and use multiple devices to drive the separate segments. The next most obvious technique is to use high-current drivers. Finally, if subdividing the load or adding drivers is not practical or does not alleviate the problem, driver outputs can be paralleled.

Enhancement-mode field-effect transistors, as used in advanced CMOS logic devices, have a positive on impedance temperature coefficient, and as a result, paralleled CMOS outputs are self-regulating with respect to load sharing. For example, if a large portion of the load current is flowing in one of several paralleled outputs, then that output tends to heat up more than the other (paralleled) outputs, and as a result, its resistance goes up and its portion of the current goes down. Thus, paralleled CMOS devices tend to share the load. Still it is best to parallel CMOS devices only in a common package.

Outputs of TTL or BiCMOS devices on the same chip or drivers in the same package can be paralleled to increase fan-out capability when there is no other alternative for achieving the needed drive. However, bipolar devices do not have a built-in mechanism for equalizing the load current, as do CMOS devices. Thus, when one is paralleling TTL or BiCMOS drivers, it is important to do so only with drivers in a common package, so that the shared drivers have similar characteristics. Drivers in a common package can be expected to see nearly the same environmental conditions. They should see the same temperature and supply voltage. They should also have similar device characteristics due to common processing. Thus, TTL or BiCMOS drivers in a common package tend to share the load, whereas devices in different packages may not. Devices in different packages may have slightly different characteristics due to different processing and environment, and thus they are less likely to share the load. If the devices do not share the load, one device may be overstressed due to having to handle a large portion of the load (such a condition is sometimes referred to as *load hogging*).

Methods of increasing drive (fan-out)

1. Separate the load and use multiple drivers.
2. Use high-current bus interface drivers.
3. Parallel outputs of devices in the same package.

9.2   Board-to-Board Interfaces

At the board-to-board level (and on large boards), signal connections tend to be dominated by bus structures that have large distributed capacitance loads and long runs across backpanels or motherboards (or large boards). Thus, the effects of large loads and the transmission-line effects caused by long runs[8] must be taken into account in the selection of most interface circuits.

9.2.1   Bus interfaces

A number of 8-, 9-, and 10-bit-wide advanced Schottky TTL, advanced CMOS, and BiCMOS drivers, latches, transceivers, and registers that are commonly designated as bus interface devices are available.

Standard AC and ACT 240 series drivers, 373 latch, 245 transceiver, and 374 register fall into the bus driver classification, but there exists a wide variance in drive capability depending upon the manufacturer. For example, National FACT AC or ACT 240, 245, 373, and 374 are specified for $\pm$ 24-mA output drive. Yet, devices with the same basic letter and number designations from other manufacturers are specified for higher current drive (at least for I_{OL}). Most devices described as bus interface devices tend to have I_{OL} ratings of 48 to 64 mA and I_{OH} ratings of 12 to 24 mA depending upon whether output *high* levels are TTL or CMOS; if TTL, the I_{OH} current rating tends to be on the low end of the listed range. For example, BCT BiCMOS bus interface logic is specified for an I_{OL} of 48 or 64 mA and an I_{OH} of 12 or 15 mA depending upon whether the device is intended for military or commercial operation. However, that is not a universal situation; Advanced Micro Device's 29C800 bus interface family is only specified for an I_{OL} of 24 mA and an I_{OH} of 15 mA.

The main issue in the selection of interface circuits is ac drive, not dc drive, and whether first incident switching is required (first incident wave switching occurs when the initial signal launched into a transmission line is of sufficient amplitude to cross the threshold of the receiving device or devices). Unfortunately, most device manufacturers do not specify dynamic drive. A few list typical values, but typical values are of limited use; guaranteed dynamic specifications are needed. Some progress is being made in that direction; the FACT databook[7] states, "...steps have been taken to guarantee incident wave switching on transmission lines with impedances as low as 50 ohms for the commercial temperature range and 75 ohms for the military temperature range." Certain vendors' advertisements for their BiCMOS bus interface logic claim first incident wave switching. Yet, individual data sheets do not specify dynamic drive.

Drive requirements for buses are complicated functions of the characteristic impedance Z_o of the bus, the location of the loads tied to the bus, and the response needed of the bus. If the bus has a long time for the signals to reach final values, then drive requirements are of little concern; but high-performance systems usually do not have a long time for buses to settle. If the effective impedance of a bus is low relative to the output impedance of the bus driver, then it will take a number of reflections between the ends of the bus and the active source for the bus to charge to a final value (see Fig. 9.4). A bus that requires a number of reflections to reach final value has less than optimum performance (i.e., it takes it a long time to settle).

It is difficult to maintain 50-Ω effective impedance in multiplayer printed-circuit boards (see Chap. 6). The typical intrinsic impedance of multilayer printed-circuit boards tends to be in the neighborhood of

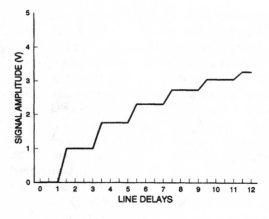

Figure 9.4 Heavily loaded bus signal transitions typically consist of a number of steps instead of smooth, fast transitions.

50 Ω, but buses with distributed loads have an effective impedance Z_o' given by Eq. (6.3) as

$$Z_o' = \frac{Z_o}{\sqrt{1 + C_{\text{LOAD}}/C_{\text{LINE}}}}$$

where C_{LOAD} is the total lumped capacitance of each device connected to the line and C_{LINE} is the total line capacitance (see Chap. 6). It is not uncommon for the effective impedance of bused lines or other lines that connect to numerous locations to be reduced to one-half the intrinsic unloaded impedance.

When line impedance is in a reasonable range and the bus drivers have adequate drive for the application (neglecting other potential transmission-line effects), a bus should take only two line delays (down and back) to settle. However, most present bus interface device specifications do not have sufficient information to allow an assessment of their actual in-circuit worst-case dynamic performance. Even when one assumes the best case (i.e., down and back), it is difficult to achieve 20-MHz or greater bus operation on large printed-circuit boards, but it can be done if the number of loads is limited. It is even more difficult to achieve 20-MHz or greater bus operation on board-to-board interfaces—particularly if it is a requirement that boards must operate on extender boards. In either case, a careful analysis using the bus driver dynamic information that is available or reasonable assumptions for bus driver dynamic characteristics is needed to establish the worst-case operating speed. Optimistic bus operating-speed projections based on typical or *hoped for* characteristics without an understanding of the many issues that affect bus speed are sure to lead to unreliable bus transfers.

9.2.2   General requirements for three-state buses

Three-state signals (buses) should not be allowed to float when unused. Floating lines tend to drift into the threshold region of the receiving circuits, and noise or other disturbances that are coupled into the line tend to cause the input structures of the receiving devices to oscillate. The oscillation tends to increase the overall system noise, particularly on the power and ground distribution systems; often the noise will reach unacceptable levels. Acceptable solutions are always to drive three-state lines or provide pull-up resistors to ensure that lines do not float near the threshold level of the receiving devices when not driven. The disadvantages of pull-up resistors include added parts and power dissipation. Selecting a pull-up resistor value is often difficult; a tradeoff between power dissipation and rise time of the line when it is not actively driven (i.e., when it is being pulled up) must be made. The use of too large pull-ups, to reduce power dissipation, may do more harm than good. Large-value pull-up resistors on lines with large capacitance loads may allow lines to remain in the critical noise-generating area near the threshold region of the receiving devices for long times. Furthermore, large-value pull-up resistors may pull signals into the threshold region that might have remained near their last active level had they not been influenced by a pull-up resistor. When power dissipation is a concern and low-value pull-up resistors cannot be used, it may be best to always drive three-state lines *high* before releasing the lines (which lets the drivers go into a high-impedance state). If three-state lines are driven *high,* then high-value pull-up resistors can be used to hold three-state lines *high.* Another alternative is to use *bus-hold* circuits or transceivers with built-in bus-hold circuits. Bus-hold circuits or devices with bus-hold circuits have low-current feedback paths that keep signals in their existing state in the absence of an active source.

Three-state drivers tied to a common line must be controlled in such a manner that contention is avoided (i.e., no more than one driver can be turned on at the same time, even for short periods during power turn-on or turnoff). The safest method of avoiding contention is to use a single hardware decoder as the source of the enables for all drivers connected to a common line; then only one driver can be on at one time (unless there is some fault). Where a single decoder for the source of all the line driver enables (for a common line or bus) is not practical, which is often the case in large systems with bus interconnects that interface to numerous units, other steps must be taken to minimize the chance for contention. For example, the system reset signal should be used to ensure that storage elements that are the source of control signals for three-state drivers are initialized to the off state during power supply transients and at power turn-on. To further ensure proper three-state driver initialization, only storage elements with dc resets should be used. Requiring the presence of the system clock, which may not always be present, due to faults or other reasons, for correct initialization of three-state buffers is an invitation to contention and part failures. Most advanced Schottky TTL, advanced CMOS, or BiCMOS three-state buffers are not rated for continuous short-circuit conditions. When buses go to multiple boards, the bus systems should be designed so that the removal of a board or unit will not result in more than one set of the remaining drivers being turned on.

9.3 Board and System Interface Guidelines

In high-speed systems, input signals to boards, racks, or systems should be received at only one place, to minimize ac loading and transmission-line effects. Signals routed to multiple devices on multiple boards have little chance of settling in a clock period as clock speeds go above 20 MHz. Output signals that are used internally and externally to a board or unit should be buffered before they are used externally to isolate the internal signals from transmission-line reflections or other external disturbances, such as short circuits, that might occur external to the unit. Signals routed to test points should be buffered to prevent test equipment from interfering with normal system operation. The transmission-line effects of long lines to test equipment are sure to corrupt internal signals, given the fast edge transitions of advanced Schottky TTL, advanced CMOS, or BiCMOS devices. In particular, a buffered clock source should be provided for logic analyzers or other test devices so that (1) clocks to test equipment can be appropriately terminated and (2) long test lines do not corrupt internal clock signals. The outputs of unbuffered clocked devices (registers, counters, flip-flops, etc.) should be buffered before being sent out of (or off) a unit (boards, boxes, etc.). Line reflections have been known to upset and change the output state of unbuffered clock elements. Most advanced Schottky TTL, advanced CMOS, or BiCMOS clock elements have built-in output buffers, but many of the older logic families do not. Devices with three-state outputs have built-in buffers due to normal three-state buffer implementation techniques.

Asynchronous input signals should never be run to multiple clocked devices within a functional unit; some of the devices within the unit may sense (sample) the signal at a slightly different time due to different line lengths or clock phasing at the multiple receiving points, and the unit may react incorrectly. When asynchronous parallel buses must be received and synchronized in a unit, it is best to capture and synchronize the bus control or strobe signals rather than to *broadside*-synchronize the entire bus. There is no assurance that all the signals on a wide bus will be properly captured when the data happens to be changing at the same time as the clock is asserted on the receiving storage elements.

Single-ended signals that traverse noisy areas, such as motherboards, should be received by devices with enhanced noise margin where practical. Some of the bus interface devices, such as the 240 and 244 buffers, are advertised as having input hysteresis and a slight bit more noise margin than standard gates. However, that is not a universal characteristic of all 240, 244, etc., buffers in all TTL, CMOS, or BiCMOS families. Schmitt trigger buffers such as the 54AC14 or 54ACT14 have higher than normal levels of noise immunity and are capable of operating with slowly changing input levels, and thus they are useful at noisy interfaces with badly corrupted signal waveforms. CMOS levels provide more noise margin than TTL levels and should be considered for critical signals such as clocks. When devices with TTL input levels are used, control signals that traverse noisy areas, such as motherboards, should have their logic polarity configured so that the predominant state (inactive state) is a *high* level. A *high* TTL level has a higher noise margin than a *low* level.

9.4 Board and System Interface Protection

Isolated board or system interface signals that connect directly to CMOS or BiCMOS devices with CMOS inputs or outputs offer the potential for a number of device faults. External connections increase the probability of exposing sensitive CMOS inputs or outputs to out-of-range dc or transient voltages which may induce latch-up. External connections also increase the probability of damage due to static electricity. Today's parts have much higher immunity to latch-up and electrostatic damage than earlier devices, but it is still a prudent design practice to add shunt low-impedance paths to V_{cc} or ground and series current-limiting resistors (see Fig. 3.17) to all external board or unit input signals that connect to CMOS inputs.[9] Shunt low-impedance paths help prevent electrostatic buildup when boards or units are isolated (e.g., when a board is out of the chassis). When a unit is in place and powered, shunt resistors prevent open inputs from floating. Series current-limiting resistors provide a means of controlling static and transient currents due to overvoltage or other abnormal conditions. Signals that overshoot or undershoot V_{cc} or ground can induce latch-up if excessive current is injected into device inputs. Series resistors are also necessary to limit input currents in applications where signal sources may be powered while receiving devices are not. In all CMOS interface applications, input currents under abnormal or worst-case transient conditions must be kept below actual specified device limits. Absolute maximum dc input limits for most CMOS logic devices are in the 20- to 30-mA range. Transient limits for most advanced CMOS and BiCMOS devices are typically near 100 mA; but caution must be exercised—some CMOS devices may latch up with injected currents as low as 10 mA.

Outputs may need series current-limiting resistors to prevent excessive output currents under abnormal conditions, such as short circuits, transients, or large transmission-line reflections. Outputs tend to be more sensitive to latch-up than inputs; i.e., outputs latch up at a lower current. In applications where high-speed signals must cross external board or unit boundaries, series current-limiting resistors may cause excessive RC delays. However, if it is not possible to use series current-limiting resistors and the possibility of excessive static or transient output currents exists, then other steps must be taken to control the situation.

9.5   Signal Interfaces between Remote Units

At the unit-to-unit level, significant ac and dc differences in the reference (ground) potential of the various units will generally be present. Furthermore, signals that are routed between units are usually exposed to a more hostile noise environment than signals that remain internal to a given unit or subsystem. Thus, communication between separate units where the actual transmitting and receiving components are *not* directly referenced to a common reference plane, such as the ground plane of a board, motherboard, or backplane, requires a signal transmission means that has a high level of noise tolerance. More noise immunity is required than is provided by standard single-ended devices with either TTL or CMOS levels. Single-ended TTL- and CMOS-level devices do not have enough noise margin to function reliably unless both the driving and the receiving devices are directly referenced to a continuous common ground plane, which is not possible for drivers and receivers that are in separate units. As shown in Chap. 4, TTL-level signal switching currents produce transient voltages across a 1-in wire that greatly exceed the static TTL *low*-level noise margin, and CMOS signal level switching currents are even worse. Thus, transient differences that exceed TTL or CMOS levels are to be anticipated between units that require several feet of wire to interconnect.

Signals transmitted between remote devices (i.e., devices not tied directly to a continuous common ground plane) must be transmitted by some method that will function reliably in the presence of high levels of noise and offset voltages. Single-ended TTL or CMOS levels are not adequate.

9.5.1 Differential unit-to-unit signal transmission

Balanced differential networks are one means of transmitting data between units. A balanced differential interface network consists of a differential line driver connected to a differential receiver by a twisted pair or a shielded twisted pair of wires. Differential receivers are insensitive to the absolute input voltage. Data is conveyed by the polarity of the voltage difference between the two inputs, not by the absolute input voltage levels.[10] Differential communication links are not upset by source or destination reference offsets which often occur as the result of dc or ac current flow in the ground reference system, since reference offset voltages appear common to both lines of a differential interunit connection (see Fig. 9.5). Also, most coupled noise appears equally on both lines of a differential connection[11] and is rejected since it is common to both lines. However, to minimize the coupling and keep the coupling below the common-mode rejection limits of the receivers used, shielded twisted-pair lines should be used in most applications, particularly for clocks and edge-sensitive interfaces.[12]

Balanced differential signal transmission has the added advantage of generating little noise in the ground system. The transient line voltages and currents tend to be equal and opposite and thus cancel. Thus, balanced differential communication between units limits the noise pollution of the local environment. Two standards used for differential communication links are the Electronic Industries Association (EIA) standard RS-422[13] for point-to-point links and RS-485 for bused differential links.

Differential unit-to-unit drivers and receivers. Figure 9.6 shows a series-terminated RS-422 unit-to-unit differential interconnection using a CMOS 26C31 driver and a 26C32 receiver. The 26C31–26C32 driver-

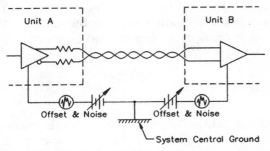

Figure 9.5 Balanced differential unit-to-unit interconnections are used to minimize possible unit-to-unit signal corruption caused by noise and offset voltage on the grounding system.

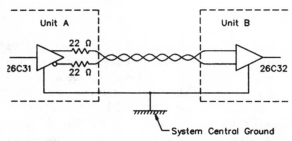

Figure 9.6 Differential drivers and receivers that meet the requirements of RS-422 are often used for differential communication between units.

receiver pair (available from National Semiconductor Corp.) meets the requirements of RS-422.[13] Those requirements include ± 7 V of common-mode capability and 0.2-V input sensitivity. In benign applications, it is possible to operate the 26C31–26C32 pair in the 30- to 40-MHz (actual signal frequency) range. However, the operating frequency is dependent on a number of factors, such as the interconnecting cable length, cable impedance, allowable error rate, etc., all of which must be carefully evaluated for each application.

Very high-speed differential unit-to-unit drivers and receivers.   For communication between separate units at, or near, the upper frequency limits of advanced Schottky TTL, advanced CMOS, or BiCMOS devices (i.e., in the data rate range of 80 to 100 Mbits/s—40- to 50-MHz clock rates), there are no off-the-shelf TTL, CMOS, or BiCMOS differential drivers or receivers. If data must be transferred at very high rates, then differential ECL line drivers and receivers or custom circuits are required. However, the common-mode noise rejection capability of ECL receivers (approximately ± 1 V) is marginal for most unit-to-unit applications. Where higher common-mode noise rejection capability is needed, high-speed bipolar analog comparators with input divider networks to increase the common-mode range are a possible solution, but care must be taken in their selection. In general, ECL drivers and receivers are required for operation above 50 MHz.

9.5.2   Low-speed unit-to-unit signal transmission

For very low-speed (less than 20 kbits/s) data transmission between separate units, single-ended driver-receiver pairs, as shown in Fig. 9.7, with signal levels that conform to the EIA standard RS-232[14] are the most common interface. RS-232 interfaces are intended for short cables (less than approximately 50 ft or 15 m). However, the

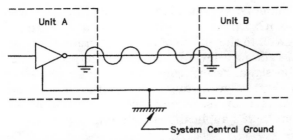

Figure 9.7 Single-ended drivers and receivers that meet the requirements of RS-232 are often used for low-frequency unit-to-unit communication.

baud rate (i.e., bits per second) and cable length can be traded off—the shorter the cable, the higher the baud rate.

Single-ended RS-232 levels are considerably larger than TTL or CMOS signal levels, and the greater the difference in the signal level and the switching threshold, the greater the immunity to noise. Worst-case minimum RS-232 *high* and *low* levels are + 5 and −5 V, respectively. Typical levels are + 9 and −9 V. The switching threshold of RS-232 receivers is near ground. The large difference between worst-case signal levels and receiver input threshold levels is sufficient to provide an acceptable amount of noise margin for most unit-to-unit applications. Large signal swings provide good noise immunity, but large signal swings have disadvantages; the slew rate must be kept slow, or else large signal swings will create a great deal of noise. The RS-232 specification defines a maximum slew rate for the specific purpose of minimizing switching edge-induced noise.

The original RS-232 driver, the 1488, required external ± 12-V supplies which complicated its use, but there are now a number of RS-232 driver-receivers from a number of manufacturers (Linear Technology, MAXIM, Motorola, and Texas Instruments) with on-board dc-to-dc conversion. Parts are available in a number of different combinations of driver and receiver within a package and with or without on-board dc-to-dc converters. For most applications, some subset of the various device configurations usually provides the exact number of receivers and transmitters required.

RS-232 interfaces require a common ground connection between units. Each unit should have a solid connection to earth ground to ensure that a unit does not float to a potential that might damage the transmitters or receivers. Floating units often take on a static charge or drift toward the ac line potential; RS-232 interfaces cannot withstand 110 V. Ideally, from a dynamic standpoint, each single-ended unit-to-unit signal should have an accompanying ground return line. Ground return lines are required to provide a direct low-impedance path for signal return currents. However, caution must be exercised when direct unit-to-unit ground connections are made.[15] Consideration must be given to the effects of interunit ground connections on overall system reference level integrity. Large ground loop currents may flow in the signal return connections, unless care has been taken in the overall system grounding to ensure that large offset voltages do not exist between units.[16] References 17 and 18 give a great deal of guidance on RS-232 applications including standard pin-outs and connector types.

9.5.3 Very low-speed unit-to-unit signal transmission

In some digital systems, a large number of very low-frequency (near dc) bilevel signals from mechanical switches, relays, solenoids, or other such external sources must be received and translated to the system internal logic levels. Signals from electromechanical devices are generally very noisy and often have large transient excursions. Yet, often little attention is given to the special interface needs of such signals. In many instances, receivers without adequate noise rejection are used with the apparent assumption being that noise is not a problem when the signal frequency is low. External signals, even if their frequencies are near dc, must be received in such a manner that unambiguous logic decisions are possible, and in such a manner that noise-accompanying signals, or signal references, do not propagate into the receiving system. Cost considerations and the need for simplicity often dictate that such signals be received with single-ended receivers. Single-ended receivers complicate the task of receiving noisy signals. If single-ended communication is used for external interfaces, signal levels must be large enough that signals can be distinguished from noise, or else signals must be heavily filtered to remove noise. Single-ended TTL or CMOS levels are inadequate for noisy external sources not solidly referenced to the same ground as the receiver.

Very low-frequency high-level receivers. High-input impedance CMOS buffers or BiCMOS buffers with CMOS input circuits are ideal for many low-frequency receiver applications. The intrinsic high input impedance of CMOS input stages provides a high level of isolation between source and load and allows the use of a number of filtering techniques that are not possible with bipolar input stages (*caution—* some BiCMOS devices have bipolar input stages). Buffers with high input impedance allow the use of very high-impedance input divider-filter networks (bipolar input stage current requirements severely restrict the signal source impedance). For example, a CMOS Schmitt trigger buffer preceded by a divider-filter network, as shown in

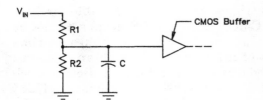

Figure 9.8 Circuit for receiving high-level low-frequency signals.

Fig. 9.8, provides a simple, inexpensive means of receiving noisy, low-frequency, high-level external signals and translating them to TTL or CMOS levels.

The input divider allows signals with level changes greater than the Schmitt trigger buffer threshold voltages to be reduced to levels compatible with the buffer input requirements, and by adjusting the divider ratio, a large range of input levels can be received. For example, bilevel signals, such as those that might originate from 12- or 28-V relays or solenoids, are easily translated to levels compatible with 5-V powered CMOS Schmitt trigger input requirements. The maximum input level is limited only by practical considerations, such as limiting voltages in digital units to safe and reasonable levels. Minimum input signal levels must at least exceed the threshold limits of the receiving CMOS Schmitt trigger buffer. Both minimum and maximum *high* and *low* signal levels must be considered in the selection of the divider network ratio, to ensure that normal signal level variations at the divider output are sufficient to ensure switching but do not significantly exceed V_{cc} or ground. However, if the divider input resistor $R1$ is large enough, then V_{cc} or ground can be exceeded without harm to the buffer. The resistance of $R1$ must be such that under all overvoltage or transient conditions the current injected into the CMOS buffer input protection circuit is less than the specified limits for the device. High-impedance input divider-filter networks also serve a number of other purposes:

1. They reduce the loading of the source.

2. They limit ground currents.

3. They limit fault or transient input currents injected into the receiving CMOS buffers to safe levels.

4. Heavy filtering of signals is possible with small-value capacitors and thus physically small capacitors.

Since filtering will slow the rise times of signals at the buffer input, buffers with minimum rise-time requirements cannot be used in such applications. Only devices that can tolerate slow rise-time inputs, such as 74/54AC14 Schmitt trigger buffers, are suitable for such applications. Most advanced CMOS and BiCMOS devices cannot be used in such applications since most have minimum rise-time requirements. Since speed is of little concern in such applications, advanced CMOS or BiCMOS devices are not required. Devices such as 4009 or 4010, or 4049 or 4050 level translator buffers, or 54HC14 Schmitt trigger buffers from the older logic families are adequate for most applications.

9.5.4 Unit-to-unit line terminations

Series (source) termination should be used for most unit-to-unit interconnections (see Fig. 9.6). Series termination provides short-circuit protection and does not increase static power dissipation, as load termination does. For optimum response, the value of the terminating resistors (plus the output impedance of the driver) should be chosen so that the line is slightly underdamped, but not too much. A line that is slightly underdamped will provide a signal at the load that reaches the threshold region of the receiver more quickly than a line that is exactly matched or overdamped. The key to successful operation and optimum performance is to not underdampen the line so much that it rings back into the threshold region of the receiving device.

9.5.5 Miscellaneous unit-to-unit considerations

All unit-to-unit signal cables must include ground lines for signal return currents. When single-ended high-level interunit communication is used (low-level single-ended signals should never be used), there should be one ground line per signal line. When balanced differential interunit communication is used, one ground line per four to eight signal pairs is a good rule of thumb. If differential signals are perfectly balanced, then no return ground lines are needed—but differential signals are never perfectly balanced. Thus, some grounds are needed to provide a direct return path for the unbalanced portion of the signal currents. However, direct unit-to-unit ground connections offer the potential for large ground loop currents (see Fig. 6.1). Thus, when unit-to-unit signal grounds are required to ensure a low-impedance path for signal return currents, care must be taken to ensure that all units have low-impedance ground connections to prevent large interunit reference voltage offsets and large ground-loop currents. If large offset voltages exist between units, ground current in the signal return lines can be great enough to disrupt system operation by introducing noise[15] and in severe cases overheat and burn out the signal return lines.

Communication between remote units generally must incorporate some form of asynchronous data transfer technique, since clock alignment between remote units is usually difficult to achieve or maintain.

9.6 Summary of Interface Guidelines

1. Communications between units mounted on a common uninterrupted reference plane can be single-ended; but care must be taken in the signal routing to limit crosstalk, and edge-sensitive signals must be properly terminated.

2. Single-ended signals that have very slow rise times should be received with Schmitt trigger buffers that have hysteresis such as 54F14s or 54AC14s that can tolerate slow input signal transitions.

3. Communications (both analog and digital) between racks or units within a rack that are not solidly referenced to a common uninterrupted ground plane should use some form of balanced differential communication with sufficient common-mode rejection capability for the application.

4. Input signals to boards, racks, or systems should be buffered at one place so as to minimize ac loading (minimizing ac loading is essential in high-speed systems).

5. Asynchronous input signals should never be run to multiple clock devices within a functional unit; some of the devices within the unit may sense (sample) the signal at a slightly different time due to different line lengths or clock phasing at the multiple receiving points, and the unit may react incorrectly.

6. When asynchronous parallel buses must be received and synchronized in a unit, it is better to capture and synchronize the bus control or strobe signals than to try to broadside-synchronize the entire bus. There is no assurance that all signals on a wide bus will be properly captured when data happen to be changing at the same time as the clock is asserted on the receiving storage elements.

7. Signals that are used internally and externally to a board or unit should be buffered before they are used externally, to isolate the internal signals from transmission-line reflections or other external disturbances, such as short circuits, that might occur external to the unit.

8. When devices with TTL input levels are used, control signals that traverse noisy areas, such as motherboards, should have their logic polarity configured so that the predominant state (inactive state) is a *high* level since *high* TTL levels have higher noise margin than *low* TTL levels.

9. The output of unbuffered clocked devices (registers, counters, flip-flops, etc.) should be buffered before it is sent out of (or off) a unit

(boards, boxes, etc.). Line reflections have been known to upset and change the output state of unbuffered clocked elements.

10. Signals routed to test points should be buffered to prevent test equipment from interfering with normal system operation. In particular, a buffered clock source should be provided for test equipment.

11. Three-state signals (buses) should not be allowed to float when unused. Floating lines tend to drift into the threshold region of the receiving circuits, causing receiving devices to oscillate and increasing system noise. Receivers with CMOS input stages may go into an excessive-current condition that can lead to device destruction.

12. Three-state drivers on a common line should be controlled in such a manner that no more than one driver can be turned on at the same time, even for short periods during power turn-on or turnoff, to prevent burnout.

13. Three-state bus controls should be designed so that the removal of a board or unit will not result in more than one set of bus drivers being turned on.

14. On multiple-drop buses (i.e., buses that go to multiple boards, cabinets, racks, etc.), the bus interface circuits must not load (clamp) the signal lines when power is not applied to a unit.

15. Unused inputs on used or spare devices must not be allowed to float, to prevent oscillation and excessive system noise or excessive current flow in CMOS input stages.

16. Inputs to CMOS and BiCMOS devices must never be allowed to float, to prevent excessive internal feedthrough current flow and burnout.

17. Static pull-up or pull-down voltage sources for unused CMOS or BiCMOS inputs should be current-limited to reduce the chance of transients inducing latch-up.

18. Board or system interface connections to CMOS or BiCMOS inputs must have pull-up or pull-down resistors, to prevent inputs from floating when normal input sources are not present.

19. Noisy board or system interface signals that connected directly to CMOS or BiCMOS inputs must have series current-limiting resistors, to prevent transients from driving the receiving devices into latch-up.

20. When CMOS or BiCMOS devices are used to receive signals from sources that have separate or independently controlled power sources, care must be taken to limit input currents and/or voltages, to prevent latch-up or other destructive conditions.

21. In *high-reliability applications,* static (dc) load limit specifications are typically derated. This is a common guideline: Do not exceed 70 percent of the manufacturer's rated drive capability when the application calls for military environmental conditions and 80 percent

when the application is for commercial conditions (unless more conservative drive derating is required by the customer).

9.7 References

1. James E. Buchanan, *BiCMOS/CMOS Systems Design*, McGraw-Hill, New York, 1991.
2. Robert K. Southard, "High-Speed Signal Pathways from Board to Board," in 81 WESCON Electronic Show & Convention Records Session 18, San Francisco, September 1981, paper 2.
3. Jack Ganssle, "Resistors in Digital Circuits," *EDN*, February 2, 1995, pp. 169–172.
4. Nathan O. Sokal, "Designer's Guide to PC-Board Logic Design—Part 2," *EDN*, November 27, 1986, pp. 229–235.
5. Gerald C. Cox, "Impedance Matching Tweaks Advanced CMOS IC Testing," *Electronic Design*, April 1987, pp. 71–74.
6. *Advanced CMOS Logic Designer's Handbook*, Texas Instruments Inc., Dallas, Tex., 1988.
7. *FACT Advanced CMOS Logic Databook*, National Semiconductor Corp., Santa Clara, Calif., 1993.
8. David Royle, "Designer's Guide to Transmission Lines and Interconnections, Part Two," *EDN*, June 23, 1988, pp. 143–150.
9. Sean Gold and Gary Maulding, "Electrostatic Self-Defense," *EDN*, Products edition, June 20, 1994, pp. 36–37.
10. Jacob Millman, *Microelectronics, Digital and Analog Circuits and Systems*, McGraw-Hill, New York, 1979.
11. Charles A. Harper, *Handbook of Electronic Packaging*, McGraw-Hill, New York, 1969.
12. Henry W. Ott, *Noise Reduction Techniques in Electronic Systems*, Wiley, New York, 1988.
13. *Electrical Characteristics of Balanced Voltage Digital Interface Circuits*, Standard RS-422-A, Electronic Industries Association, Washington, August 1978.
14. *Interface between Data Terminal Equipment and Data Communication Equipment Employing Serial Binary Data Interchange*, Standard RS-232-C, Electronic Industries Association, Washington, August 1969.
15. H. C. Brown, "Get Rid of Ground-Loop Noise," *Electronic Design*, no. 15, July 19, 1969, pp. 84–87.
16. Edward R. Oates, "Good Grounding and Shielding Practices," *Electronic Design*, no. 1, January 4, 1977, pp. 110–112.
17. Joe Campbell, *The RS-232 Solution*, 2d ed., SYBEX Inc., Alameda, Calif., 1989.
18. Martin D. Seyer, *RS-232 Made Easy*, Prentice-Hall, Englewood Cliffs, N.J., 1984.

General reference for bus interfaces:

Di Giacomo, Joseph: *Digital Bus Handbook*, McGraw-Hill, New York, 1990.

10

Noise-Tolerant Logic Architectures

It is impractical, if not impossible, with today's high-speed logic devices to keep noise due to reflections, ringing, crosstalk, and ground bounce (or power supply droop) on all signals to levels that do not exceed input switching thresholds. The only solution is to use logic system implementations, such as synchronous architectures, that tolerate high noise levels.[1]

10.1 Synchronous Design

Synchronous architectures maximize the noise immunity of systems by utilizing the time quantization of their clock to provide a filtering effect. In synchronous systems, clock inputs of storage elements, such as flip-flops, registers, counters, and state machines, are only driven by the system clock.[2,3] Signals generated in combinational logic paths are never used to clock storage elements. Noise-sensitive asynchronous inputs, such as presets or resets, are never used to perform operational system logic functions. Asynchronous inputs are only used for system initialization at power turn-on or for test initialization. In synchronous systems, storage element state changes are controlled by the logic conditions on the control inputs. Thus, noise on control signals, except at the critical time near a clock transition, will not cause false storage element changes.

Output transitions are the major source of noise in most digital systems. Synchronous systems tolerate a great deal of switching noise without upset or error because switching noise in synchronous systems occurs only following clock transitions.[4] If there is sufficient

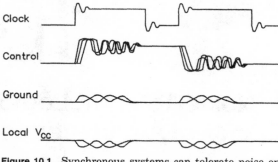

Clock

Control

Ground

Local V_{CC}

Figure 10.1 Synchronous systems can tolerate noise on signals, power, and ground following the active clock edge if there is time for the noise to die out before the next active clock edge.

time for all switching transients to subside before the next clock transition, then quiet signals are available to be sampled when the clock transitions (see Fig. 10.1). Ideally, synchronous systems have only one clock frequency and one phase to optimize the quiet time.

Synchronous systems are easy to understand, analyze, test, and change, if necessary. In synchronous systems, signals flow in an orderly manner from one clocked element to the next. Thus, systems are partitioned into manageable and understandable sections. In the ideal synchronous system, all clocked elements are clocked with the same clock; hence a fixed and known quantum of time is established for all operations, which simplifies the timing analysis. Test and design verification are also simplified since clock rates can be increased or decreased to determine timing margins without logic malfunctions occurring due to special timing paths or requirements.

A perceived disadvantage of synchronous design is that decisions can be made only at clock times, and thus timing paths cannot be optimized; i.e., synchronous designs are perceived to be slower than asynchronous designs.[3] In synchronous designs, the clock period must be long enough to accommodate the slowest signal path, and all other signal paths are forced to accommodate that clock period whereas theoretically each signal path can be optimized[2] in asynchronous designs. Perhaps each signal path can be optimized in experimental setups operating in benign laboratory environments, but in production systems that is usually not practical. Production systems, whether with synchronous or asynchronous designs, must allow for worst-case timing parameter variations. When proper allowance is made for worst-case timing changes due to aging, process, and environmental conditions, asynchronous designs have little, if any, speed advantage.

10.2 Important Synchronous Design Issues

Three critical issues must be understood to successfully implement synchronous designs:

1. Clock signal requirements
2. Signal *hold-time* requirements
3. Synchronization of asynchronous inputs

10.2.1 Clock requirements

The ideal synchronous system uses only one clock frequency and one phase, so that all storage elements are clocked at the same time. Such an arrangement establishes when a system will be noisy and when it will be quiet. If the clock period is sufficient to allow for the worst-case signal propagation path, then all signals will be quiet at the next clock edge, allowing unambiguous logic decisions to always be made (see Fig. 10.1). If multiple clock sources or clock phases are used, noise will be present more of the time, and for a given system cycle time, the time for noise to subside is reduced.

When it is necessary to store, process, or transfer data at time intervals that differ from the primary clock frequency, it is usually best to generate enable signals and use devices with clock enable input controls (see Fig. 10.2) rather than use different clock frequencies. When enable signals are used, state changes are initiated by the primary clock, not the enable signal, so noise due to state transitions remains locked to the primary clock. Enable signals are easier to use and to generate than multiple clock frequencies. It is very difficult to maintain the alignment needed for synchronous data transfers

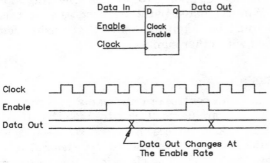

Figure 10.2 When it is necessary to store, process, or transfer data at time intervals that differ from the primary clock frequency, it is usually best to generate enable signals and use devices with clock enable input controls.

between different frequency domains when multiple clock frequencies are used.

Clock signals require an optimal electrical environment. Clock signal quality, uniformity of propagation delays (skew), and noise tolerance must be closely controlled throughout clock distribution networks. Clock signals must be as nearly perfect as possible. Excessive ringing and glitches cannot be tolerated on clock lines. Thus, clock distribution circuitry must incorporate some form of line termination for waveshape control.[2] Clock signals must be routed to their destinations via reasonably well-controlled impedance paths so that proper termination can be selected.

Clock distribution networks (trees) must be designed to minimize skew between clock signals. To accomplish the needed alignment, clock distribution circuitry must be standardized. Propagation delays must be matched throughout clock distribution networks. Clock drivers at each level must be identical generic devices of the same logic family. Where possible, all drivers in a given level should be located in a common package. Drivers and loads must be arranged so that loads are equalized. Clock lines must be very short so that wiring propagation delays are insignificant, or lines must be of nearly equal length in each distribution level to equalize physical propagation delays.

Clock signal paths must be isolated from other signals to minimize crosstalk. Parallel runs adjacent to other signals or other clocks must be kept as short as possible, to minimize the opportunities for cross-coupling. When multilayer printed-circuit boards are used, clock signals should be isolated and shielded from other signals by locating clock traces between reference planes. On welded-wire or wire-wrap circuit boards or backpanels, clock interconnections should use coaxial cable, shielded twisted-pair lines, or twisted-pair lines where practical (i.e., where the lines are not too short), to provide shielding and control of line impedance. Where twisted pairs are used, the clock is twisted with ground. Care must be taken to ensure that unshielded clock lines do not get bundled with other signals.

10.2.2 Hold-time requirements

Hold time is the time that an input control or data signal to a clocked element must remain stable after an active clock edge (see Fig. 10.3). Ensuring that all signals to clocked devices meet the required hold time is one of the most difficult tasks in a synchronous design. It is usually impossible to show that hold-time violations fail to occur under worst-case conditions using worst-case data sheet minimum and maximum timing specifications. Yet, in practice, when attention is paid to the conditions that most often cause hold-time violations, synchronous systems can be built that operate reliably.

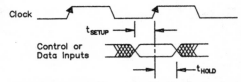

Figure 10.3 Signal setup and hold times relative to the active edge of the clock.

Hold-time violations most often occur

1. Where clock alignment is poor
2. Where signals go directly from one clocked device to another with no combinational logic between them
3. Where control signals are gated with clocks to form gated clocks
4. Where signals go from a fast device to a much slower device
5. Where logic families or technologies are mixed

Good clock alignment is essential for preventing hold-time violations. If clock alignment is poor, control signals from a device with an "early" clock may go away before a receiving device with a "late" clock is clocked, but perfect alignment can never be achieved. Thus, all signal paths must have some allowance for slight misalignment. Adding extra delay elements, such as additional buffers, or requiring that there be some combinational logic between clocked elements can help alleviate hold-time problems. However, care must be taken since minimum propagation times are generally not specified for the exact load conditions of a given situation. Minimum propagation times, when specified, are for a standard load (50 pF for most advanced Schottky TTL, advanced CMOS, and BiCMOS devices). Yet, in many cases, the actual load will be much less than the standard load, particularly when devices are used as delay elements. When the load is less than a standard load, the actual minimum propagation delay will be less than the specified value. Package type can also influence minimum propagation delays. The minimum propagation times shown in the data books for some logic families are specifically for devices in dual-in-line packages. Devices in packages with less lead inductance, such as leadless chip carriers (LCCs), will have smaller minimum propagation times than those shown in the data book.

Of special concern is the situation where a signal originates from a high-speed device and is received by a much slower-speed device from one of the older logic families. When signals flow from fast devices to slow devices, it is generally difficult to meet hold-time requirements. Likewise, when technologies are mixed, for example, BiCMOS and

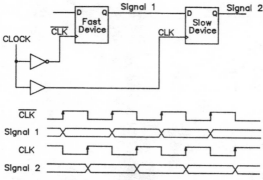

Figure 10.4 Off-phase clocking.

CMOS or CMOS and Schottky TTL, hold-time violations may occur at temperature extremes, since propagation delays and setup and hold times of different technologies may change at different rates with temperature. Several levels of combinational logic between devices may provide adequate hold time, but care must be exercised in all such cases because of the uncertainty of minimum propagation times.

Off-phase clocking, as shown in Fig. 10.4, which is undesirable in synchronous systems, is one means of transferring data and preventing hold-time violations where clock alignment is poor or other of the above conditions are present. However, off-phase clocking using the basic system clock is usually not practical for data transfers where the basic clock rate exceeds 20 MHz. Ideally off-phase clocking occurs in the middle of the basic clock period, but some timing allowance must be made for setup time and clock misalignment. Thus, off-phase clocking more than doubles the effective clock rate since data must be stable within less than one-half of the normal clock period. In most cases where clock frequencies are above 20 MHz, it is difficult to ensure that data will stabilize in less than one-half of a clock period.

10.2.3 Synchronizing asynchronous inputs

Signals coming into synchronous systems are generally asynchronous to the internal system clock, since most systems must interact with external sources that operate independently with respect to the internal system clock. Signals from independent sources (i.e., with separate clock sources) appear random with respect to the clock in the receiving system. To be used, asynchronous input signals must be synchronized to the local clock. Such signals should be physically isolated from the internal synchronous logic (since the system clock will not act as a filter) and synchronized as soon as possible at one place only. It is impor-

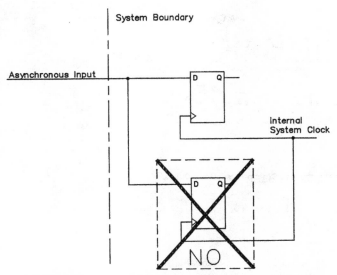

Figure 10.5 Synchronize asynchronous inputs at one place only.

tant that asynchronous inputs be synchronized at only one point (Fig. 10.5). If multiple synchronizers are used, one synchronizer may have significantly different characteristics from another and may detect an input on different clock edges as the internal clock and the external signal shift with respect to one another. Capturing signals at different times in parallel synchronizers can result in some portions of a system being out of phase with other portions.

Metastability. At asynchronous interfaces there is always the problem of, and the possibility of, synchronizing devices going into metastable states.[5] *Metastable* means "in between." when metastable malfunctions occur in digital devices, outputs may linger for some indeterminate period in the unknown-logic-level region (i.e., in between valid logic levels), or they may go to a valid logic level but be unstable and not remain in that state (see Fig. 10.6). The possibility of metastable operation of clocked devices is inherent and impossible to prevent at asynchronous interfaces.[6] All bistable devices, flip-flops, registers, latches, etc., have the possibility of going to a metastable state if their input signals do not meet all the required specifications for input levels or setup and hold times. Since it is impossible to meet such conditions at asynchronous interfaces, care must be taken to ensure that metastable operation of synchronizing devices does not upset system operation.[7] The recovery time for a part that goes into a metastable state can be much longer than the specified propagation delay for the part in a normal operating mode.

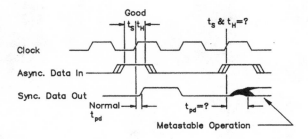

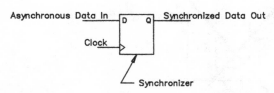

Figure 10.6 Metastable operation of a synchronizing flip-flop.

Thus, at asynchronous interfaces, the question is, How long to wait before you use the synchronized data (see Fig. 10.6)?[8] The higher the system speed, the greater the concern since the higher the speed, the less time there is for recovery.[9]

In general, faster logic families, such as today's advanced Schottky TTL, advanced CMOS, and BiCMOS logic families, have a smaller window of susceptibility to metastable conditions and recover faster from metastable states. Older, slower logic families, such as LS or HC, have very poor metastable recovery characteristics[8] and should not be used to synchronize data in high-speed systems.[10] Programmable devices such as PALs, PLAs, or other such devices should be used only if their metastable performance is known and meets system requirements (see Refs. 9, 11, and 12 for metastable data on some common PLDs). Programmable devices tend to have a wide range of susceptibility, and there is a tendency to overlook the possibility of asynchronous signals being routed to multiple internal flip-flops and synchronized at multiple places.

The probability of occurrence of metastable operation depends on the device technology, clock frequency, and frequency and phase of the input data. The worst-case data condition is when the data are always changing near the active edge of the clock. That condition occurs when the input data frequency is 0.5 times the clock frequency and the data are aligned so that they are always changing in the critical area where setup and hold times are violated. Metastable state

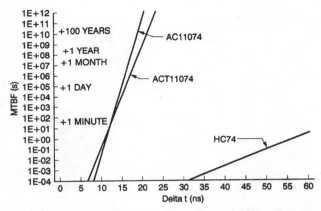

Figure 10.7 Metastability performance of Texas Instrument's advanced CMOS AC11074s and ACT1140s with the metastability performance of HC74s shown for comparison. (*Reprinted by permission of Texas Instruments.*)

recovery is related to device technology; the faster the device technology, the faster the recovery. Advanced Schottky TTL, advanced CMOS, and BiCMOS devices tend to have a very high probability of recovery after 20 to 25 ns (see Fig. 10.7 for typical advanced CMOS characteristics). Typically, after 20 to 25 ns the chance of a metastable failure is reduced to 1 in 100 or more years. Note, though, that at 10 to 15 ns the chance of a failure is reduced to approximately 1 per minute. In most systems, 1 failure per minute is intolerable. Any failure is undesirable, but metastable failures will occur at asynchronous interfaces. The only recourse is to allow a long enough recovery time that the probability of a metastable failure is insignificant. Yet, at 20 MHz or higher, the recovery time needed for a high probability of not suffering a metastable failure is a significant portion of the clock period. Metastable recovery time must be added to the normal device delays in a signal path to determine the maximum usable clock frequency of an asynchronous interface. For example, in Fig. 10.8 the maximum clock period is the recovery time of $U1$ (not the normal maximum propagation time) plus the propagation delay of $U2$ plus the setup time of $U3$.

The recovery time for given failure, data, and clock rates can be calculated if curves of the mean time between failures (MTBF) versus recovery time Δt are available for the device of interest. The general equation for the metastable failure rate (1/MTBF) is

$$\frac{1}{\text{MTBF}} = K_1 f_{\text{data}} f_{\text{clock}} \, \varepsilon^{-K2 \, \Delta t} \tag{10.1}$$

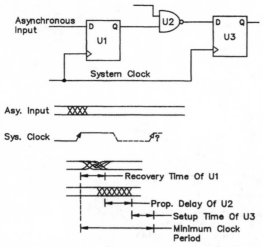

Figure 10.8 The minimum clock period is equal to the recovery time of $U1$ plus the delay of $U2$ plus the setup of $U3$.

where $K1$ and $K2$ describe the metastable characteristics of the synchronizing device and Δt is the time given the device to come out of the metastable condition. Different manufacturers present metastable data in slightly different forms, so one must be sure when calculating 1/MTBF that the constants, Δt, and the failure rate used in the MTBF equation are compatible. Since metastable characteristics are neither guaranteed nor tested, except in a few isolated cases it is best to design with a recovery time that provides a very high probability of recovery. In general, with today's devices, allowing 25 ns or more for recovery will be sufficient for most applications; but in critical cases or where less recovery time is allocated, the synchronizing devices should be tested for their metastable characteristics (Refs. 7 and 8 show and describe test circuits).

Synchronizing asynchronous buses. Where asynchronous buses are received, it is better to capture and synchronize the strobes or control signals (assuming that the timing of the bus is such that it is possible to do so) than to try to synchronize an entire bus (see Fig. 10.9). Such an arrangement minimizes the chance of metastable operation, since only the control signals must be synchronized. The entire bus is not subjected to the possibility of incorrect setup or hold times. Attempting to synchronize an entire bus widens the window of susceptibility to metastable operation and increases the possibility that one or more bits may go into metastable operation. Not all the receiving devices will be identical; some will be slower and others faster, and the clock phasing may be slightly different at each device.

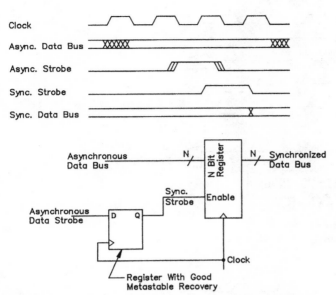

Figure 10.9 It is better to capture and synchronize the data strobe than to try to synchronize an entire bus.

Synchronizing wide pulses. Asynchronous pulses wider than the internal clock period may need either to be synchronized and used with their width unmodified (except for the quantization effect of the internal clock) or converted to one clock time pulse at either the leading or trailing edge of the input pulse. If wide pulses only require synchronization, all that is required to synchronize them is to clock them through a resistor that has good metastable recovery characteristics. If wide pulses need to be synchronized and converted to a one-clock time pulse that follows the leading edge of the input pulse, a leading-edge detector (LED) circuit such as shown in Fig. 10.10 is typically used. The circuit operates as shown in the timing diagram of Fig. 10.10. Register $U1$ in Fig. 10.10 must have a metastable MTBF sufficient to meet the system reliability requirements at the system clock speed. If the asynchronous input transitions in the metastable zone of $U1$ (near the clock edge), the LED output may glitch due to metastability, as shown in Fig. 10.11. However, if $U1$ has a sufficiently fast recovery time, the LED output will be stable at the next clock edge. If a clean full-clock-time wide pulse is required, then an additional register must be used between the input signal and the LED circuit to synchronize the signal before it reaches the LED circuit.

A trailing-edge detector (TED) and synchronizer are implemented as shown in Fig. 10.12. The TED circuit issues a one-clock time pulse during the clock time following the absence of the wide input signal, as shown in the timing diagram in Fig. 10.12.

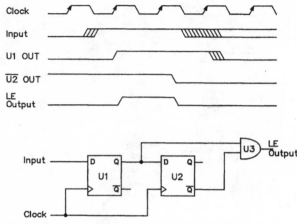

Figure 10.10 Leading-edge detector and synchronizer circuit.

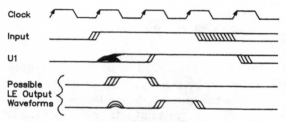

Figure 10.11 Possible leading-edge detector output waveforms when the asynchronous input changes in the metastable zone of the synchronizing register.

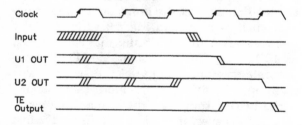

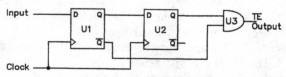

Figure 10.12 Trailing-edge detector and synchronizer circuit.

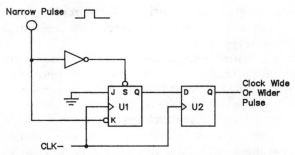

Figure 10.13 Circuit for capturing and synchronizing pulses narrower than the system clock period.

Synchronizing narrow pulses. Asynchronous pulses narrower than the internal clock period cannot be captured and synchronized with a simple clocked register. A narrow pulse may not be present at a clock edge. Thus, some form of asynchronous capture is necessary that can hold the pulse until a clock edge occurs. One circuit that is used to capture and synchronize narrow pulses is shown in Fig. 10.13. The circuit in Fig. 10.13 operates as follows: The presence of a narrow input pulse (but one sufficiently wide to be recognized by $U1$) asynchronously forces $U1$ to a 1, where it remains until the clock edge following the absence of the input pulse. The second register, $U2$, captures and synchronizes the changes in the output of $U1$ to the system clock. If the input pulse is wider than the internal clock period, the pulse width is maintained (less quantization variability). If a synchronized one-clock time pulse is needed, a LED or TED circuit can be implemented by using $U2$ as the first stage, followed by an additional register and gate (see Figs. 10.11 and 10.12).

10.3   Devices Incompatible with Synchronous Design

Certain devices are inherently incompatible with synchronous logic design. They include one-shots (multivibrators), transparent latches, and master-slave devices.

10.3.1   One-shots

One-shots should not be used in synchronous systems. One-shot output changes are not clock-controlled. Thus, one-shots clearly violate the synchronous design requirement that all signals change relative to the active edge of the system clock. In addition to violating synchronous design requirements, there are several practical reasons for not using one-shots in modern digital systems. One-shot time-out periods are difficult to control or determine accurately, and as a result worst-case time-out limits are generally greatly underestimated. One-shots are also difficult to test. Most automatic testers used for digital hardware testing cannot test one-shots.

However, there is often a temptation to use one-shots when long time delays or long time-out periods are needed and board space is at a premium. Long time-out periods using standard 4-bit counters may require a number of packages to achieve the same time-out period as can be achieved with a single one-shot (package), a resistor, and a capacitor (most one-shots require an RC timing network, as shown in Fig. 10.14). However, one-shots with long time-out periods tend to have much greater variations in time-out period than expected. One-shots with long time-out periods require RC timing networks with large-value resistors and capacitors. Yet, large-value resistors and capacitors are generally not available in close tolerances, and they tend to have large tolerance variations with temperature and aging.

Several sources of leakage current exist that contribute to time-out errors, including capacitor leakage current, board leakage current, and one-shot timing port input current (one-shot input current is technically not a leakage current, but the effect is the same). Worst-case leakage currents for large tantalum capacitors are often in the microampere range. Board leakage depends on environmental conditions and the physical arrangement of the interconnections. It is not uncommon for board impedance to be as low as 100 kΩ in high-humidity conditions and as low as 10 kΩ in some extreme salt air conditions. One-shot timing port input current is usually not specified, and thus its effect on the time-out period is usually unknown. If all the leakage sources are near maximum and a high-value timing resistor is used, time-out may never occur. Leakage currents may load the RC timing network to the extent that it never reaches a level sufficient to trigger the one-shot and as a result the one-shot never times out (see Fig. 10.15).

Given the possibility that one-shots with long time-out periods may not time out, or that if they do time out, the variation in time-out period may be very large, long time-out one-shots should be avoided if at all possible. When long time-out periods are needed, a number of microprocessor support chips have long counter chains, and there are

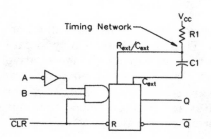

Figure 10.14 Typical one-shot timing network.

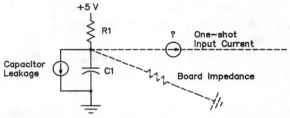

Figure 10.15 Leakage currents and stray board impedance can prevent one-shot time-out.

a number of long ripple counters (in a single package) in the HC/HCT
logic family. Counters are a better solution than one-shots in most
applications requiring long time-out periods.

10.3.2 Latches

Latches, depending upon how they are used, may violate the requirement that all signals change relative to the active edge of the clock.
Latches also may impose restrictions on latch control signals that are
difficult to meet in a synchronous, single-phase clock system. Great
care must be taken to ensure that latch control signals are timed so
that hold-time violations do not occur at latch inputs or at devices
receiving latch outputs.

10.3.3 Master-slave devices

Master-slave devices reduce the amount of quiet time in a system.
Master-to-slave transfers are completed on the off-phase edge of the
clock, which reduces the signal settling time by one-half (for a 50 percent duty cycle clock).

10.4 Summary of Synchronous Design
Practices

> In synchronous designs, storage elements are allowed to change states only in
> response to clock transitions on clock inputs.

1. Clocked elements should be clocked by only the system clock.

2. Use only clock signals of a single phase and single frequency.

3. All clocked elements should be edge-triggered (as opposed to
    latches or master-slave devices).

4. Clocked devices with TTL input levels should be selected so that
    all clocks are on the *low*-to-*high* clock transition to maximize the
    noise margin.

5. Asynchronous presets and resets on clocked elements should never be used for performing operational system logic functions due to susceptibility to noise.

6. Unclocked feedback paths (such as cross-coupled gates) should not be used because of their susceptibility to being upset by system noise.

7. Never use a counter carry or a decoder output as a clock (such outputs are expected to have spikes).

8. Never use a simple multiplexer to switch clocks. Multiplexers typically spike or glitch when switched.

9. Do not route asynchronous signals to multiple points within a functional unit until they are buffered and synchronized to the internal clock.

10. Monostable multivibrators (one-shots) should not be used.

10.5 References

1. Richard Funk and James Nadolski, "Advanced CMOS—Pinouts Are Not the Crucial Factor," *Electronic Engineering Times*, August 4, 1986, p. 33.
2. Morris M. Mano, *Digital Design*, Prentice-Hall, Englewood Cliffs, N.J., 1984.
3. William I. Fletcher, *An Engineering Approach to Digital Design*, Prentice-Hall, Englewood Cliffs, N.J., 1980.
4. John P. Hayes, *Computer Architecture and Organization*, 2d ed., McGraw-Hill, New York, 1988.
5. Lindsay Kleeman and Antonio Cantoni, "Metastable Behavior in Digital Systems," *IEEE Design & Test of Computers*, December 1987, pp. 4–19.
6. Steven R. Masteller, "Design a Digital Synchronizer with a Low Metastable-Failure Rate," *EDN*, April 25, 1991, pp. 169–174.
7. Hoang Nguyen, "How to Detect Metastability Problems," *ASIC & EDA*, February 1993, pp. 16–24.
8. Thomas J. Chaney, "Measured Flip-flop Responses to Marginal Triggering," *IEEE Transactions on Computers*, vol. C-32, no. 12, December 1983.
9. Tom Bowns, "Control Metastability in High-Speed CMOS Circuits," *Electronic Design*, September 26, 1991, pp. 74–80.
10. *Advanced CMOS Logic Designer's Handbook*, Texas Instruments Inc., Dallas, Tex., 1988, pp. 3-29–3-36.
11. Sean Dingman, "Determine PAL Metastability to Derive Ample MTBFs," *EDN*, August 5, 1991, pp. 147–154.
12. *Advanced Micro Devices PAL Device Data Book*, Advanced Micro Devices, Sunnyvale, Calif., 1988, pp. 3-164–3-169.

10.6 Bibliography

Fletcher, William I.: *An Engineering Approach to Digital Design*, Prentice-Hall, Englewood Cliffs, N.J., 1980.
Goodrich, Richard: "Pinpointing Metastable Problems Leads to More Reliable Designs," *Communications Systems Equipment Design*, February 1985, pp. 33–35.
Mano, Morris M.: *Digital Design*, Prentice-Hall, Englewood Cliffs, N.J., 1984.

Worst-Case Timing

High-speed digital systems require a careful timing analysis of all signal paths to establish the maximum usable system clock frequency. Too often, unrealizable operating speeds are forecast based on typical device timing parameters with no allowance made for worst-case component delays and little or no allowance made for signal wiring propagation delays and transmission-line effects. For system performance goals to be met, realistic worst-case propagation delays of each component in each signal path, plus the physical propagation delays and settling time of each interconnection within the paths, must be determined and factored into the projected operating speed. Signal interconnection and settling time delays are a significant part of most signal propagation delay paths when system operating speeds approach 20 MHz or greater. At 20 MHz, interconnection delays average 20 percent of signal delays. At 50 MHz, interconnection delay may average 50 percent or more of total delay.[1]

At present, most system and board level timing analysis of critical signals must be done on an individual net basis by hand calculations or by SPICE or other similar circuit analysis tools. Computer-aided design (CAD) tools that combine logic device timing and PC boards or backpanel interconnection system transmission-line response characteristics capable of handling a complete PC board or motherboard of digital circuitry exist,[2,3] but they are not available to most designers. Without such CAD tools, a thorough timing analysis of every signal on complex high-speed PC boards or motherboards is an impossible task. Yet, without a thorough timing analysis, there is little hope of producing reliable high-speed systems.[4] Fortunately, a technique exists for structuring systems so that a thorough timing analysis is a manageable task. Synchronous design is the key. In synchronous systems, data flow in an orderly manner from one clocked device to another with signal path propagation requirements clearly defined by the system clock period. In contrast, in asynchronous systems, data tend to flow through long, irregular paths that are dependent on many conditions, with the consequence being that a proper timing analysis is usually difficult, or impossible, to achieve.

Worst-case timing analysis.   Traditionally what is commonly called *worst-case* timing analysis is used to analyze digital circuit and interconnection delays. Worst-case timing analysis methodology consists of adding the maximum delay value for each element in the delay path for the *maximum worst-case delay* and likewise adding all the minimum delay values for the *minimum worst-case delay;* i.e.,

$$t_{path} \text{ max worst-case delay} = t_p \text{ max(device 1)} + t_p \text{ max(device 2)}$$
$$+ t_p \text{ max(device 3)} + \cdots + t_p \text{ max(device } N) + t_p \text{ max(interconnect 1)}$$
$$+ t_p\text{max(interconnect 2)} + \cdots + t_p \text{ max(interconnect } N)$$

$$t_{path} \text{ min worst-case delay} = t_p \text{ min(device 1)} + t_p \text{ min(device 2)}$$
$$+ t_p \text{ min(device 3)} + \cdots + t_p \text{ min(device } N) + t_p \text{ min(interconnect 1)}$$
$$+ t_p \text{ min(interconnect 2)} + \cdots + t_p \text{ min(interconnect } N)$$

Here the timing path t_{path} is a given independent path, devices 1 to N and interconnections 1 to N are individual elements within the path, and t_p max, t_p min, t_p max, and t_p min are the maximum and minimum delays, respectively, of the individual elements (devices and interconnecting nodes) in the path. In simple single-path timing loops that encompass common elements, worst-case maximum and minimum timing results are treated independently. In dual-path to common-element situations, maximum and minimum delay times for the two paths must be compared. If there are a large number of components in the dual paths, it is usually very difficult with absolute worst-case maximum and minimum analysis to show that proper timing relationships (for the two paths) exist.[5] Statistical analysis is usually required in such cases (see below).

When a worst-case analysis shows that all paths meet their timing requirements with some margin, the system should perform in a reliable manner. But what is a reasonable or adequate margin? If all delay values used are truly worst-case with all loading, transmission-line, temperature, etc., effects accounted for, then little or no extra margin is needed. If all effects are not accounted for, which is the usual case, then some margin is required. A common goal is to have at least 20 percent margin when all *known* effects have been accounted for (to allow for those that are not known) and to have from 50 to 100 percent margin when the timing analysis is based on typical component timing values. The advantage of worst-case timing analysis is that it is simple to use and is supported by most CAD timing tools. The disadvantage of worst-case timing analysis is that it produces conservative results which may cause circuits to be overdesigned or system performance goals to be reduced.

Statistical timing analysis. Statistical timing analysis is an alternate approach to worst-case analysis. Statistical timing analysis provides a means of quantifying the risks of performance and manufacturing goals versus device timing parameter variations.[5] Statistical methods are often the only realistic approach for timing paths with many components and multiple paths that eventually must merge (i.e., must maintain some timing relationship). Statistical methods tend to be a less useful approach when timing paths consist of a very small number of components. That is particularly the case if one component contributes a major portion of the path delay, such as timing paths that include a memory device (which are typically the predominant portion of the path delay). Two statistical approaches to worst-case timing are root-sum-squared (RSS) and Monte Carlo.

Root-sum-squared timing analysis. Root-sum-squared timing analysis methodology consists of determining a nominal or typical delay value for each element in the delay path of interest, which is then modified by the standard deviation of each circuit's timing attribute probability distribution above and below the nominal (mean value) for a *maximum RSS delay* and a *minimum RSS delay*. That is,

$$t_{\text{path}} \text{ max RSS delay} = t_{\text{path}} \text{ typ}$$
$$+ \sqrt{(t_P \text{ max1} - t_P \text{ typ1})^2 + \cdots + (t_P \text{ max} N - t_P \text{typ} N)^2}$$

or, in words,

t_{path} max RSS delay = $[t_P$ typ(device 1) + t_P typ(device 2)
+ t_P typ(device 3) + $\cdots$ + t_P typ(device N) + t_p typ(interconnect 1)
+ t_p typ(interconnect 2) + $\cdots$ + t_p typ(interconnect N)]
+ square root of {[t_P max $- t_P$ typ(device 1)]^2
$$+ [t_P \text{ max} - t_P \text{ typ(device 2)}]^2 + \cdots \}$$

and

$$t_{\text{path}} \text{ min RSS delay} = t_{\text{path}} \text{ typ}$$
$$- \sqrt{(t_P \text{ typ1} - t_P \text{ min1})^2 + \cdots + (t_P \text{typ} N - t_P \text{ min} N)^2}$$

and again, in words,

t_{path} min RSS delay = $[t_P$ typ(device 1) + t_P typ(device 2)
+ t_P typ(device 3) + $\cdots$ + t_P typ(device N) + t_p typ(interconnect 1)
+ t_p typ(interconnect 2) + $\cdots$ + t_p typ(interconnect N)]
$-$ square root of {$[t_P$ typ $- t_P$ min(device 1)]^2

$$+ [t_P \text{ typ} - t_P \text{ min(device 2)}]^2 + \cdots \}$$

Here path t_{path} is a given independent path; devices 1 to N and inter-connections 1 to N are individual elements within the path; and t_P typ, t_P max, t_P min, t_p typ, t_p max, and t_p min are the typical, maximum, and minimum delays, respectively, of the individual elements (devices and interconnects) in the path. In simple single-path timing loops (i.e., an independent path that is not dependent on other signals), RSS maximum and minimum timing results are treated independently. In dual-path to common-element situations, maximum and minimum RSS delay times for the two paths must be compared. If there are a large number of components in dual or multiple paths, RSS analysis is usually the most practical approach.

An RSS analysis predicts the probability of the circuit timing attributes falling within the required limits. The results of an RSS analysis are generally more realistic than those of absolute worst-case analysis for circuits with a large number of components, but errors are possible due to assumptions of linearity of sensitivity and normal distributions of timing parameters.

Monte Carlo timing analysis. The Monte Carlo analysis process consists of determining a histogram of the circuit timing attribute's probability distribution by repeatedly selecting random sets of circuit delay values. In general, designers do not have sufficient timing parameter distribution information, the means of getting the needed information, or the tools to use Monte Carlo analysis. Monte Carlo analysis typically yields accurate results, given a knowledge of the variability of the timing parameters of the parts.

11.1   Device Delays

Manufacturers' device specification sheets or data books provide some very useful timing information, but it requires interruption and translation to the actual load and environment conditions of each application.

11.1.1   Device timing specifications

Most SSI and MSI advanced Schottky TTL, advanced CMOS, and BiCMOS device data sheets have three columns of timing specifications.[6,7] They typically list

1. Minimum, typical, and maximum timing parameters at + 25°C

2. Minimum and maximum timing for commercial rated devices

3. Minimum and maximum timing for military rated devices

Traditionally, commercial rated devices were specified for operating conditions of 0 to +70°C and ±5 percent from nominal power supply limits. However, there is little consistency in the temperature range or power supply range limits for commercial rated parts today. Some are specified for −40 to + 85°C, which has traditionally been called the *industrial range*. Some commercial rated advanced CMOS parts are specified with ± 10 percent power supply limits instead of ± 5 percent. Specification limits are much more consistent for military rated devices. Most military rated devices are specified for operating conditions of −55 to +125°C and ±10 percent power supply variations from nominal. The timing information supplied for LSI and VLSI devices is usually less complete than that for SSI and MSI devices; in many cases no typical or minimum data are supplied.

Unfortunately, not all manufacturers use the same load conditions when specifying timing. Most SSI and MSI advanced Schottky TTL, advanced CMOS, and BiCMOS logic devices are specified with a 50-pF load. Many LSI and VLSI devices, such as memories, are specified with a 30- or 35-pF load. The load resistance used to specify timing varies considerably; load resistance does not have a large impact on device timing. However, variations in load resistance make interpreting and comparing timing specifications difficult when differences are small, e.g., when a logic family is claimed to be 1 or 2 ns faster than another family. Load resistors that limit *high* levels when devices are tested to TTL-level test thresholds (1.5 V) tend to improve *high*-to-*low* propagation times. It takes less time to transition a shorter distance (across a smaller voltage difference). If the actual load varies significantly from the load used to specify the device timing, the timing must be adjusted to reflect the actual load conditions. Loading of control signals and local data lines seldom exceeds 50 pF. Thus, in most cases, manufacturers' maximum and minimum specified timing can be used without adjustments since most signals fall into the control signal or local-data categories. Buses usually exceed 50 pF, but most buses are long-line and thus are not lumped loads and should not be treated as such (they should be treated as transmission lines—see Chap. 7).

11.1.2 Timing parameter adjustments for worst-case conditions

If worst-case timing is not specified, some derating criteria must be applied for worst-case operating conditions and possible process vari-

ations. The manufacturer is the best source of information on parameter limits when they are missing and should be contacted for the
missing information. However, when the manufacturer does not have
the specific parameter limits needed or is unwilling to supply them,
the following paragraphs describe some of the major device variables
and list typical variability rates that can be used to estimate timing
parameter limits.

Timing changes due to process variations.   Timing changes due to
process variations typically range from $\pm$ 30 to $\pm$ 50 percent.[6] Process
variations increase the spread in device timing parameters more than
any other single factor, and there is little that the system designer
can do to influence process limits. For integrated circuits to be cost-
effective and producible, a great deal of processing tolerance is
required. System designers are often misled into believing that
devices with tighter process tolerances can be purchased, but it is
usually neither practical nor cost-effective to do so.

Timing adjustments for temperature.   Propagation delays of advanced
Schottky TTL devices typically change by less than $\pm$ 2 ns over the
military temperature range.[7]

Propagation delays of advanced CMOS devices typically change by
a factor of 0.3 percent per degree Celsius[8] which corresponds with the
rate of change in transconductance g_m and output current of
MOSFETs with temperature.[9]

The typical change in propagation delay versus temperature is 0.3 percent per
degree Celsius for most advanced CMOS devices.

Over the military temperature range, that means an approximate
change of $\pm$ 30 percent. Note that propagation delay has a positive
temperature coefficient so CMOS propagation delays are worst (slowest) at high temperatures. At cold temperatures, CMOS devices speed
up, which increases the danger of hold-time violations—signals may
go away too fast. Most manufacturers provide curves of propagation
delay versus temperature for their logic families. Knowing the propa-
gation-delay-versus-temperature behavior of devices can help narrow
specification limits for time-critical applications. For example, if all
parts in a critical subsystem are grouped together, it can be assumed
that all are at the same temperature (and supply voltage), which nar-
rows the range of variability of timing parameters. Narrowing the
range of timing parameters may provide justification for a higher-per-
formance design.

Not a great deal of delay-versus-temperature data are available for
BiCMOS devices or logic families. However, since BiCMOS output
stages are similar to advanced Schottky TTL output stages, their

change in delay should be similar to that of advanced Schottky devices. Advanced Schottky devices typically change less than ± 2 ns over the military temperature range.[7] The improved stability of propagation versus temperature of BiCMOS devices relative to advanced CMOS devices is one of their great advantages.

Timing adjustments for power supply voltage levels. Propagation delays of advanced Schottky TTL devices do not change significantly with power supply variations—only on the order of 1 ns over the -55 to $+$ 125°C military temperature range. Most of the change in propagation delay due to power supply level changes is a result of the change in output drive capability of the output stage. Output *high* drive tends to go up with higher power supply levels, but output *low* drive tends to decrease, which means that the output high turn-on time tends to decrease and output *low* switching time tends to increase. Because of conflicting trends, propagation delay changes cannot be relied on to track with power supply voltage changes, but propagation changes due to power supply changes (1 ns or less typically) are not a major factor when advanced Schottky TTL devices are used.[7]

Propagation delays of advanced CMOS devices typically change by a factor of about -10 percent per volt change in power supply voltage.[6]

The typical change in propagation delay versus power supply voltage is -10 percent per volt for most advanced CMOS devices.

Worst-case change is in the neighborhood of -20 percent per volt.[6] Over the military power supply limits of ± 10 percent (± 0.5 V), that means an approximate change of ± 5 percent typically and ± 10 percent worst-case at the extremes of the power supply voltage limits. The propagation-delay-versus-voltage coefficient is negative. High supply voltage means higher speed and less propagation delay. The larger the voltage applied to gate-source or gate-drain junctions of MOSFETs, the lower the on impedance. Lower on impedance means less RC delay. Thus, for operation near the limits of CMOS technology, it is best to keep the supply voltage level on the *high side* of the normal operating range. For example, in large high-performance systems, it is often best to set the supply voltage at 5.2 V to optimize device speed and to help compensate for ac and dc losses in the power distribution system.

Propagation delays of BiCMOS devices are less sensitive to power supply variations than those of CMOS devices. The majority of the change in propagation delay due to power supply level changes is a result of the change in output drive capability of the output stage. Output drive characteristics of BiCMOS bipolar outputs change with the power supply voltage, but not as much or in as consistent a manner as does the drive of CMOS outputs. Output *high* drive tends to go up with higher power supply levels, but the turnoff time of *low* outputs tends to increase. Because of the conflicting trends, propagation delay changes cannot be relied on to track with power supply voltage changes, but propagation changes due to power supply changes are not a major factor when BiCMOS devices are used.

Rule of thumb for quick estimates of device timing parameter limits.   For a quick estimate of worst-case timing parameters, the following rules of thumb can be used to convert + 25°C, + 5-V timing parameters, i.e., propagation delays or setup and hold times, to worst-case over temperature and supply limits:[10]

Rule-of-Thumb Timing Parameter Conversion Factors

■ To convert typical + 25°C timing parameters to worst-case values over the commercial temperature range, multiply by a factor of 1.5.

■ To convert typical + 25°C timing parameters to worst-case values over the military temperature range, multiply by 2.

■ To convert maximum (or minimum) + 25°C timing parameters to worst-case values over the commercial temperature range, multiply by 1.25.

■ To convert maximum (or minimum) + 25°C timing parameters to worst-case values over the military temperature range, multiply by 1.5.

Timing adjustments for actual load conditions.   When the signal line length is less than the *critical line length,* line loading appears as lumped.[11] When lines are less than the critical length, transmission-line effects are not significant, but signal transition and propagation times may be slowed due to capacitance. If the capacitance loading is different (which it will usually be) from the value at which the timing is specified, in critical applications the timing must be adjusted to take into consideration the actual loading. Propagation delays for most SSI and MSI advanced Schottky TTL, advanced CMOS, and BiCMOS devices are specified with 50-pF loads. In contrast, propagation delays for most memory devices and many other LSI devices are specified with 30- or 35-pF loads. However, in many situations actual loads will exceed 50 pF, particularly in many bus driving applications. In those cases where loads exceed 50 pF (or 35 pF for memories), some adjustment must be made to the specified output response time of the driving device. In some cases, device manufacturers provide graphs that show the typical change in output response versus load capacitance.

The typical change in propagation delay versus load capacitance is 15 to 25 ps/pF for most advanced Schottky TTL, advanced CMOS, and BiCMOS devices.[6,7]

Worst-case response versus load capacitance is seldom provided. Multiplying typical values by a factor of 1.5 for commercial operation and a factor of 2 for military operation provides a reasonable estimate of worst-case change in response versus load capacitance. The factors 1.5 and 2 are based on possible device characteristic changes due to process variations and operation at the limits of the temperature and supply voltage ranges. When minimum propagation delay is a concern, e.g., to ensure the hold time, minimum specified propagation times should be adjusted by using the propagation-delay-versus-load-capacitance factors.

When delay versus load capacitance is not provided (and a verification of the typical number above is needed), an estimation of the increased delay due to larger-than-specified load capacitance can be determined from Eq. (4.14),

$$\frac{dv}{dt} = \frac{I_{OS}}{C}$$

where I_{OS} is the output short-circuit current of the output driving device and C is the increase in load capacitance beyond the specified load value. For TTL and BiCMOS devices, or CMOS devices with TTL output levels (those with source-follower pull-up output stages), the value of I_{OS} is different for *high* and *low* outputs. In most cases, *low*-to-*high* transition times are slower than *high*-to-*low* transition times because *high*-level I_{OS} is less than *low*-level I_{OS} due to the construction of TTL-level output stages. TTL and BiCMOS totem-pole outputs have current-limiting pull-up resistors, and most CMOS devices that have TTL output levels use n-channel source followers for output pull-ups. Source-follower circuits tend to have less *high* output drive than conventional complementary CMOS outputs that switch to V_{cc} or ground.

Load capacitance. Total signal load capacitance must be established to determine the signal response. Total signal capacitance consists of the input or output capacitance of each device connected to the line plus the line capacitance.

Device input or output capacitance is usually included on data sheets. If it is not, capacitance loading due to standard SSI or MSI device connections can be estimated by using the following values:

5 pF for inputs

7 pF for outputs

15 pF for bidirectional ports

However, the input-output capacitance of some parts will vary considerably for the above, so data sheets should be consulted to ensure that proper values are used. The input and output capacitances of LSI and VLSI devices and of devices in large packages may be much larger than the values listed above.

Typical interconnection (wiring) capacitances are

2 to 4 pF/in of PC board track

1 to 2 pF/in for welded-wire or wire-wrap wire

The actual interconnection capacitance should be used in timing calculations when available. However, in many applications, the actual capacitance of a given signal interconnection is difficult to determine due to great variations in conductor and ground-reference spacing. Wire spacing relative to reference planes or other conductors on welded-wire or wire-wrap boards varies a great deal. Even where the conductor topology is known, it is difficult to determine the exact line capacitance due to interaction of nearby conductors. Thus, most line capacitance calculations are made under only the assumptions of an isolated conductor and a nearby reference plane.

For most applications, lumped loading due to interconnection (wiring) capacitance can be estimated by using the following values:

3 pF/in of PC board track

1.5 pF/in for welded-wire or wire-wrap wire

Guidance for calculating more exact interconnection capacitance values can be found in a number of the references covering transmission lines listed at the end of Chap. 7.

Timing adjustments for simultaneous switching. Some degradation of propagation delay normally occurs in multiple-output devices when several outputs switch simultaneously. Most data sheet propagation times are for only one output switching. Propagation delay is typically increased by 0.2 to 0.3 ns per simultaneously switched output.[12]

Propagation delay increases approximately 0.2 ns per simultaneous switched output for multiple-output devices.

However, many factors influence the actual change. Load conditions, device technology and inherent speed, internal and external noise levels, efficiency of the package and external power and ground distribution, and decoupling all impact speed degradation. Thus, 0.2 to 0.3 ns of degradation per switched output should be used only as a rough guideline. Actual system degradation may be much worse. Octal and wider parts may have serious degradation if all devices switch at once. In time-critical applications, system designers need specific data for the actual devices being used.

Timing effects of package style. Package style and lead inductance influence the response time of devices. Surface-mounted packages with short leads tend to respond faster than devices in large dual-in-line packages. Some data books specify (in very fine print) that the listed times are for devices in dual-in-line packages and that the minimum times shown may be shorter for devices in other package styles. Quantitative data for package style effects on device timing are not readily available. Nonetheless, the system designer should be aware that package style does influence the timing parameter limits.

11.1.3 *Caution:* Beware of F_{max}

The parameter F_{max}, which is listed as the maximum toggle rate or maximum clock rate on data sheets for clocked devices such as counters, flip-flops, and shift registers, should never be used as an indication of the useful speed of a device.[13] It is a measure of what might be achieved with an individual part under ideal conditions with no restrictions on input pulse widths or load conditions.[13] Since most digital systems must operate under conditions that vary greatly from ideal, and since devices must communicate with other devices to serve a useful purpose, F_{max} is of little use for actual system timing. Actual signal path propagation times—not F_{max}—must be used to determine the maximum operating speed of systems.

11.2   Circuit Board Interconnection Delays

Interconnection delays consist of the conductor propagation delay and signal settling time delay. *Signal propagation delay* is the time required for a signal to traverse a physical conductor. *Signal settling time* is the time required for a signal to transition to a proper logic level or to settle to a proper logic level if it overshoots and rings. Signal settling time is of most concern when signal lines are long, i.e., where lines behave as transmission lines.

11.2.1 Interconnecting line propagation delay

Calculation of interconnection delays due to load and transmission-line effects is not straightforward. Yet, both effects may add significant time to signal delays. For PC boards, the intrinsic propagation delay t_{pd} is approximately 2 ns/ft, and for welded-wire or wire-wrap boards, t_{pd} is approximately 1.5 ns/ft. For extremely time-critical circuits or very long lines (several feet), more exact intrinsic propagation delay times should be calculated (see Chap. 7 and the various transmission-line references at the end of Chap. 7). However, for most applications the above per-unit-length intrinsic signal propagation values are sufficient. Distributed loads along a line modify the propagation time of signals. The actual delay is called the *effective delay* t'_{pd}. Actual conductor delay is equal to the per-unit-length effective propagation delay t'_{pd} of electric energy in the interconnection media multiplied by the length of the interconnection.

11.2.2   Line propagation delay with distributed loads

Lines with distributed loads slow the propagation of signals by a factor equal to

$$t_{pd}(\text{slowdown factor}) = \sqrt{1 + \frac{C_{\text{LOAD}}}{C_{\text{LINE}}}} \tag{11.1}$$

Thus, where loads are distributed, the actual propagation time t'_{pd} is given by Eq. (6.4),

$$t'_{pd} = t_{pd}\sqrt{1 + \frac{C_{\text{LOAD}}}{C_{\text{LINE}}}} \tag{6.4}$$

When lines have distributed loads, t'_{pd} should be used in Eq. (7.1) to determine the critical line length.

11.2.3   Line delay due to transmission-line effects

Transmission-line effects become a concern in high-speed systems when line lengths exceed the critical line length (see Chap. 7). The common definition of the *critical line length* is given by Eq. (7.1),

$$\text{Critical line length} = \frac{1}{2}\frac{t_r}{t'_{pd}} \tag{7.1}$$

where t_r is the rise time of the driving source (typically measured from 20 to 80 percent) and t'_{pd} is the actual loaded per-unit-length (i.e., per foot) propagation delay of the line. More conservative versions of the rule cut the ratio to one-fourth or one-fifth of the signal rise time relative to the propagation delay.[3,14]

If a line does not fall into the critical-line category, i.e., if it is shorter than the critical length, then the line delay used in the timing budget is the one-way propagation delay of the line (t'_{pd} times the line length). If a line exceeds the critical line length, some allowance for transmission-line effects must be incorporated into the timing analysis, unless the line is terminated in such a way that it is stable at all loads after a one-way delay. For the general category of control and data signals, it is impractical to terminate all lines. Thus, additional time beyond the one-way line delay must be allowed for most signals to settle to acceptable logic levels. For most lines in excess of the critical line length, allowing five line delays will provide adequate time for transmission-line reflections to subside (see Chap. 7).

> A rule of thumb to expedite most timing analysis: Allow five line delays for unterminated lines to settle.

However, it is difficult to generalize the response of very complex transmission lines. For example, receivers with very low-impedance clamp diodes on their inputs may extend the settling time to seven or nine line delays. Time-critical situations must be carefully analyzed with good timing analysis tools.[15]

Caution: Allowance for any additional signal length that might be added to signal paths during system test or troubleshooting should be made in the worst-case timing analysis where appropriate. One example is the added circuit-board-to-motherboard signal length that occurs when extender boards are used to extend circuit boards for troubleshooting.

11.3   Backpanel Interconnection Delays

The same device and line delay considerations must be addressed for backpanel or motherboard signal interconnections as for circuit board interconnections (see Sec. 11.2). However, most backpanel interconnections must be treated as transmission lines. Most backpanel interconnections will exceed the critical line length.[16] In addition to the normal backpanel signal path interconnection distance, backpanel signal interconnection length and delay calculations must include an allowance for extender cards (extender cards allow circuit boards to be extended out of a chassis so that test equipment can be connected for troubleshooting). All systems will have faults; thus it is essential that board-to-board signals have adequate timing margins so that extender cards can be used for troubleshooting. The extra length of an extender board is certain to increase backpanel interconnections beyond the critical line length when advanced Schottky TTL, advanced CMOS, or BiCMOS signals are routed between boards. Thus, additional time beyond the one-way line delay must be allowed for unterminated backpanel signals to settle to adequate logic levels, or else signals must be terminated to reduce the uncertainty of the settling time. For most backpanel lines, allowing five line delays will provide adequate time for transmission-line reflections to subside (see Chap. 7). However, as noted above, receivers with very low-impedance clamp diodes on their inputs may extend the settling time to seven or nine line delays. If system timing requirements are met with five line delays (or seven or nine for low-impedance clamps), then no further analysis is required. If the extra line delays are unacceptable, then further analysis with more sophisticated techniques, such as signal integrity tools, is required. Signal integrity tools may show that the signal(s) of interest will settle faster than anticipated; but if that is not the case, some form of termination may be required to improve the settling time.

11.4   Unit-to-Unit Interconnection Timing

Timing analysis of signal interconnections between remote units (i.e., units that do not have a common backpanel or motherboard) must allow for transmission-line effects. In most cases, unit-to-unit signal paths will exceed the criterion for critical line length, regardless of the logic family being applied. Thus, signals traversing unit boundaries must be properly terminated, or time must be allowed for signals to settle to valid logic levels (see Chap. 7).

Most unit-to-unit interconnections consist of some form of cabling using twisted-pair or shielded twisted-pair lines, coaxial cable, or flat cable. Cable manufacturers' specifications should be consulted for cable propagation times.[17] *Caution:* Cables with polyvinyl chloride (PVC) dielectrics may have very long per-unit propagation delays—on the order of 3.5 ns/ft.

Synchronous transfer of data between remote units is generally not practical due to the difficulty of maintaining clock alignment, which means extra time must be allotted for synchronization. If synchronous transfers are planned, some allowance for clock alignment uncertainty must be included in the timing analysis.

11.5   Examples of Worst-Case Timing

The signal path shown in Fig. 11.1 is representative of signal paths commonly encountered in large synchronous systems where data and control signals flow between boards mounted on a common motherboard or backpanel. A signal originates at the output of a clocked device (flip-flop $U1$) and proceeds through buffer $U2$ and off circuit board 1 on to the motherboard. It then goes to circuit board 2, where it goes through buffer $U3$ and then to a control input on a clocked device (flip-flop $U4$). Large systems typically require a number of similar data paths for board-to-board data transfers. In some cases, the

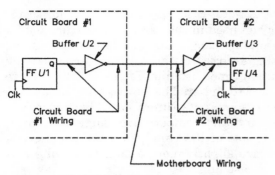

Figure 11.1 Typical board-to-board signal path.

output buffer $U2$ and receiving buffer $U3$ may not be needed, but they are required in many cases. Furthermore, it is standard (good design) practice to buffer signals at board interfaces. Even if the buffers are not required from a functional or good-design standpoint, they may be needed to ensure an adequate hold time at the receiving flip-flop $U4$. In high-speed systems, it is difficult to keep clock signals on separate boards sufficiently aligned to make reliable direct register-to-resister transfers. Buffer or other delay elements may be needed to ensure the hold time.

In the example circuit (Fig. 11.1), the worst-case signal propagation time is determined by the time required for a signal to travel from flip-flop $U1$ on board 1 to flip-flop $U4$ on board 2. The incremental signal path delays are as follows:

1. The maximum propagation delay from the clock to the output of flip-flop $U1$

2. The time required for the signal to propagate from the output of flip-flop $U1$ to the input of buffer $U2$ and the time required for the signal to stabilize at the desired logic level

3. The maximum propagation time of output buffer $U2$

4. The time required for the signal to traverse the backpanel (motherboard) and to stabilize at the desired logic level at the input of receiving buffer $U3$ on board 2 (transmission-line effects, such as ringing, must be considered)

5. The maximum propagation time of buffer $U3$ on board 2

6. The time required for the signal to propagate from output buffer $U3$ to the control input of the receiving flip-flop $U4$ and stabilize at the transmitted logic level

7. The setup time required by flip-flop $U4$

Tables 11.1 to 11.6 show the worst-case signal path delay for several of today's logic families when used in the example configuration (of Fig. 11.1). The tables are useful for comparing logic family speeds and as a guide for maximum single-clock-time signal transfer rates. The flip-flop and buffer propagation times listed in Tables 11.1 to 11.6 are for the 374 register and the 240 buffer. The propagation delay and setup times listed are worst-case manufacturers' data sheet specifications for operation over the military temperature range and power supply variation limits. The use of RSS analysis or of commercial device specifications would give slightly more optimistic results, but the objective is to show worst-case limits.

The interconnection delay calculations are based on PC board 1 and 2 track lengths of 6 in and a backpanel plus extender card interconnection length of 1.5 ft. Two nanoseconds per foot is used for board and backpanel signal track propagation delays. It is assumed that the two signal interconnections on the boards do not ring and are stable after a one-way line propagation delay. It is assumed also that the interconnection between boards does ring and that five line delays are required for the backpanel interconnection to settle. All on-board signal capacitance loads are assumed to be 50 pF.

Summary of times listed in Tables 11.1 to 11.6. The path delays for the various logic families listed in Tables 11.1 to 11.6 are not a great deal different from each other. Three are in the 45- to 51-ns range. The ABT and FCT-A families are slightly below 40 ns, and the AC11 fami-

TABLE 11.1   Example Circuit—Worst-Case Delay with National 54F240s and 54F374s

Signal path delay	Time, ns
1. Flip-flop $U1$ propagation delay	
Maximum value of t_{PHL} or t_{PLH} over $T_A = -55$ to $+125°C$	10.5
2. Circuit board 1 track delay	
Output of flip-flop $U1$ to input of buffer $U2$ track delay	1.0
3. Output buffer $U2$ propagation delay	
Maximum value of t_{PHL} or t_{PLH} over $T_A = -55$ to $+125°C$	7.5
4. Backpanel propagation delay	
Assume a 1.5-ft interconnection:	
5×2 ns/ft$\times1.5$ ft =	15.0
5. Input buffer $U3$ propagation delay	
Maximum value of t_{PHL} or t_{PLH} over $T_A = -55$ to $+125°C$	7.5
6. Circuit board 2 track delay	
Output of receiving buffer $U3$ to input of flip-flop $U4$	1.0
7. Flip-flop $U4$ setup time	
Largest value of minimum t_{SH} or t_{SL} over $T_A = -55$ to $+125°C$	2.5
Total propagation delay	45.0

Source: Ref. 7.

TABLE 11.2   Example Circuit—Worst-Case Delay with TI BiCMOS 54ABT240s and 54ABT374s

Signal path delay	Time, ns
1. Flip-flop $U1$ propagation delay Maximum value of t_{PHL} or t_{PLH} over $T_A = -55$ to $+125°C$	7.6
2. Circuit board 1 track delay Output of flip-flop $U1$ to input of buffer $U2$ delay	1.0
3. Output buffer $U1$ propagation delay Maximum value of t_{PHL} or t_{PLH} over $T_A = -55$ to $+125°C$	5.5

4. Backpanel propagation delay
   Assume a 1.5-ft interconnection:
   5×2 ns/ft $\times 1.5$ ft $=$
	15.0

5. Input buffer $U3$ propagation delay Maximum value of t_{PHL} or t_{PLH} over $T_A = -55$ to $+125°C$	5.5
6. Circuit board 2 track delay Output of receiving buffer $U3$ to input of flip-flop $U4$	1.0
7. Flip-flop $U4$ setup time Largest value of minimum t_{SH} or t_{SL} over $T_A = -55$ to $+125°C$	2.5
Total propagation delay	38.1

Source: Ref. 19.

TABLE 11.3   Example Circuit—Worst-Case Delay with IDT FCT-A 54FCT240As and 54FCT374As

Signal path delay	Time, ns
1. Flip-flop $U1$ propagation delay Maximum value of t_{PHL} or t_{PLH} over $T_A = -55$ to $+125°C$	7.2
2. Circuit board 1 track delay Output of flip-flop $U1$ to input of buffer $U2$ delay	1.0
3. Output buffer $U2$ propagation delay Maximum value of t_{PHL} or t_{PLH} over $T_A = -55$ to $+125°C$	5.1

4. Backpanel propagation delay
   Assume a 1.5-ft interconnection:
   5×2 ns/ft $\times 1.5$ ft $=$
	15.0

5. Input buffer $U3$ propagation delay Maximum value of t_{PHL} or t_{PLH} over $T_A = -55$ to $+125°C$	5.1
6. Circuit board 2 track delay Output of receiving buffer $U3$ to input of flip-flop $U4$	1.0
7. Flip-flop $U4$ setup time Largest value of minimum t_{SH} or t_{SL} over $T_A = -55$ to $+125°C$	2.0
Total propagation delay	36.4

Source: Ref. 20.

TABLE 11.4   Example Circuit—Worst-Case Delay with TI AC 54AC11240s and 54AC11374s with V_{cc} = 3.3 V

Signal path delay	Time, ns
1. Flip-flop $U1$ propagation delay	
Maximum value of t_{PHL} or t_{PLH} over $T_A = -55$ to $+ 125°C$	15.2
2. Circuit board 1 track delay	
Output of flip-flop $U1$ to input of buffer $U2$ delay	1.0
3. Output buffer $U2$ propagation delay	
Maximum value of t_{PHL} or t_{PLH} over $T_A = -55$ to $+ 125°C$	12.8
4. Backpanel propagation delay	
Assume a 1.5-ft interconnection:	
5×2 ns/ft$\times 1.5$ ft =	15.0
5. Input buffer $U3$ propagation delay	
Maximum value of t_{PHL} or t_{PLH} over $T_A = -55$ to $+ 125°C$	10.2
6. Circuit board 2 track delay	
Output of receiving buffer $U3$ to input of flip-flop $U4$	1.0
7. Flip-flop $U4$ setup time	
Largest value of minimum t_{SH} or t_{SL} over $T_A = -55$ to $+ 125°C$	2.5
Total propagation delay	57.7

Source: Ref. 21.

TABLE 11.5   Example Circuit—Worst-Case Delay with TI AC 54AC11240s and 54AC11374s with V_{cc} = 5V

Signal path delay	Time, ns
1. Flip-flop $U1$ propagation delay	
Maximum value of t_{PHL} or t_{PLH} over $T_A = -55$ to $+ 125°C$	11.1
2. Circuit board 1 track delay	
Output of flip-flop $U1$ to input of buffer $U2$ delay	1.0
3. Output buffer $U2$ propagation delay	
Maximum value of t_{PHL} or t_{PLH} over $T_A = -55$ to $+ 125°C$	9.2
4. Backpanel propagation delay	
Assume a 1.5-ft interconnection:	
5×2 ns/ft$\times 1.5$ ft =	15.0
5. Input buffer $U3$ propagation delay	
Maximum value of t_{PHL} or t_{PLH} over $T_A = -55$ to $+ 125°C$	9.0
6. Circuit board 2 track delay	
Output of receiving buffer $U3$ to input of flip-flop $U4$	1.0
7. Flip-flop $U4$ setup time	
Largest value of minimum t_{SH} or t_{SL} over $T_A = -55$ to $+ 125°C$	2.5
Total propagation delay	50.7

Source: Ref. 21.

TABLE 11.6 Example Circuit—Worst-Case Delay with National FACT
54AC240s and 54AC374s

Signal path delay	Time, ns
1. Flip-flop $U1$ propagation delay	
Maximum value of t_{PHL} or t_{PLH} over $T_A = -55$ to $+125°C$	12.0
2. Circuit board 1 track delay	
Output of flip-flop $U1$ to input of buffer $U2$ delay	1.0
3. Output buffer $U2$ propagation delay	
Maximum value of t_{PHL} or t_{PLH} over $T_A = -55$ to $+125°C$	8.5
4. Backpanel propagation delay	
Assume a 1.5-ft interconnection:	
5×2 ns/ft$\times1.5$ ft =	15.0
5. Input buffer $U3$ propagation delay	
Maximum value of t_{PHL} or t_{PLH} over $T_A = -55$ to $+125°C$	8.5
6. Circuit board 2 track delay	
Output of receiving buffer $U3$ to input of flip-flop $U4$	1.0
7. Flip-flop $U4$ setup time	
Largest value of minimum t_{SH} or t_{SL} over $T_A = -55$ to $+125°C$	5.0
Total propagation delay	51.0

SOURCE: Ref. 6.

ly with $V_{cc} = 3.3$ V is at 57.7 ns. Since the circuitry and interconnections used represent the minimal circuitry needed for board-to-board data transfers, the resulting total signal path propagation times shown in Tables 11.1 to 11.6 are indicative of the maximum clock frequency that could be safely used for single-clock-time data transfers in a system with similar signal paths using similar logic devices (see Table 11.7).

The maximum clock frequencies listed in Table 11.7 represent the best-case system clock speed for the listed logic families, assuming all data transfers must occur in one clock time. To build systems with the logic families listed that will operate reliably with a higher clock frequency, either signal path lengths must be reduced, or all time-criti-

TABLE 11.7 Maximum System Clock Frequency for Listed Logic Families

Logic family	Maximum signal path delay, ns	Maximum system clock frequency, MHz
FAST (F)	45.0	22.2
ABT	38.1	26.2
FCT-A	36.4	27.5
LV AC11	57.7	17.3
AC11	50.7	19.7
FACT (AC)	51.0	19.6

cal board-to-board signals must be terminated to reduce settling times. Some may argue that the assumptions made are too pessimistic and that not all elements in a delay chain will exhibit worst-case propagation delays simultaneously—and that is normally true. However, if worst-case timing numbers are used for all elements, a system will have some margin to compensate for those items that are overlooked—and there are always some of those.

The maximum clock frequencies listed in Table 11.7 are much below the frequencies being projected for advanced CMOS and BiCMOS systems. Why the discrepancy? What is the upper clock frequency limit for systems using devices with TTL or CMOS signal levels? Possible clock frequency depends on system size and architecture. Small compact systems where all lines are short can achieve higher operating speeds than large systems with long interconnections. It is possible to operate small compact groups of advanced CMOS or BiCMOS devices in the 40- to 100-MHz range (e.g., today's microprocessor chips), but as Tables 11.1 to 11.6 illustrate, 20 to 25 MHz, depending upon the logic family, is near the limit for point-to-point single-clock-time data transfers in large systems where signals must travel from board to board across a motherboard. For example, personal-computer I/O buses run much slower than the processor chip. Actual systems tend to have much more complex data paths than the simple example, such as heavily loaded buses, which will have long delays. In large systems, interconnection delays limit the system operating speed.

11.6 Signal Timing Summary

A great deal of care and attention to details must be given to system timing when advanced Schottky TTL, advanced CMOS, or BiCMOS devices are used.[18] The optimistic typical timing specifications prominently displayed on the first page of most data sheets have little value and should be disregarded. The parameter F_{max}, which is listed as the maximum toggle rate or maximum clock rate on data sheets for clocked devices such as counters, flip-flops, and shift registers, should never be used as an indication of the useful speed of a device.[13] In all high-speed applications, actual in-circuit worst-case device timing parameters must be used to establish system timing limits. System timing must allow for signal interconnection delays since interconnection delays are generally a major portion of most signal delays in high-speed systems.

Timing faults will be minimized by (1) carefully following synchronous design practices so that system timing requirements can be understood and analyzed, (2) structuring the design so that a measure of the actual operating speed can be determined, and (3) providing a method for inserting a variable-frequency test clock so that actual system performance can be determined during development and individual unit performance can be verified during production. Under ideal conditions (that is, + 25°C and nominal supply voltage level), a well-designed system with the margin to allow for worst-case military operating conditions and degradation with time should operate at nearly twice the design speed. Systems with less than 20 percent speed margin under ideal conditions, even if intended for benign conditions, present a high level of risk due to the variability of parts, actual operating conditions, and degradation of parts with age.

11.7 Signal Timing Checklist

1. Use absolute worst-case or worst-case RSS timing parameters based on worst-case system operating conditions (i.e., temperature, load, and supply voltage levels). Never base a design on typical device timing information.

2. Adjust manufacturers' maximum timing values for load capacitance in excess of that at which the timing is specified. Adjust minimum timing vales when the actual load is less than the specified load. Use manufacturers' timing adjustment guidelines, or estimate the change in delay for advanced Schottky TTL, advanced CMOS, and BiCMOS devices by using 20 ps/pF$\times\Delta C$, where ΔC is the actual load minus the specified load.

3. The signal line capacitance needed for timing calculations is the sum of the input and output capacitances of all devices connected to the line plus the line capacitance. The actual device input or output capacitance should be used when available. If the actual input-output capacitance is not available, for standard SSI and MSI parts use

   5 pF per input
   7 pF per output
   15 pF per bidirectional port

For VLSI parts such as PLDs, gate arrays, etc., manufacturers' data must be consulted. Estimate line capacitance, using

   1.5 pF/in for welded-wire and wire-wrap interconnections
   3 pF/in for PC board traces

4. To estimate unloaded interconnection propagation delays, use

   1.5 ns/ft for welded-wire and wire-wrap interconnections
   2 ns/ft for PC board traces

For cables or twisted-pair lines, consult manufacturers' data.

Caution: Some PVC insulated cables have very slow propagation times (greater than 3 ns/ft).

5. Take into account the slowing effect of distributed loads on line propagation delay. As a very rough rule of thumb, allow an additional 0.15 ns per load.

6. Allow for the additional length of extender boards or test cables in the timing analysis when appropriate (e.g., board-to-board signals).

7. Allow five line delays for unterminated long lines to settle.

8. Terminate long signal lines (greater than the critical length) that have critical timing or waveshape requirements. In the timing analysis, allow one line delay for load-terminated lines and two line delays for source-terminated lines.

11.8 References

1. Mike Meredith, "Analyzing Interconnection Timing," *Electronic Engineering Times,* September 11, 1989, p. T6.
2. Ravender Goyal, "Managing Signal Integrity," *IEEE Spectrum,* March 1994, pp. 54–58.
3. Richard A. Quinnell, "CAD Tools Help Cure Transmission-Line Woes," *EDN,* March 1, 1991, pp. 47–52.
4. Mike Donlin, "Signal-Integrity Concerns Slip into the Mainstream," *Computer Design,* September 1994, pp. 52–54.
5. James J. Vorgert, "Quantify Critical-Timing Risks with Statistical Analysis," *EDN,* February 17, 1994, pp. 95–102.
6. *FACT Advanced CMOS Logic Databook,* National Semiconductor Corp., Santa Clara, Calif., 1993.
7. *FAST Advanced Schottky TTL Logic Databook,* National Semiconductor Corp., Santa Clara, Calif., 1990.
8. *LSI Logic 0.7-Micron Array-Based Products Databook,* LSI Logic Corp., Milpitas, Calif., 1990.
9. Thomas M. Frederiksen, *Intuitive CMOS Electronics,* McGraw-Hill, New York, 1989.
10. James E. Buchanan, *CMOS/TTL Digital Systems Design,* McGraw-Hill, New York, 1990.
11. David Royle, "Transmission Lines and Interconnections, Part One," *EDN,* June 23, 1988, pp. 131–136.
12. *Bus Interface Products 1988 Data Book,* Advanced Micro Devices Inc., Sunnyvale, Calif., 1987.
13. *Bipolar Microprocessor Logic and Interface Data Book,* Advanced Micro Devices Inc., Sunnyvale, Calif., 1981.
14. David Royle, "Rules Tell whether Interconnections Act Like Transmission Lines," *EDN,* June 28, 1988, p. 131.
15. Dileep Divekar, Raj Raghuram, and Paul K. U. Wang, "Simulate Transmission-Line Effects in High-Speed PCB and MCM Systems," *Electronic Design,* April 11, 1991, pp. 113–122.
16. David Royle, "Transmission Lines and Interconnections, Part Two," *EDN,* June 23, 1988, pp. 143–150.
17. Ronald A. Crouch, "Choose Cable with Care to Optimize System Design," *EDN,* November 5, 1978, pp. 113–116.
18. Richard Nass, "PC-Board Speeds Skyrocket," *Electronic Design,* September 28, 1989, pp. 31–38.
19. *ABT Advanced BiCMOS Technology Data Book,* Texas Instruments Inc., Dallas, Tex., 1993.
20. *High-Performance Logic 1994 Data Book,* Integrated Device Technology Inc., Santa Clara, Calif., 1994.
21. *Advanced CMOS Logic Data Book,* Texas Instruments Inc., Dallas, Tex., 1993.

System Initialization and Low-Voltage Sensing

Most digital systems need some means of initialization to a known starting condition when power is turned on, following undervoltage (low-voltage) transients, and for test. Many systems also need some means of preventing unsafe or possibly destructive conditions, such as bus contention or random outputs, and preventing false writes to nonvolatile memories as power turns on or off and during power transients.[1] Overvoltage needs to be sensed to protect logic circuits from damage, and low or undervoltage conditions need to be sensed to prevent erroneous operation.

In most systems, overvoltage and undervoltage sensing circuitry is located in the power supply, and the power supply provides a *volts-good* signal to the system. The volts-good signal is used to initialize the system at power turn-on or to shut down the system under abnormal voltage conditions. If the power supply does not have circuitry to generate a volts-good signal, an equivalent signal must be generated elsewhere. In most applications, the volts-good signal is ORed with software-generated reset signals, hardware time-out signals, and in some cases manual reset signals to form a *master reset* signal. The master reset signal is buffered and distributed to each unit, board, etc., in the system that requires a reset, or initialization,* signal.

A central master reset signal is needed to ensure that all sections of a system are initialized at the same time and under the same conditions. Distributed reset signal generators, particularly those imple-

---

*Reset and initialization are often used in an interchangeable manner. In general, initialization is the action required which is accomplished with a reset signal.

mented with RC networks, should not be used because of the uncertainty of operation of RC-generated resets. Distributed reset signal generators introduce the possibility that sections of a system may not be initialized, or that sections may not be initialized at the same time.

The master reset signal, controlled by the volts-good signal and any required time-out counters, should be asserted (i.e., applied) when system power is turned on or when the supply voltage V_{cc} falls below the actual level at which the logic devices in the system no longer operate. When the master reset signal is applied, it should remain on until the system V_{cc} stabilizes at the proper operating level. During power turnoff or during low-voltage transients, the master reset signal should be applied immediately to prevent false outputs or random conditions. In most system applications, it is not practical to set the trip point (threshold) of the voltage level sensing circuit (i.e., the volts-good circuit) at exactly the minimum rated digital logic device supply voltage level; some allowance for system noise and an allowance for inherent accuracy limitations of practical level-sensing circuits are needed. In most cases, it is acceptable to set the trip point 0.25 to 0.5 V below the rated low power supply operating level of the system logic components with the highest minimum rating. Some allowance is needed to avoid excessive tripping due to noise and to provide an allowance for error in the level-sensing circuitry. Most TTL, CMOS, or BiCMOS systems designed with reasonable safety margins will continue to operate with supply levels slightly below rated minimum levels. However, when a system must either operate properly or shut down to prevent hazardous outputs or damaging internal conditions when low voltage occurs, the reset circuit trip point must be set above the point at which the system stops operating.

The low V_{cc} limit[2] for most 5-V advanced Schottky TTL devices rated for military environmental conditions is 4.5 V, and for most commercial rated TTL devices the low limit is 4.75.

The recommended low V_{cc} limit is 4.5 V for most 5-V advanced CMOS and BiCMOS devices with TTL input levels for both commercial rated devices and for military rated devices. However, most CMOS or BiCMOS devices with TTL inputs will operate at much lower voltages; but device input-output levels may not meet TTL specifications and speed is reduced. Most 5-V advanced CMOS devices with CMOS input levels (TTL or BiCMOS SSI or MSI devices are typically not available with CMOS input levels) have a rated low supply operating limit of either 2 or 3 V, but the device speed decreases significantly at reduced supply levels. Thus, it is best to sense a minimum supply level well above the allowable low supply limit. Most systems will consist of a mixture of TTL, CMOS, and BiCMOS; thus in most cases the system reset signal generator threshold should be set near the low supply operating limit for the devices with TTL levels used in the system.[2,3]

Low-voltage (3.3-V) devices are typically specified for operation down to 2.7 or 3 V depending on the vendor. In all cases, vendor specifications should be checked and adhered to.[4,5]

12.1   Initialization Signal Generation

A volts-good signal used to initialize or reset a digital system should be generated by using an analog voltage level sensing circuit—not an *RC* circuit. Simple *RC* networks should not be used to initialize or reset systems due to the uncertainty of their delay and the unpredictability of their response to power supply transients or power supply turn-on or turnoff rates. Simple *RC* circuits may operate as expected in the laboratory, but when exposed to actual system power turn-on or turnoff rates, they may not function as expected; actual system power supply turn-on rates tend to be much slower than those of breadboard setups or test stations. If the power supply turns on very slowly, simple *RC* delay circuits may not have sufficient delay to generate a valid reset signal. Furthermore, most automatic test equipment cannot test *RC*-generated resets that time out as a function of the application of V_{cc} to the unit under test. In contrast to crude *RC* networks, analog comparator circuits can be designed to accurately sense a predefined V_{cc} level.

Today a number of integrated-circuit (IC) power monitor chips, typically called *supply voltage supervisors* or *microprocessor supervisory circuits,* are available that contain circuitry for accurately sensing supply voltage levels (they contain analog comparators).[6,7] Their features typically include

1. True and complementary reset outputs

2. Reset time-out adjustable by external capacitors

3. Inputs for injecting other sources of reset

4. Circuitry for write protection of nonvolatile memories

5. Microprocessor watchdog timers for some

6. Battery switchover circuits for some

For applications where an existing power monitor chip does not meet system requirements or the needs of a particular situation, a discrete circuit power supply voltage level sensor is shown in Fig. 12.1. The circuit configuration is described below along with its operation. The analog comparator network in Fig. 12.1 is configured to generate a volts-good signal when the supply voltage V_{cc} is above a prede-

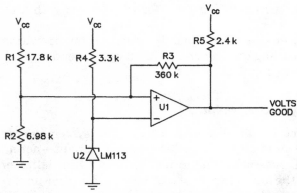

Figure 12.1 Volts-good signal generator implemented with an analog comparator.

fined level.[8,9] The comparator (Fig. 12.1) operates as follows: The LM193 IC analog comparator $U1$ compares the 1.22-V reference input from the LM113 voltage reference to the output of the divider network, $R1$ and $R2$.[10] When the voltage level-out of the divider network is greater than the reference, the output of the comparator is a *high* level (pulled up to V_{cc} by $R5$). When the output of the divider network is lower than the reference, the output of the comparator is a *low* level (near ground). Selection of the values of $R1$ and $R2$ controls the level of the sensed voltage (V_{cc} in this case) at which the comparator output switches. With the resistor values shown in Fig. 12.1, the comparator switches states at about 4.3 V. Resistor $R3$ provides a small amount of hysteresis to prevent oscillation of the comparator when the sensed voltage is near the threshold level. Unless hysteresis is used, oscillation tends to occur due to amplification of noise riding on the sensed voltage or the referenced voltage. Spurious oscillations need to be avoided where possible to keep system noise as low as possible and to reduce the chance of system malfunctions.

In noisy applications (which most applications are), filter capacitors should be used at the two inputs of the comparator, to reduce the chance of noise triggering the comparator to the volts-bad state. When filter capacitors are used, a diode may need to be added in parallel with $R1$ (cathode to V_{cc}) to quickly discharge the filter capacitor on the divider input and speed up the reaction of the comparator when power is lost. A capacitor in parallel with $R2$ can also delay the volts-good state and provide a small amount of extra time for V_{cc} to stabilize. If a volts-good or reset signal must be asserted for a significant time after the supply voltage is good, a digital time-out circuit (i.e., a counter) started with a volts-good signal should be used; RC delays are not reliable.

Two areas of the comparator circuit are critical with respect to threshold accuracy: the divider network $R1$ and $R2$ and the reference $U1$. To achieve an accurate threshold level, resistors with a tolerance of 1 percent or better should be used for $R1$ and $R2$. The tolerance of the other resistors in the circuit is not critical. Reference uncertainty tends to be the largest source of error in a level-sensing circuit. Low-voltage precision IC references, such as the LM113, are required to meet reasonable threshold tolerance limits. Low-voltage zener diodes do not have sufficient accuracy for most applications. Divider networks connected to system V_{cc}, or other supply voltages, should not be used as a reference; normal supply voltage levels usually are not precise enough and are often noisy. In all applications, the worst-case threshold limits should be determined from the worst-case tolerances of the components selected. If the results are unsatisfactory, higher-quality components should be selected. A worst-case threshold tolerance of ± 0.25 V is achievable with low-cost standard components.

In most applications, the system reset signal generator must be powered by the same supply V_{cc} that is being sensed.[11] There is often no other (higher) supply voltage available. If higher voltages, for example, ± 12 or ± 15 V, are available and they are guaranteed to be stable when V_{cc} is transitioning, then a number of analog comparators can be used to sense V_{cc}.[10] If higher voltages are not available, it is important to select a comparator and reference that will operate predictably when their supply voltage V_{cc} is less than 4.5 V for 5-V devices and less than 2.7 or 3 V (depending on the vendor) for LV devices. It would serve no useful purpose to employ a low-voltage sensing circuit that might not work correctly when the supply level that it must sense (and be powered by) is lower than the nominal power supply operating range. The sensing circuit should be designed to operate from a low supply level well below the minimum operating supply voltage level of the system components to a high level equal to, or above, the absolute maximum upper limit of the devices in the system; i.e., the sensing circuit should have at least as much high-voltage tolerance as the digital components. The LM193 comparator and the LM113 voltage reference used in the low-voltage sensing circuit shown in Fig. 12.1 have a suitable range for such applications. The LM193 is specified for operation with a supply voltage as low as 2 V and as high as 36 V. The LM113 provides a 1.2-V reference level for a wide range of input current. Resistor $R4$ must be selected so that the current supplied to the LM113 is adequate for the LM113 to be in regulation at a V_{cc} level much below the desired low V_{cc} threshold level.

If a volts-good signal must be combined with other reset signals and if the combined reset signal must be asserted under marginal power conditions to prevent unsafe operation (e.g., false outputs, bus

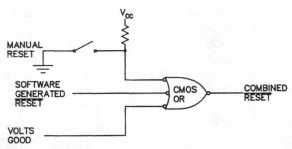

Figure 12.2 CMOS gates that operate with low power supply voltage should be used to combine reset and volts-good signals.

contention, or write signals to nonvolatile memories), then CMOS gates that operate with low supply levels should be used to combine the signals (for an example see Fig. 12.2). Most 5-V bipolar devices are not suitable since they are specified only for operation above 4.5 or 4.75 V, but CMOS OR gates are available that are specified for operation with supply voltages as low as 2 V (see Ref. 3).

If the only objective is to initialize a system to a known starting point and it is certain that it is not necessary to guard against unsafe conditions during power excursions, then there is no need to use special components to combine multiple reset signals. In those cases where it is sufficient for the reset signal to be issued a short time after V_{cc} stabilizes at the operating level, devices from any of the logic families can be used to combine reset signals. For parts commonality, the device(s) used should be selected from the logic family being used to implement the system.

12.2 Reset Signal Distribution

Great care must be taken in the design of the electrical and physical network used to distribute reset signals. Reset signals must not be degraded by excessive loading or noise. The central reset signal generator output should be buffered with multiple buffers to fan out the reset signal to the various subunits (component, board, etc.) in the system. Each subunit does not have to have a dedicated driver; buffers can be shared, but the loading needs to be reasonable. Where a reset signal enters a unit or subunit (such as a board), it should be buffered so that each unit or board presents only a single load to the central source.

Buffers used to drive the reset signal should not be mixed in a common package with buffers driving other signals. Large transient-load currents may cause local power supply droop, which will appear as negative-going spikes on the reset lines. If a *low* inactive reset signal polarity is used (in TTL-level systems), it is very important to have the reset signal buffers isolated from other buffers driving heavy loads. Ground-bounce spikes on inactive *low* reset lines are much more serious than those on *high* inactive lines, since *low* TTL-level signals have less noise margin than *high* signals. However, in spite of the desirability of isolating reset signals, board space limitations often make it impractical to isolate reset signal buffers. If reset signal buffers must share a package with other active buffers, there are two keys to avoiding system operational problems: (1) Use buffers that have minimal inherent ground bounce, and (2) make sure that the other buffers are very lightly loaded (the ac load is the greatest concern).

12.3 Reset Signal Phasing

The inactive state of reset signals should be the logic state with the maximum noise immunity since most reset (set, clear, or preset) inputs on TTL, CMOS, or BiCMOS logic devices are asynchronous and thus sensitive to noise spikes. When devices with TTL levels are used, the inactive state should be the *high* state, since devices with TTL levels have more noise margin in the *high* state. Since most systems consist of a mixture of logic families and technologies, reset signals should be phased to be in a *high* inactive state throughout the interconnection system, to take advantage of the higher *high*-level noise margin of those devices with TTL input levels. The inactive level of all TTL-level reset signals that must pass through noisy areas, such as motherboards, should be the *high* level. Most reset (clear) or preset (set) inputs on most devices take advantage of the higher noise margin of the *high* state at the device level by requiring an active *low* input level for resetting (or presetting). Either polarity is acceptable when devices have CMOS input levels since most CMOS devices with CMOS levels have symmetric noise margins.

To further enhance the noise margin of *high* inactive reset signals, pull-up resistors should be used in each electrically isolated reset signal line segment to provide additional noise margin. A pull-up resistor will ensure that an inactive reset line is near 5 V, which will provide an additional 1.5- to 2-V noise margin under typical conditions and near 2.5 V under worst-case conditions (without a pull-up resistor the worst-case minimum output *high* level for most 5-V devices with TTL output levels is 2.5 V). Pull-up resistors also serve to keep open reset lines (a line not connected to a source) in the inactive state. For example, pull-up resistors are often necessary at major interfaces to ensure that reset signals are not asserted during checkout or test, when not all input signals may be present.

12.4 Reset Signal Loading

It is important to limit the number of loads on reset lines. There is often a temptation to connect an excessive number of loads to reset lines since reset signals are perceived as *slow* dc signals. The rationale is that advanced Schottky TTL, advanced CMOS, and BiCMOS devices have the capability to drive many loads, and speed is of no concern. However, for practical purposes, the number of loads should be limited. For example, 10 loads is a reasonable and practical number to deal with. Troubleshooting a shorted signal line that runs to a great number of loads can be very time-consuming and difficult. Also, driving a large number of loads results in very long signal runs, which increases the possibility of coupled noise which must be avoided since most reset inputs are asynchronous.

12.5 Reset Signal Timing

Reset signals should be asynchronously asserted and synchronously removed. Reset signals need to be asynchronously asserted so that under fault conditions, such as the absence of the system clock, the systems can be reset to a benign state with no bus contention, false nonvolatile memory writes, or false outputs that could initiate unsafe conditions. Thus, reset signals must be asserted through combinatorial logic paths that have no clocked elements in the path. The presence of the system clock should not be a condition for asserting reset signals.

In contrast to being asynchronously asserted, reset signals should be removed synchronously to ensure that all clocked elements are properly initialized on the same clock edge. If reset signals are removed from clocked devices, such as multiple-stage counters, asynchronously and if the reset recovery time t_{rec} is violated, there is no assurance that all the clocked elements will remain reset.[12] A metastable reaction may upset some stages (see Chap. 10). If some stages remain reset and others do not, the system may not operate as expected. Two logic configurations that provide asynchronously asserted and synchronously removed reset signals are shown in Fig. 12.3.

The circuits shown in Fig. 12.3 operate as follows:

Circuit A. When $\overline{\text{RESET}}$ goes *low,* the $\overline{\text{LOCAL RESET}}$ signal is asynchronously activated through AND gate $G1$. When $\overline{\text{RESET}}$ goes *high,* the transition of $\overline{\text{LOCAL RESET}}$ to a *high* level is delayed until $F1$ is clocked *high.*

Circuit B. When $\overline{\text{RESET}}$ goes *low,* LOCAL RESET is asynchronously activated through the asynchronous reset input of $F2$. When

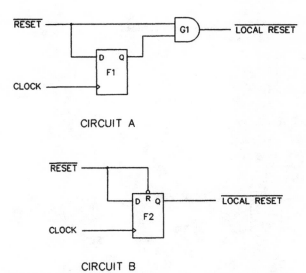

CIRCUIT A

CIRCUIT B

Figure 12.3 Two circuits for asynchronously applying and synchronously removing reset signals.

$\overline{\text{RESET}}$ goes *high,* the transition of the output of $F2$, $\overline{\text{LOCAL}}$ $\overline{\text{RESET}}$, to a *high* level is delayed until the next clock edge.

Note that the output of either circuit in Fig. 12.3 may glitch due to metastable behavior if $\overline{\text{RESET}}$ goes away during the undefined time near the active clock edge, but high-speed advanced Schottky TTL, advanced CMOS, or BiCMOS devices should recover by the next clock. A glitch following a clock edge that recovers by the next clock edge should not cause a problem in most applications since the $\overline{\text{LOCAL RESET}}$ signal was stable (at the other clocked elements on the board) until after the clock edge. If a glitch could cause a problem, $\overline{\text{RESET}}$ can be double-registered as shown in Fig. 12.4, which will remove the possibility of $\overline{\text{LOCAL RESET}}$ glitching.

In low-frequency applications with good clock alignment, the reset synchronizing circuitry can be located at the central source of the reset signal or in a central location in each given unit. However, when a system is operating near the upper end of the speed capability of the logic family being used, reset signals may need to be synchronized at the local circuit board level due to clock phasing uncertainty. If a synchronizing circuit must operate, i.e., supply an active reset signal, during undervoltage conditions, then the circuit must be implemented with advanced CMOS devices that will operate with a low supply voltage.

The synchronizing circuit also provides a convenient location to add a time-out circuit. Some reset signals require a fixed time to have

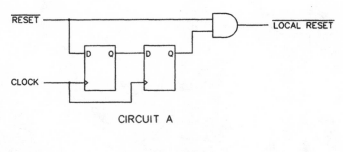

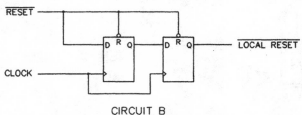

Figure 12.4 Circuits for double-registering asynchronously applied and synchronously removed resets so that the local reset signal does not glitch owing to metastable operation.

elapsed after V_{cc} stabilizes at the operating level. A timer synchronously started when LOCAL RESET goes inactive provides one means of adding a fixed time-out to the removal of the system reset after V_{cc} has reached the normal operating level.

12.6 Write Protection of Nonvolatile Memories

In most system applications, nonvolatile electrically alterable memory devices that are alterable with normal system supply voltage levels require some form of write protection during power turn-on or turnoff and during low-voltage transients.[13,14] Devices that typically need protection are battery-backed CMOS RAMs, EEPROMs, and NOVRAMs. Most UV EPROMs and some flash EPROMs do not; they typically require a programming voltage higher than the normal V_{cc}, but flash EPROMs are available that program with normal V_{cc}. In most cases where UV and flash EPROMs are used that require a higher programming voltage, the higher voltage is not present in the actual system application so false writes cannot occur. However, if the voltage needed for programming is present in the system and if the memory devices are connected to control signals that allow in-circuit alteration, then some form of write protection is needed during power sequencing. When V_{cc} is below the normal operating range, memory interface signals may be out of control and randomly glitch to a state that indicates a memory write should occur. It is also possible for some microprocessors to be out of control and inadvertently issue write commands during the first few clock cycles after power-up. Random glitches on write control lines may start write cycles even when they do not meet minimum pulse-width requirements. Data sheets define the minimum writer pulse width that will ensure proper writes under all conditions, but under most conditions much shorter write pulses will have sufficient write energy to cause data upsets.

Most of today's single-voltage alterable memories have some form of built-in write protection. Some have both internal hardware and software protection. Internal hardware protection typically consists of one or more of the following:

1. A power supply level sensor that locks out writes when V_{cc} is low

2. A noise filter on the write enable ($\overline{WE}$) input that prevents a write cycle unless $\overline{WE}$ is at least a certain width (typically 15 to 20 ns)

3. A power-up delay that prevents writes until a fixed time after V_{cc} stabilizes at the operating level

Internal software write protection typically requires certain data patterns be written to several internal write protection control registers before data can be written. The data pattern required to allow writing is such that it has a very low probability of randomly occurring. Devices with software and low-V_{cc} lockout circuitry usually do not require further write protection, but devices that have only low-V_{cc} and other of the hardware lockout features generally require some form of external protection. Internal V_{cc} sensors cannot be built economically with the accuracy needed to provide complete protection. To ensure that internal V_{cc} level sensors do not interfere with normal operation, their thresholds must be set much below the normal V_{cc} operating range. Most internal V_{cc} sensors' lockout writes below 3 to 3.5 V for 5-V parts, for V_{cc} levels above the internal protection circuit's threshold and the minimum operating V_{cc} level of the logic devices controlling the nonvolatile memory (usually 4.5 or 4.75 V for 5-V parts) is a danger zone. When V_{cc} is in the danger zone, the conditions of system and memory control signals are undefined; write and chip select signals may become active and may initiate unintended writes.[13]

Inadvertent data writes to electrically alterable memories without adequate internal protection must be prevented by forcing the signals that can initiate writes to nonwrite states during the critical portion of power transitions. Writes to most EEPROMs can be prevented by keeping chip enable ($\overline{CE}$), which is called *chip select* ($\overline{CS}$) on some data sheets, write ($\overline{\text{W}}$ or $\overline{\text{WE}}$), or out enable ($\overline{\text{OE}}$) in the nonwrite state. The nonwrite state for $\overline{\text{CE}}$ and $\overline{\text{W}}$ is *high* and for $\overline{\text{OE}}$ is *low* for most EEPROMs. If $\overline{\text{CE}}$, $\overline{\text{W}}$, or $\overline{\text{OE}}$ is forced into a nonwrite state when V_{cc} is between 3.0 and the V_{cc} level at which the control logic is stable and under control, writes cannot occur. The forcing circuitry has the same basic requirements as a volts-good signal generator:

1. It must operate at low voltage.

2. It must be insensitive to power supply turn-on or turnoff rates.

3. It must be insensitive to noise.

4. It must have a precise threshold.

Simple RC networks are inadequate; they do not meet requirement 2 or 4. A circuit similar to the reset signal generator shown in Fig. 12.1 combined with a CMOS gate is needed that will operate at low voltage.[3] For example, Fig. 12.5 shows how CMOS gates can be used to combine system-generated $\overline{\text{CE}}$, $\overline{\text{W}}$ or $\overline{\text{OE}}$ signals with a $\overline{\text{RESET}}$ signal from a low-voltage sensing circuit to force $\overline{\text{CE}}$, $\overline{\text{W}}$, or $\overline{\text{OE}}$ signals for battery-backed CMOS RAM or nonvolatile memories, such as EEPROMs or flash EPROMs, to a nonwrite state during critical power-up or power-down times.[13,14] The CMOS gate or gates used and the low-voltage sensing comparator must maintain control until V_{cc} is below the trip point of the internal voltage level sensor, i.e., below 3 V in most cases.

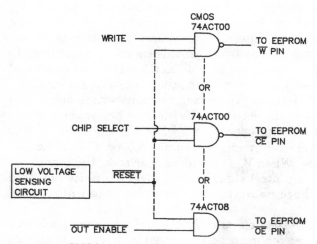

Figure 12.5 CMOS gates that operate with low V_{cc} should be used with the system reset signal to force system-generated $\overline{\text{CE}}$, $\overline{\text{W}}$, or $\overline{\text{OE}}$ signals to nonvolatile memories, such as EEPROMs, to a nonwrite state during critical power-up or power-down times.

Holding $\overline{\text{CE}}$ *high* is generally the safest method of preventing memory writes. Holding $\overline{\text{CE}}$ *high* prevents writes and ensures that EEP-ROM data outputs remain in a high-impedance state during power-on or power-off, thereby eliminating any possibility of output data drivers being in contention. Holding $\overline{\text{OE}}$ *low* causes outputs to be in the driven state during power excursions, which increases the chance of contention between data outputs and other devices that might share the data bus.

Some of today's supply voltage level sensors, such as the Maxim MAX691 and MAX697, have a built-in circuit for controlling $\overline{\text{CE}}$ during power transients.[6]

12.7   Logic Initialization to Prevent Hazardous or Damaging Conditions

Many systems need some means of initialization to prevent unsafe or possibly destructive conditions, such as bus contention or random outputs, during power excursions.[15]

If a system has three-state buses or three-state control signals, the system reset signal should be used to ensure that the controls which enable the three-state drivers are initialized to the off state during power supply transients and at turn-on. Requiring the presence of the system clock, which may not always be present owing to faults or other reasons, for correct initialization of three-state buffers is an invitation to device failure. Most advanced Schottky TTL, advanced CMOS, or BiCMOS three-state buffers are not rated for continuous short-circuit conditions. Ideally, three-state drivers connected to a common line are controlled in such a manner that no more than one can be turned on at the same time, even for short periods during power turn-on or turnoff. The safest method of achieving that is to use a single hardware decoder as the source of the enables for all drivers connected to a common line; then only one driver can be on at one time (unless there is some fault). Where a single decoder for the source of all the line driver enables (for a common line or bus) is not practical, which is often the case in large systems with bus interconnects that interface to numerous boards, the system reset signal must be used to ensure that three-state drivers are in the high-impedance state during power supply transients and at turn-on.

Some systems have critical outputs that must be controlled at all times to prevent harm to personnel and physical damage. One means of controlling critical outputs when V_{cc} is low is to use the reset signal to force the signals to harmless states. The reset signal and all circuits beyond the point where the reset signal is introduced to a critical output data path must be capable of operating at low voltage. The reset signal used to control critical outputs must have a direct asynchronous path. Control of outputs that may cause potentially hazardous conditions must not rely on the presence of the system clock, which may be absent due to faults or other reasons.

12.8   Summary of Initialization and Low-Voltage Sensing Techniques

1. Use a single volts-good circuit as the central source for system master reset signals.
2. Generate volts-good signals by using a power monitor, such as an analog comparator circuit or integrated power monitor chip, that can accurately sense when V_{cc} is out of tolerance.
3. Do not use RC networks to generate reset signals. Their response is unpredictable.
4. Do not overload reset signal drivers or allow reset signal buffers to share packages with buffers driving large loads, to prevent ground bounce or power supply droop interference.
5. Buffer reset signals where they enter units, boards, etc., so that each destination presents only a single load to the central source.
6. Pull up reset signals where they enter units, boards, etc., so that reset will not be asserted when the normal source is absent.
7. The phasing of TTL-level reset signals should be such that reset lines are *high* in the inactive state, to maximize the noise margin.
8. Pull up *high* inactive TTL-level reset signals for extra noise margin.
9. Reset signals should be asynchronously asserted to prevent damage and synchronously removed to prevent metastable conditions.
10. Where it is important for reset signals to be asserted to prevent unsafe conditions or false writes to nonvolatile memories during transient power supply conditions, CMOS logic components that will operate with low supply voltage should be used throughout the reset signal path.
11. The system reset should be used to ensure that three-state drivers are in the off state during power transients and at power turn-on.

12.9   References

1. J. E. Buchanan, "A Normally ON FET Control Circuit for TTL Logic Systems," *Computer Design*, June 1972, pp. 83–85.

2. *FAST Advanced Schottky TTL Logic Databook,* National Semiconductor Corp., Santa Clara, Calif., 1990.
3. *FACT Advanced CMOS Logic Databook,* National Semiconductor Corp., Santa Clara, Calif., 1990.
4. *ABT Advanced BiCMOS Technology Data Book,* Texas Instruments, Dallas, Tex., 1993.
5. *High-Performance Logic, 1994 Data Book,* Integrated Device Technology, Inc., Santa Clara, Calif., 1994.
6. *Maxim 1992 New Release Data Book,* Maxim Integrated Products, Sunnyvale, Calif., 1992.
7. *Linear Circuits Data Book,* vol. 3, Texas Instruments, Dallas, Tex., 1993.
8. Thomas M. Frederiksen, *Intuitive Operational Amplifiers,* McGraw-Hill, New York, 1988.
9. *Linear Applications Databook,* National Semiconductor Corp., Santa Clara, Calif., 1986.
10. *Linear Databook 1,* National Semiconductor Corp., Santa Clara, Calif., 1988.
11. W. H. Austin, J. E. Buchanan, and C. W. Nelson, "Precise Voltage Level Detector," *Digital Design,* August 1973, p. 30.
12. Thomas J. Chaney, "Measured Flip-flop Responses to Marginal Triggering," *IEEE Transactions on Computers,* vol. C-32, no. 12, December 1983, pp. 1207–1209.
13. *Atmel Corporation CMOS Integrated Circuit Data Book 1993–1994,* Atmel Corp., San Jose, Calif., 1993.
14. *Xicor Nonvolatile Solutions 1992 Data Book,* Xicor, Inc., Milpitas, Calif., 1992.
15. James E. Buchanon [*sic*], "How to Use the On/Off Relay Action of Junction Field-Effect Transistors," *Digital Design,* July 1977, pp. 26–34.

Memory Subsystem Design

Most high-performance digital systems are speed- and performance-limited by the speed and storage capability of their memory subsystems. In turn, memory subsystems are limited by available memory device speed and density. Even though memory device technology continues to make huge strides, system requirements stay slightly ahead of memory device technology. In most cases today, available memory devices are more likely to meet density requirements than speed requirements. That is fortunate since system designers have little choice with regard to memory device density; they are limited to what is commercially available. That is also true of device speed, but device speed does not give a complete picture of memory subsystem speed. Memory subsystem speed is determined by both memory device speed and memory subsystem design. A common mistake is to assume that a memory subsystem can operate at a cycle time near the access time of the memory devices used. Memory data paths or loops have many other sources of delay in addition to the actual memory devices. Interconnection delays and interface circuitry such as address drivers and data buffers or transceivers add significant delays in high-speed systems.[1,2] Signal integrity is particularly important in memory subsystems. Degraded signals mean extra time must be allotted for them to stabilize, and extra signal settling time means longer memory cycle times. System designers must guard against accepting or perpetuating unrealistic memory cycle time expectations. Memory devices keep getting faster, but memory interface circuitry and interconnection delays are near their limits and both become a larger percentage of total delay as memory devices and memory subsystems get faster. Poor interface and interconnection designs often severely degrade memory subsystem speed and waste inherent memory device speed.

Not long ago most memory subsystems typically consisted of several boards that contained mostly memory devices along with a few address and data line buffers. That is no longer the case; today with denser memory devices and higher speed requirements, most memory devices are distributed among the circuitry they support. In most cases, the needed density can be achieved with a small number of memory chips located near the processor or other memory user. Speed requirements also force memory devices to be collocated with the devices that use them. Long signal paths, such as required to go from one board to another, cannot be tolerated when 50-ns or less memory cycle times are needed.

13.1   Semiconductor Memory Devices

Semiconductor memory devices fall into two broad categories: volatile and nonvolatile. Volatile devices lose their contents (data) when power is removed; nonvolatile devices do not. Dynamic random-access memories (DRAMs), static random-access memories (SRAMs), latches, registers, and register files are examples of volatile memory devices; they can store data as long as power is present, but once power is removed, they lose their contents and must be reloaded when power is restored. Examples of nonvolatile memory devices (i.e., memory devices that retain their data contents when power is absent and do not have to be reloaded when power is restored) are read-only memories (ROMs) and programmable read-only memories (PROMs) such as electrically erasable (EE) and flash, and ultraviolet (UV) erasable PROMs (EPROMs). Power is required to read a nonvolatile device, but not to retain data.

Volatile memory devices usually have relatively fast read and write cycle times (i.e., the time it takes to read or write a location and prepare for the next operation), and the control signals required to initiate a read or write are relatively simple to generate. Read and write cycle times are approximately the same. Nonvolatile devices, however, have relatively fast read cycles but long write cycles and require special procedures to write or load data. ROMs are the least flexible nonvolatile memory devices from a system design standpoint; data can only be entered, or *programmed,* as it is called, once. Some ROMs are mask-programmable at the factory. Others can be programmed by the purchaser, but they require special programming tools of which there are a number of commercial ones available. In either case, once data are entered or programmed in ROMs, the data cannot be changed. PROMs, however, can be reprogrammed and in most cases while in the circuit. EEPROMs and flash EPROMs are designed to be in-circuit programmable. EEPROMs are the most flexible nonvolatile memory devices; individual locations or words can be modified. Write cycles take much longer than read cycles, but today's EEPROMs require no special voltages for writing or programming. Flash EPROMs are next in flexibility. They can be modified while in circuit, but not on an individual word or location basis. Most, but not all, flash devices must be completely erased before they can be written, which means all locations must be rewritten. However, some flash devices can be erased on a sector basis. Most flash EPROMs require a voltage higher than the normal operating V_{cc}, such as 12 V for writing, but others are available that require only the normal operating voltage. The UV PROMs are the least flexible of the reprogrammable memory devices; they must be erased with a UV light source before they are rewritten, which means the devices or the board on which they are mounted must be removed from the equipment. Removing devices or boards from equipment is an undesirable and risky procedure. The chance of creating problems is greatly increased when equipment is opened or devices are handled.

How often data must be changed and the initial device cost are two of the factors that determine which type of nonvolatile memory should be used in a given application. Mask-programmable ROMs are the least expensive if they are used in large volume and if the content does not have to be changed. In the reprogrammable category, UV PROMs are the least expensive and EEPROMs the most expensive; but device cost is not the only consideration. The time required and the simplicity of reprogramming are also important cost factors. As a rule of thumb, UV EPROMs are most cost-effective if the data have to be changed only once every 2 or 3 years; flash EPROMs are most cost-effective if the data have to be changed only once or twice a year; and EEPROMs are most cost-effective when the data have to be changed on a daily, weekly, or monthly basis.

13.1.1 Typical memory device

From the system designer's viewpoint, semiconductor memory devices are places to store and retrieve large amounts of data. To apply these devices, system designers must understand how the devices function logically and what the interface requirements are. Most LSI and VLSI memory devices, regardless of whether they are RAMs or ROMs, are structured as shown in the block diagrams of Figs. 13.1 and 13.2. They consist of an array of memory storage elements surrounded by address buffers, address decoders, data buffers, and controls. The address buffers and decoders are used for selecting particular locations in the memory element array. Data in buffers (if an alterable device) minimize the load for the source and isolate the memory array from external disturbances. Data output buffers isolate

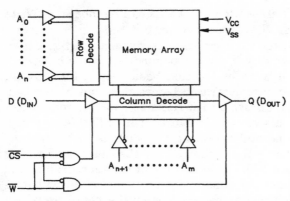

Figure 13.1 Block diagram of a typical alterable memory device with separate input and output data paths.

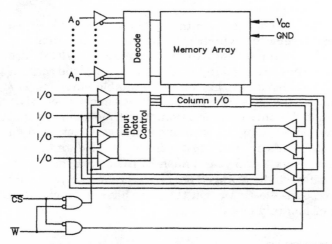

Figure 13.2 Block diagram of a typical alterable memory device with common input and output data paths.

the memory array and provide drive for external loads. Alterable memory devices come in two basic data input-output configurations: Some have separate input and output pins, as shown in the block diagram of Fig. 13.1, and others have common input-output (I/O) data connections, as shown in the block diagram of Fig. 13.2. Memory devices with separate I/O data pins are generally easier to use if the system architecture is such that advantage can be taken of separate data paths; separate I/O memories require more package pins. Common I/O memories save package pins, but complicate data bus control. They compound the risk of data bus contention between memory device outputs and data input sources.

Control signals common to most memory devices. Memory control signals fall into three basic categories: chip selects, out enables, and write controls. Not all memory devices have all three; most have chip selects, some have out enables, and only those that are *in-circuit alterable* have write controls. In general, these controls function as follows (check data sheets for specific devices).

Chip-select signals (sometimes called *chip enable signals*) typically serve to activate memory devices for either read or write cycles. Most memory device chip-select inputs are level-sensitive, not edge-sensitive. Most SRAMs, PROMs, UV EPROMs, and flash EPROMs require chip-select signals to be active throughout a read or write cycle (if alterable). Most EEPROMs require chip-select signals to be active throughout a read, but may not require the chip-select signal to be active throughout a write cycle (only at the start). Synchronous static RAMs typically use a clock or latch enable signal to capture the chip-select signal (as well as address, data, and write signals). Chip-select signals to synchronous RAMs only have to be valid within the setup and hold-time window around the clock edge or latch enable signal. Synchronous RAMs greatly simplify chip-select signal generation in high-speed applications. Dynamic RAMs typically require multiple chip-select or chip enable control signals (e.g., they typically require a row chip-select signal called $\overline{RAS}$ and a column chip-select signal called $\overline{CAS}$). The timing of dynamic RAM chip-select controls tends to be device-specific, and it is difficult to generalize the requirements. Up-to-date manufacturers' data sheets must be consulted for specific chip-select timing requirements.

Memory devices are typically implemented so that *low* chip-select signals activate I/O circuitry and start memory cycles; i.e., when chip-select signals are *low,* most memory devices are active, and when chip-select signals are *high,* most memory devices are inactive. Memory access time is usually measured from the time the chip-select signal is applied or from the time when all address lines are stable (whichever is later). In most applications, chip-select signal timing controls memory access time because chip-select signals are generally decoded for upper address signals, and as a result, chip-select signals usually stabilize some time later than address signals. For most memory devices, chip-select signals must be active for outputs to be active; when chip-select signals are not active, outputs are typically in a high-impedance (tristate) condition. When chip-select inputs are level-sensitive (in contrast to edge-activated), chip-select signals cannot be removed before data are read.[3] Memory deselect time is usually measured from the time the chip-select signal is removed (i.e., goes inactive). When chip-select signals are inactive, most peripheral circuits on most memory devices power down to conserve power and to minimize chip temperature.

Out enable signals, on those memory devices that have them, control whether outputs are in an active or high-impedance state. Out enable circuits in memory devices are usually implemented so that a *low* out enable signal causes outputs to be active and a *high* out enable signal causes outputs to be in a high-impedance or tristate mode. Out enable controls greatly simplify data bus control when memory devices have common I/O.

Write control signals (on those devices that have them) control when data is written into in-circuit alterable memory devices such as DRAMs, SRAMs, and EEPROMs. Flash EPROMs and UV EPROMs, although alterable in the circuit, typically do not have a write control input as such; instead, write signals are controlled by a certain combination of other control signals and the application of a special programming voltage to a V_{pp} pin. If V_{pp} is not present in normal operation, then data cannot be modified by erroneous signals or operation. In applications where devices can be modified in normal operation, write signals are extremely critical signals. Noise or glitches cannot be tolerated in those circumstances. Any disturbance on a write signal may cause an inadvertent write to memory, which corrupts the memory data. Noise, glitches, or other disturbances on write signals to high-speed SRAMs are a particular problem, since most SRAMs have asynchronous write inputs and are sensitive to very narrow pulses at any time. Data sheets may call out a minimum write pulse width, but under typical conditions much narrower pulses may cause writes. Write signal timing with respect to address and data is extremely critical and must be given a great deal of attention, to ensure that address and data setup and hold times relative to write signals are not violated. Write signal timing violations account for a large percentage of memory problems.

13.1.2 High-speed advanced CMOS and BiCMOS memory devices

A brief status report of size and speed, and a description of the basic characteristics of several of the major memory device categories utilizing advanced CMOS and BiCMOS technology are provided for those readers with little exposure to semiconductor memory devices and applications. Memory technology moves so fast that an attempt to report current memory device status in a book such as this is certain to be out of date before the book is published. The best that can be accomplished is to identify the present state of the art in each major memory device category and to indicate near-future expectations. A comprehensive coverage of all memory device types and the many subgroups and their characteristics is beyond the scope of this book as well as an impossible task in a single chapter. A chapter or more would be needed for each major category and perhaps for several of the subgroups, which means the book size would have to more than double due to the great variety of memory devices. Again, the best that can be accomplished is to provide a broad overview of the basic characteristics of several of the major categories.

In general, devices designed for low-voltage (typically 3.3-V) operation are available in each major memory device category, but most of today's devices are designed for 5-V operation. Most of the very high-density memory devices in development, such as 64 Mbit DRAMs, will be available only for operation at low voltage.

Static RAMs. Static RAMs, often called *SRAMs,* are used for high-speed random-access memory (RAM) applications such as cache, scratchpad, and control memories. Density and speed requirements drive static RAM technology, and advanced CMOS and BiCMOS process technologies have allowed density to be pushed up and access time down.[4,5] Static RAMs are now available in production quantities in 4-Mbit densities; 16-Mbit devices will soon be available, and 64-Mbit devices are in development.[6] Smaller static RAMs, such as 16-Kbit devices, are available with 3-ns access time, and 1-Mbit parts are available with a 5-ns access time.[7] Static RAMs are the fastest memory devices available. From the system designer's standpoint, static RAMs are one of the essential building blocks for high-speed digital computers and processors. No other memory device can match SRAM speed or simplicity of operation for either read or write cycles. Static RAMs are required to keep up with processors running in the 20-MHz or higher range unless extra clock times[8,9] (wait states) or other special techniques such as interleaving are used for memory cycles.

Static RAMs come in a number of configurations[5,6] by 1, 4, 8, 9, 16, and 18 data bits wide and with constantly increasing depths (i.e., number of words or bits deep) as technology improves. Small devices tend to be faster than large devices. One-bit-wide devices tend to be faster than multiple-bit-wide devices. Multiple-bit-wide static RAMs generally have common I/O pins (some 4-bit-wide devices are available with separate I/O). Most static RAMs are asynchronous devices. Address, data, and controls are not latched and must be present throughout a memory cycle. Because they are asynchronous devices, SRAMs are sensitive to noise or erroneous signals at any time, which means extra care is required to prevent crosstalk or glitches on signals. Extra care is also required to ensure proper write pulse widths and timing of write pulses, to avoid setup and hold-time violations. In the past when system clock periods were much longer, write pulse requirements could usually be met with a minimum of effort, but as memory speed increases and clock periods decrease, it becomes extremely difficult to meet write pulse requirements. In very high-speed applications it becomes almost impossible to shape write pulses.[10] Self-timed or synchronous RAMs[11,12] are less sensitive to noise and require no external write pulse shaping. The write pulse shaping is done internal to the device. Synchronous RAMs latch or register address, data, and control signals depending upon their exact implementation so that address, data, and control signals including write signals only have to meet setup and hold times relative to a clock edge, which greatly reduces the window over which signals must be valid. Because of the reduced timing constraints on inputs, self-timed or synchronous RAMs offer a great advantage in high-speed applications. The disadvantage of synchronous RAMs is that they usually must be used in a "pipeline" fashion (i.e., address and controls must have a clock time to setup before they are clocked in, or data require an extra clock time to be clocked out depending upon whether the device has input or output data registers—see synchronous RAM data sheets).

Most—but not all—advanced CMOS and BiCMOS static RAMs are designed to power down the peripheral or I/O circuitry when the chip-select signal is not active to conserve power and to keep the chip temperature as low as possible. Some designed specifically for very high-speed applications keep the I/O circuitry powered up and active, to gain a few nanoseconds in speed. Where memory devices are in use most of the time, there is little advantage to powering down, but in most applications that is not the case. In most applications where a large number of RAMs are used, only certain banks or subgroups are active at any one time, and in those cases RAMs that power down should be used. Static RAMs that power down when the chip select is not active (as well as those that are always active) typically dissipate 300 to 600 mW when active. When the chip select is not active and in the powered-down standby mode, they typically dissipate under 100 mW with TTL-level inputs, and some dissipate under 10 mW with CMOS-level inputs. Note that standby power is higher with TTL input levels than CMOS because TTL input levels do not completely turn off the complementary input pairs. When input pairs are not completely cut off, direct current flows between V_{cc} and ground, and power goes up. Wherever possible, RAMs that do power down when inactive (in standby) should be used. They offer a significant power saving where not all memory chips are active all the time. Memory subsystem power dissipation and memory device reliability are often major factors in determining overall system reliability, so it is important to keep memory power dissipation as low as possible. Another technique that sometimes can be used to conserve system power and maintain memory data integrity when static RAMs are not in use is to reduce the RAM power supply to a *holding* level which is typically in the 2- to 3-V range. Most advanced CMOS and BiCMOS static RAMs will maintain data at reduced power supply levels, but data sheets must be consulted for specific limits and reduced voltage operating requirements.

Dynamic RAMs.   Dynamic RAMs, called *DRAMs,* are used where very large quantities of alterable memory are required. Dynamic RAMs are, in general, the densest-commodity semiconductor devices available. They push the state of the art in semiconductor process technology development.[13] Today 5-V and 3.3-V 16-Mbit dynamic RAMs are commercially available; 64 Mbit 3.3-V parts will be available shortly.[14] Because dynamic RAM cells require only one transistor whereas static RAM cells require at least four transistors, dynamic RAM density will lead static RAM density by factor of 4 until the limits of technology are reached. Dynamic RAMs typically have been available in 1- and 4-bit-wide versions. In most applications, several are used in parallel to store a word or byte of data, but as density goes up, there is need for wider versions in many applications. Often 16 M words or more of memory is not needed, but denser (and wider) devices are needed to reduce component count. Most 16-Mbit and larger dynamic RAMs are 8 bits wide or wider.

Dynamic RAMs are not as fast as static RAMs, but are faster than most other memory devices. Dynamic RAMs are available with access times under 50 ns, but access time is not the whole story. Dynamic RAM data sheets specify both access times and cycle times, and cycle times are longer than access times. Even access time specifications are confusing and can be misleading since the typical dynamic RAM data sheet lists two or three access times measured from different control signals. Cycle time is usually a better measure of memory subsystem performance when dynamic RAMs are used. The *cycle time* is the time required to make a true random read or write. Cycle time usually takes approximately twice the longer of the listed (on data sheets) access times to complete. Cycle time is longer than access time because certain dynamic RAM internal signals must be precharged before each random access. Today some 1-Mbit devices are available with random access cycle times as low as 100 ns, but most 1- and 4-Mbit devices have cycle times of 125 to 180 ns, which translates to 150- to 200-ns system cycle times when some allowance is made for practical limitations of generating the required control signals. In general, it is very difficult to meet all the address, data, and control signal timing requirements needed for minimum cycle times. Most systems do not have clock signals of the frequencies or shapes needed to meet all the interrelated control, address, and data timing specifications when running at the minimum cycle time.

Dynamic RAMs, even without a precharge time penalty, are slower and more complicated to use than static RAMs because address information is loaded in two steps or words. For example, 22 address bits is required to decode 1 of 4,194,304 storage locations. Parallel entry of that many address bits would mean a very large package; so to conserve pins and package size, traditionally dynamic RAMs have loaded address information in two steps (or words). To overcome cycle time limitations, a great number of specialized DRAM configurations have been developed, such as video DRAMs (VDRAMs), cache DRAMs (CDRAMs), enhanced DRAMs (EDRAMs), RAMBUS DRAMs (RDRAMs), and burst extended-data-out DRAMs (burst EDO DRAMs).[15,16] Most of these specialized dynamic RAMs have some form of what is often called *page mode operation* whereby they can be accessed at a higher rate than the normal cycle time for a limited number of address locations (e.g., a page). Page mode operation can be used to advantage in pipeline sequential operations where only a limited amount of the address information (bits) has to be changed to access a new location. However, at page boundaries and for true random accesses, time must be allotted to allow loading of multiple address words and for precharging. Interleaving is another technique used to compensate for the slower speed of dynamic RAMs. Interleaving banks of dynamic RAMs allows overall memory system speed to match that of high-speed processors.[17]

Aside from the speed issue, the main disadvantage of dynamic RAMs from the system users' standpoint is their requirement for refresh cycles. Dynamic RAMs, as their name implies, must be constantly accessed, or else the data go away. Data are stored on very small capacitors, and unless the charge on each capacitor is restored periodically, the charge leaks off and the data are lost. Most modern high-density (1-Mbit or greater) dynamic RAMs require the charge to be refreshed at a 4- to 16-ms rate. Refresh circuitry adds to system complexity and in certain cases slows memory response, but in most cases refresh cycles can be made to happen in the background and can be transparent to the memory user. A number of semiconductor manufacturers have developed and market LSI/VLSI dynamic RAM control circuits that provide refresh timing and control, and in most cases these are much better solutions than discrete implementations.

UV EPROMs. The UV EPROMs have served as the mainstay of reprogrammable nonvolatile memories for a number of years. They have led the way in density; 8- and 16-Mbit units are available now,[18] and 32- and 64-Mbit units are in development. They are also the least expensive of the reprogrammable memories on a per-bit basis, and they are available from a large number of sources, which simplifies procurement and keeps the cost low. Until recently most UV EPROMs were relatively slow (most older EPROMs had access times above 200 ns), but that is no longer true. Now many units are available with access times under 100 ns, and some of the smaller EPROMs have access times under 30 ns. In the past, in most high-speed applications, special techniques had to be used to compensate for the slow access times for the available EPROMs. They were often interleaved to decrease the average access time, or the data stored in them were downloaded to high-speed RAM at start-up (or at other times), to allow the operational memory to keep up with the processor or other circuits it might be serving. Interleaving memories decreases flexibility and increases complexity. Downloading to RAM increases hardware; both RAMs and EPROMs are required. Now that under-30-ns UV EPROMs are available and faster ones are in development and will be available soon, the opportunity exists to run directly from EPROMs and eliminate the RAM used for downloading.

Most UV EPROMs come in 8-bit-wide configurations, but as density goes up, 16-bit-wide units are also available. For example, $131{,}072 \times 8$ bits and $65{,}536 \times 16$ bits and $262{,}144 \times 8$ bits and $131{,}072 \times 16$ bits are standard configurations for 1- and 2-Mbit EPROMs. The UV EPROM packages tend to be large. Address inputs are not multiplexed as they are for dynamic RAMs, which means that as density goes up, a large number of pins are required for address inputs—256-kbit EPROMs fit in 28-pin packages, but 1-Mbit units need more than 28 pins and are typically packaged in 32- or 40-pin DIPs or 32- or 44-pin leadless chip carriers.

One advantage of UV EPROMs compared to fuse-link-type PROMs is that data in UV EPROMs can be changed a limited number of times—normally the limit is about 100 times. The small number of erase and write cycles allowed is usually not a problem since UV EPROMs are intended for applications that do not require frequent data changes. But care must be exercised during board or system test to avoid inadvertently exceeding or approaching the limit. In general, when data are changed, the complete chip must be erased or cleared (except for one special case) with an ultraviolet light before it is rewritten or programmed, as it is called. An erase cycle is not required when data only have to be changed from the erased or neutral state to the programmed state; but if data bits have to be returned to the neutral state, then the complete chip must be erased and all bits or words reprogrammed. Most UV EPROMs require a voltage higher than $+5$ V for writing in data or programming. Older devices often required $+20$ V, or a level in that vicinity, to program, but the newer, higher-density devices typically require a voltage in the neighborhood of $+12$ V. Programming voltage requirements also vary from vendor to vendor, even for similar parts. Because of the variations and special voltage levels required for programming, UV EPROMs are generally programmed before installation with one of the commercially available programming tools. They can be programmed in the circuit if provisions are made for applying the proper programming voltage, data, and controls. If the programming voltage is normally present in the system, care must be taken to ensure that it and the control signals needed for programming do not get applied during transient conditions such as might occur during power turn-on and turnoff times (see Chap. 12). Another complication with in-circuit programming is that parts from different vendors often have different programming sequences and timing requirements as well as programming voltage level requirements, so parts from different vendors cannot be mixed. Also, some means of identifying the type of part that is in the circuit must be provided. When in-circuit programming is used, data sheets must be studied thoroughly to ensure that all programming requirements are met.

Flash EPROMs.   Flash EPROMs are expected to displace UV EPROMs and to be used in most nonvolatile memory applications in the future. The technology used to build flash EPROMs is similar to that used for UV EPROMs, and their operation and speed are similar, but flash EPROMs have the advantage that they are electrically erasable and do not have to be removed from the circuit (nor does the equipment have to be opened) as do UV EPROMs. In-circuit erase capability is viewed as a significant advantage in most quarters. Anytime equipment is opened or components are handled, the chance of problems increases significantly. Mechanical damage, ESD damage, and a host of other potential sources of damage are always possible when equipment is opened.

Flash EPROMs are programmed similarly to UV EPROMs. They must be erased before they are programmed. Like UV EPROMs, flash EPROMs are specified for a very limited number of erase-write cycles—first-generation flash EPROMs were specified for as low as 100 cycles; most of today's parts have 10,000 to 100,000 erase-write cycle duration, but some have 1 million write and erase cycles. Flash EPROMs are available that require approximately + 12 V for programming, but others are available that do not require special programming voltages.[18] Devices that do not require special programming voltages are a mixed blessing. They simplify the programming task, but they open the possibility for inadvertent write during power transients or normal power supply on-off transitions unless special precautions are taken. Regardless of what the programming voltage level is, if it is normally present in the system, care must be taken to ensure that it and the control signals needed for programming do not get applied during transient conditions such as might occur during power turn-on and turnoff times (see Chap. 12). Another complication with in-circuit programming is that flash devices from different vendors have different programming sequences and timing requirements as well as programming voltage level requirements, so parts from different vendors cannot be mixed. The situation with respect to standardization is even worse for flash devices than for UV devices. To date, flash EPROM users have had to deal with a complete lack of standardization. Thus, when flash devices from different vendors are used, some means of identifying the type of part that is in the circuit must be provided as well as some means of changing the programming algorithm. When in-circuit programming is used, data sheets must be studied thoroughly to ensure that all programming voltage levels and timing requirements are met.

> *Caution:* When in-circuit programming of flash EPROMs is possible, care must be taken to ensure that the specified erase-write cycle limit is not inadvertently exceeded or approached by unnecessary mode changes or test routines. Particular care must be exercised during board or system test.

Flash PROM technology and device density tend to lag UV technology slightly; 8- and 16-Mbit devices are available in production quantities, and sample quantities of 32-Mbit devices are available; 64-Mbit units are still in development. Flash EPROMs are available with pinouts compatible with both UV EPROMs and EEPROMs (see UV PROM section above for typical package size). As with UV EPROMs, most low-density flash EPROMs come in 8-bit-wide configurations, but as density goes up, 16-bit-wide units are available.

EEPROMs. EEPROMs are the most versatile of the alterable nonvolatile memories. They can be written on a word-by-word basis. Write cycles are much longer than read cycles, and some devices require that a word be erased before it is written; but the flexibility exists to modify individual words in a true random fashion. EEPROM read times have typically been in the 200-ns range, but now devices are available with access times under 100 ns. Write times are typically 1 to 10 ms. Read cycle operation is similar to that of static RAMs, UV, or flash EPROMs. Address and chip-select inputs are not latched or registered and must be present for the duration of the cycle. In contrast, during write cycles most EEPROMs latch or register address, data, and some or all control inputs. Some EEPROMs are self-timed and latch address and all control signals, which allows the controlling circuitry to do other tasks while write cycles are in progress. EEPROMs have limitations on the number of writes allowed, just as do other alterable memory devices; some are rated for 10,000 cycles, but others are rated for 100,000 cycles, and a few are rated for 1 million cycles.[18]

> CAUTION: When EEPROMs are used, care must be taken to ensure that specified erase-write cycle limits are not exceeded or approached during board or system test.

EEPROM internal circuits and storage cells are more complicated than those of UV or flash EPROMs, and as a result, EEPROMs lag UV and flash in density. The progression to each new generation of EEPROMs has been slow. The 4-Mbit EEPROMs are in development, 1-Mbit EEPROMs are available, but 256-kbit devices, which have been available for some time, remain the most popular in the EEPROM arena. Most EEPROMs come in byte-wide configurations, but there are some serial EEPROMs and other special-purpose devices.

13.2   High-Speed Memory Subsystem Design

It would seem that memory subsystem design should get easier as memory devices get larger and faster, but device characteristics never seem to catch up with system requirements. Memory subsystem or circuit design is extremely critical to the success of most systems. System speed and performance are generally a direct function of memory circuit speed. System reliability and owner satisfaction are generally a direct function of memory reliability. An old and true adage is, "A digital system is only as reliable as its memory subsystem or circuits."

Memory subsystem or circuit design is not as easy as it may first appear. Most memory devices are asynchronous devices and thus are sensitive to noise at any time. Yet, memory circuits generate a great deal of noise. Many address and data lines tend to switch at once, which causes large transient currents, which in turn cause lots of noise. Timing constraints are often difficult to meet and are often misunderstood and violated, particularly when system requirements push memory subsystems and devices to their limits.[19] Noise and timing violations typically do not cause outright failure, but create intermittent memory problems. Intermittent troubles are the worst kind. They are typically data-pattern-sensitive, and depending upon the degree of the noise or timing violations, they may occur very infrequently. Memory errors that occur very infrequently are extremely difficult to find and correct. Yet, until the trouble is found, the equipment is unreliable and in most cases useless. A single-bit error in a memory storing millions of bits of instruction code usually means that the machine gets lost and ceases to perform its function.

13.2.1   Typical memory subsystem

A typical memory subsystem consists of several memory devices interconnected to a source of address and control, to a source for data (if it is an in-circuit alterable device), and to a destination for data.

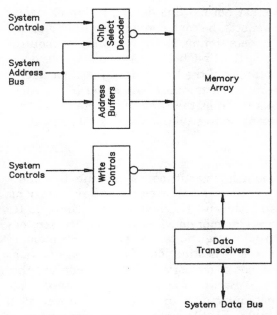

Figure 13.3 Block diagram of a typical memory subsystem.

For example, a block diagram of a typical memory subsystem is shown in Fig. 13.3.

When high-speed memory devices are used, regardless of whether they are RAMs or ROMs and regardless of what type of memory function they are used to implement, certain fundamental issues must be addressed for their successful application. Those fundamental issues include

1 Board layout for minimum signal routing

2. Control signal generation and timing (including write signal generation if RAM)

3. Worst-case address, data, and control path timing

4. Crosstalk control

5. Data bus contention avoidance

6. Power and ground distribution and decoupling

Physical arrangement, timing, and crosstalk control are interrelated. It is impossible to do the timing analysis until the approximate signal line lengths and physical arrangements are known. Interconnection delays are a direct function of line length, and crosstalk is a direct function of the physical arrangement of memory interconnections. Not only must normal line delays, including delays caused by transmission-line effects, be considered in the timing analysis, but crosstalk may also impact timing. Extra time may be required for crosstalk to subside. Thus, the first task in a memory subsystem design is to make a rough estimate of the layout or physical packaging of memory devices. The layout must minimize all signal interconnections to minimize line delays while at the same time minimizing the chance for cross-coupling among address, data, and control lines.

13.2.2 Memory circuit layout

The prime objective when one is laying out memory circuits is to minimize interconnecting line lengths. The shorter the interconnections, the more quickly signals settle and the less chance there is for crosstalk. When only one or two memory devices are used, the strategy for minimizing line length is straightforward: Locate the memory devices as close to the source and destination of interface signals as possible.[20] When a large number of memory devices function together (sometimes referred to as an *array* of devices), the typical strategy is to locate the source and destination circuitry in the center of the array of memory devices. For example, Fig. 13.4 shows a typical memory processor layout used when maximum possible speed is needed.[2] By locating the processor in the center between two equal groups of memory devices, the address, control, and data lines are minimized. When address and data lines have separate sources and destinations, an arrangement such as shown in Fig. 13.4, where address buffers are located in the center and data buffers or transceivers above or below the memory array, tends to be the best strategy for minimizing line lengths. Once a basic layout is determined, the next step is to interconnect the circuitry by using the techniques described below for minimizing signal settling time and controlling crosstalk. Often several iterations are required before the required performance is achieved.

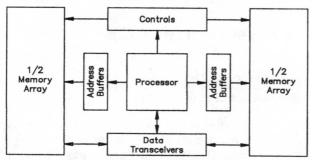

Figure 13.4 Memory and processor layout that minimizes signal length.

13.2.3 Control signal generation and timing

The first step in any memory device application is to thoroughly read and understand the control signal timing requirements specified on the memory device data sheet. That is often not easy. Many data sheets have several pages of timing specifications. Dynamic RAMs in particular have many critical timing requirements. Failure to read and understand data sheet requirements remains one of the leading causes of memory system problems. It is easy to be lazy when one is faced with several pages of timing diagrams. Yet, unless all timing requirements are met, there is no hope of achieving a reliable memory system. *Read the timing requirements over and over and over.*

The functional timing for a typical memory device read cycle is shown in Fig. 13.5. Good data appear at the destination some time after both the address and chip-select inputs to the memory array stabilize and after the memories and the output data paths have time to react. Delays through the subsystem include

1. The propagation delays from clock to output of address and chip-select sources

2. The interconnection delays between the source of address and chip-select signals and the address and chip-select buffers

3. The address and chip-select buffer delays

4. The interconnection delay between the address and chip-select buffers and the memories

5. The access time of the memories

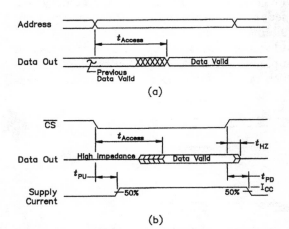

Figure 13.5 Functional timing for a typical memory read cycle. (*a*) Address-controlled; (*b*) chip-select-controlled.

6. The interconnection delay between the memories and the data buffers

7. The data buffer delays

8. The interconnection delays between the data buffers and the final destination

9. The setup time of receiving devices

The functional timing for a typical write-signal-controlled write cycle (for those devices that are in-circuit alterable) is shown in Fig. 13.6. Address and chip-select functionality and timing are the same as for a read cycle. The difference is that in a write cycle, data must be supplied to the memories in addition to a write signal. Write signal timing is always critical. Input data and all address lines must be stable and meet setup and hold times relative to write signals. In high-speed memory subsystems, that is usually not easy to accomplish.[3] Also, data contention between memory outputs and data input buffers is difficult to avoid during the start of write cycles when common I/O memories are used, and the high currents caused by data contention can upset memory devices and change data (see Sec. 13.2.6). In a write-signal-controlled write, memory devices first react as though a read cycle is starting; outputs become active and drive data out. Active memory outputs may conflict with data being driven in unless care has been taken to ensure that the data input drivers are not enabled until the write signal is active. To avoid problems with data contention, chip-select-controlled write cycles, as shown in Fig. 13.7, which are possible with most memory devices, are preferred and safer in most cases. In a chip-select-controlled write, memory outputs remain in a high-impedance state throughout the memory write cycle, eliminating any possibility of contention.

In high-speed SRAM subsystems such as cache memories, write cycles usually must be completed in one clock cycle of the highest-frequency clock available, which means there are no other clock frequen-

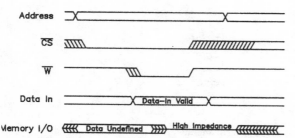

Figure 13.6 Functional timing for a typical write-controlled memory write cycle.

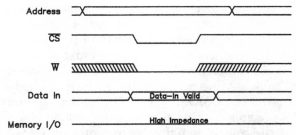

Figure 13.7 Functional timing for a typical chip-select-controlled write cycle.

cies or phases to shape write signals to satisfy address and data setup and hold times. In those cases where there are no other clock frequencies or phases, write signals are typically generated by gating the clock with the write control signal as shown in Fig. 13.8. Such an arrangement works fine at the start of a write cycle. Address and data have one-half clock period to stabilize before the write pulse becomes active. The danger with such an arrangement is that the address or data may go away before the write pulse goes away. If the address goes away first, data may be written to incorrect locations. If the data go away before the write pulse, incorrect data may be written to the

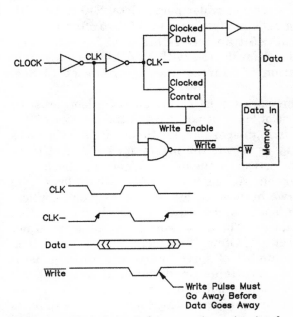

Figure 13.8 Typical circuit for generating write signals to RAMs.

selected address. Usually only one level of gating is possible without skewing the write signal into the danger zone. The gating structure and the write signal interconnections must be faster than the address and data buffers and their interconnections. Great care must be taken if PALs are used to gate write signals with the clock or other control signals: PALs tend to have more ground bounce than discrete advanced Schottky TTL, advanced CMOS, or BiCMOS gates. Ground bounce must be avoided since spikes on write lines can cause inadvertent write signals. Thus, write control signal gates or buffers must not be mixed in packages with address, chip-select, or other heavily loaded buffers. Other potential sources of spikes are decoders and multiplexers. Decoders must not be used for generating write signals unless a decoder disable signal is available that is guaranteed to disable the decoder during all possible times when decoder data inputs are changing. Multiplexers must never be used for write signals. Most multiplexers will spike when different inputs are selected, even when the input signals are in states that do not call for an output change.

Selection of memory address and data buffers or transceivers requires a great deal of care. Address and data buffer characteristics must be matched to the application. Typically, buffers must have the capability to drive large capacitances in a short time. Most advanced Schottky TTL, advanced CMOS, and BiCMOS buffers are suitable for such tasks, particularly the bus interface devices. Board space limitations usually dictate octal or wider parts. Octal 240 or 244 drivers with series damping resistors (see Sec. 13.2.4) are often used for address drivers, and octal 245 transceivers are used for data interfaces. Today a number of similar devices with built-in series resistors are available. Termination of address lines is discussed in Sec. 13.2.4.

When large banks of memories must be driven, a tradeoff must be made between the number of loads per driver and the number of drivers. As a rule of thumb in high-speed applications (50-ns cycle times or less), about 16 memory devices is the maximum number of loads (memories) that should be driven by one driver. When speed is important, it is usually best to split signals with larger than 16 loads into two groups and to use two buffers. In high-speed memory applications, a tradeoff between speed and hardware must be made. More speed requires more hardware. The above rule of thumb is often not followed in DRAM applications. Often 30 or more DRAMs are driven by one address buffer. A number of special-purpose address generators and multiplexers are available for dynamic RAMs that are designed to drive large numbers of DRAMs, but there is so much variation in the operation and functionality of these special-purpose parts

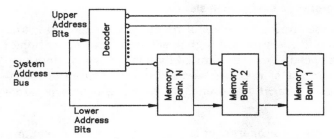

Figure 13.9 Chip-select signals are typically decoded from upper address bits, which causes the start of memory cycles to be delayed by the propagation delay of the decoder.

that it is impractical to cover them in a book such as this. The reader is referred to manufacturers' data books.

Chip-select timing often limits memory subsystem speed. Chip-select signals are typically decoded from upper address bits and as a result are delayed beyond the address signals at a minimum by the propagation time of the decoder used (see Fig. 13.9). Special high-speed decoders are available for address decoding, but they still have some delay. Some advanced CMOS and BiCMOS decoders have propagation delays under 5 ns, so it is possible to approximately match address buffer and chip-select decoder delays if possible decoder glitches do not have to be masked.

Caution. In some applications, it is important that chip-select signals do not glitch. For example, it is important that RAS and CAS signals to dynamic RAMs do not glitch, and in some cases chip-select signals to asynchronous static RAMs must not glitch. In most cases, glitches do not upset stored data in asynchronous memories, but glitches may affect operation. For example, glitches may reduce access time, so it is best to check with the manufacturer. Even if glitches do not directly upset a memory device, they increase system noise directly and by temporally selecting banks of memory cause transient power supply disturbances. In most cases, power supply current goes up significantly when chip-select inputs are active. To minimize equipment temperature and improve long-term reliability, chip-select control circuitry should be designed so that all chip-select signals are inactive when none of the memory devices are in use (when the memory devices being used power down when the chip-select signal is inactive). That means if a decoder is used to generate chip-select signals, it must be controlled by an enable signal that forces all decoder outputs to the inactive state when none of the memory subsystem is in use.

13.2.4   Memory worst-case timing analysis

A careful worst-case timing analysis of memory address, data, and control path timing is essential for high-speed memory applications.[2] System operating speed is usually limited by memory subsystem loop speed, so establishment of realistic worst-case loop timing is essential. The analysis is typically approached from one of two possible standpoints:

1. To establish the system operating speed, given a certain memory device speed

2. To establish that the memory devices available are adequate for the required system speed

In either case, it is essential to carefully determine the delay for each device in each signal path and the delay for each segment of the interconnection network and then to show that the sum of the delays is less than the required memory cycle time. In general, statistical timing analysis is not used for memory subsystems since most memory devices are tested at the factory and sorted into groups with similar performance characteristics.[21] Worst-case analysis is used because memory devices (which are graded by speed) contribute a significant portion of most memory loop delays and because memory loops tend to consist of a very limited number of devices (memory devices plus address buffers and data transceivers).

To ensure that the memory address, data, and control signal timing requirement is met and that no issues are overlooked, a complete timing diagram showing the worst-case *maximum* and *minimum* timing relationship of each control signal relative to worst-case address and data timing is an essential memory design practice. CAD tools that account for both device delays and interconnection delays (which are generally significant in high-speed memory applications) are a necessary aid. However, they must be used with caution. They may not account for loading effects, etc., which may be significant in critical memory loops.[22]

Worst-case device delays.   Data sheet device propagation times and memory access times must be adjusted for worst-case environmental conditions and actual load conditions. Propagation times for most advanced Schottky TTL, advanced CMOS, and BiCMOS bus interface devices, such as might be used for address and data buffers, are specified for worst-case commercial and military conditions and require no further derating for temperature or power supply level limits. However, most devices require some adjustment to propagation times for actual load capacitance since most are specified with 50-pF loads (excluding memories and some special memory address drivers). In many memory system applications, the actual load capacitance will exceed 50 pF. In those cases, device timing should be adjusted by using the techniques described in Chap. 11. Memory device access times are usually given as worst-case values over the specified operating conditions and do not require any adjustment for temperature or power supply voltage variations. However, access time is usually specified with a 30- or 35-pF load, which is typically less than actual load conditions. Memory access times are adjusted for actual load conditions by using the same techniques as for discrete devices.

Interconnection delays.   Interconnection delays often account for a large part of memory loop delays. Address and control lines, and data lines to a lesser extent, typically go to a large number of devices, which means they are inherently long lines with long propagation times. Line delays are further increased because of large distributed loads (where a large number of devices are connected to the line) which cause the intrinsic propagation delay time t_{pd} to be increased by the factor (see Chap. 11)

$$\text{Propagation delay time factor} = \sqrt{1 + \frac{C_{\text{LOAD}}}{C_{\text{LINE}}}}$$

where C_{LOAD} is the sum of the input and output capacitances of all devices connected to the line and C_{LINE} is the line capacitance. Determination of C_{LOAD} is straightforward: C_{LOAD} is the sum of the input (or output, as the case may be) capacitance of all the devices connected to the line. Determining C_{LINE} requires that the per-unit-length line capacitance C be known ($C_{\text{LINE}} = C \times$ line length). For printed-circuit boards, C is typically 2 to 4 pF/in, and for welded-wire and wire-wrap boards C is typically 1 to 2 pF/in. When the correction factor is applied, the actual interconnection propagation delay times t'_{pd} are given by Eq. (6.4), which is

$$t'_{pd} = t_{pd} \sqrt{1 + \frac{C_{\text{LOAD}}}{C_{\text{LINE}}}} \tag{6.4}$$

In most cases where a large number of memory devices are interconnected, it will be found that the interconnection delay is substantially greater than the intrinsic line delay. In many cases, the actual delay may be 4 or 5 ns/ft instead of the intrinsic printed-circuit board value of 2 ns/ft.

Line delay due to transmission-line effects.   Signal delays caused by transmission-line effects must also be considered in the calculation of memory interconnection delays. Transmission-line effects are a concern when line lengths exceed the critical line length (see Chap. 7).

The common definition of critical line length is given by Eq. (7.1):

$$\text{Critical line length} = \frac{1}{2}\frac{t_r}{t'_{pd}} \tag{7.1}$$

where t_r is the rise time of the driving source and t'_{pd} is the actual loaded per-unit-length (i.e., per foot) propagation delay of the line.

If a memory interconnection exceeds the critical line length, and many will, then some allowance for transmission-line effects must be incorporated into the timing analysis, unless the line is terminated in such a way that it is stable at all loads after a one-way delay. In most memory applications, it is impractical to terminate all lines. Thus, additional time beyond the one-way line delay must be allowed for most signals to settle or reach acceptable logic levels. Two conditions must be considered: underdamped lines and overdamped lines. When only a small number of memory devices (perhaps one to five) are interconnected, most lines will be underdamped and will ring unless terminated. The rule of thumb for the settling time for underdamped unterminated long lines is to allow five line delays for signals to settle (see Chap. 7). For printed-circuit boards, that means approximately 1 ns/in [(2 ns/ft ÷ 12 in/ft)×5] must be allowed for interconnection delays. Assuming five line delays for long unterminated lines simplifies and expedites the timing analysis task. If the memory loop timing meets the system requirements with that assumption, it is usually safe to proceed. However, it is difficult to generalize a very complex phenomenon. Critical situations must be carefully analyzed. If the timing requirements are not met with the five-line-delay assumption, the next step is to determine the actual line response. It may not require five line delays for the lines of interest to stabilize. If, after the actual settling time is determined, the system timing requirements are still not met, then there is little choice but to use faster memories and interface devices or to find some way of matching impedance levels so that the lines responsible for the largest delays can be effectively terminated.

When a number of memory devices (perhaps 6 to 15) are interconnected, most interconnecting lines are overdamped. When a large number of memory devices (16 or more) are interconnected, signals are normally severely overdamped. Overdamped signals normally require at least one trip down the line and back to reach threshold levels. Severely overdamped signals typically require several reflection cycles, as shown in Fig. 13.10, to reach the threshold level of the receiving devices.[23]

Whether a signal is underdamped or overdamped depends on the ratio of the signal dynamic source impedance to the effective line impedance. If the source impedance is less than the line impedance,

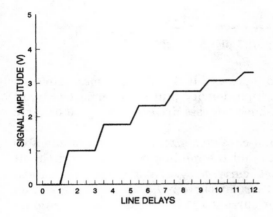

Figure 13.10 Address lines connected to a large number of memory devices are typically severely overdamped and require several reflection cycles to reach threshold levels.

signal waveforms will be underdamped. If the source impedance is greater than the line impedance, signal waveforms will be overdamped. The ideal case occurs when the source and line impedances are equal, but that seldom occurs in the real world. Dynamic source impedance is seldom given on buffer or memory data sheets. However, the output short-circuit current I_{OS}, or dynamic output current I_{OD} is usually given, and it can be used to calculate the voltage step size V_{STEP} if the effective interconnection impedance is known. That is,

$$V_{STEP} = I_{OS} \times Z_o'$$ (13.1)

Effective interconnection impedance Z_o' is found with Eq. (6.3),

$$Z_o' = \frac{Z_o}{\sqrt{1 + \dfrac{C_{LOAD}}{C_{LINE}}}}$$ (6.3)

where C_{LOAD} is the total lumped capacitance (inputs and outputs) of each device connected to the line and C_{LINE} is the total line capacitance (see above and Chap. 6 for further definition of C_{LOAD} and C_{LINE}). Where a large number of memory devices are connected to a line, the effective line impedance may be as low as 20 Ω. For example, consider the case of a memory address line that originates at a buffer and goes to 16 memory address inputs. Assuming 7 pF for buffer output capacitance and 5 pF for memory address input capacitance, C_{LOAD} is 87 pF (7 pF + 16×5 pF). Assuming the line is 9 in long and is a PC board with an intrinsic impedance of 40 Ω and a per-unit-length line capacitance of 3 pF/in, C_{LINE} is 27 pF (3 pF×9 in). The effective impedance Z_o' of the line is

$$Z_o' = \frac{40\ \Omega}{\sqrt{1 + 87\ \text{pF}/27\ \text{pF}}} = \frac{40\ \Omega}{\sqrt{4.22}} = 19.5\ \Omega$$

This example is not an unrealistic case. It is difficult to maintain high intrinsic line impedance in high-density multilayer printed-circuit boards, and it is common to have address drivers driving 16 or more memory devices.

Once Z_o' is known, the worst-case step size, i.e., the minimum step size, is found from Eq. (13.1) and the minimum output short-circuit current I_{OS} or dynamic output current I_{OD}. Unfortunately, the maximum—not minimum—short-circuit current I_{OS} is usually given on data sheets. Dynamic output current I_{OD} is specified as a minimum value and is typically more appropriate (for minimum-step-size calculations). For example, FACT 54AC240 or 54ACT240 octal buffers have a minimum dynamic output current rating of 50 mA (75 mA for 74AC or ACT 240s). The initial voltage step for a 50-mA buffer driving a 20-Ω line is

$$V_{\text{STEP}} = 50\ \text{mA} \times 20\ \Omega = 1.0\ \text{V}$$

which means the signal must propagate down the line and back several times, depending upon the starting level of the signal and the thresholds of the receiving memory devices, before a new level is recognized. If the signal starts near V_{cc} and the receiving devices have TTL levels, it must transition 4.5 V, which means 10 line delays (five round trips) are needed for the signal to safely cross the *low* TTL threshold. Ten line delays at approximately 3 ns each (4 ns/ft×9 in×$\frac{1}{12}$ ft/in) is a significant and intolerable delay in most applications. The situation may be even worse when signals originate from memories or special-purpose devices, processors, ASICs, etc. They often have very low drive, and their dynamic output drive may not be specified. Where the short-circuit output current I_{OS} or dynamic output current I_{OD} is not given on data sheets, it can be estimated by the following rule of thumb: Typically the dynamic output current is approximately 10 times the static (dc) output rating. That is,

When dc I_o is 4 mA, I_{OD} is typically 40 mA.

When dc I_o is 8 mA, I_{OD} is typically 80 mA.

When dc I_o is 16 mA, I_{OD} is typically 160 mA.

Etc.

Low effective line impedance is not always a problem in memory systems. Sometimes the line impedance is too high relative to address or data line drivers. High line impedance means signals are under-damped and ring, which causes extra delay. When the line impedance is high, one solution is to terminate lines. Either source or load termination can be used. Source termination has the advantage of requiring fewer parts (than load termination) and of dissipating less dc power. The disadvantage of source-terminated lines is that at least two line delays are required for all points to transition to valid new logic levels (see Chap. 7). Signals start at one-half amplitude (assuming an exact match in source and line impedances) and must propagate to the load and reflect back to the source to reach final value. Load-terminated lines have the advantage of requiring only one line delay to reach final value (assuming the source impedance is much less than the line impedance). When the signal reaches the end of the line or the last load on the line, all loads have new valid logic levels. The disadvantages of load-terminated lines are high dc power dissipation and greater number of parts. Load termination typically must be implemented with split or Thevenin's terminations, so at least two resistors are required per load termination. Split termination is required because few advanced Schottky TTL, advanced CMOS, or BiCMOS buffers, even those designed for memory address driving applications, have the capability to drive 60-Ω, or less, terminations connected directly to ground or V_{cc}. The advantage of a Thevenin termination is that it provides a means of matching lower line impedances while minimizing driver current source and sink requirements.

Another solution, when signals are underdamped, is to lower the impedances of the interconnections until they more nearly match the output impedance signal sources. The simplest technique and the one most frequently used is to locate the signal source, e.g., an address buffer, in the middle of the line. The source (buffer) sees two lines in parallel, which means that the effective impedance seen by the source is one-half the normal line impedance. The source must be near the middle of the line, or reflections may not cancel. Another technique, which is similar and has the same effect as center-driving lines, is to loop lines back to the source. The advantage of looping lines to lower impedance is that it removes any question of whether the driver is in the middle of the line. The disadvantage is that most PC board autorouters will not loop lines. If center driving or looping does not lower line impedance sufficiently, lines to memory arrays (i.e., groups of memory devices) can be connected in a grid to lower the effective impedance. Connecting lines in a grid, in effect, is the same as paralleling a number of lines, which means the effective impedance of a grid interconnection is lower by a factor equal to the number of lines paralleled. One disadvantage of lowering line impedance to control ringing is that it increases the switching currents in the signal sources and in the power and ground system. Center driving, looping, and gridding memory interconnections tend to reduce worst-case signal propagation paths (as well as ringing) which helps improve memory system response.

In high-speed memory applications, each interconnecting path must be carefully analyzed and optimized. When it is found that performance does not meet requirements, definitive steps must be taken to improve the situation. Lines must be shortened or broken into segments so that multiple drivers can be used; higher-current drivers and memories may be required along with some of or all the above-described special termination and interconnection techniques. High-speed memory operation does not come easy.

13.2.5 Crosstalk control

The fast edge speeds of advanced Schottky TTL, advanced CMOS, and BiCMOS address and data buffers and transceivers and of CMOS and BiCMOS memory devices greatly increase the possibility of the memory subsystem being degraded by crosstalk. Crosstalk is a special concern in memory subsystems because most memory devices are asynchronous and are subject to disruption at any time. Crosstalk may not only cause erroneous memory operation, but also slow memory access times. Extra time may have to be allotted to allow crosstalk to subside if it is not controlled. Extra time is usually not available when today's memory devices are applied; the goal is often to achieve the highest possible operating speed.

Cross-coupling between any combination of memory input or output signals as well as crosstalk between nearby unrelated signals can be disruptive and must be guarded against. Crosstalk to RAM write control signals is a particular concern; it may cause inadvertent write signals. Crosstalk between address and data buses is a common problem; bused signals tend to change at the same time, which means more coupling energy. Crosstalk between buses tends to be data-pattern-sensitive and is worse when all address or data lines change in the same direction at the same time. Excessive cross-coupling from memory data lines to address lines during read cycles can result in positive feedback that degrades the response time of the memory device and in extreme cases can cause unstable oscillatory operation. During write cycles, the danger is that data-to-address-line cross-coupling may upset address lines sufficiently to cause write signals to incorrect memory locations.

Crosstalk is a function of the separation between signal lines, the linear distance that signal lines run parallel with each other, and the height above a ground, or other, reference plane. Standard techniques for controlling cross-coupling between signals include these:

1. Run signals at right angles to each other.

2. Keep lines as close as possible to ground or reference planes.

3. Isolate signals from one another by ground traces and reference planes.

Multilayer PC boards simplify the task of isolating and controlling crosstalk in memory interconnection systems; as a minimum, address, data, and control signals can be routed at right angles on different layers, and in more critical applications, voltage and ground planes can provide isolation for critical memory signals. Where high-speed RAMs are used, multilayer PC boards are essential; address, data, and control signals (particularly write signals) must be isolated by reference planes. All write control signals must be isolated from other signals by reference planes and extrawide line-to-line spacing. Critical write signals can be further protected by running a ground trace on each side of signal traces. If each signal layer in the PC board is not separated by a reference plane, care must be taken to ensure that there is not a noisy signal running parallel and directly above or below a critical signal.

On welded-wire or wire-wrap boards or backpanels, memory interconnection wiring must be as direct as possible between points so as to randomize the routing, and the wiring must be kept as close as possible to the board or backpanel ground (or voltage) plane. Care must be taken to ensure that wiring is not channelized. Particular care must be taken to ensure that critical write signals are not channelized with address or data buses or any noisy signals for that matter.

13.2.6 Data bus contention prevention

Bus contention occurs when two or more devices with opposing output states are enabled to the same line at the same time. Contention, even for short times, causes high currents in the device outputs in contention. High currents cause noise that can cause system and device upsets and destroy devices.[24] Even if immediate destruction does not occur, extended periods of bus contention can impact long-term device reliability. Bus contention problems in memory subsystems are most apt to occur when common I/O memory devices are used, but contention can be a problem anywhere two or more tristate devices are connected to a line.

Write-enable-controlled write cycles to common I/O memories are rife with opportunities for data bus contention[25] and are the most common cause of contention problems. In a write-enable-controlled write cycle (see Sec. 13.2.3), the chip-select and write timing is such that the chip-select signal is applied before and removed after or coin-

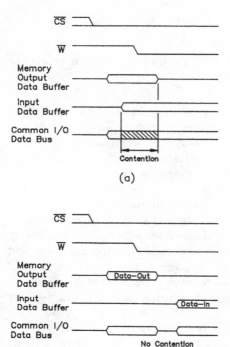

Figure 13.11 (a) Data contention at the beginning of a write cycle; data input is enabled before memory outputs are disabled. (b) No data contention; data input is enabled after memory outputs are disabled.

cident with the write signal. Contention occurs because until the write enable is applied, memory outputs are active following the application of the chip-select signal. If the input data buffer is enabled before the write signal forces the memory outputs to a high-impedance state (see Fig. 13.11), then contention exists for the period until the write signal is activated and the memory outputs go to a high-impedance state. Contention can also exist at the end of the cycle if the memory address changes, if the input data change, or if there is faulty operation (see Fig. 13.12). As long as the memory address and input data remain the same and the device is operating correctly, the output data are the same as the input data (since it should be reading out what was just written in) and no contention should occur. Applying chip select at the same time as write, or slightly after write and removing it slightly before removing write, or using a chip-select-controlled write cycle as described in Sec. 13.2.3 eliminates most contention problems and should not be used where possible. Write-controlled write cycles should not be used unless the timing is such that it can be guaranteed that no contention will occur; careless use of write-controlled write cycles often leads to devices being in

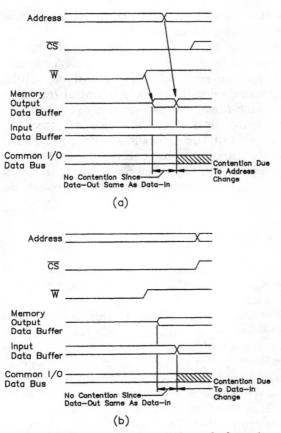

Figure 13.12 Data contention at the end of a write cycle. (*a*) Contention due to address changes; (*b*) contention due to data input changes.

contention for one-half clock cycle or more, which can cause data corruption and device failure.

In high-speed applications it is usually very difficult to eliminate all possibilities of contention at cycle boundaries. In the past, when memory devices were much slower, a few nanoseconds of contention seldom caused a problem, but that is no longer the case. Many high-speed RAMs, particularly those with access times under 25 ns, are extra sensitive to data contention; very short periods of contention will cause data errors. When high-speed memories are used, steps must be taken to control memory chip-select signals or out enables and bus driver enables so that contention does not occur. In some cases contention problems can be cured by limiting the contention current. Contention currents can be limited by series resistors in the

22- to 100-Ω range, but series resistors slow response and may cause voltage offsets that in turn may cause logic level errors.

It is important to prevent bus contention at power-on to prevent damage to bus drivers and memory chips. Some memory devices have built-in circuits to limit output currents at start-up, but not all do, and most bus interface drivers do not. Thus, it is essential that tristate buses be controlled in such a way that all drivers are initialized off or only one is on when power first comes on. All bus control circuits should be asynchronously initialized by the system reset signal so that all bus control signals start up in the inactive state. The presence of the system clock should not be required for a safe start-up at power-up. Under fault conditions and during initial system checkout, the clock may not be present.

13.2.7 Power and ground distribution and decoupling

High-speed memory subsystems require low-impedance power and ground planes to distribute power. No other means of power distribution should be considered. Most memory devices have very large transient-current demands when they are first selected, often in the 100- to 200-mA range. Only very low-impedance planes are capable of supplying such large transient currents without severe voltage drops. If universal boards are used, package power and ground pins must be connected directly to power and ground planes with solder clips or washers (see Chap. 5). The inductance of any length of wire sufficient to make a connection will be excessive. Even when power and ground planes are used, decoupling capacitors are needed. The memory device manufacturer's decoupling recommendations must be followed exactly to ensure a reliable memory subsystem. Most manufacturers recommend one decoupling capacitor of at least 0.1 μF for each memory device below 256 kbits and one of at least 0.22 μF for each memory device of 256 kbits and above. All address and data buffers must be decoupled since they tend to have very high transient-current demands.

Ceramic capacitors with good high-frequency response are required for memory decoupling (see Chap. 5). Leads need to be as short as possible to minimize inductance. Surface-mounted ceramic capacitors are ideal since they have the shortest possible leads. Decoupling capacitors must be connected directly to power and ground planes; there should be no wiring or long PC board tracks. The capacitors must be located as close as possible between the power and ground pins of the package being decoupled. A row of capacitors on the edge or center of a board does little good when high-frequency devices are used.

In addition to local decoupling, when a large number of memory devices are collocated and a large number are accessed at the same time, then as large as physically possible bulk storage capacitors should be located near where power enters the board and around the perimeter of the memory devices (see Chap. 5 for guidelines on selecting bulk decoupling capacitors). Bulk decoupling capacitors help replenish the charge on local decoupling capacitors so that the local ones are back to full charge at the start of the next memory cycle.

13.2.8 Failure rates and error detection and correction

Errors are always a concern in memory systems, and the larger the memory subsystem, the greater the chance of errors. An early decision that must be made in any memory subsystem design turns on whether some means of flagging and reporting errors is needed or whether some form of error detection and correction circuitry is needed to meet error rate requirements. Memory subsystem error rates are mainly a function of memory device error rates since most of the devices in a memory subsystem are memories. Memory devices are usually pushing the state of the art, and devices that push technology are often more prone to failures or errors. The sheer size and number of transistors in large memory devices greatly increase the chances of manufacturing defects including latent defects that do not show up until after devices have been installed in systems. Some of the large memory devices are built with redundant sections that the manufacturer activates as needed during initial test to overcome fatal manufacturing faults and improve yield. Others have built-in error detection and correction circuits that are transparent to the user and become active when needed. Regardless of the manufacturing approach used to ensure to the manufacturer a reasonable yield, most of today's LSI/VLSI memory devices have a reasonably low failure rate, given the complexity of the devices. Failure rate (or more correctly projected failure rates since state-of-the-art devices usually have little actual failure rate history) are specified in failures in test (FITs) per billion device hours. Given the assumption that the memory devices are the main contributors to memory subsystem failure, the memory subsystem failure rate is the memory device failure rate times the number of memory devices. If it is possible to find and use memory devices that have a sufficiently low failure rate to meet system requirements, that is a much better solution than adding error detection and correction circuits. Error detection and correction circuits do not come free; extra circuitry is required, and the cost and the benefits of the extra circuitry must be weighed carefully. In some cases, the size and complexity of the extra circuitry may negate the perceived benefits. The extra circuitry may also slow throughput. Extra time is required for error detection and correction circuitry to make decisions. The simplest and most used technique for detecting memory subsystem errors is to use byte or word parity checking. Byte or word parity checking requires 1 additional bit of storage per byte or word and one additional buffer or transceiver in the data paths to and from the memory subsystem, which is not a severe overhead. Actual error correction significantly increases the overhead. Logic implementations for detecting and correcting errors are out of the scope of this book. They are covered in most books on logic design.

13.3 Memory Subsystem Testing

As memory subsystem size and speed go up, it becomes more important that subsystems be thoroughly tested; but as size goes up, the time required for test becomes significant. Tradeoffs must be made between component testing and subsystem testing in production situations. The time required to find all possible memory faults in a large memory subsystem is prohibitive and not cost-effective in a production environment. Thus, it is important that memory subsystems be designed with adequate operating margins so that production testing does not have to "weed out" those units where the components are all in specification but all the tolerances fall in the wrong direction. To ensure that memory subsystems are not operating on "the edge" or have pattern-sensitive problems, all memory subsystems must be thoroughly tested during the design verification process or when major components or interconnection systems (e.g., PC boards) are changed. High-speed buffers and memory outputs increase the chances of crosstalk, and high-speed memory devices, particularly static RAMs, are more sensitive to crosstalk on address, data, and write signals. Both crosstalk and ground-bounce disturbances are a function of the data pattern and are typically worse during all-1 to all-0 or all-0 to all-1 data patterns.

Testing a large memory subsystem is not easy, and the requirements and the degrees of flexibility are much different for RAM systems than for ROM or PROM systems. Little flexibility exists for changing data patterns in a ROM or PROM memory. However, ROM or PROM memory subsystems can and should be checked at the extremes of the specified power supply and temperature limits, and at the extremes there should be sufficient frequency margin left to ensure operation with worst-case process variations (see Chap. 11). RAM-based systems should be checked for timing margin and for pattern sensitivity at the extremes of the allowed operating conditions. High-speed RAMs are extremely sensitive to noise, and noise is generally a function of data patterns.

Often RAM memory tests are started with simple data patterns that check for basic functionality. For example, 1s are written to all locations and read back, and then 0s are written to all locations and read back. Such a test is easy to implement, and fast to run, and it quickly indicates gross problems; but it will not catch data lines short-circuited to each other, address malfunctions, or data pattern sensitivity problems. Another simple test that is often run and is a little more comprehensive is an alternate 101010–0 and 010101–1 bit and word data pattern, called a checkerboard pattern, followed by its complement (see Table 13.1). A checkerboard pattern checks for adjacent data bit short circuits but is still a very limited check for address or pattern sensitivity problems. All but the least significant address line could be stuck; yet, no problem would be indicated since the data are the same in all odd and even locations. Even more complex RAM tests are often misleading because RAM systems may repeat what is written regardless of where it is written. For example, if address lines are malfunctioning, data may be written to an incorrect location, but nonetheless they are written somewhere in the memory. If the data are not overwritten, when a request is sent to read the data, it comes back correct because the address malfunction also causes data to be read from the (same) incorrect location. Even for the extreme case where all address lines are stuck, if only one pattern or if only one word is written and then read before another word is written, then the address malfunction is not apparent. Thus, detection of address malfunctions requires special test patterns that are unique for given locations.[26] The same is true for detecting some forms of interaction, such as crosstalk, between address and data lines.

To check for address malfunctions, the test data must be a function of the address. For example, data equal to the address or some portion of it (generally the least significant bits) can be written into the

TABLE 13.1 Checkerboard and
Complement Data Patterns

Address	Data
First Test	
0	01010101
1	10101010
2	01010101
3	10101010
⇓	etc.
Second Test	
0	10101010
1	01010101
2	10101010
3	01010101
⇓	etc.

TABLE 13.2 Address and Complement Data Patterns

Address	Data
First Test	
0	000000···
1	100000···
2	010000···
3	110000···
4	001000···
⇓	etc.
Second Test	
0	111111···
1	011111···
2	101111···
3	001111···
4	110111···
⇓	etc.

memory array and then checked (Table 13.2). If address lines are stuck, then data will be overwritten (in most cases), and it will be obvious that a fault exists when the memory is read.

To check more than basic functionality, more complicated patterns than those described above are required, and the time required for the tests goes up significantly. In most cases, the time goes from a function of N, where N is the number of words in the memory, to a function of N^2, and the time required for a single test can take hours and days as memory size goes above 256 K words. However, to check for data-dependent crosstalk or ground-bounce-induced problems, patterns must be run that change a word and check all other words, or some subset of other words, to see if they have been disturbed. One such test is called a *marching 1/0 pattern*.[26] A marching test initializes a memory to all 0s, then sequentially writes words of all 1s into the memory, and after each write checks all the previous locations to see that they have not been disturbed. Then it sequentially writes words with all 0s and again sees that the previous locations have not been disturbed (Table 13.3). A more thorough variation of the marching test checks all locations above as well as below the location where the last all-1s or all-0s word was written, to see if any other location was disturbed by the write operation.

Another pattern that checks for disturbances is called the *walking 1/0 pattern*.[26] In the walking pattern, the memory is initialized to all 0s or all 1s; then a word of the opposite sense, e.g., all 1s if the memory has been initialized to all 0s, is written to a location, and all other locations are checked to see that they have not been disturbed. That location is then returned to all 0s, and the process is repeated until

TABLE 13.3   Marching 1/0 Data Pattern

Address	Data
	First Test
0	1111111...
1	1111111...
⇓	⇓
X − 1	1111111...
X	1111111... Write address X, check all previous locations.
X + 1	0000000...
⇓	⇓
N	0000000...
	Second Test
0	0000000...
1	0000000...
⇓	⇓
X − 1	0000000...
X	0000000... Write address X, check all previous locations.
X + 1	1111111...
⇓	⇓
N	1111111...

all locations are checked with 1s, and then the memory is written with all 1s and the process repeated for words of all 0s.

One of the most extensive patterns is called a *galloping pattern*. A galloping pattern checks all possible read-read transitions.[26] A galloping test starts by initializing a memory to an all-0s or an all-1s state. Then a word of the opposite sense of all 1s or all 0s is written to a location, and all other words in the memory are checked one at a time with the initial word checked after each of the other words is read to see that it has not changed. The process is repeated until each word in the memory has been used as the reference word. The galloping read-read pattern is useful for checking internal device ineraction as well as system read problems, but is not a good check of system write problems caused by crosstalk and ground bounce. A more useful test from a system standpoint is called a *galloping write-recovery pattern*. In a galloping write-recovery test, the memory is initialized to all 1s or all 0s, a word is changed to the opposite state, and a second word is changed to the opposite state. The first word is checked, the second word is changed back to its initial state, and the first word is checked again. The process is repeated until all other words are checked. Then a new reference word is picked, and the process is repeated until all words in the memory have served as the reference word.

These special memory test patterns take a long time to run, but they, or variations of them customized to specific applications, must be run during the design verification process when high-speed RAM devices are used. The faster the RAM chips, the more likely crosstalk, ground-bounce, and other interactions are to cause problems. Noise, glitches, or other disturbances on write signals to high-speed SRAMs are a particular problem since most SRAMs have asynchronous write inputs and are sensitive to very narrow pulses at any time. Data sheets may call out a minimum write pulse width, but under typical conditions much narrower pulses may cause writes. Static RAMs that are specified for 20-ns-minimum write pulses often can be written with 3- or 4-ns pulses under typical conditions. Thus, high-speed RAM subsystems must be checked for possible data-dependent interaction problems even though long times are required for the tests. It is much less costly to find problems before a large number of systems are out in the field. As a minimum, both the enhanced marching 1/0 test (where all other locations are read to check for changes) and the walking 1/0 test should be run. Ideally, the galloping write-recovery test should be run, but in large memory systems (e.g., above 256 K words) the time required is often prohibitive. Table 13.4 shows the number of memory cycles or operations required for the various test patterns, where N is the number of words in the memory subsystem.

The time for a particular test is determined by multiplying the number of cycles for a test by the time required for a memory cycle, or the time required for the test system to complete a cycle. Often a test setup has significant overhead and cannot exercise a memory at its normal operating speed. Note that to read or write each location in a 1 M words memory with a 100-ns test cycle time per operation (i.e., a read or a write) requires 104.86 ms ($1,048,576 \times 100$ ns), which is not long from a system test standpoint; but an improved marching 1/0 test for the same memory requires 2.199×10^{12} cycles, which translates to 2.199×10^5 s or 61 h. Thus, the more complicated patterns are practical only for small high-speed memory subsystems, such as high-speed cache memories.

TABLE 13.4   Number of Memory Cycles per Memory Test

Test pattern	Number of cycles where N = number of memory locations
All 1s and then all 0s	$4N$
Checkerboard and complement	$4N$
Address pattern and complement	$4N$
Marching 1/0	$N+2N!$
Improved marching 1/0	$N+2N^2$
Walking 1/0	$2(2N+N^2)$
Galloping 1/0	$2(N+4N^2)$
Galloping write-recovery 1/0	$2(N+12N^2)$

13.4   Summary of High-Speed Memory Design Techniques

1. High-speed memory address and data signals must be isolated from one another by reference planes and extrawide horizontal spacing to prevent cross-coupling. Running memory address and data signals at right angles may not be adequate when high-speed devices are used.

2. Memory control lines such as chip selects, out enables, and write signals must be isolated from address and data lines and other noisy signals.

3. Memory write lines require the highest possible degree of isolation from crosstalk. They must be isolated by reference planes and by extrawide line-to-line spacing from other signals, particularly other memory chip-select signals and address and data buses.

4. When prototyping boards such as welded-wire or wire-wrap boards are used, address and write lines must be run at right angles to data lines.

5. Use a decoupling capacitor of the value recommended by the manufacturer for each high-speed CMOS or BiCMOS memory device (typically recommendations are from 0.1 to 0.22 µF).

6. When a large number of memory devices are collocated and accessed at the same time, use as large as physically possible bulk storage capacitors near where power enters the board and around the perimeter of the memory devices.

7. Minimize signal path lengths for all memory address, data, and control signals to minimize interconnection delays.

8. Protect electrically alterable nonvolatile memories from false write signals during transient power supply conditions (see Chap. 12).

9. Do not tie memory data inputs or outputs directly to backplane or system buses. Memory devices typically do not have a great deal of drive, and they are often sensitive to damage from transient conditions.

10. Make sure there is no bus contention on memory data buses. Particular care is required for common-I/O memory devices.

11. Do not mix write signal buffers with buffers driving address, chip-select, data, or other heavily loaded signals in a common package. Ground bounce may cause interaction.

12. Study data sheet timing cycles thoroughly. Ensure that all setup and hold times as well as all ac operating conditions are met. *Read the requirements over and over and over.*

13. Prepare a complete timing diagram that shows all *maximum* and *minimum* times for each component and interconnection segment in all memory address, data, and control paths, to ensure that an adequate timing margin exists.

14. Terminate or dampen all address, control, and data paths to minimize signal settling times in very high-speed applications.

15. Do not allow contention between memory outputs and data bus drivers.

13.5 References

1. Lisa Maliniak, "Nix Physical Design Flaws before Layout," *Electronic Design*, May 30, 1994, pp. 71–74.
2. Joseph P. Altnether, "High-Speed Memory Takes Fast Chips and Little Delay," *Electronic Design*, July 10, 1986, pp. 135–140.
3. Jeff Chritz and Al Reddy, "The 10- and 5-ns Solution to SRAM Contention," *Electronic Products*, April 1, 1987, pp. 43–46.
4. Milt Leonard, "Density and Speed Drive Static RAM Technology," *Electronic Design*, December 8, 1988, pp. 63–70.
5. Markus Levy, "A Thumbnail Sketch of Cache Memory," *EDN*, January 19, 1995, pp. 30–34.
6. Dave Bursky, "Digital Technology Achieves New Plateaus," *Electronic Design*, December 16, 1994, pp. 71–78.
7. Jeff Child, "RISC and Pentium Drive Demand for SRAMs That Are Fastest of the Fast," *Computer Design*, March 28, 1994, pp. 47–54.
8. Raymond M. Leong, "Purge RISK-Based Systems of Wait States," *Electronic Design*, February 9, 1989, pp. 69–72.
9. "Source List: Cache RAMs," *Electronic Products*, June 1994, pp. 36–41.
10. Dave Bursky, "Advanced Self-Timed SRAM Pares Access Time to 5 ns," *Electronic Design*, February 22, 1990, pp. 145–147.
11. Kathy Rogers, "SRAMS Are Self-timing," *Electronic Engineering Times*, March 5, 1990, pp. 44–45.
12. Richard Quinnell, "Synchronous Memories," *EDN*, August 4, 1994, pp. 56–66.
13. Milt Leonard, "IEDM Tackles Fresh Design Approaches," *Electronic Design*, November 23, 1989, pp. 41–46.
14. Jeff Child, "Low-Power DRAMs Head for Mainstream," *Computer Design*, March 28, 1994, pp. 42–46.
15. Markus Levy, "The Dynamics of DRAM Technology Multiply, Complicate Design Options," *EDN*, January 5, 1995, pp. 46–56.
16. Ron Wilson, "Burst EDO DRAMs Burst on the Scene," *Electronic Engineering Times*, January 16, 1995, p. 10.
17. Nagi Mekhiel, "Speed System Memory by Interleaving DRAM Accesses," *Electronic Design*, October 12, 1989, pp. 65–72.
18. Dave Bursky, "Choices Abound for Nonvolatile Memories," *Electronic Design*, April 26, 1990, pp. 39–52.
19. John Springer, "Designers' Guide to Semiconductor Memory Systems," *EDN*, September 5, 1974, pp. 49–56.
20. Lisa Gunn, "The Problems of RISK-Based Designs," *Electronic Design*, November 23, 1989, pp. 69–74.
21. James J. Vorgert, "Quantify Critical-Timing Risks with Statistical Analysis," *EDN*, February 17, 1994, pp. 95–102.
22. Dan Strassberg, "Signal-Integrity Tools Don't Yet Replace EEs Intelligence," *EDN*, January 19, 1995, pp. 61–68.
23. Joel Martinez, "BTL Transceivers Enable High-Speed Bus Design," *EDN*, August 6, 1992, pp. 107–112.
24. Nathan O. Sokal, "Check List Helps You Avoid Trouble with MOS and Memory ICs," *EDN*, November 27, 1986, pp. 229–235.

25. *Bus Contention Considerations,* Application Note 5, INMOS, Colorado Springs, Colo., December 1982.
26. Martin Marshall, "Through the Memory Cells—Further Exploration of IC's in Testingland," *EDN,* February 20, 1976, pp. 77–85.

13.6 Bibliography

Child, Jeff: "DRAM Vendors Juggle with New Architectures to Increase Performance," *Computer Design,* March 1995, pp. 71–86.
Child, Jeff: "New DRAM Types Target Graphics and More," *Computer Design,* October 1994, pp. 45–49.

Using PLDs, FIFOs, and Other LSI Devices

Programmable logic devices (PLDs), first-in first-out devices (FIFOs), dualport and multiport memories, and a host of other LSI and VLSI devices available today have greatly simplified the system designer's task. They make it possible to keep the parts count, cost, and power down while increasing performance. They provide flexibility that allows designers to develop new equipment faster and get products to market sooner. However, as with all new devices, they bring new problems. Large-scale devices exacerbate most of the power and signal integrity problems inherent in high-speed applications. Ground bounce, transmission-line effects, and noise all are worse and cause more problems when LSI devices are used. The use of LSI devices, particularly PLDs, often leads to neglect of important decisions in the early phase of designs. Often it is assumed that system requirements can be met with PLDs or some other LSI devices when in actuality they cannot. It is important to avoid the trap of assuming a function can be performed by an LSI device before it is certain that it can.

14.1 PLD Application Tips

Programmable logic devices provide system designers with a great deal of flexibility and in many applications are an excellent alternative to standard SSI and MSI logic devices. PLDs reduce the parts count and save board area. They offer a means of upgrading existing systems where board space is limited.[1] They may, if properly applied, optimize performance and improve reliability and testability. They shorten the design cycle and reduce the time to market. Large programmable logic arrays (PLAs) provide a minimal-risk alternative to application-specific integrated circuits (ASICs) in many lower-gate-count applications (up to approximately 20K of usable gates).

Today PLDs are available in a great assortment of sizes and logic structures which are sold under a confusing hodgepodge of names such as programmable array logic (PAL), programmable logic array, complex PLD (CPLD),[2] field-programmable logic array (FPLA), and erasable programmable logic device (EPLD).[3] Vendors tend to specialize in a given configuration, and each stresses the advantages of its own implementation. However, the purpose of this chapter is not to describe the advantages or fine points of various PLD implementations or to survey the devices available, but to list some general system application concerns that are universal to all PLD applications.

Speed and size are two of the foremost concerns when PLDs are considered for an application, and speed is often more of a limiting factor than density in high-performance system applications.[4] High equivalent gate count is always desirable, but if a PLD will not function at the speed needed, it is of no use. In applications where large PLDs are used, speed and utilization must be traded off. Interconnection delays become significant when several levels of logic must be interconnected. Careful evaluations of actual routed delays are essential before one commits to a PLD solution.

Great care must be taken if PLDs are used to synchronize asynchronous signals. Metastability must be addressed, and multiple synchronizers (for a given signal) must be avoided. Metastable operation of synchronizing circuits is always a possibility, and the higher the speed of an application, the greater the demands for good metastable recovery characteristics. First-generation PLDs tended to have poor metastable characteristics.[5-7] However, today's advanced CMOS FPLAs and PLDs tend to have good (i.e., fast) metastable recovery characteristics.[8,9] Their recovery times tend to be on the same order as discrete advanced CMOS devices (see Fig. 10.7). Nevertheless, some extra delay (i.e., recovery time) beyond the normal propagation time of the synchronizing flip-flops must be allotted for the signal settling time to reduce the chance of system faults due to metastable conditions on synchronizer outputs.

When PLDs are used to synchronize signals, there is always the danger that an asynchronous input will inadvertently be routed to two or more flip-flops. Attempting to synchronize an asynchronous signal in two or more places introduces the risk that the signal will not be captured at the same time at all locations. No matter how good the metastable characteristics of the synchronizing flip-flops, there is always the chance that different flip-flops will react in a different manner when their setup and hold-time requirements are violated. Thus, when PLDs are used to synchronize asynchronous inputs, the logic configuration must be controlled so that a given asynchronous input signal goes to only one clocked element (beware of automatic logic optimization)—a given asynchronous input must not be allowed to change two clocked elements on the same clock edge.

An additional reason for not synchronizing asynchronous signals in PLDs is that it mixes asynchronous and synchronous signals in the same device and in the same board area, which increases the danger of noise and crosstalk-induced faults.

Care must be taken to properly initialize PLDs. Do not assume a power-up state. Some manufacturers design PLDs to power up with all internal registers in a given state, and others do not. Where an asynchronous reset or initialization input is available, it should be used in conjunction with the system reset signal to initialize PLDs and to reduce the chance for output contention or other possible abnormal start-up conditions that could cause operational faults or damage parts (see Chap. 12).

See Sec. 14.3 for other important system design considerations in the use of PLDs.

14.2   FIFO Application Tips

The exchange of data between different frequency domains is greatly simplified by FIFOs. They allow asynchronous data to be loaded and output data to be read at the same time under control of signals that have no relative phase or frequency relationship. Today FIFOs are available in two basic control configurations, asynchronous and synchronous. Both types are used to transfer data across asynchronous boundaries. The difference is that asynchronous FIFOs require control of the shape and width of the write and read signals where synchronous FIFOs do not. Synchronous FIFOs have clock inputs (for both in and out) and capture control signals on the clock edges. Most modern FIFOs have clock inputs (for both in and out) and capture control signals on the clock edges. Most modern FIFOs are 8 or 9 bits wide and 64 bits, 512 bits, 1 kbit, 4 kbit, 8 kbit, or 16 kbits deep. Most early FIFOs of the 64-bit-deep or smaller variety were the register fall-through type. Resister fall-through FIFOs suffer from the disadvantage, from a test standpoint, that data availability at the output is not fixed in time relative to a clock. Data fall-through time (i.e., the time data take to move from the input port to the output port) varies with temperature and other environmental conditions as well as inherent device speed and depth. Fall-through register designs are not practical for large FIFOs, so most larger FIFOs, 512 bits and above, are memory-based with pointers to write and read data from a memory array. Memory-based FIFOs with pointers have a fixed fall-through time independent of FIFO size, which is usually no longer than a write and read cycle. As with PLDs and other LSI devices, FIFO speed is often a greater concern than size or depth. The larger FIFOs have trouble running at the speeds needed for most very-high performance CPU and processor applications, but higher-speed FIFOs are constantly being introduced.[10]

Some asynchronous FIFOs have write and read pulse requirements that are difficult to meet on a clock-to-clock basis in high-speed single-phase synchronous systems. In high-frequency applications, FIFO write and read pulse-width requirements may exceed one-half the clock period, which means that a simple gated clock cannot be used to generate write or read pulses. Thus, either multiple clock periods must be used for data transfers, which is usually not acceptable, or special circuitry must be added to generate properly shaped write and read pulses. Figure 14.1 shows one scheme for generating proper write and read pulses by using a delay line.

When one is generating write and read pulses, care is required to avoid data hold-time violations on FIFO inputs and at FIFO output data receivers. When data are loaded into FIFOs, the write pulse must go away before the input data go away (check data sheets for hold-time requirements—some FIFO data inputs have significant

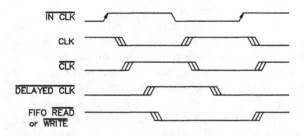

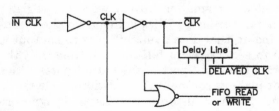

Figure 14.1 Delay line scheme for generating proper-width FIFO write and read pulses for a single-clock-time write or read in a system with only a single phase and frequency clock.

hold-time requirements). Thus, any special circuitry required to shape write pulses must not cause extra delay. Write pulses must go away with the clock or slightly before (see Fig. 14.1). Read pulses have the opposite requirement; read pulses must not go away before the active clock edge occurs at the receiving device since the output state of the typical large FIFO is controlled by the read pulse. Most FIFOs are designed so that outputs are active when the read pulse is present and are inactive or in a high-impedance (tristate) mode when the read pulse is not present (some FIFOs have output enables, but most do not). In most applications, read pulses are not present at all times, which means FIFO outputs are in a high-impedance state most of the time. Thus, pull-ups are required on FIFO outputs to prevent the output data lines from floating when a FIFO is not selected (i.e., the read pulse is not active) and during start-up or fault conditions. Floating lines may cause oscillation of the receiving circuits which will increase system noise, and floating lines may cause overcurrent damage to any CMOS receivers on the line (see Sec. 14.3.2 and Chap. 3). In cases where there are multiple FIFOs or other sources bused together, an alternate method of preventing floating lines is to keep one source active at all times, but such an arrangement increases the chance for bus contention, which must also be avoided.

See Sec. 14.3 for other important system design considerations in the use of FIFO devices.

14.3   Important Considerations in the Use of LSI Devices

14.3.1   Ground-bounce and output pin interaction

Ground-bounce and power supply droop are a particular concern when PLDs, FIFOs, and other LSI devices are used. Most such devices have a large number of outputs that can switch at once, but most LSI devices do not have sufficient ground or V_{cc} pins to support heavy simultaneously switched loads without severe output pin interaction. Some of the new high-speed PLDs are going to center ground pins to reduce ground-bounce effects, but center ground pins only reduce ground bounce—they do not eliminate it. The only recourse of system designers is to limit output loads and control the mix of signals in LSI devices where that is possible (see below). In general, most of the rules for controlling ground bounce in SSI and MSI devices covered in Chap. 4 must be followed when PLDs and other LSI devices are used. For example, the following classes of signals should not be sourced from a common LSI device:

1. Signals going to asynchronous inputs and signals driving heavy loads

2. Clock enable signals and signals driving heavy loads

3. Write enable signals to RAMs and other heavily loaded signals

4. Clock signals of different frequencies

In general, PLDs should not be used as clock drivers because of potential ground-bounce problems and other possible interactions.

Byte-wide FIFOs and other devices with byte-wide outputs (where it is possible for all bits to change at once) may need to be buffered and redriven to prevent ground bounce from disrupting internal operation. FIFOs are of special concern; most FIFOs are asynchronous and extremely sensitive to spikes on ground or V_{cc}. Outputs of byte-wide devices must be lightly loaded to guard against ground-bounce upsets.

14.3.2   Proper connection of unused inputs

Proper connection of unused inputs on PLDs and other LSI devices is essential for reliable system operation. Inputs should never be left unconnected. *Open* or *floating inputs* may cause

1. Input stages to go into oscillation, causing noise which may disrupt the operation of the device as well as the operation of other nearby devices

2. Excessive V_{cc}-to-ground current (if the input drifts into the intermediate region between a valid logic *high* or *low,* both input MOSFETs may turn on), which may cause overheating and parts failure (see Chap. 3)

Unused PLD outputs that serve as feedback paths or as alternate inputs must not be neglected. They must be tied to a valid *high* or *low* logic level, or else the associated output must be programmed to an active *high* or *low* logic level. Programming unused outputs that serve as alternate inputs so they are active (i.e., not in a tristate mode) is usually the safest approach. Tying outputs to a common pull-up or pull-down voltage introduces some risk—one of the outputs might be inadvertently programmed to an opposite level, which would cause contention and possible damage.

14.3.3   Proper termination of inputs

Many advanced CMOS LSI devices, including PLDs, do not have effective input clamp diodes. Signals terminated at devices without effective clamps or some form of termination may ring and take a long time to settle. Since input clamping characteristics are usually not specified on data sheets, when signal settling time or waveshape are of concern, there are two alternatives. (1) Parts must be characterized for dynamic input characteristics, and parts with good input clamps must be selected; or (2) conventional termination techniques can be used to prevent ringing.

If it is decided to characterize inputs, then device input dynamic characteristics can be determined with a simple test setup, as shown in Chap. 7. The test consists of observing input waveforms while inputs are driven by a buffer or gate (from the logic family being used to implement the system) through a 2- or 3-ft length of coaxial cable (of approximately the characteristic impedance of the system interconnection system). If the device under test has good input clamps, input signals will overshoot a small amount (1 or 2 V) but will not undershoot back into the threshold region. If the device under test does not have good input clamps, input signals will ring and undershoot back into the critical threshold region. Testing devices for input characteristics is usually not a good long-range solution. It is expensive and time-consuming, and there is no guarantee that future parts will behave as those tested. Manufacturers often change designs and processes, and functionally identical devices from different manufacturers can have very different clamping characteristics. Often the best overall solution is to assume that LSI devices will not have clamps and eliminate the chance of ringing (on critical lines) by using conventional line-terminating techniques or by ending critical signal lines at devices with effective clamps. Lines feeding multiple devices (including devices without clamps) can be arranged so that critical lines always end with a device with an effective input clamp. Signal strings without devices with effective input clamps can be clamped by the addition of a buffer at the end of the string that has an effective clamp. However, input clamping effectiveness is not specified on the data sheet; it must be determined experimentally (see Chap. 7). In many cases, the clamping buffer may serve no other useful purpose than to clamp the line, but in some cases clamping buffers can be used to drive signals to test ports or test connectors. Conventional termination techniques are often less desirable than clamps for several reasons: Termination resistors may cause logistics and handling problems in surface-mounted applications, source termination slows signal settling time depending upon the location of loads relative to the source, and load termination increases power dissipation.

The longer the signal lines and the faster the signal sources switch, the greater the chance of system operational problems due to unclamped inputs. Very short lines—those less than the critical line length (see Chap. 7)—may not cause waveshape corruption and the resulting system faults. Long lines, such as at board interfaces, are a particular concern. Devices without input clamps should not be used to receive signals at board or system interfaces. Not only is there danger of operational malfunctions due to ringing, but also there is danger of damage to devices. Excessive ringing, such as might occur on long lines at board or system interfaces, may exceed input level specifications and damage device inputs.

Clamping of all signals is not always required. In most applications, some signals are more critical from a waveshape or timing standpoint than others. For example, clock signals to PLDs are generally much more critical than data or control signals. Read and write controls to FIFOs are generally more important than data inputs. Clock and read-write signals must not ring, but data inputs can ring if there is time for them to settle and if the amplitude of the ringing is not sufficient to damage parts. Thus, clock and read-write signals should be clamped in most applications, but clamping of data and control inputs depends on the application.

14.3.4   Decoupling needs of LSI devices

Large-scale ICs have special decoupling needs. They often have a large number of outputs that switch at once, and they may have large internal switching currents, both of which can cause large transient currents in power and ground. To avoid potential device malfunction, manufacturers' recommendations as to the amount and placement of decoupling capacitors should always be followed. Data sheets for LSI devices usually specify the decoupling requirements; if a data sheet does not, the manufacturer should be consulted for recommendations. In addition, regardless of what the manufacturer recommends, practical engineering judgment should be used when one is specifying decoupling for LSI devices. The worst-case simultaneously switching load capacitance must be determined, and a value of decoupling capacitance must be used that will keep the local V_{cc} at a proper level (see Chap. 5). The general rule of thumb is that the local decoupling capacitance should be at least 100 times the simultaneous switched load capacitance.

14.4   Summary of Design Techniques for PLDs, FIFOs, and Other LSI Devices

1. Add clamps or terminate all time- or waveshape-critical input signals to LSI devices that do not have high-speed input clamps.

2. Do not use LSI devices without high-speed input clamps to receive signals at board or system interfaces.

3. Be very careful when you use PLDs to synchronize asynchronous signals—make sure only one flip-flop synchronizes a given signal.

4. Follow manufacturers' recommendations for decoupling LSI devices.

5. Do not let unused PLD inputs or output feedback paths float.

6. Do not let CMOS or BiCMOS FIFO inputs float.

7. Do not drive large buses or otherwise heavily load LSI device outputs.

8. Do not mix signals going to asynchronous inputs and signals driving heavy loads in PLDs or other LSI devices.

9. Do not mix clock enable signals and signals driving heavy loads in PLDs.

10. Do not mix write enable signals to RAMs and other heavily loaded signals in PLDs.

11. Do generate and buffer clock signals of different frequencies or phases in a common PLD.

12. Do not use PLDs as clock drivers because of potential output skew, ground bounce, and other interactions.

14.5 References

1. Richard Nass, "ASICs: The Latest Alternative," *Electronic Design,* October 12, 1989, pp. 51–60.
2. Christopher Jones, "Knowing Your CPLD Maximizes Its Resources," *EDN,* January 5, 1995, pp. 117–124.
3. David L. Greer, "A New IC Classification Act," *Electronic Engineering Times,* February 26, 1990, pp. 37 and 72.
4. Stan Baker, "Silicon Bits—Beyond the Gate-Count Wars," *Electronic Engineering Times,* January 1, 1990, p. 30.
5. *PAL Device Data Book,* Advanced Micro Devices Inc., Sunnyvale, Calif., 1988, pp. 3-164 to 3-169.
6. Sean Dingman, "Determine PLD Metastability to Derive Ample MTBFs," *EDN,* August 5, 1991, pp. 147–154.
7. Stan Baker, "PLD Designers Cope with Metastability," *Electronic Engineering Times,* March 9, 1992, pp. 37–39.
8. *The Programmable Gate Array Data Book,* Xilinx Inc., San Jose, Calif., 1992.
9. *GAL Data Book 1992,* Lattic Semiconductor Corp., Hillsboro, Oreg., 1992.
10. Kathy Rogers, "FIFO Race Revs to 15 ns," *Electronic Engineering Times,* January 29, 1990, p. 48.

ASIC Application Tips

The purpose of this chapter is not to describe the advantages and disadvantages of CMOS and BiCMOS application-specific integrated circuits (ASICs), most of which are well known.[1] Nor is the purpose here to survey CMOS and BiCMOS ASIC types and availability[2,3] or to cover general ASIC applications. ASIC devices and technology change so rapidly even current magazine articles often miss several manufacturers' latest announcements. Instead, this chapter discusses several topics that may not be obvious to those new to ASIC applications,[4] and it covers several system-level signal and power integrity concerns that may not be covered or sufficiently emphasized in ASIC device manufacturers' data books or application information. For specific gate array, standard cell, or other ASIC device family capabilities, characteristics, and application information, readers are referred to ASIC manufacturers' most recent data books and application manuals. In all cases, manufacturers' application information must be studied closely and followed precisely.

The great majority of ASICs used today are fabricated with advanced CMOS processes. BiCMOS ASICs are mainly used in a performance niche between the upper limits of comfortable CMOS operation and below those very high-performance applications that require ECL. Typically BiCMOS ASICs make possible at least a 50 percent improvement in operating speed over CMOS-only circuits with similar features.[5] However, BiCMOS processing costs more than CMOS.

BiCMOS ASICs with bipolar output stages offer a level of performance that is not possible with CMOS-only devices. Bipolar output circuits reduce both transient switching currents and propagation times, and propagation times do not degrade as much with environmental conditions such as high temperature, low supply voltage levels, or high capacitance. A major benefit of bipolar outputs is that transient switching currents are reduced by as much as 65 percent relative to CMOS-only output stages.[6] Lower transient switching currents mean that fewer ground and power pins are required, or alternately outputs can have higher drive. Bipolar output stages make it possible to interface directly to buses without requiring an impractical number of power and ground pins. BiCMOS ASICs are available with drive capability of up to 72 mA per output.[7]

Not all BiCMOS ASIC vendors combine CMOS and bipolar circuits in the same manner. Some arrays are fabricated with CMOS-only cores surrounded by bipolar input and output circuits. Other vendors combine CMOS and bipolar circuits throughout the array[8] (see Fig. 15.1) or at least have internal sections with an option of using bipolar output stages for driving critical signals such as clocks and buses. Some BiCMOS ASICs have an option on a cell-by-cell basis that allows internal bipolar output stages to be activated or not activated as needed for drive. Bipolar internal drivers are seen as the key to the next level of performance. In CMOS ASICs, heavily loaded internal interconnections often contribute a significant portion of signal delay and limit overall performance. In contrast, BiCMOS internal cells experience little performance degradation as the load is increased. Internal bipolar drivers significantly reduce fan-out propagation time degradation of heavily loaded internal interconnections[9] (see Fig. 15.2 for comparison of CMOS and bipolar internal interconnection delay[10]).

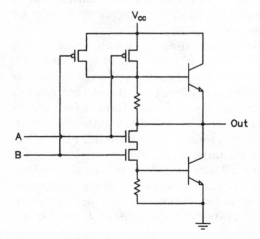

Figure 15.1 Schematic of AMCC Q24000 series BiCMOS two-input NAND showing bipolar output circuit used with internal CMOS logic cells. (*Reprinted with permission of Advanced Micro Circuits, Corp.*)

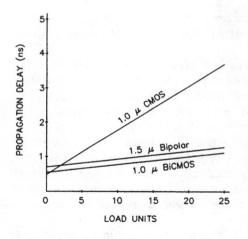

Figure 15.2 Fan-out degradation comparison of internal BiCMOS and CMOS drivers as a function of loading. (*Reprinted with permission of Advanced Micro Circuits, Corp.*)

15.1   Logic Structures to Avoid in ASICs

Special design techniques are often required for special devices, and ASICs are no exception. Certain logic structures that offer many advantages in discrete implementations may be undesirable in ASIC implementations. One example is tristate buses. Tristate buses often simplify circuit board or motherboard wiring and reduce the parts count. However, tristate buses usually complicate ASIC internal signal routing. Buses that go to a large number of locations tend to use up a great deal of the available on-chip signal interconnection resources and block other needed interconnections. Buses also tend to have slow response because long interconnections and many loads mean large line capacitance. Internal drivers often do not have the drive to quickly drive large-capacitance loads. Large buses also cause internal power to go up. Slow signal transitions through the region where both MOSFETs in complementary input pairs are on cause increased V_{cc}-to-ground current. Tristate buses also offer the potential for internal bus contention and possible damage to parts. In general, multiplexers are a better choice than tristate buses for combining signals in ASICs. In discrete implementations, multiplexers often require an excessive number of packages, but in ASICs they may be a more efficient use of silicon (than tristate buses). If tristate buses must be used, they should be controlled with an internal decoder circuit that only allows one node to be on (the bus) at any given time. If a combinational decoder circuit is not possible, all storage elements that control bus drivers must have some means of asynchronous initialization that is activated by the system reset or volts-good signal. However, asynchronous initialization only ensures a proper start-up.

Unless an exclusive decoder is used, there is no guarantee that invalid or erroneously issued control signals will not cause bus contention during operation.

Tristate circuits also offer the potential for contention at ASIC interfaces. Contention at ASIC interfaces can be more damaging than internal contention since output drivers typically have much more current capability than internal drivers. Furthermore, interface bus contention is often more difficult to control than internal contention. At ASIC interfaces it is often not possible to use a single central decoder to enable the various sources on a bus; often each ASIC and its interface are independently controlled. Bidirectional interface ports are special cases of tristate buses and offer the same potential for contention as other tristate buses as well as additional complications (see Sec. 15.2.2).

Buried circuits with internal feedback paths should be avoided. If operational malfunctions occur in buried feedback circuits with no visibility, it may be impossible to determine the cause of the malfunction. Ideally, all feedback paths should be connected externally, but external feedback is often not practical in high-speed application—on and off chip propagation times are too long. If internal feedback must be used, e.g., in high-speed state machines, then all storage element outputs should be brought out so that they are visible, or else provisions should be made to disable feedback paths by external controls.

Circuits that require a long time to initialize should be avoided. They complicate tests and in extreme cases make tests prohibitively expensive. All ASIC storage elements should utilize asynchronous reset circuitry to ensure rapid initialization.

15.2   Guidelines for Selecting Input-Output Characteristics

System or circuit designers have a great deal of control over the parameter that controls the signal integrity of ASIC interface signals. In contrast to discrete logic devices where the input-output characteristics are determined by the manufacturer, ASIC designers get to pick input and output logic levels, output drive, and in some cases the slew rate.

15.2.1   CMOS or TTL levels?

Most of today's ASIC vendors offer some choices for interface levels. CMOS ASICs are typically available with CMOS or TTL interface levels. BiCMOS ASICs are typically available with ECL and TTL levels and sometimes CMOS levels. When the choice is between CMOS or TTL levels, it is usually better to select TTL levels (in very high-speed applications, the choice should be ECL).[11] TTL levels generate less noise than CMOS levels and are compatible with most standard devices and test equipment.[12] CMOS levels offer more noise margin (than TTL), but they create more noise and cause compatibility problems with other parts. Many LSI devices, such as PLDs, FIFOs, RAMs, and ROMs, are not available with CMOS levels. In some critical-signal cases, such as clocks, CMOS levels may provide some advantage from a noise margin standpoint. However, CMOS levels complicate the termination of clock lines (see Chap. 8), and clock signal waveshape must be controlled.

15.2.2 Do not let CMOS or BiCMOS ASIC inputs float

Damage to CMOS or BiCMOS ASICs due to open or floating inputs is a serious concern. Most CMOS and BiCMOS ASICs have complementary MOSFET input circuits that may conduct excessive and damaging currents between V_{cc} and ground if inputs are allowed to remain in the indeterminate region between valid *high* and *low* logic levels (see Chap. 3). The danger is greatest during initial system test or when parts are first tested. Test routines or test equipment may not operate as expected during initial test. Proper signals may not be present due to software or hardware errors which may allow inputs to float (with damaging results). A careful checkout of component test setups prior to first installing expensive ASICs is essential to prevent floating inputs. The checkout must ensure that all inputs, including bidirectional ports functioning as inputs, are driven with valid logic levels at all times during test. Bidirectional ports present a special problem during test. The question is, When is a bidirectional port functioning as an input or an output? If the direction of a bidirectional port is controlled by an external signal, then control of direction is straightforward, but if the direction is controlled by an internal signal, then it is difficult to prevent illegal conditions (either floating or bus contention). When a bidirectional port is controlled internally, a signal should be brought out to indicate port direction for use of testers or external buffers that might have to be used to buffer the port for test loads or other reasons.

It is not good practice to connect ASIC inputs directly to signals that originate on other circuit boards or that originate from external sources. Expensive ASICs should be buffered and isolated from potentially damaging transients. Transients may cause direct damage or initiate latch-up that can cause damage (see Chap. 3). If ASICs must be connected directly to board or system interfaces, then pull-up resistors should be used on all lines where there is a chance for the signal source to be disconnected. Series current-limiting resistors should also be used to limit injected transient current to prevent latch-up or other damaging effects (see Chap. 9 for recommended board or system interface circuits). Pull-up and current-limiting resistors add parts and complicate board layout. To avoid adding pull-up resistors to board or test stations and to reduce the chance of damage due to improper operation of interface signals either during test or during normal in-circuit operation, in most cases it is best to specify internal pull-up resistors or current sources for all ASIC inputs and bidirectional ports. Most CMOS or BiCMOS ASIC vendors offer low-current pull-up or pull-down resistors. Some vendors offer only one value, but others offer two or three choices. For example, one ASIC vendor[13] offers current sources of 5, 95, and 400 μA. For most applications, where the objective is to prevent floating inputs during initial checkout or under other similar circumstances, 50-kΩ pull-up or pull-down resistors or equivalent current sources are appropriate. Pull-up or pull-down resistors must have enough current capability to provide the worst-case input current requirement, but should have no more current capability than is necessary to limit power dissipation. *Caution:* Source pull-up or pull-down current values are not precise. They typically vary 4 to 1 with normal temperature, voltage, and process variations. Due to the possible large variation in characteristics, internal pull-up or pull-down resistors should be used only to prevent floating inputs, not for dynamic signal pull-up operation (unless the possible large variations in pull-up or pull-down times can be tolerated).

15.2.3 Output drive selection

Most CMOS or BiCMOS ASIC vendors offer output drivers with various current and slew rate limits. In general, output drivers with the lowest current and slowest slew rate compatible with system requirements should be selected.[14] More current capability than is necessary increases the chance for ground bounce and other system upsets due to transient switching currents. A greater slew rate than is necessary increases transient currents plus increases crosstalk and transmission-line effects. Package ground and power pin requirements are a function of output driver current and slew rate. Power and ground pin requirements increase significantly for high-current high-slew-rate output buffers, and package pins are usually at a premium.

15.3 Early Determination of Number of Ground and Power Pins

It is important to establish the number of package power and ground pins early in a design. Speed is a function of output drive, and the number of power and ground pins is a function of output drive characteristics and the number of outputs that switch at once. Transient switching currents cause fluctuations in internal power and ground levels that cause spikes on unswitched outputs (which can cause system upsets) and may also disturb internal logic. It is easy to underestimate the number of power and ground pins required in high-performance applications. Often optimistic guesses are made that severely limit design options later on. High-speed high-current outputs (for example, 12 mA or higher) often require a ground and power pin per two outputs and in some cases may require a power and ground pin per output. Unless proper allowance has been made for power and ground pins, a larger package may have to be used, which may complicate the planned packaging arrangement, or performance may have to be decreased. Slower lower-current outputs that require fewer power and ground pins may have to be used, and this means lower performance.

Most ASIC vendors have strict rules as to power and ground pin requirements and will not fabricate devices that do not meet their requirements. Thus, it is important to understand the requirements early in a design so that proper allowance is made. Vendor application information must be thoroughly studied. However, many system application issues also affect power and ground pin requirements. The ASIC vendor may not understand the system issues and should not be relied upon to establish the requirements. The system designer is in the best position to understand all the issues and must take responsibility for establishing the required number of power and ground pins. Even if the ASIC vendor takes the initiative to establish the number of pins, the system designer should check the results.

Important system application issues that affect the number of power and ground pins required are the

1. Number of simultaneously switching outputs

2. Output speed and current driver requirements

3. Package pin inductance

4. Ground-bounce and power supply droop tolerance

Items 1 and 2 are system issues that the ASIC vendor has little knowledge of prior to the later stages of ASIC designs, and they must be determined by the system designer. Package pin inductance is usually available from the ASIC vendor unless a custom package is used. If a custom package is used, it is important that either the user or the ASIC vendor determine the package lead inductance. Interconnection inductance between package power and ground pins and circuit board power and ground planes must also be considered. Ideally, package power and ground pin connections should be made directly to power and ground planes so as to avoid adding inductance, but that is sometimes not possible with certain surface-mounted techniques. If it is not possible to make a direct connection to circuit board power and ground planes, then the inductance of interconnecting traces must be added to the package pin inductance and the total used to calculate power and ground pin requirements.

15.4   Guidelines for Interface Timing

Timing of ASIC input-output signals relative to circuit board or system clock signals and system signals is a major issue that is often overlooked. ASIC vendors and their software tend to concentrate on internal signal relationships and ignore system issues, as expected. The system designer must take the initiative to ensure that all system components including ASICs have the ability to communicate where required. To simplify communication between ASICs and other components, all ASIC interfaces should be synchronous. The more complicated the device, the more important it is to follow synchronous design practices (see Chap. 10). Furthermore, most ASIC vendor software only supports synchronous design, which means that if asynchronous interfaces are used, they often cannot be simulated.

When synchronous ASIC interfaces are used, the input signal timing parameters of greatest interest are the setup and hold times relative to the local board or system clock signal. Thus, it is important to establish ASIC input timing parameters with respect to the clock signal phasing at the ASIC package interface, not to some internal clock phase.

Setup time requirements are usually straightforward. Input signals must propagate to internal clocked devices in sufficient time to be captured by the next clock edge. The less setup time required, the better. Setup times are usually worse at high temperatures, where CMOS and BiCMOS devices slow down the most.

Hold-time requirements cause most ASIC input interface problems. Inputs to clocked devices tend to have long hold-time requirements because internal clock networks tend to have long propagation paths. Long clock paths mean that internal clocked devices are clocked sometime later than when the clock edge occurs at the package interface. Unless input signal paths have an equal delay, they must be held until the internal clock edge occurs. Because of the uncertainty of minimum propagation times of discrete devices or ASICs, it is usually impossible to guarantee a given amount of hold time in synchronous systems. Thus, ASICs should be designed to have zero or negative hold-time requirements, as most MSI and commodity LSI devices do. ASIC vendors do not like to design for zero hold times because it is an extra complication for them (and board level interface problems are not their concern). Zero hold-time interfaces also simplify second sourcing of ASICs. System operation is less dependent on device-to-device match of input-output propagation times.

Hold-time faults are most apt to occur where devices are fastest, and CMOS and BiCMOS devices speed up as the temperature goes down and as the power supply voltage goes up (see Chap. 11). Thus, in systems using advanced CMOS and BiCMOS ASICs, hold-time faults occur most often at cold temperatures and when the operating power supply voltage level is on the high side.

15.5 Summary of System Application Tips for ASICs

1. Use output drivers with the lowest current and slowest slew rate compatible with system requirements.

2. Use output circuits with TTL levels where possible to reduce transient switching currents.

3. Inputs to clocked elements should be designed to have zero or negative hold-time requirements.

4. Avoid tristate internal connection.

5. Avoid buried feedback circuits that have no visibility.

6. Use internal pull-up or pull-down resistors on all inputs and bidirectional ports.

7. Use internal and I/O storage circuits with asynchronous reset capability to allow rapid initialization.

8. Provide an output signal to indicate the direction of internally controlled bidirectional interface ports.

9. Buffer signals to and from external board or system destinations or sources to protect ASIC inputs and outputs from transients and ESD damage.

15.6 References

1. "Source List: Gate Arrays," *Electronic Products,* February 1994, pp. 36–41.
2. Bill Arnold, "Standard Cells Pace CMOS ASIC Growth," *ASIC & EDA,* March 1994, pp. 36–51.
3. Richard Nass, "ASICs: The Latest Alternative," *Electronic Design,* October 12, 1989, pp. 51–60.
4. Alan Heckman, "Designing ASICs: Be Prepared for Changes," *Electronic Design,* January 11, 1990, pp. 133–140.
5. Dave Bursky, "Digital ICs in the 1990s: Nearly Unlimited On-Chip Resources," *Electronic Design,* January 11, 1990, pp. 97–106.
6. *ASIC Action: The ASIC Newsletter,* LSI Logic Corporation, Milpitas, Calif., January 1990, p. 6.

7. "BiCMOS Arrays Boost Density, Speed, I/O Drive, and Usable Gates," *Electronic Products,* April 1, 1988, p. 60.
8. Liang-Tsai Lin and Richard Spehn, "Fast, Low-Powered Logic Array Unites CMOS and Bipolar," *Electronic Design,* April 16, 1987, pp. 82–88.
9. *Q24000 Series BiCMOS Logic Arrays Device Specification,* Applied Micro Circuits Corp., San Diego, Calif., 1990.
10. *Network Products Data Book,* Applied Micro Circuits Corp., San Diego, Calif., 1994.
11. Michael Chester, "Action Brews in BiCMOS Arrays," *Electronic Products,* June 1, 1987, pp. 22–24.
12. Stan Baker, "Extending TTL," *Electronic Engineering Times,* October 16, 1989, pp. 41, 52.
13. *TSC500 Series 1-μm CMOS Standard Cells Data Manual,* Texas Instruments Inc., Dallas, Tex., 1988.
14. J. Scott Runner and Larry Roffelsen, "The Pitfalls of ASIC Interfaces," *Electronic Engineering Times,* November 28, 1988, pp. T30–T32.

15.7 Bibliography

"ASIC Design Methodologies Change to Keep Up with Deep-Submicron Geometries," *Computer Design's ASIC Design,* October 1994, pp. A16–A22.
Chou, Tai-Yu: "Signal Integrity Analysis in ASIC Design," *ASIC & EDA,* May 1994, pp. 70–81.
"CMOS Cell-Based Products," *ASIC & EDA,* March 1994, pp. 44–51.
"CMOS Gate Array Products," *ASIC & EDA,* March 1994, pp. 36–43.
"CMOS Gate Array Products," *Integrated System Design,* February 1995, pp. 44–51.
"CMOS Standard Cell-Based Products," *Integrated System Design,* February 1995, pp. 36–43.
Duvall, Steven G.: "A Practical Methodology for the Statistical Design of Complex Logic Products for Performance," *IEEE Transactions on Very Large Scale Integration (VLSI) Systems,* vol. 3, no. 1, March 1995.
Sicard, Etienne, and Antonio Rubio: "Analysis of Crosstalk Interference in CMOS Integrated Circuits," *IEEE Transactions on Electromagnetic Compatibility,* vol. 34, no. 2, May 1992, pp. 124–129.

A.1 Conversion Factors

$$1 \text{ ft} = 30.48 \text{ cm}$$
$$1 \text{ ft} = 0.3048 \text{ m}$$
$$1 \text{ in} = 2.54 \text{ cm}$$
$$1 \text{ mil} = 2.54 \times 10^{-3} \text{ cm}$$
$$1 \text{ mil} = 10^{-3} \text{ in}$$

A.2 Definition of Symbols and Acronyms

ABT	designation used for TTL compatible BiCMOS logic devices
ac	alternating or dynamic current
AC	designation used for advanced CMOS logic
AC11	designation used for advanced CMOS logic with center ground and power pins
ACL	advanced CMOS logic
ACT	designation used for TTL compatible advanced CMOS logic
ACT11	designation used for TTL compatible advanced CMOS logic with center ground and power pins
ALS	designation used for advanced low-power Schottky TTL logic devices
ALU	arithmetic logic unit
AMD	Advanced Micro Devices Inc.
AND	logic circuit whose output is a 1 state only when every input is in the 1 state
AS	designation used for advanced Schottky TTL logic devices
ASIC	application-specific integrated circuit
AWG	American Wire Gage

b	distance between reference planes in printed-circuit boards
BC	designation used for Motorola and Toshiba TTL compatible BiCMOS logic
BCT	designation used for TTL compatible BiCMOS logic
BiCMOS	bipolar and complementary metal-oxide semiconductor
Bi-CMOS	acronym used by Motorola and Toshiba for semiconductor devices that combine bipolar and CMOS technologies
C	designates a CMOS device
C	capacitor
CAD	computer-aided design
CAS	column access strobe
$\overline{\text{CAS}}$	column access strobe, active *low*
C_d	decoupling capacitance
$\overline{\text{CE}}$	chip enable, active *low*
C_{IN}	input capacitance
C_L	load capacitance
CLK	designates a clock signal
$\overline{\text{CLK}}$	designates an inverted clock signal
C_{load}	total load capacitance which includes signal track plus device input and output capacitance
C_{LOAD}	total capacitance (i.e., input and output capacitance) of all devices connected to a line
C_{LINE}	total line capacitance (i.e., signal track capacitance)
C_m	mutual capacitance between lines
CMOS	complementary metal-oxide semiconductor
C_{pd}	internal device capacitance used for power calculations
CPU	central processing unit
$\overline{\text{CS}}$	chip select, active *low*
°C	degrees Celsius
ΔC	difference in specified and actual load capacitance
d	diameter of a wire conductor
D	diode
D	drain terminal of field-effect transistor
dc	direct or static current
DIP	dual-in-line package
DRAM	dynamic random-access memory
ECL	emitter-coupled logic
EEPROM	electrically erasable programmable read-only memory

EMI	electromagnetic interference
EIA	Electronic Industries Association
EPROM	electrically programmable read-only memory
EPLD	erasable programmable logic device
ESD	electrostatic discharge
ESL	effective series inductance
ESR	effective series resistance
f	frequency (hertz)
F	node toggle frequency
FACT	National advanced CMOS logic (was Fairchild advanced CMOS logic)
FACT QS	National advanced CMOS logic with output slew rate control and other features that reduce ground bounce
FAST	National advanced Schottky TTL logic (was Fairchild advanced Schottky TTL logic)
FBT	designation used for fast BiCMOS TTL compatible logic devices
FCT	designation used for fast CMOS TTL compatible logic devices
FCT-T	designation used for fast CMOS TTL compatible logic devices with TTL output levels
FCT-A	designation used for very fast CMOS TTL compatible logic devices
FET	field-effect transistor
FIFO	first-in first-out storage device
FITs	failures in test, per billion device hours
F_{MAX}	maximum toggle rate of a clocked logic device
FPLA	field-programmable logic array
G	gate terminal of field-effect transistor
GND	ground
h	height of a conductor above a reference plane
HC	designation used for high-speed CMOS logic devices
HCT	designation used for TTL compatible high-speed CMOS logic devices
I_b	base current
IC	integrated circuit
I_c	collector current
I_{cc}	device supply current
I_D	drain current
IDT	Integrated Device Technology, Inc.

I_{IH} or $I_{\text{in high}}$	rated (maximum) input *high* current
I_{IL} or $I_{\text{in low}}$	rated (maximum) input *low* current
$I_{\text{in total}}$	total input current
I_{IN}	input current
I_L	load current
I_o	output current
I/O	input-output
I_{OD}	dynamic output current
I_{OH}	rated output *high* current
I_{OL}	rated output *low* current
I_p	peak internal feedthrough current
I_{OS}	output short-circuit current
ΔI	change in current
K	constant
K_C	capacitive coupling coefficient
K_L	inductive coupling coefficient
l	unit length of a transmission line
l, w, t	length, width, and thickness, respectively
L	self-inductance
L	inductor
LCC	leadless chip carrier
LED	leading-edge detector
L_m	mutual inductance between lines
L_p	package pin inductance
L_p	parallel inductance
L_s	source inductance including power source inductance
LS	low-power Schottky TTL logic
LSI	large-scale integration
LV	low-voltage (typically designates a logic device designed to operate with a 3.3-V supply)
MOSFET	metal-oxide semiconductor field-effect transistor
MSI	medium-scale integration
MTBF	mean time between failures
n	semiconductor material with an excess of electrons
N	number of turns in an inductor
N	number of words in a memory subsystem
NAND	logic device whose inputs must all be in a 1 state to produce a 0 state output

NOR	logic device where any one input or more having a 1 state will yield a 0 state output
NOVRAM	nonvolatile random-access memory
$\overline{\text{OE}}$	out enable, active *low*
OR	logic device where any one input or more having a 1 state is sufficient to produce a 1 state output
p	semiconductor material with a deficiency of electrons
PAL	programmable array logic
PC	printed circuit, as in printed-circuit board
P_d	dynamic power dissipation
PLA	programmable logic array
PLCC	plastic leaded chip carrier
PLD	programmable logic device
P_q	quiescent power dissipation
PROM	programmable read-only memory
Q	transistor
Q_i	initial charge
Q_f	final charge
R	resistor
RAM	random-access memory
RAS	row access strobe
$\overline{\text{RAS}}$	row access strobe, active *low*
R_{CL}	current-limiting resistor
RF	radio frequency
R_L	load resistance
R_o or R_{out}	output resistance
ROM	read-only memory
R_{ON}	bipolar transistor collector-to-emitter or field-effect transistor drain-to-gate on resistance
$R_{\text{pull-up}}$	pull-up resistor
R_S	source resistance
RSS	root sum squared
S	source terminal of field-effect transistor
S	switch
SCR	silicon controlled rectifier
SRAM	static random-access memory
SSI	small-scale integration
t	time (seconds)

t	thickness of printed-circuit board conductors or planes
T_A	ambient temperature
TED	trailing-edge detector
t_f	fall time
t_{HL} or t_{PHL}	propagation time from an input change to an output *high*-to-*low* transition
t_h or t_{hold}	time that a signal to a clocked device must be stable after application of active clock edge
TI	Texas Instruments, Inc.
t_{LH} or t_{PLH}	propagation time from an input change to an output *low*-to-*high* transition
t_{LINE}	propagation delay of a line
t_p	propagation delay of a designated length of conductor
t_P	propagation time from an input change to an output transition
t_{path}	propagation time for a given group of devices and their associated interconnections
t_{pd}	intrinsic propagation delay time of medium
t'_{pd}	effective propagation delay of loaded conductor
t_{prop}	propagation time of a device
t_r	rise time
t_{rec}	reset recovery time (to next active clock edge)
t_s or t_{setup}	time that a signal to a clocked device must be stable before the arrival of active clock edge
t_{SH}	time that a *high*-level signal to a clocked device must be stable before the arrival of active clock edge
t_{SL}	time that a *low*-level signal to a clocked device must be stable before the arrival of active clock edge
TTL	transistor-transistor logic
Δt	change in time for an event
U	integrated circuit
UV	ultraviolet
UV EEPROM	ultraviolet erasable electrically programmable read-only memory
V_B	voltage amplitude of backward crosstalk
V_{BE}	bipolar transistor base-to-emitter voltage
V_{cc}	positive logic device supply voltage
V_{cc} min	minimum rated supply voltage
V_{CE}	bipolar transistor collector-to-emitter voltage
$V_{CE}(\text{sat})$	bipolar transistor collector-to-emitter voltage when fully on

V_f	final voltage or diode forward voltage
V_F	voltage amplitude of forward crosstalk
V/I	voltage-current characteristics of a node
V_{IL}	rated maximum input *low* voltage
$V_{IL\,MAX}$	rated maximum input *low* voltage
V_{IH}	rated minimum input *high* voltage
$V_{IH\,MIN}$	rated minimum input *high* voltage
V_{IN}/I_{IN}	input voltage and current characteristics
V_{IN}	input voltage
V_L	voltage at the load
V_{loss}	voltage drop across a ground or power plane
VLSI	very large-scale integration
V_{OH}/I_{OH}	output *high* voltage-current characteristics
V_o or V_{out}	output voltage
V_{OL}	rated output *low* voltage
V_{OH}	rated output *high* voltage
V_{pp}	programming voltage
V_{STEP}	voltage step magnitude when a wave is launched into a transmission line
$v(t)$	time-varying voltage
V_x	voltage at a distance x on a transmission line
ΔV	change in voltage level
ΔV	signal swing
w	width of a square section of plane
$\overline{W}$ or $\overline{WE}$	write enable, active *low*
x	variable, e.g., distance from a point
XTK	acronym for Quad Design's crosstalk calculation program
Z_o	characteristic impedance
Z_o'	effective characteristic impedance

Greek symbols

ε	relative dielectric constant
ε_0	dielectric constant (permittivity) of free space (8.85×10^{-12} F/m)
μ	permeability
ρ	resistivity (the resistivity of copper is 1.724×10^{-6} $\Omega-$cm at 20°C)
ρ_L	load reflection coefficient
ρ_s	sheet resistance

ρ_S source reflection coefficient

ϕ magnetic flux (webers)

A.3 Trademarks

FAST, FACT, and FACT QS are registered trademarks of National Semiconductor Corporation.

PAL is a registered trademark of Advanced Micro Devices, Inc./Monolithic Memories, Inc.

A.4 CMOS and BiCMOS Power Dissipation Calculations

Calculating the power dissipation of CMOS and BiCMOS systems is an extremely difficult task because the largest portion of the power dissipation is a function of operating conditions and environment. Quiescent or static power dissipation of most CMOS and BiCMOS devices, which is easy to calculate, is generally insignificant. The majority of the power dissipated in high-speed CMOS and BiCMOS systems is a function of signal switching rates and actual load capacitance, both of which are very often difficult to determine. In contrast, in TTL systems, most of the system power dissipation is due to intrinsic device dissipation. System dc power dissipation is easy to calculate by using data book dc specifications which are provided on most data sheets. System dynamic power dissipation, on the other hand, is difficult to calculate since dynamic power is dependent on the system application rather than on the inherent device characteristic. Dynamic power dissipation is a function of node frequency, capacitance, and signal voltage swing. Thus, the operating conditions of each system signal, or node, are needed to calculate the system dynamic power. Even though individual device dc dissipation tends to be insignificant, in a large system overall dc dissipation "adds up." So to calculate the system power, both the quiescent power and the dynamic power of all devices must be determined:

$$P_{\text{TOTAL}} = P_{\text{quiescent}} + P_{\text{dynamic}} \qquad (A.1)$$

A.4.1 Quiescent power dissipation calculations

Most advanced CMOS SSI and MSI logic devices in the AC and ACT logic families are built with complementary circuits (see Figs. 3.21,

3.23, and 3.24) that have no dc path between V_{cc} and ground, and as a result, most AC and ACT advanced CMOS devices dissipate very little dc power. The same is true of BiCMOS SSI and MSI devices in the ABT logic family. In the ABT logic family, the core and input stages are built with CMOS circuits and the output stages are built with bipolar totem-pole structures (see Fig. 3.11) that likewise have no dc path between V_{cc} and ground. When devices are built exclusively with complementary and totem-pole structures, device dc or quiescent power is a function of internal device leakage current and any dc load that may exist.

Quiescent power P_q is the product of the supply voltage V_{cc} and the quiescent supply current I_{cc}:

$$P_q = V_{cc}I_{cc} \tag{A.2}$$

Quiescent supply current I_{cc} is listed on most data sheets and is typically given as a maximum value. It is usually specified at $+ 25°C$ and at the worst-case high operating temperature (typically $+ 125°C$) with V_{cc} at 5.5 V in both cases. Worst-case quiescent I_{cc} for AC and AC11 parts is shown as 4 µA at $+ 25°C$ and 80 µA $+ 125°C$ with all inputs at either V_{cc} or ground.[1,2] (*Caution:* I_{cc} is higher when inputs are at TTL levels—see below.) When I_{cc} is strictly due to leakage current, its value at other temperatures can be estimated when needed, since leakage currents in semiconductors approximately double for each 10°C increase in temperature.[3] That is, for positive changes (i.e., increases) in temperature

$$I_{cc} \text{ at a higher } T_O = (I_{cc} \text{ at } T_s) \times 2^N \tag{A.3}$$

and for negative changes in temperature

$$I_{cc} \text{ at a lower } T_O = \frac{(I_{cc} \text{ at } T_S)}{2^N} \tag{A.4}$$

where N in Eqs. (A.3) and (A.4) is

$$N = \left| \frac{T_O - T_S}{10} \right| \tag{A.5}$$

and T_S is the initial temperature at which I_{cc} is known (specified) and T_O is the operating temperature at which a value for I_{cc} is needed.

Quiescent current is not low in all CMOS and BiCMOS devices. For example, most CMOS and BiCMOS memories and PALs dissipate significant dc power. Texas Instruments' BCT bus interface family data sheets show quiescent I_{cc} currents as high as 80 mA for some BCT parts, depending upon input conditions. Most CMOS and BiCMOS devices with TTL compatible input structures, i.e., ACT and FCT devices, dissipate significantly more power when driven with TTL-level signals than with rail-to-rail CMOS-level signals. Complementary input structures, even when optimized for TTL levels, may not cut completely off when they are driven with TTL-level signals; V_{IH} may not be sufficiently high. No operational problem is caused, but I_{cc} may be higher than expected unless the system designer carefully reads all the fine print on data sheets. Typically, maximum I_{cc} is on the order of 1.5 mA for ACT parts driven with TTL *high*-level signals. Most devices in the FCT logic families have source follower output stages and as a result have quiescent I_{cc} currents, even when driven with rail-to-rail input signals. Typical I_{cc} value for FCT devices is 1 to 2 mA when driven with rail-to-rail signals and approximately double that for nominal TTL *high*-level inputs (FCT data book TTL-level input I_{cc} specifications are typically given for $V_{IN} = 3.4$ V and 0 V).[4]

A.4.2 Dynamic power dissipation calculations

The equation for calculating dynamic power P_d is [1]

$$P_d = (C_L + C_{pd})(\Delta V_s)^2 F \tag{A.6}$$

where C_L is the line and device load (both input and output) capacitance, C_{pd} is the internal device capacitance, ΔV_s is the signal swing (which is approximately equal to V_{cc} for CMOS devices with CMOS output levels), and F is the node toggle frequency. Signal voltage swing is easily established, and C_{pd}, which represents internal device capacitance, is provided on most CMOS and BiCMOS data sheets; but line and load capacitance and the frequency of each node are usually difficult to establish. Yet, if a reasonably accurate estimate of system power is needed, then a reasonably accurate estimate of the toggle rate and capacitance of each node is needed to calculate system power dissipation. In most situations, the best that can be done is to neglect all low-frequency control signals and to concentrate on data paths, where some assumptions as to average toggle rate and load capacitance can be made.

It is generally assumed that CMOS systems dissipate less power than equivalent TTL systems. Perhaps that is true at low frequencies, since certain CMOS devices dissipate little dc power, but as system operating speeds increase, the power advantage of first-generation advanced CMOS systems decreases. First-generation CMOS devices have greater output voltage swings than TTL, BiCMOS, and second-generation advanced CMOS devices with TTL output levels. Thus, dynamic power dissipation is greater in CMOS systems with true CMOS levels than in TTL-level systems, since dynamic power is a function of the signal voltage swing squared—see Eq. (A.6). Typical true CMOS output voltage swings are 5 V where typical TTL output voltage swings may be as low as 3 V or even less, depending upon loading (worst-case minimum TTL voltage swing is 2 V). Since dynamic power is a function of the signal swing squared, on a typical basis, CMOS-Level dynamic power is greater than TTL-level dynamic power by a factor of

$$\frac{5^2}{3^2} = \frac{25}{9} \approx 2.8$$

The difference between CMOS- and TTL-level dynamic dissipation is illustrated in the following example: The dynamic load power dissipation for a CMOS-level signal driving a 50-pF load at 20 MHz is [from Eq. (A.6)]

$$P_d = (50 \text{ pF})(5 \text{ V})^2(20 \text{ MHz}) = 25 \text{ mW}$$

and for the same load and signal switching frequency, the TTL- and low-voltage CMOS-level signal dynamic power is

$$P_d = (50 \text{ pF})(3 \text{ V})^2(20 \text{ MHz}) = 9 \text{ mW}$$

From the above example, it follows that BiCMOS, second generation advanced CMOS devices with TTL output levels, and low (supply) voltage CMOS offer significant dynamic power savings. At high signal toggle rates, individual first-generation 5-V advanced CMOS devices may provide little or no power advantage over bipolar TTL devices. Yet, in most cases, on an overall basis, high signal level 5-V CMOS systems dissipate less power than equivalent TTL systems because most control signals toggle at relatively low rates; it is usually only a few signals that toggle at high rates and have high dynamic power dissipation. However, if all signals toggle at very high rates, for example, 40 MHz or greater, then the dissipation of a 5-V true CMOS-level system may exceed the dissipation of an equivalent bipolar TTL system. The BiCMOS ABT logic family and the FCT-T TTL-level CMOS families offer the best of both bipolar and CMOS technologies—low static and dynamic dissipation.

A.4.3   References

1. *Advanced CMOS Logic Designer's Handbook,* Texas Instruments Inc., Dallas, Tex., 1988.
2. *FACT Advanced CMOS Logic Databook,* National Semiconductor Corp., Santa Clara, Calif., 1993.
3. H. C. Lin, *Integrated Electronics,* Holden-Day, San Francisco, 1967.
4. *High-Performance Logic, 1994 Data Book,* Integrated Device Technology Inc., Santa Clara, Calif., 1994.

Glossary

Active edge   A *low*-to-*high* or *high*-to-*low* signal transition that initiates an action.

Active *high*   A logic *high* asserts or causes an action.

Active *low*   A logic *low* asserts or causes an action.

Active sense or signal   The logic level that asserts or causes an action.

Advanced complementary metal-oxide semiconductor (CMOS) logic devices or families   Advanced-performance logic devices or family of devices fabricated with state-of-the-art CMOS processes.

Advanced Schottky transistor-transistor logic (TTL) devices or families   Advanced-performance bipolar logic devices or family of devices fabricated with state-of-the-art bipolar processes.

Analysis tools such as signal integrity or circuit   Software used to determine signal characteristics or circuit operation.

AND gate   A logic circuit whose output is a 1 state only when every input is in the 1 state.

Application-specific integrated circuit (ASIC)   An integrated circuit that is tailored for a particular application. Includes devices such as gate arrays, standard cells, complete custom integrated circuits, and field-programmable devices.

Assert   To cause a signal to change from its inactive to its active state.

Asynchronous or dc set or reset inputs   Set or reset inputs on storage elements which are level-sensitive, i.e., activated by a level, rather than a level transition or a level plus a clock transition.

Asynchronous inputs or asynchronous interfaces   Signals with no fixed frequency or phase relationship to the receiving device or system clock signal.

Asynchronous logic   Logic circuits that are not clocked by a system clock.

Asynchronous operation   The completion of one operation triggers the next. Operations do *not* occur in step with a clock.

Backpanel   A panel used for mechanical support of several interconnected circuit boards and support of the board-to-board interconnections.

Backplane   A power or ground plane that is an integral portion of a backpanel.

Balanced differential communication   Transmission of digital data on a pair of lines (wires) using a true and complementary signal pair; i.e., each signal of the pair is always the inverse of the other. In a balanced differential pair, currents tend to be equal but opposite in direction, so that the net current flow at any point is small.

Bandwidth   The frequency at which the gain of the device or network is 3 dB below its nominal frequency value.

Bare die   An integrated circuit or other circuit element that has not been packaged.

Bidirectional   A circuit, typically a buffer, that passes signals in both directions between two nodes or pins.

Bilevel signals   Signals with two defined levels.

Binary or binary data   Data belonging to a number system that has 2 as its base. Data that are expressed as a logic 1 or 0 or as a logic *high* or *low*.

Bipolar and complementary metal-oxide semiconductor (BiCMOS)   A semiconductor device composed of bipolar and CMOS devices operating in tandem.

Bipolar device   A semiconductor device whose operation depends on the flow of both holes and electrons.

Bipolar transistor   A three-layer semiconductor device whose operation depends on the flow of both holes and electrons.

Bistable   A logic device with two stable states.

Bit   One unit of binary data.

Buffer   A device used to provide extra drive and to isolate low-drive devices from heavy loads.

Bulk decoupling capacitor   A capacitor located near the power entrance points of a circuit board or other electronic module that is used to supply low-frequency transient supply current needs and to help suppress transmission of internal noise.

Bypass capacitor   See **decoupling capacitor.**

Byte   Eight bits.

Characteristic impedance Z_o   The apparent real impedance (resistance) of a transmission line when a signal with a sufficiently high-frequency content is applied.

Circuit   A combination of electrical components such as capacitors, resistors, transistors, diodes, and inductors that perform a specific function.

Circuit model or equivalent circuit   A functional representation of a circuit for a limited set of conditions that uses simpler and more easily understood circuit elements.

Clear   To force a digital circuit to a logic 0 or *low*. Also see **reset.**

Clock   The source or the periodic signal used to synchronize synchronous systems. The periodic signal applied to clocked elements such as flip-flops, counters, etc., to activate logic operations.

Clocked device or element   A digital circuit that requires a clock input to change states.

Clock frequency   The clock repetition rate.

Clock period   The time interval between two active clock edges. The inverse of the clock frequency.

Clock signal   The periodic signal applied to clocked elements such as flip-flops and counters to activate logic operations.

Clock switching edge   The clock edge transition that initiates state changes of clocked elements.

Combinational logic   A combination of digital circuits such as gates and buffers that has no memory or data storage capability.

Commercial devices or parts   Traditionally, digital devices rated to operate from 0 to + 70°C and ± 5 percent power supply variations, but many of the newer, commercially rated devices have broader temperature and supply operating ranges. Part numbers for commercial rated devices in many of the logic families start with 74.

Common-mode voltage   The portion of the input signal magnitude (measured with respect to the device ground reference) that is common to both inputs of a differential line receiver, comparator, or amplifier.

Comparator   (1) An analog device that compares the magnitudes of two voltages or currents and indicates their relationship, or (2) a digital device that compares the magnitudes of two digital data words or quantities and indicates their relationship.

Complementary metal-oxide semiconductor (CMOS)   An integrated-circuit technology that uses complementary isolated gate field-effect transistors to implement digital circuits.

Complementary signal   A signal that is *high* when a related signal is *low* or *low* when a related signal is *high.*

Control signal or signals   A Signal that controls the operation of digital circuits such as registers, counters, and multiplexers or that controls the functional operation of a system or a portion of a system.

Counter   A digital circuit that counts events by progressing through a sequence of binary states.

Critical line length   When the line length is equal to one-half the rise or fall time of the signal divided by the actual loaded propagation delay of the line.

Critical path   A signal path that could limit the speed of operation of the circuit.

Crosstalk or cross-coupling   Undesirable signal coupling between adjacent or nearby signal lines.

Daisy chain   Several devices connected in serial fashion. Wires or other forms of interconnections routed from one device or node to the next.

Daughterboard   A circuit board that plugs into (via some form of connector) or otherwise attaches to a motherboard.

Deassert To cause a signal to change from its active to its inactive state.

Decoder A digital circuit that converts coded digital information to a more usable form.

Decoupling capacitor A capacitor used to supply the transient switching currents associated with digital circuits.

Delay The time between the occurrence of an event at one point in a circuit and its occurrence at another point in the circuit.

Derating or drive derating A safety factor applied to the current drive rating specified by logic device manufacturers to ensure that a device will function in a system over a long lifetime and under the extremes of the expected operating conditions.

Design verification The process of confirming or validating that the design meets the required specifications.

Destination or load termination A load impedance that has a prescribed relationship to the interconnecting line impedance Z_o.

Device or digital device A digital circuit, generally an integrated circuit.

Die A basic circuit element such as an integrated circuit. The active circuit element. A bare die is a die that has not been packaged.

Differential line driver A line driver with a true and complementary output used for balanced digital data transmission.

Differential line receiver A line receiver used in balanced digital data transmission applications that requires a true and a complementary input signal.

Differential signals A pair of signals one of which is always the complement of the other.

Digital circuit A circuit that switches between two levels and makes logic decisions, performs logic operations, or stores data.

Digital data Data conveyed by means of bilevel signals.

Don't-care inputs Inputs that are not sensitive to logic level; i.e., the circuitry will operate correctly with a logic *high* or *low* input.

Driver A device used to provide extra drive and to isolate low-drive devices from heavy loads.

Dual-in-line package A type of package for electronic devices that has two rows of pins on two parallel sides of the package. The pins are at right angles to the package and typically on 0.1-in centers.

Dual stripline or dual stripline conductor A form of interconnection where two layers of conductors are enclosed between two ground or reference planes. Conductors within each layer are routed parallel to each other, but conductors in the two adjacent layers are typically routed at right angles, to minimize crosstalk between layers.

Dynamic loading The capacitance and inductance associated with a digital signal line, i.e., the capacitance and inductance that must be driven when a digital signal switches states.

Dynamic power dissipation Power dissipated while charging and discharging internal and load capacitances when a signal switches states.

Dynamic random-access memory (DRAM) A memory device that allows data to be written and retrieved from random locations, but requires some means of continuously refreshing the data because the data consist of small packets of stored charge that tend to leak away unless refreshed.

Edge-triggered Activation of a digital circuit by the edge of a pulse rather than the level of the signal.

Electrically erasable programmable read-only memory (EEPROM) A memory device that can be programmed on a bit or word-by-word basis in random order and reprogrammed a number of times. Parts are available with allowable write cycles (reprogramming cycle) that range from 10^3 to 10^6.

Electrically programmable read-only memory (EPROM) A memory device that can be programmed one time by the user.

Electrostatic discharge (ESD) The transfer of electrostatic charge between bodies at different electrostatic potentials, caused by direct contact or induced by an electrostatic field.

Element or logic element A digital circuit, generally an integrated circuit.

Emitter-coupled logic (ECL) Digital integrated circuits that use nonsaturating bipolar transistors to implement cascade differential amplifiers that are coupled via the emitters (hence, emitter-coupled).

Enable A control input or signal that allows a circuit to respond to an input. For example, a clock enable allows a circuit to respond to its clock input.

Encoder A digital circuit that converts digital data to a coded format.

Equivalent circuit A functional representation of a circuit for a limited set of conditions using simpler and more easily understood circuit elements.

Erasable programmable logic device (EPLD) Field-programmable parts that can be erased and reprogrammed by the user.

Fall time t_f The time interval between two reference levels on a negative-going signal transition, typically measured between 10 and 90 percent or 20 and 80 percent of the signal transition.

Fan-out The number of logic device inputs that a given output is capable of driving while maintaining correct logic levels.

Feedthrough current The transient current that flows through a device, i.e., from the supply voltage to ground, when a device switches states.

Ferrite bead or shield bead A bead made of ferrite material that is used to absorb high-frequency energy in fast signal transitions. Ferrite beads located at the signal source help minimize transmission-line ringing and overshoot.

Field-programmable logic A standard product that the user can configure to specific applications.

Field-programmable logic array (FPLA) A standard product that the user configures to specific logic functions. FPLA typically refers to a relatively large programmable device.

Flash EPROM   A memory device that can be programmed and reprogrammed by the user after it is erased. Some flash EPROMs can be erased in blocks, but others operate such that the complete device is erased.

Flip-flop   A circuit having two stable states and the ability to change from one to the other on application of external signals.

Gate   A combinational logic circuit.

Gate array   A digital integrated circuit with uncommitted elements that are interconnected as required for specific applications.

Glitch   A short-duration voltage or current spike that is typically unwanted.

Ground bounce   Transient reference (ground) shifts caused by transient-current flow to ground being impeded by the inductance of device ground pins and other connections between the switching device and the system reference level.

Hold time t_h   The time interval that a signal on an input pin of a clocked logic device must be retained after an active (triggering) clock transition.

Inactive state or level   The logic state or level that does not initiate action or cause an operation to occur.

Indefinite (logic) level   When the logic level is not known.

Indeterminate (logic) level   When the logic level is not known.

Indeterminate state   Where the conditions of the input signals, reference, or power to a device are such that the response of the device is undefined. For example, if the power supply voltage to a device is less than the specified minimum operating level, the device may not function.

Initialize   Establish an initial condition or starting state for logic circuits such as counters and registers and for associated functional groups of logic circuits (i.e., digital systems).

Input or input line   A circuit node that provides an input data or control path to a circuit or system.

Input level   The actual voltage at an input terminal of a device.

Input loading   The input impedance of a circuit, board, or system. For digital circuits, input loading is typically given in terms of current and capacitance.

Input-output circuits   The circuitry on the boundary (interface) of a device, circuit board, or unit, i.e., the circuitry that connects to other devices, boards, or units.

Integrated circuit (IC)   An electronic device in which all the components are fabricated on a single piece of semiconductor material.

Interconnection   The wire, printed-circuit board trace, or other physical means used to connect two or more electric circuit nodes.

Interface   The electrical boundary of a device, system, or subsystem.

Interface circuitry   The circuitry used at device, system, or subsystem boundaries.

Intermediate (logic) level   A signal level that does not meet the defined requirements for a logic *high* or *low* level.

Inverter   A logic device that changes the input logic level from a *high* to *low* or *low* to *high,* i.e., a circuit whose output is the opposite of the input.

Large-scale integration   Commonly defined as an integrated circuit that has the functional equivalent of 100 to 10,000 simple gates.

Latch   A flip-flop that is level-controlled rather than edge-triggered.

Latch-up   A disruptive and possibly destructive low-impedance condition that occurs in CMOS devices when parasitic SCRs are triggered on by extraneous substrate currents. Once triggered on, the parasitic SCR remains on until power is removed from the part.

Leadless chip carrier   An integrated-circuit package without leads that is used for surface mounting.

Leakage current   Current that flows due to imperfections or nonideal characteristics of components and their mounting or attachment hardware.

Level translator   A circuit for interfacing forms of logic having different logic levels.

Line capacitance   The capacitance associated with a given signal interconnection, i.e., wire, PC board trace, or other physical means of interconnection.

Line driver   A digital circuit suitable for driving long lines.

Line receiver   A digital device used to receive signals from long lines.

Load capacitance   The total capacitance of a signal interconnection or in some transmission-line equations the capacitance of discrete device inputs and outputs connected to a signal line, but not including that of the interconnecting signal line.

Load or destination termination   A load impedance that has a prescribed relationship to the interconnecting line impedance Z_o.

Local-decoupling capacitor   A capacitor located near the power pins of a device that supplies the transient supply current needed to charge related stray and load capacitances when the associated device switches states.

Logic family   A group of logic devices fabricated with a common semiconductor technology that have similar electrical characteristics, i.e., speed and power.

Logic *high* level   The more positive of the two logic levels.

Logic *low* level   The more negative of the two logic levels.

Long line   An interconnection that exceeds the criterion for the onset of transmission-line effects.

Lumped capacitance load   Capacitance located within a distance equivalent to less than one-half the rise time of the signal.

Master or central reset signal   A signal used to initialize an entire digital system to a known starting condition.

Master-slave A binary element containing two independent storage stages with a definite separation of the clock function (edges or levels) used to enter data into the master and transfer them to the slave.

Matching impedance A network used to match the source or load impedance to the impedance of the interconnecting line.

Medium-scale integration Commonly defined as a digital circuit that has the functional equivalent of 10 to 100 simple gates.

Memory device A digital device capable of storing 1 or more bits of digital data or digital words.

Metastable An unknown or unstable output condition that can occur when the inputs to a clocked device do not meet the required timing relationships or levels.

Metal-oxide semiconductor field-effect transistor (MOSFET) The most common insulated gate field-effect transistor. The transistor is constructed so that when a voltage is applied to the gate, a transverse electric field is produced in the adjoining semiconductor material, which causes the resistance of the semiconductor material to decrease. By varying the gate voltage, the resistance can be controlled.

Microstrip or microstrip conductor A form of interconnection where layers of conductors are routed adjacent to a ground or reference plane.

Military device, part, or military rated device A digital device rated to operate from -55 to $+125°C$ and ± 10 percent power supply variations. Part numbers for most military rated TTL, CMOS, or BiCMOS digital devices start with 54.

Monostable multivibrator (one-shot) A digital circuit with two output states, one of which is stable and the other temporary, which can be triggered into the temporary state for a period of time determined by an associated RC network.

Motherboard A large printed-circuit board that serves as the electrical and mechanical interface for daughterboards and that provides the interconnections between daughterboards and external signals.

Multilayer printed-circuit (PC) board A board used to interconnect electric circuits with more than two layers of etched interconnections determined in the manufacturing process by printed masks.

Multiple-emitter transistor and multiple-emitter input A bipolar transistor with more than one emitter. Such transistors are typically used to implement the input stage of standard (original) and Schottky TTL circuits.

Multiplexer A digital circuit used to route digital data from multiple sources to a common destination.

NAND gate A logic device whose inputs must all be in a 1 state to produce a 0 state output.

Net A group of circuit nodes that are interconnected.

Node An identifiable point in a circuit.

Noise immunity   A measure of how good a circuit is at rejecting extraneous signals.

Noise margin   The amount of extraneous voltage that a signal can tolerate before the signal is no longer recognized as the intended logic level.

Nonvolatile memory   A memory, i.e., a digital data storage device, not requiring continuous power to maintain its contents.

NOR gate   A logic device where any one input or more having a 1 state will yield a 0 state output.

Off-phase clocking   Clocking of signals at some time other than when the normal active clock edge occurs. Typically, off-phase clocking is done at the midpoint between normal active clock edges.

One-shot (monostable multivibrator)   A digital circuit with two output states, one of which is stable and the other temporary, with an input or inputs for triggering to the temporary state. When triggered into the temporary state, they remain there for a time determined by an associated RC network.

Operating speed   The speed at which a logic circuit or system must make decisions.

OR gate   A logic device where any one input or more having a 1 state is sufficient to produce a 1 state output.

Output level   The actual output voltage level at the output terminals of a logic device.

Overshoot   A signal that goes beyond its normal range or steady-state level. A digital signal that goes below ground or above the power supply level.

Overvoltage   Overvoltage with respect to digital circuits means that the power supply voltage is greater than the maximum specified operating level.

Parallel or split termination (sometimes described as Thevenin's termination)   A termination network consisting of two series-connected resistors with Thevenin's impedance (at the junction) with a prescribed relationship to the interconnecting line impedance. One of the resistors is connected to the supply voltage and the other to ground. The line is connected to the junction.

PC board   Printed-circuit board.

Plane   A continuous layer or sheet of material in which any voids or cutouts are small with respect to the wavelength of the highest frequency of interest.

Power integrity   Power connections or distribution networks with proper integrity meet their ac and dc voltage tolerance limits and other specifications.

Power supply droop   The shift in device supply voltage caused by transient-current flow through the inductance of the package power pins and other power supply connections to the device.

Programmable logic device (PLD)   A logic device that is customized by the user and retains the programmed logic structure when power is off.

Programmable read-only memory (PROM)   A memory device customized by the user that retains the programmed data when power is off.

Propagation delay (1) For digital circuits, the time difference between the change of an input signal, or clock, and the change of the output. (2) For interconnections, the time difference between two reference points in the interconnection.

Prototyping board A universal circuit board without dedicated locations for circuit components that can be used to quickly implement and test the operation of a new circuit.

Pull-down resistor A resistor connected to ground used to pull down unused inputs or lines that have the potential to float to an undefined logic level.

Pull-down voltage A voltage used to provide a static *low* input level to unused inputs.

Pull-up resistor A resistor connected to the positive supply voltage used to pull up unused inputs or lines that have the potential to float to an undefined logic level.

Pull-up voltage A voltage used to provide a static *high* input level to unused inputs.

Pulse width The time between the leading and trailing edges of a pulse.

Quiet time The time interval in a synchronous system between the time when all signals have settled and the next active clock edge.

Random-access memory (RAM) A memory device that allows data to be written or retrieved in a random fashion from any address.

Read-only memory (ROM) A memory device that is programmed to the customer's specification by the manufacturer. Data cannot be changed once a part is fabricated.

Register A digital device (a flip-flop) used for temporary storage of digital data.

Reset or clear input An input used to return a storage element to its logic 0 state.

Reset signal A signal used to initialize a system at power-on, following a power transient, or under other conditions.

Ringing This occurs when a signal overshoots and undershoots the final steady-state level a number of times following a logic level transition.

Rise time t_r The time interval between two reference levels on a positive-going signal transition. Typically measured between 10 and 90 percent or 20 and 80 percent of the signal transition.

Route The configuration of the interconnection between circuit nodes.

Routing The process of configuring interconnections between nodes.

Schmitt trigger buffer A buffer with hysteresis between the positive-going and negative-going input thresholds that provides greater noise margin than conventional buffers.

Schottky transistors Transistors that use a low-drop diode between the base and collector to prevent saturation.

Schottky transistor-transistor logic (TTL) Digital integrated circuits that use Schottky transistors to achieve higher speed with less power than earlier TTL devices.

Set To force a digital storage element to a logic 1.

Set input An input to a storage element that causes it to go to the logic 1 state.

Setup time t_s The time that the input data to a clocked logic device must be stable before the active (triggering) clock transition.

Short-circuit current I_{sc} The maximum output current which a device will put into a short circuit or that is available to charge load capacitance.

Signal integrity Signals with the required waveshape and that are free of noise and other degradation when they are being sampled or when they can initiate an action.

Signal integrity tools Software used to determine crosstalk, transmission-line effects, ground bounce, and other signal- and power-corrupting effects.

Single-ended signals Signals with one discrete observable interconnection, i.e., a single wire, where the current loop must be completed by the power or ground system.

Slew rate The rate of change of an output.

Small-scale integration References to traditional standard digital logic components such as NAND, NOR, and OR gates and other devices having 1 to approximately 10 logic gate equivalents.

Solder clips A small clip used to make direct solder connections between welded-wire pins and ground or power planes on welded-wire boards with universal pin fields.

Solder washer A small washer used to make direct solder connections between wire-wrap pins and ground or power planes on wire-wrap boards with universal pin fields.

Source or series termination An impedance in series with a line located near the driven end of the line that has a prescribed relationship to the interconnecting line characteristic impedance Z_o.

Spike A very narrow voltage or current pulse.

Split termination See **parallel termination.**

Standard cell A predefined mask-level design of a logic function or functional element.

State The condition of a logic signal, i.e., whether it is *high* or *low* or a logic 1 or logic 0.

Static random-access memory (SRAM) A bistable memory device that can be written and read in a random manner. The data are lost when power is removed, but data do not have to be continuously refreshed when the device is powered.

Storage element A flip-flop (see **flip-flop**).

Stripline or stripline conductor   A form of interconnection where a layer of conductors is enclosed between two ground or reference planes.

Switching time   The time required for a signal to transition from *high* to *low* or vice versa. Generally measured from 10 to 90 percent or 20 to 80 percent of the signal transition.

Synchronous   All devices are clocked in step with a master clock signal.

Synchronous logic   Clocked logic circuits in which all functional signal changes follow and are caused by clock transitions.

Synchronous system   A digital system in which all sending and receiving clocked devices are clocked with a common-clock frequency and phase.

Termination   Provision of a source or load impedance that has a prescribed relationship to the interconnecting line impedance.

Thevenin's termination   See **parallel termination.**

Three-state   Logic systems or devices with three states: defined *high* and *low* levels and an undefined high-impedance state.

Threshold voltage   The input voltage level at which the output logic level is no longer defined.

Timing analysis   Evaluation of circuit and interconnection delays to determine whether signals arrive at their destination at the proper time.

Timing margin   The excess operating speed that a circuit or system has beyond the specified operating speed.

Timing verification   Actual checking of circuits or systems to verify that they function at the required operating speed with worst-case environmental conditions.

Toggle   A digital storage element changes to the opposite state.

Toggle rate   The rate at which a flip-flop is toggling.

Transistor-transistor logic   Integrated-circuit logic devices that use bipolar-transistor technology.

Transition time   The time required to transition from *high* to *low* or *low* to *high* logic levels.

Transmission line   An interconnecting signal line comparable to the wavelength of the signal frequency.

Transmission-line effects   Ringing, overshoot, undershoot, loading, and line propagation delays are effects of transmission-line interconnections. Transmission-line effects delay signal settling.

Transmission-line load   The effective impedance (i.e., load) of a transmission line is equal to the characteristic impedance Z_o of the line.

Tristate   Logic devices or signals with three states: defined *high* and *low* levels and an undefined high-impedance state or floating state.

Twinex   A form of shielded twisted-pair cable with controlled characteristic impedance Z_o. The dimensions between the pair of conductors and the conductors and the shield and other cable parameters are closely controlled so that the cable impedance is consistent and within a tight absolute tolerance.

Ultraviolet erasable electrically programmable read-only memory (UV EPROM)   A user-programmable memory device that can be erased by using ultraviolet light and then can be reprogrammed.

Undefined logic level or condition   The input or output level is not a defined *high* or *low*.

Undershoot   When a digital signal rings back toward or across the nearest logic level threshold; i.e., when a digital signal transitions, it may overshoot and then ring back or *undershoot*.

Undervoltage   Undervoltage with respect to digital circuits means that the power supply voltage is less than the minimum specified operating level.

Unit   Distinct, separate housing, such as a rack, cabinet, or chassis, of electronic equipment.

Unit load   Generally the load for one *high* or *low* input for a given TTL family, but in some cases the load for one input of the standard (original) TTL family (*high* and *low* unit loads are different).

Unknown level or state   When the state of a signal is unknown. Typically it is due to bistable devices that have not been initialized, but it also occurs during circuit operation while signals are transitioning to new states.

Very large-scale integration   Commonly defined as an integrated circuit with more than 10,000 transistors.

Vias   Connections between layers in multilayer printed-circuit boards.

Volatile   A memory or other digital storage element with the attribute of losing the stored information when power is removed.

Volts-good signal   A signal from a level-sensing circuit or circuits that indicates that the system power supplies are at their proper operating levels.

Waveform   The shape of a signal, particularly during signal transitions between states.

Welded-wire board, backpanel, or motherboard   An interconnection technique that uses discrete insulated wires (typically AWG no. 30) that are attached to the circuit nodes by a welding process.

Wire-wrap board, backpanel, or motherboard   An interconnection technique that uses discrete insulated wires (typically AWG no. 30) that are attached to the circuit nodes by stripping a short section and wrapping the bare wire around square posts which are located at each circuit node.

Index

Advanced CMOS logic circuits (*see* CMOS logic circuits; CMOS logic devices; CMOS logic families; Logic families)

Advanced Schottky TTL devices:
  circuit operation, 40
  dynamic operational characteristics of, 16
  input-output capacitance of, 83
  input circuits, 40
  internal circuit structure, 40
  internal switching currents in, 76–78
  NAND, 40
  noise margin change with temperature, 32
  noise margin of, 31
  noise margin of (table), 31
  output circuits, 41
  standard test load, 16, 83, 229
  (*See also* Advanced Schottky TTL logic families; Logic families; TTL logic circuits; TTL logic devices; TTL logic families)

Advanced Schottky TTL logic families:
  input-output voltage levels (table), 30
  input currents, 20
  input currents (table), 21
  input voltage levels, 19
  output voltage levels, 21
  output voltage levels (table), 23
  worst-case buffer speed (table), 17
  worst-case register speed (table), 17
  (*See also* Logic devices)

ASIC applications:
  general discussion, 331, 332
  guidelines for interface timing, 338
  guidelines for selecting input-output levels, 334
  logic structures to avoid, 333, 334

ASIC applications (*Cont.*):
  output drive selection, 336
  power and ground pin requirements, 336, 337
  prevention of floating inputs, 335, 336
  summary of application tips, 339

Asynchronous applied reset signals, 270, 271

Asynchronous buses, synchronizing, 212, 234

Asynchronous data transfer:
  device-to-device, 230
  unit-to-unit, 221

Asynchronous designs:
  disadvantage of, 226
  speed of operation, 226

Asynchronous inputs:
  synchronizing of, 230, 234
  synchronizing of in PLDs, 322
  for system initialization, 225
  use of, 225

Asynchronous interfaces, 230, 234
Asynchronous logic design, 226
Asynchronous signals, 212, 230, 234

Balanced differential interfaces, 215
Balanced differential transmission, 215
Bandwidth:
  needed versus rise time, 4
Bergeron plots, 162
BiCMOS gate, internal circuitry, 58, 59
BiCMOS logic circuits:
  advantages of, 57
  dc input current limits, 65
  ESD protection networks, 64–66
  implementation of, 57, 58
  input circuit operation, 60, 61

BiCMOS logic circuits (*Cont.*):
  inputs, reflection coefficient of, 157
  internal switching currents in, 76–78
  latch-up in, 62
  noise margin of, 33
  noise margin of (table), 33
  optimum input-output impedance, 169
  outputs, reflection coefficient of, 157
  totem-pole output stage, 59
  transmission-line response of, 162, 166, 167
BiCMOS logic devices:
  adjustments for worst-case conditions, 246
  advantages of, 57
  ASIC NAND, 332
  available interfaces, 10
  conditions for timing specifications, 15, 245
  dc input current limits, 65
  dynamic operational characteristics of, 16
  ESD protection networks, 64–66
  implementation of, 57, 58
  input-output capacitance of, 83, 249
  input circuit operation, 60, 61
  internal switching currents in, 76–78
  latch-up in, 62
  optimum input-output impedance, 169
  paralleling of, 208
  standard test load, 16, 83, 174, 229, 245
  timing adjustments for actual load, 248, 249
  timing adjustments for package style, 251
  timing adjustments for process, 246
  timing adjustments for simultaneous switching, 250
  timing adjustments for temperature, 246
  timing adjustment for V_{cc} level, 247
  totem-pole output stage, 59
  transmission-line response of, 162, 166, 167
  (*See also* BiCMOS logic circuits; BiCMOS logic families)
BiCMOS logic families:
  conditions for timing specifications, 245
  features of, 14
  input-output voltage levels (table), 30
  input currents, 20
  input currents (table), 21
  input voltage levels, 20

BiCMOS logic families (*Cont.*):
  listing of, 14
  output voltage levels, 24
  output voltage levels (table), 23
  worst-case buffer speed (table), 17
  worst-case register speed (table), 17
  (*See also* BiCMOS logic circuits; BiCMOS logic devices; Logic devices; Logic families)
Bidirectional ports, capacitance of, 249
Board-to-board clocks:
  summary of distribution techniques, 194
  termination of, 188–192
Board-to-board interconnections:
  clock distribution, 187–192
  CMOS level clock distribution, 191
  signal interconnections, 199, 208–210
  typical signal path, 254, 255
  (*See also* Interconnections)
Board ground pin requirements, 193
Board interface protection, 65, 213
Board leakage current, 238
Board level clock distribution, 177–180
Board level clock tree, 178–180
Buffer speed:
  worst-case for Adv Sch TTL Logic (table), 17
  worst-case for BiCMOS logic families (table), 17
  worst-case for CMOS logic families (table), 17
Bulk capacitance, 101
Bulk capacitors:
  caution on use, 101
  caution on use of, 118
  sizing of, 101, 118
  use of, 117, 118
Bulk decoupling (*see* Capacitors; Bulk capacitors; Bulk capacitance)
Bus-hold circuits, 211
Bus contention:
  avoidance of, 211
Bus interfaces, 208–210
Bypass capacitors (*see* Decoupling capacitors)

Capacitance:
  of device inputs and outputs, 83, 249
  of interconnections, 83, 249
  of standard test load, 16, 83, 174, 229, 245

Capacitor voltage rate of change:
for constant current drive, 81, 82, 249
Capacitors:
bulk, 101, 117, 118
decoupling needs of LSI devices, 328
leakage current effects in one-shot appl,
238
local decoupling, need for, 113
Central reset signal generator, need for,
264
Characteristic impedance:
as a function of load, 131, 303
basic equation for, 128, 131
effective, equation for, 131, 303
of a welded-wire board, 133
of a wire-wrap board, 133
of a wire above a reference plane, 133
of buried microstrip conductor, 134,
135, 137
of common interconnection structures,
133
of dual-stripline conductor, 136
of epoxy glass pc boards, 136
of microstrip conductor, 134
of off-center stripline conductor, 136
of stripline conductor, 135, 137
of welded-wire board, 181
of wire-wrap board, 181
Circuit models (*see* Equivalent circuit)
Clamp termination (*see* Diode clamp termination)
Clamped inputs:
effect on line response, 163, 170
test circuit for, 170
Clock alignment, 178, 179
Clock alignment, in synchronous systems,
228, 229
Clock distribution:
board-to-board routing, 187–192
board-to-board with CMOS levels, 191
board level, 177–180
categories of, 177
circuit for test clock, 196
component-to-component, 177–180
crosstalk, control of on motherboards,
189, 192
general guidelines, 173–177
load grouping on circuit boards, 178, 184
maximum line length, 185
need to control skew, 173
on circuit boards, 177–180
routing of, 173
summary of board-to-board, 194

Clock distribution (*Cont.*):
summary of board level techniques, 186
summary of unit-to-unit, 196
unit-to-unit, 194, 195
(*See also* other Clock entries)
Clock drivers:
for board-to-board applications,
188–194
for unit-to-unit applications, 195
Clock frequencies, not mixing in package,
175, 179, 180
Clock frequency:
maximum for logic families, 259, 260
maximum for logic families (table), 259
of synchronous designs, 226, 227
Clock lines:
load placement on, 178, 184
maximum line lengths, 185
Clock phasing:
preferred active edge, 35
Clock receivers:
for unit-to-unit applications, 195
Clock requirements, for synchronous systems, 227
Clock signals:
gating of, 186
phasing for maximum noise immunity,
175, 176
routing of, 188–192
shaping (duty cycle), 176
termination of, 188–192
Clock termination:
at the board level, 182–186
board-to-board, 188–192
unit-to-unit, 195
Clock tree:
for board-to-board, 188
for boards, 178–180
Clocked devices, unbuffered, 212
CMOS buffers:
equivalent circuit of, 78, 79
for high-voltage signal receivers, 218,
219
for very low-speed receivers, 218, 219
CMOS circuits:
supply current versus input voltage, 61,
79, 204, 205
CMOS input stage:
circuit of, 61, 204
equivalent circuit of, 61, 79, 204
CMOS inputs:
reflection coefficient of, 157
unused, connection of, 205

CMOS inverter:
  equivalent circuit of, 54
  equivalent circuit of when switching, 78, 79
  equivalent circuit of with open input, 61, 204
  implementation of, 54, 61, 78, 79, 204
  input impedance, 55
CMOS levels:
  advantages of, 28
CMOS logic circuits:
  complementary circuit structures, 54, 78, 79, 204
  dc input current limits, 65
  devices used to implement, 52
  ESD protection networks, 64–66
  implementation of, 53, 54
  input circuit operation, 60, 61
  input impedance, 55
  internal switching currents in, 78, 79
  inverter, 54, 61, 78, 79, 204
  latch-up in, 62
  NAND gate, 56
  NOR gate, 56
  optimum input-output impedance, 169
  output impedance change with state, 57
  output implementation of, 56
  supply current versus input voltage, 61, 79, 204, 205
  transmission-line response of, 162–165
  (See also CMOS logic devices)
CMOS logic devices:
  (See also CMOS logic families)
  adjustments for worst-case conditions, 246
  complementary circuit structures, 54, 78, 79, 204
  conditions for timing specifications, 15, 245
  dc input current limits, 65
  dynamic operational characteristics of, 16
  dynamic output current, 304
  ESD protection networks, 64–66
  four-layer pnpn structures, 62
  input-output capacitance of, 83, 249
  input circuit operation, 60, 61
  input impedance, 55
  input threshold levels, 55
  interface protection, 65, 213
  inverter, 54, 61, 78, 79, 204
  latch-up in, 62
  NAND, 56

CMOS logic devices (Cont.):
  noise margin of, 32
  noise margin of (table), 32
  noise tolerance, 5
  NOR, 56
  optimum input-output impedance, 169
  output impedance change with state, 57
  output impedance of, 56
  paralleling of, 207, 208
  parasitic SCR structures in, 62
  power dissipation of, 54
  standard test load, 16, 83, 174, 229, 245
  supply current versus input voltage, 79
  timing adjustments for actual load, 248, 249
  timing adjustments for package style, 251
  timing adjustments for process, 246
  timing adjustments for simultaneous switching, 250
  timing adjustments for temperature, 246
  timing adjustments for V_{cc} level, 247
  timing specification (table), 15
  transmission-line response of, 162–165
  (See also CMOS logic circuits)
CMOS logic families:
  acceptance of, 13
  conditions for timing specifications, 245
  devices used to implement, 52
  first generation definition, 11
  input-output voltage levels (table), 30
  input currents, 20
  input currents (table), 21
  input voltage levels, 19, 20
  letter designators, 12
  listing of, 12
  output voltage levels, 21
  output voltage levels (table), 23
  second generation definition, 11
  worst-case buffer speed (table), 17
  worst-case register speed (table), 17
  (See also CMOS logic circuits; CMOS logic devices; Logic devices; Logic families)
CMOS NAND gate, 56
CMOS NOR gate, 56
CMOS output:
  reflection coefficient of, 157
Common-mode rejection:
  interconnection needed for, 215
  need for on unit-to-unit lines, 215
Communication, between separate units, 214

Complementary CMOS circuit, 61, 204
Complementary pair, 53, 54
Component-to-component:
  clock distribution, 177–180
  signal interconnections, 199, 201
Conductor delay:
  calculation of, 251
  microstrip conductor, 134
  stripline conductor, 135
  typical pc board, 153, 154, 251
  welded-wire, 251
  wire-wrap, 251
Conductors (*see* Dual-stripline conductor;
    Microstrip conductor; Stripline con-
    ductor; Wire above ground)
Connector pins:
  location of power and ground pins, 99
  needed for power and ground, 7, 99
  number of ground pins needed, 193
Connections, between dissimilar metals,
    106, 107
Constant current drive:
  capacitor rate of change of voltage, 81,
    82, 249
Contention:
  avoidance of on buses, 211
  on memory data buses, 293, 307, 308,
    53
Copper conductor (stranded), resistance,
    104
Coupled lines, 143
Coupling (*see* Crosstalk)
Critical line length:
  definition of, 4, 153, 252
  equation for, 153, 302
  signal waveshape as a function of, 154
Crosstalk:
  backward, discussion of, 142–146
  backward, equation for, 144
  control of in memory subsystems, 293,
    306, 307
  control of on motherboards, 189, 192
  control of on welded-wire boards, 142
  control of on wire-wrap boards, 142
  curves of for buried microstrip, 147
  curves of for dual stripline, 147
  curves of for stripline, 148
  forward, discussion of, 142–146
  forward, equation for, 144
  general discussion of, 141
  in a homogeneous material, 145
Current limited pull-down voltages:
  sources of, 206

Current limited pull-up voltages:
  sources of, 206

dc input current limits, 65
Decoupling capacitors:
  bulk, 101, 117, 118
  charge transfer from, 114, 115
  circuit model for, 115
  effect of ESL, 116, 117
  effect of ESR, 116, 117
  for LSI devices, 328
  local, 113
  local bulk, 101, 117, 118
  need for, 98, 113
  placement of, 114
  selection of, 115
  sizing of, 113, 114
Derating factor, 206, 207
Destination termination (*see* Load termi-
    nation)
Detector:
  leading edge, 235, 236
  trailing edge, 235, 236
Device operating speed:
  to utilize, 2
Device timing adjustments:
  for load conditions, 249
  for worst-case conditions, 18, 248
  versus load capacitance, 249
Different supply voltages:
  logic devices with, 27
  transferring signals between, 27
Differential drivers:
  for clocks, 195
  for high-frequency signals, 216
  for RS-422 signal transmission, 216
Differential receivers:
  for clocks, 195
  for high-frequency signals, 216
  for RS-422 signals, 216
  frequency capability of, 216
Differential signal transmission, 215
Diode clamp termination:
  of board clock lines, 184
Diode forward voltage drop, 42, 43
Diode voltage temperature coeffiient, 42,
    43
Diodes, equivalent circuits for, 41–43
Dissimilar metals, connections between,
    106, 107
Distributed loads:
  effect on propagation delay, 252

Distributed reset signals, reason to avoid, 264
Drive capability:
  increasing, 207, 208
Drivers, differential, 216
Drivers, differential high speed, 216
Drivers, RS-232, 216, 217
Drivers, RS-422, 216
Dual-stripline conductor:
  basic configuration, 136
Dynamic loading:
  when inputs are paralleled, 206
Dynamic noise immunity, 33
Dynamic output current, 304
Dynamic power dissipation:
  calculation of, 348–350
  TTL versus CMOS, 350, 351
Dynamic RAMs (DRAMs), 280, 283, 284, 287, 288

ECL logic circuits:
  advantages of, 9
  disadvantages of, 9
Edge speed:
  of advanced logic devices, 4
EEPROMs:
  write protection of, 272–274
Electrostatic protection networks, 64–66
EMI ground, 110
Enhancement-mode field-effect transistor, 52
Equivalent circuit:
  CMOS inverter with open input, 61, 204
  for diodes, 41–43
  for MOSFETs, 53
  for TTL gate, 47–51
  of CMOS inverter, 54
  of CMOS inverter when switching, 78, 79
ESD, control of at board interfaces, 66
ESD ground, 110
ESD protection networks, 64–66
ESD ratings:
  classes of, 67
  of logic families, 67
  packages marking for, 67
Extender boards:
  need to include in timing analysis, 253

F_{MAX}, caution on use of, 18, 251, 260
Failure rates:
  of memory devices, 311
Fan out:
  means of increasing, 207, 208
Faraday's law, 74
Feedthrough current:
  in CMOS circuits, 79
  in CMOS inverters, 79
  in totem-pole output stages, 76–78
Ferrite beads:
  advantages of for termination, 191
  for series termination, 181, 182, 191
  for source termination, 180
  impedance of, 182
First-in first-out (FIFO) devices:
  application issues, 323–325
  control pulse issues, 324
First incident switching, 128–130
Flash EPROMs, 280, 281, 283, 284, 290, 291
  write protection of, 272–274
Floating buses, prevention of, 211
Floating inputs (see Open inputs)
Floating signals, prevention of, 211
Flux density, 72
Functional design, limitations of, 39

Gated clocks, 186
Ground, single point, 102
Ground-loop currents, 220
Ground bounce:
  calculation of, 87, 88
  causes of, 86
  connector ground pins needed to prevent, 99
  definition of, 85
  due to package ground pin inductance, 86
  due to wired ground connection, 94
  general discussion of, 85, 86
  in clock buffers, 179, 180
  in FIFOs, 325
  in LSI devices, 325
  in PLDs, 325
  spikes, 86–88
  techniques for minimizing, 88, 89
Ground connection to devices:
  inappropriateness of wiring, 94
Ground lines, between units, 220
Ground loop currents, prevention of, 102

Ground loops, 127
Ground offsets, between units, 215
Ground pins:
  needed for clock signals, 193
Ground planes:
  need for, 95
Grounding:
  for EMI control, 110
  for ESD control, 110
  for lightning protection, 108
  for power sources, 108
  for safety, 108
  for signals, 109
  general issues, 108
  ground loops, 127
  summary, 110

High-level signal receivers, 218, 219
High-voltage receivers, 218, 219

Incident wave, 157
Inductance:
  electrical factors that influence, 72
  equations for, 73
  general discussion of, 71
  means for reducing, 73
  measure of, 71
  of a plane, 97
  of component power connections, 94
  of number 30 wire, 94
  of package pins, 86
  physical factors that influence, 72, 73
Inductive effects:
  with respect to digital signal levels, 72
Inductor, transient voltage drop across,
  74
Initialization (*see* System initialization)
Initialization signal (*see* Reset signal)
Input-output levels:
  TTL compatible CMOS, 30
Input-output protection networks, 64
Input-output voltage levels (table), 30
Input capacitance:
  of logic devices, 249
Input current:
  calculation of for a TTL gate, 47, 48
Input currents (table), 21
Input levels, TTL compatible CMOS, 20
Input threshold levels:
  control of, 55
Input voltage levels, 19, 20

Interconnection delays:
  board-to-board, 253
  calculation of on circuit boards, 251
  component-to-component, 251
  need to allow for, 260
  no allowance for, 2
  on backpanels, 253
  on motherboards, 253
  unit-to-unit, 254
Interconnections:
  as low-pass networks, 3
  bandwidth requirements, 4
  board-to-board, 125, 199, 208–210
  capacitance of, 83, 250
  categories of, 124, 199, 214
  component-to-component, 125, 199, 201
  delay of typical pc board track, 153, 154
  general considerations, 199
  impedance of, 127, 129
  imperfections, 3
  in memory subsystems, 293, 300–305
  loaded impedance of, 132
  minimum impedance requirements of,
    130
  of board-to-board clocks, 187–192
  of breadboard circuits, 138
  of signals, 123
  optimum impedance of, 127, 129, 132
  physical means of, 124
  single-ended, 199, 200
  sources of delay, 251
  summary of guidelines, 221, 222
  summary of techniques, 149
  transmission-line effects on, 153
  typical signal path, 254, 255
  unit-to-unit, 126
Interface networks, balanced differential,
  215
Interface protection, 65, 213
Interface requirements:
  CMOS-to-TTL, 26
  TTL-to-CMOS, 25, 26
Inverter, CMOS, 54, 61, 78, 79, 204

Latch-up:
  as a function of temperature, 63, 64,
    204
  causes of, 62, 204
  conditions that increase susceptability,
    63
  definition of, 62
  in CMOS devices, 62

Latch-up (*Cont.*):
  mechanism in CMOS integrate circuits,
    62
  military specification for test of, 63
  prevention of, 62, 66, 202
Latches, 237, 239
Lattice diagram:
  for a transmission line, 157
Leading-edge detector, 235, 236
Lightning ground, 108
Line capacitance, estimating, 250
Line delay:
  due to transmission-line effects, 158,
    252, 253
Line delays (*see* Conductor delays;
    Interconnection delays)
Line settling time, rule of thumb, 158,
    253
Load capacitance:
  used to specify propagation time, 245,
    248
Load placement, on clock lines, 178, 184
Load termination:
  of board clock lines, 181
  of clock lines, 191, 192
  of transmission lines, 158, 159
Loading, special cases:
  parallel inputs, 206
Logic device delay adjustments:
  for worst-case operating conditions, 18,
    248
Logic devices:
  adjustments for worst-case conditions,
    246
  conditions for timing specifications,
    244, 245
  delay adjustments for load conditions,
    249
  drive derating of, 206, 207
  dynamic output current, 304
  increasing drive, 207, 208
  input-output capacitance of, 249
  need to understand noise tolerance, 5
  selection of, 9
  tradeoffs versus system requirements,
    9
  worst-case parameters of, 1
  (*See also* Advanced Schottky TTL
    devices, families; BiCMOS circuits,
    devices, families; CMOS logic cir-
    cuits, devices, families; Logic fami-
    lies; TTL logic circuits, devices,
    families)

Logic families:
  compatibility of, 25, 26
  input-output voltage levels (table), 30
  input level requirements, 201
  interface requirements, 25, 26
  speed, comparison of, 17
  (*See also* Advanced Schottky TTL
    devices, logic families; BiCMOS
    logic circuits, devices, families;
    CMOS logic circuits, devices, fami-
    lies; Logic devices; TTL logic cir-
    cuits, devices, families)
Low-speed signal transmission, 216–218
LSI devices:
  important application issues, 325
  summary of application tips, 328, 329
Lumped loads, definition of, 248

Magnetic flux, 74
Master-slave devices, 237, 239
Master reset, description of, 263, 264
Maximum system clock frequency:
  for logic families, 259, 260
  for logic families (table), 259
Maximum toggle rate, caution on use of,
    18, 251, 260
Memory devices:
  alterable, 284
  dynamic RAMs (DRAMs), 280, 283,
    284, 287, 288
  failure rates, 311
  flash EPROMs, 280, 281, 283, 284, 290,
    291
  functional timing, 295–299
  high speed, 284
  standard test load, 16, 245
  static RAMs (SRAMs), 280, 283–286
  typical circuit arrangement, 281–283
  typical controls, 281–283
  UV EPROM, 280, 281, 283, 284,
    288–290
Memory subsystems:
  board layout, 293, 294
  control of contention on data buses,
    293, 307, 308
  control of crosstalk, 293, 306, 307
  control signal generation, 293, 295–299
  decoupling requirements, 293, 310
  delay due to transmission-line effects,
    301, 303, 304
  device delays, 300
  devices used in, 280

Memory subsystems (*Cont.*):
    effective interconnection impedance,
        303
    error detection and correction, 311
    failure rates, 311
    for high performance, 292
    functional timing, 295–299
    general discussion of, 279, 280, 292
    high effective line impedance, 305
    interconnection delays, 300, 301, 303
    low effective line impedance, 304
    optimization of line impedance, 305
    power and ground distribution, 293,
        310
    signal routing, 293, 294
    summary of design techniques, 317
    testing of, 312–316
    typical arrangement, 292
    worst-case timing, 293, 300, 301
Metastable:
    condition, 231, 232
    failure rate (equation), 233
    failure rate (graph), 233
    operation, 231, 232
    recovery of PALs, 322
    recovery time, 232, 233
    state, 231, 232
Microstrip conductor:
    buried in a dielectric, 134
    buried, 135
    equations for, 135
    graph of impedance, 137
    on the surface, 134
MOSFET:
    enhancement-mode operation, 52
    off equivalent circuit, 54
    on equivalent circuit, 54
    on impedance, 61, 204
    operation of, 52
    schematic symbol, 52
    threshold voltage of, 55
Motherboard:
    power supply connections, 100

NAND, 40, 46, 56
    internal BiCMOS ASIC, 332
Noise:
    major source of, 225
    noise tolerant logic architectures,
        225
    peak time, 226, 227
Noise generation, 35

Noise immunity:
    of synchronous designs, 225
Noise margin, static:
    of Advanced Schottky TTL, 31
    of Advanced Schottky TTL (table), 31
    of BiCMOS logic families, 33
    of BiCMOS logic families (table), 33
    of CMOS logic families, 32
    of CMOS logic families (table), 32
    TTL change with temperature, 32
Noise margin:
    definition of, 29
    dynamic, 33
    dynamic (graph), 34, 35
    general discussion of, 30
    means of optimizing, 35
    need to understand, 30
    static (table), 31, 32
Nonvolatile memories:
    description of, 280
NOR, 56

Off-phase clocking, 230
One-shot:
    time out period, 238
    time out period variations, 238
    use of in synchronous systems, 237
    with long time out periods, 238
Open inputs, 204
    control of for ASICs, 335, 336
    effects of, 205
    effects on BiCMOS devices, 203, 204
    effects on CMOS devices, 203, 204
    effects on TTL devices, 202, 203
    (*See also* Unused inputs), 204
Operating speed:
    maximum for ABT system (table), 257,
        259
    maximum for AC system (table), 259
    maximum for AC system (tables), 258
    maximum for F system (table), 256, 259
    maximum for FACT system (table), 259
    maximum for FCT-A system (table),
        257, 259
    need for margin, 260
Output capacitance:
    of logic devices, 249
Output impedance:
    of CMOS NOR gate, 56, 57
Output levels:
    TTL compatible CMOS, 22
    TTL compatible CMOS (table), 23

Output response:
  versus load capacitance, 249
Output voltage:
  at specified current (table), 23
Output voltage levels, 21
Output voltage levels (table), 23
Overshoot:
  definition of, 163
Overvoltage protection, of logic circuit,
    107

Package pin inductance, 86
Package style:
  timing adjustments for, 251
Parallel inputs:
  disadvantages of, 206
  dynamic loading, 206
  effect on dynamic performance, 206
Parasitic SCR structures, in CMOS, 62
PLD applications:
  summary of application tips, 328, 329
Power connections to devices:
  inappropriateness of wiring, 94
Power dissipation:
  calculation of, 348, 349
  dynamic, 349, 350
  quiescent, 348, 349
  static, 348, 349
  TTL versus CMOS, 350, 351
Power distribution:
  effects of inductance, 71
  summary of techniques for, 119–121
Power distribution:
  general discussion of, 93
  on clock boards, 185
  summary of, 110
Power ground, 108
Power planes:
  need for, 95
Power supply, overvoltage protection, 107
Power supply:
  minimum voltage needed for logic
    devices, 103
  overshoot, 101
  undershoot, 101
Power supply connections:
  supply-to-motherboard, 100
  to multiple units, 103
  to multiple units (loads), 102
  to reference (ground), 102
  to remote supplies, 100–102
  to return line, 102

Power supply droop:
  calculation of, 87, 88
  causes of, 86
  definition of, 85
  general discussion of, 85, 86
  techniques for minimizing, 88, 89
Power supply voltage, minimum for logic,
    103
Printed circuit (pc) board:
  capacitance of interconnections, 250
  conductor thickness, 136
Programmable logic devices (PLDs):
  application issues, 69, 321–323
  metastable characteristics, 322
  synchronizing signals in, 322
  unused inputs, 326
Propagation delay:
  as a function of load, 131
  basic equation for, 128
  effective, equation for, 131
  of a wire above a reference plane, 133
  of buried microstrip conductor, 135
  of lines, 251
  of lines with distributed loads, 252
  of microstrip conductor, 134
  of stripline conductor, 135
  (See also Interconnection delays)
Protection:
  from electric shock, 108
  of board interface circuits, 65, 213
  of system interface circuits, 65, 66, 213
Pull-down resistors:
  loading of, 206
  selecting the value, 206
Pull-down voltages, current limited, 206
Pull-up resistors:
  loading of, 205
  rule of thumb for loading, 205
  selecting the value, 206
  use of with pull-up resistors, 269
Pull-up voltages, current limited, 206

Quiescent power dissipation:
  calculation of, 348, 349
Quiet times, in synchronous systems, 226,
    227

Radial resistance, of a plane, 105, 106
Rail-to-rail levels:
  definition of, 54
RC resets, reasons to avoid, 264, 265

Receivers, differential, 216
Receivers, differential high-speed, 216
Receivers, RS-232, 216, 217
Receivers, RS-422, 216
Receivers, very low-speed, 218, 219
Refection diagram:
    for BiCMOS logic devices, 166, 167
    for CMOS gate with input clamp, 164
    for CMOS gate without input clamps,
        165, 166
    for TTL logic devices, 166, 167
Reflection coefficient:
    definition of, 156
    equation for, 156
    of BiCMOS inputs, 157
    of BiCMOS outputs, 157
    of CMOS inputs, 157
    of CMOS outputs, 157
    of TTL outputs, 157
Reference offsets, between units, 215
Reflections, 156
Register speed:
    worst-case for Adv Sch TTL logic
        (table), 17
    worst-case for BiCMOS logic families
        (table), 17
    worst-case for CMOS logic families
        (table), 17
Remote units, signal connection between,
    214
Reset signal:
    asynchronously apply, 270, 271
    buffering of, 268
    circuits for, 265, 270
    combining of, 267, 268
    distribution of, 268
    distribution, summary of, 268, 276
    general description of, 263, 264
    generation, summary of, 276
    generator, typical circuit, 12, 265–267
    isolation of buffers, 268
    loading of, 268, 269
    metastable considerations of, 270, 271
    ORing of, 267, 268
    phasing of, 269
    prevention of metastable conditions, 271
    recommended pull-up resistor value of,
        269
    requirements of, 263, 264
    summary of, 276
    synchronously remove, 270, 271
    timing of, 269
    use of pull-up resistors with, 269

Reset signal generator:
    general requirements, 264, 265
    recommended circuit operating limits,
        267
    trip point, 264
    typical circuit, 265–267
Resistance, of stranded copper conductor,
    104
Resistance, radial, of a plane, 105, 106
Resistance of a plane, 96
Resistors:
    pull down, 205
    pull up, 205
Rise-time requirements:
    in BiCMOS and CMOS circuits, 62
Routing guidelines:
    analog signals, 140
    for buses, 139
    for clock signals, 139
    for ECL signals, 140
    for memory address and data lines, 139
    for memory chip select lines, 139
    for memory write lines, 139
    for strobes, 139
    general discussion of, 138
    routing order, 140
Routing order, 140
RS-232 drivers, 216, 217
RS-232 receivers, 216, 217
RS-422 drivers, 216
RS-422 receivers, 216
RS-422 signal transmission, 216
Rule of thumb:
    for number of connector ground pins, 99
    for pull-up loading, 205
    for settling of unterminated lines, 158,
        253
    for sizing decoupling capacitors, 114
    to convert timing parameters to worst
        case, 18, 248

Safety ground, 108
Schottky clamped transistor, 45
Schottky diode clamps, use of, 45
Schottky diode forward voltage drop, 42,
    43
SCR structures:
    in BiCMOS and CMOS circuits, 62
Self-inductance, 72
Separate units, communication between,
    214
Series termination (*see* Source termination)

Settling time, for unterminated lines, 157, 158, 253
Sheet resistance, 96
Sheet resistance, of copper, 96
Shield beads (see Ferrite beads)
Signal connection between remote units (see Interconnections; Unit-to-unit)
Signal ground, 109
Signal interconnections:
  effects of inductance, 71
  (See also Interconnections)
Signal interfaces:
  single ended, 199, 200
Signal propagation delays (see Interconnection delays)
Signal settling time:
  rule-of-thumb for, 253
Signal timing checklist, 261
Signal timing summary, 260
Silicon diode forward voltage drop, 42, 43
Simultaneous switching:
  timing adjustments for, 250
Single-ended interconnections:
  requirements for, 200
Single-ended interfaces, 199, 200
Single point ground, 102
Slew rate:
  noise as a function of, 75
Source follower, 54, 55
Source termination:
  for CMOS clock lines, 180–183
  of board clock lines, 180–183
  of transmission lines, 158, 160, 161
  resistor value, 180, 181, 183
Source termination resistors:
  for clock lines, 180–183
Specified load capacitance:
  for logic families, 248
Spikes, due to ground bounce, 86–88
Split termination:
  circuit for, 159
  of clock lines, 191
  Thevenin's impedance of, 191, 192
  typical value for, 191, 192
  (See also Load termination)
Standard test load, 16, 83, 174, 229, 245
Static input-output characteristics, 18 (table), 19
Static RAMs (SRAMs), 280, 283–286
Stripline conductor:
  basic configuration, 135
  equations for, 135
  graph of impedance, 137

Stripline conductor (Cont.):
  off center, 136
Stripline transmission lines, 135
Switching currents:
  techniques for minimizing effects of, 88–90
  when driving distributed loads, 84
  when driving transmission lines, 84
  with a constant rate of change of voltage, 81, 82, 249
  with lumped capacitance loads, 80, 81
Switching transitions:
  frequency of, 3
  harmonic content, 3
Synchronizing asynchronous buses, 234
Synchronizing asynchronous inputs, 230, 234
Synchronizing narrow pulses, 237
Synchronizing wide pulses, 235
Synchronous logic design:
  advantages of, 260
  description of, 225
  general practices, 225
  noise immunity of, 226
  summary of practices, 239, 240
Synchronous removal, of reset signals, 270, 271
Synchronous systems:
  advantages of, 226
  clock alignment, 228, 229
  clock requirements, 227
  design issues, 227–230
  disadvantages of, 226
  hold time requirements, 228, 229
  quite time in, 226, 227
  summary of design practices, 239, 240
System ground, 108
System initialization:
  requirements of, 263, 264
  to prevent damage, 275
  to prevent hazardous conditions, 275
System operating speed:
  maximum with ABT devices (table), 257, 259
  maximum with AC devices (table), 259
  maximum with AC devices (tables), 258
  maximum with F devices (table), 256, 259
  maximum with FACT devices (table), 259
  maximum with FCT-A devices (table), 257, 259
  neglect of interconnection delays, 1
  not compatible with device timing, 1

System timing:
  general considerations, 260
  neglect of interconnection delays, 1
  not compatible with device timing, 1

Tantulum capacitors:
  note of caution on use of, 118
Temperature coefficient:
  of Schottky diodes, 43
  of silicon diodes, 43
Terminating resistors:
  value for optimum response, 220
Termination:
  ac, 159
  at load, 159
  at source, 160, 161, 180–183
  of clock lines, 173, 178, 180–183,
      187–193, 195
  of signals to LSI devices, 326–328
  of signals to PLDs, 326–328
  of transmission lines, 154
  of unit-to-unit interconnections, 220
  split, 159, 191
  with diode clamps, 184
  (See also Load termination; Source ter-
      mination)
Test circuit:
  for clamping efficiency, 170
Test clock input port, 196
Test patterns:
  for memory subsystems, 312–316
Test points, signals routed to, 212
Testing:
  of memory subsystems, 312–316
Thevenin's termination (see Split termi-
      nation)
Thickness, of pc board copper planes, 136
Three-state buses, treatment of, 211
Three-state drivers, control of, 211
Three-state signals, treatment of, 211
Timing adjustments:
  for actual load conditions, 248, 249
  for package style, 251
  for power supply voltage level, 247, 248
  for process variations, 246
  for simultaneous switching, 250
  for temperature, 246
Timing analysis, worst-case:
  example of with ABT devices (table),
      257
  example of with AC devices (tables),
      258

Timing analysis, worst-case (Cont.):
  example of with F devices (table), 256
  example of with FACT devices (table),
      259
  example of with FCT-A devices (table),
      257
  examples of, 254, 255
Timing analysis:
  general discussion, 241
  Monte Carlo, 244
  root-sum-squared, 243, 244
  statistical, 243
  structure system for, 260
  worst case, 241, 242
Timing checklist, 261
Timing effects:
  of package style, 251
Timing parameters:
  adjustments for worst-case conditions,
      17, 18, 245–249
  converting to worst case, 17, 248
Totem-pole output stage:
  circuit of, 57, 58
  internal switching currents in, 76–78
  voltage swing, 59, 60
Trailing-edge detector, 235, 236
Transient current generation:
  need to understand, 5
Transient load currents:
  general discussion of, 80
  when driving distributed loads, 84
  when driving transmission lines, 84
  with a constant rate of change voltage,
      81, 82, 249
  with lumped capacitance loads, 80, 81
Transient suppressors, use of, 107
Transient switching currents:
  due to load, 75
  frequency components of, 3, 4, 71
  general discussion of, 75
  internal to devices, 75
  techniques for minimizing effects of,
      88–90
Transistors:
  as back-to-back diodes, 43, 44
  equivalent circuit for, 44, 45
Transmission-line reflections:
  time needed to subside, 157, 158
Transmission lines:
  basic considerations of, 154
  basic equations for, 128, 131
  basic theory of, 154
  effects of, 153

Transmission lines (*Cont.*):
 equivalent circuit for, 128
 ideal response, 155
 lattice diagram, 157
 load termination of, 158, 159
 loaded impedance of, 130, 132
 microstrip on a surface, 134
 reflection coefficients of, 156
 reflections on, 156
 response of, 158
 response of BiCMOS devices in, 162,
  166, 167
 response of CMOS devices in, 162–165
 response of TTL devices in, 162, 166,
  167
 series termination of, 158, 160, 161
 source termination (*see* Series termination)
 stripline, 135
 summary of techniques for dealing
  with, 171
 termination of, 158
 typical response of, 158
 with distributed loads, 252
Tri-state (*see* Entries beginning with
  Three-state)
TTL gate:
 equivalent circuit, 46–51
 high output voltage, 49, 50
 input-output current flow, 47
 low input current, 47, 48
 low output voltage, 51
TTL level threshold, 16
TTL levels:
 advantages of, 28
TTL logic circuits:
 internal switching currents in, 76–78
 operation of a 54/7400 NAND gate, 46
 optimum input-output impedance, 169
 transmission-line response of, 162, 166,
  167
TTL logic devices:
 adjustments for worst-case conditions,
  246
 circuit operation, 40
 conditions for timing specifications, 245
 input-output capacitance of, 83
 input circuits, 40
 internal circuit structure, 40
 internal switching currents in, 76–78
 optimum input-output impedance, 169
 output circuits, 41
 paralleling of, 208

TTL logic devices (*Cont.*):
 reflection coefficient of inputs, 157
 reflection coefficient of outputs, 157
 standard test load, 245
 timing adjustment for V_{cc} level, 247
 timing adjustments for package style,
  251
 timing adjustments for process, 246
 timing adjustments for simultaneous
  switching, 250
 timing adjustments for temperature,
  246
 transmission-line response of, 162, 166,
  167
TTL logic families:
 conditions for timing specifications, 245
TTL NAND gate, 46
Twisted-pair lines:
 advantages of, 142
Typical device timing:
 to convert to worst case, 18, 248

Unbuffered clocked devices, outputs of,
  212
Undershoot:
 control of, 168
 definition of, 163
Unit-to-unit:
 asynchronous data transfer, 220
 clock distribution, 194, 195
 clock termination, 195
 differential signal transmission, 215
 ground lines, 220
 interconnection delays, 254
 line terminations, 220
 low speed signals, 216–218
 miscellaneous considerations, 220
 miscellaneous signal considerations,
  220
 signal interconnections, 199, 214
 signal interconnections, 214
 (*See also* Interconnections)
 summary of clock distribution techniques, 196
 very low-speed signals, 217, 218
Unit (system) interface protection, 65,
  213
Unreliable systems, cause of, 3
Unterminated lines:
 behavior of, 154
Unused inputs:
 CMOS, connection of, 205

Unused inputs (*Cont.*):
connection of for LSI devices, 326
connection of for PLDs, 326
treatment of, 202–206
treatment of on TTL devices, 202, 203
(*See also* Open inputs)
UV EPROMs, 280, 281, 283, 284, 288–290
write protection of, 272–274

Very low-speed receivers, 218, 219
Very low-speed signal transmission, 218
Volatile memories:
description of, 280
Voltage drop (*see* Voltage loss)
Voltage loss:
ac across a plane, 97
dc across a plane, 95
in power conductors, 103
in power connections, 104

Welded-wire board:
capacitance of interconnections, 250
impedance of, 181, 192
Wire-wrap board:
capacitance of interconnections, 250

Wire-wrap board (*Cont.*):
impedance of, 181, 192
wire inductance, 94
Wire:
capacitance of, 250
inductance of, 94
resistance of, 104
Wire above ground:
characteristic impedance, 133
equations for, 133
propagation time, 133
Worst-case propagation delays:
converting to from typical, 18, 248
Worst-case timing analysis, 241
example of with ABT devices (table), 257
example of with AC devices (tables), 258
example of with FACT devices (table), 259
example of with FCT-A devices (table), 257
examples of, 254, 255
(*See also* Timing analysis)
Write protection:
of EEPROMs, 272–274
of flash EPROMs, 272–274
of nonvolatile memories, 272–274
of UV EPROMs, 272–274

ABOUT THE AUTHOR

James E. Buchanan is a senior advisory engineer at
Westinghouse Electric Corporation's Electronic Systems
Division in Baltimore, MD. He has more than 30 years of
design experience and holds 15 patents, most of which cover
analog-to-digital converter and digital-to-analog converter
circuits. He is the author of two other books, *CMOS/TTL
Digital Systems Design* and *BiCMOS/CMOS Systems
Design,* both published by McGraw-Hill, and is a contributor
to the *Computer Engineering Handbook,* also published by
McGraw-Hill.

CPSIA information can be obtained
at www.ICGtesting.com
Printed in the USA
LVHW102154160822
726147LV00002B/4